Multi-Platform Code Management

Multi-Platform Code Management

Kevin Jameson
ISA Corp.

O'Reilly & Associates, Inc.
103 Morris Street, Suite A
Sebastopol, CA 95472

Multi-Platform Code Management

by Kevin Jameson

Copyright © 1994 O'Reilly & Associates, Inc. All rights reserved.
Printed in the United States of America.

Editor: Andy Oram

Production Editor: Stephen Spainhour

Printing History:

August 1994: First Edition.

This book is printed on acid-free paper with 50% recycled content, 10-15% post-consumer waste. O'Reilly & Associates is committed to using paper with the highest recycled content available consistent with high quality.

ISBN: 1-56592-059-7

Table of Contents

3: *A Hands-on Tour: Part 2* 97

4: *Designing a Code Management System* 129

List of Figures

List of Tables

Preface

This book describes a set of policies, procedures, and tools for performing code management activities on software projects of three kinds:

- Single-person, single-platform projects (SPSP)

- Single-person, multi-platform projects (SPMP)

- Multi-person, multi-platform projects (MPMP)

It is intended to be read by people who are interested in code management problems on software projects—people such as programmers, managers, software engineers, and quality assurance personnel.

The main goal of this book is to provide a specific, tested, and relatively complete solution to software code management problems. The solution described here is specific because it's well defined and uses detailed examples. It's tested because it has been used before on projects ranging from 50 to 100,000 lines of code. And it's complete because it includes the source code for all the necessary software tools. In short, this book is a simple, "one-stop-shopping" solution for the code management problem.

Code management is important because poor code management costs more money and time than good code management. The reasoning is simple—if you lose a bug fix, or have to back it out a few days later, or clobber the latest version of a module before you've saved it properly, it costs time and money to do the work over again. Or if you can't share reusable files easily among multiple products, or can't easily find out which programs are using a file that you want to change, or if you have problems propagating changes in a file to all of the programs that share it, you're probably spending more time and money on the problem than you want to. This book shows you how to avoid or solve many of those problems, and thus can help you to reduce your development costs.

The main ideas in this book are platform independent, so you should be able to use them on any computer. Currently, the software included with the book runs on the following platforms:

AIX	Irix	NeXt
Amiga	Linux	Solaris 2.0
Apollo Domain	MS-DOS with Borland make and compiler	Sun4 OS
Dell PC	MS-DOS with Microsoft make and compiler	Ultrix
HP-UX	NetBSD	

Other platforms are implicitly supported, since the source code and shell scripts for the tools can be modified easily for other mainframes and personal computers. Most of the tutorial examples have been written for DOS because it is almost universally available and understood by everyone. Some of the more complex examples have been written for UNIX because they use symbolic links.

The tools can be used effectively by a single programmer or a team of programmers. They have very low overhead and automatically generate directory structures and makefiles. They automatically import include files and export finished programs, and keep a record of which programs use shared include files. The tools have been tested and used on both large and small projects. They use ASCII files. And perhaps best of all, the source code for over 30 software tools is included with the book so that you can tune the tools to run the way you like, on your particular machine. (The source code contains DOS batch files, UNIX shell scripts, C code, and *gawk* and *sed* scripts.)

The major ideas discussed in this book are:

- Standard directory structures for source files

- Standard directory structures for sharing, alpha testing, and releasing products

- Standard makefile structures for common software products

- Isolation of platform-dependent code in separate source files

- Support for explicit importing of shared include files

- Storage of code in a version control system (such as RCS)

- Logging of all RCS transactions

- Automated tool support for all of these ideas

The main benefits of this approach are:

- Increased productivity through automation

- Simplified user interfaces to many code management operations

- Increased stability of the development environment

- Increased flexibility in directory structure reorganizations

- Increased information about source code changes

- Increased knowledge of file sharing relationships

The main drawback of this approach is that it limits programming freedom in a few small areas. The software tools can provide advanced support only if they can make some assumptions about the way you do things on your software projects. For example, some freedom is lost in naming directories. The tools currently expect platform directory names to end in *.plt* (such as *sun4gcc.plt, msc.plt*). They also expect to use lowercase *rcs* for RCS subdirectories, and *s* for directories that hold source code. The tools also make assumptions about where code is placed, about how source code checkins are done, and about how makefiles are constructed. The book even recommends that machine-specific **#ifdefs** be disallowed in your code, to promote the readability and portability of the code (other kinds of **#ifdefs** are okay). (Of course, you can change all these assumptions if you want, since the source code is included with the book.)

In summary, the main benefit of this book is that it describes a tested and efficient solution to SPSP, SPMP, and MPMP code management problems. The main drawback of the solutions are that they restrict your programming freedom a little bit. But if you can accept these relatively small restrictions, then it's likely that you'll rarely have to fight common code management problems ever again.

Intended Audience

This book is a technical book of medium difficulty and is intended for both programmers and managers who have a reasonable understanding of the daily operation a software development environment. At a minimum, you should know how to write and compile C programs, and have some familiarity with the *make* utility.

During the review process, several people who commonly worked on UNIX computers read the tutorial example (which uses DOS command lines), and commented that the book "was about DOS." But the opposite also occurred—some DOS users felt that the book "was about UNIX." One conference review committee even became divided over the material. Part of the committee thought that the book was "too DOS-centric," while others argued that the material was platform independent. It seemed that no one could agree on which platform the book "was about." (Interestingly, the Amiga and OS/2 developers weren't bothered by this confusion at all.) The whole situation puzzled me for a while, because I thought the title of the book accurately described the contents.

I eventually realized that the breadth of the topic contributed to the confusion, because the book discussed multiple platforms instead of just one particular platform. I also learned that most people tended to look at the book through their own experiences because they were in search of solutions that would work in their own environments. This is, of course, a reasonable thing to do. (But it makes writing a book about multiple environments more challenging.)

Intended Goals

Some people who have read this book had unfair expectations of the included software. Some people expected a lot from the software, and some people expected almost nothing. People who expected a lot of the book software tended to compare it with commercial code management products, and sometimes felt that the book software fell short of equality with those products. Other people (who expected less of the software) seemed quite pleased that the software could provide so much functionality.

Whatever else this book and the software inside it might be, they were never intended to be any of the following things:

- A set of commercial code management tools, supported by a whole company of programmers, and sold for hundreds or thousands of dollars

- A set of universal code management tools that would fit the specific needs of all people, on all projects, in all organizations, on all platforms

- A way of doing things that would smoothly integrate with existing code management practices on all platforms

Instead, the goals of this book are much more modest. They are:

- To be a book, that is sold for the price of a book, even though it contains source code for a fairly complete set of code management tools

- To identify and discuss most of the important issues in "fully dimensioned" development environments (such as multi-person, multi-platform sites)

- To present some new ideas that can help to resolve most of the issues, on many— but not all—computing platforms

- To provide a useful set of prototype tools that can demonstrate the feasibility of the proposed solutions, on many—but not all—platforms

Understanding these design goals should help you to see the book and the software tools for what they were originally intended to be, rather than for something they'll never be.

Scope of This Book

There are really two complementary goals pursued in this book. The first is to explain in general terms what you need for a useful code management system, what your choices are, and so on. The second is to teach you how to use one specific code management system—the tools on the disk.

The first chapter of the book introduces the concepts and problems that are commonly found in programming environments. This sets the basis for the two kinds of chapters found in the rest of the book.

One kind of chapter takes you on a tour through the tools—this includes Chapters 2, 3, and 8. The idea here is to show you code management in action. You can master the tools by following along and typing in each command as you see it. But even more important, you learn the processes that are needed to keep code consistent on complex projects.

The other kind of chapter describes the theory of code management: requirements, design, and so on. Early chapters are very general, while later ones describe the solutions used by the tools in this book.

Because most people prefer to see a concrete implementation before learning abstract ideas, two of the tour chapters come early in the book, before the theory chapters. If you are the type who likes to work from theory to practice, you can go right to Chapter 4, *Designing a Code Management System*, where the abstract part begins.

Chapter 1, *Introduction*, describes some common software development problems, and outlines the solutions used by this book.

Chapter 2, *A Hands-On Tour: Part 1*, introduces the ideas and tools in this book by working through several practical code management examples. In particular, the tour begins with a good example of how *not* to do code management, and leads you through a corrective process with two more examples.

Chapter 3, *A Hands-on Tour: Part 2*, continues with a fourth example that shows how to work with multiple platforms.

Chapter 4, *Designing a Code Management System*, discusses the requirements of good code management systems and the key decisions that must be made when setting one up. The systems should help to increase project stability, developer productivity, and convenience and functionality within the development environment. Decisions must be made on platform issues, corporate issues, directory structure issues, makefile issues, and source code style issues.

Chapter 5, *Directory Structures*, describes the directory structures used in this book.

Chapter 6, *Makefile Architectures*, describes the makefile structures used in this book. It also discusses the relative virtues of tree walking with recursive makefiles or linear sequences of *chdir* and *make* commands.

Chapter 7, *File Sharing*, describes the file sharing solution used in this book. It tells how to share, log, and inspect the sharing relationships that arise when include files are shared between software products.

Chapter 8, *A Hands-on Tour: Part 3*, completes the tour with two examples that show how to perform bulk RCS operations with tree walker scripts and how to support multiple developers in UNIX environments.

Chapter 9, *Code Management Environments for DOS and UNIX*, describes and justifies a set of policy decisions for two important platforms.

Chapter 10, *Conclusion*, summarizes and evaluates the key ideas in this book. It also contains a list of open questions and possible areas for future research into better code management systems.

Appendix A, *Code Management Software Tools*, describes the detailed features of all the software tools included with the book. It contains simple descriptions of all the tools and how to use them.

Appendix B, *Other Useful Tools*, discusses compatibility issues between my tools and third party RCS implementations. It also describes and recommends some tools that I've found to be very useful in my personal code development environment.

After reading this book, you should be able to design a set of code management policies to suit your needs, and then implement those policies using the software provided with this book.

Typographical Conventions

The following typographical conventions are used in this book:

Bold	is used for commands that the user must directly type in, and to emphasize topic sentences.
Italic	is used for file and directory names, program and command names, and to emphasize new terms.
`Constant Width`	is used in examples to show the contents of files or the output from commands, and to indicate environment variables, targets and macro names.
`Constant Bold`	is used in examples to show commands or other text that should be typed literally by the user.

Software Included with This Book

Source code for many software tools is included with this book. Earlier in this preface I listed the platforms to which the code has been ported. It should be straightforward to port the code to other platforms too, since the existing platform-dependent files can be used as examples.

Acknowledgments

I remember that when I used to read books as a child, I'd always wonder about the long lists of names that appeared in the acknowledgments sections of books that I had read. I couldn't understand why so many people had to be involved in the production. The author just wrote it, and then you printed it, right? Now I know better. Here's my own long list of people who helped to make this book a reality.

Financial Support: To Grant and Liz Lakeman at ISA Corp., who let me take time off from my job while I was writing this book, and who continued to support me when my money ran out; and to Rob Park, who made the financial numbers look good to Grant and Liz, and who offered constant encouragement on the rare days when I was part of his busy schedule.

Editorial Support: To Andy Oram at O'Reilly & Associates, my editor, who made several major suggestions that significantly improved the quality of the book, as well as countless minor ones; and who maintained his kind and very supportive attitude throughout the entire two years that it took to create this book—(I hope to meet you one day, Andy!).

Production Support: To the many other people at O'Reilly who made a difference; to Stephen Spainhour, who brought the book through a new production system and edited it very intelligently, finding many minor inconsistencies in the content; to Mary Anne Weeks Mayo, who helped copy edit the book; to Chris Reilley and Karla Tolbert, who turned my rough sketches into wonderfully professional figures; to Edie Freedman, who created the amusing and artful cover; and to Clairemarie Fisher O'Leary, who wrote the Colophon.

Technical Content: To Murray Peterson and Alan Covington, who first taught me the directory structure and makefile strategies that now form part of the central foundation of this book.

General Reviewers: To Richard Budrevich, Dan Freedman, Steve Hole, David Grubbs, and John Lazzaro, who made general comments during the technical review.

Technical Reviewers: To Andrew Ginter and Stephen Walli, who both turned in beautifully detailed, full-scale reviews that identified more awkward spots in the text than I could ever imagine would be there (:-\}).

Software Porting Support: And especially to those people who helped to port the code to other platforms: Heinz Wrobel (Amiga), who dedicated his work to Joan Thuesen, Arnout Grootveld (Amiga), Scott Stark (Next), Mark Alexander (OS/2), Jim Quick (Next), and Jason Simmons (Apple IIGS).

Hardware Porting Support: To Dan Freedman, Theo Deraadt, Herb Peyerl, and Wayne McCormick, who let me use their (many) different UNIX machines for porting my code.

Thank you. This book wouldn't have been possible without your help.

Kevin Jameson, 1994

Comments and Corrections

If you have comments or suggestions for improving this book or software, please feel free to contact me. You can send electronic mail to *mpcm@realcase.com*, or write to:

Kevin Jameson
2010 Ulster Road NW Suite 506
Calgary, Alberta
Canada T2N 4C2

Software Installation

The two floppy disks included with this book contain my own software as well as some free tools. Most of the software has been condensed into a few files through the *tar* utility, which is well-known to UNIX users, then compressed using the *zip* command. You are expected to have access to an *unzip* utility, and non-MS-DOS systems also need *tar* to unpack the files. For MS-DOS users, I have included an executable version of *tar*.

The installation process goes something like this:

1. Install the software into a temporary directory.

2. Set your environment variables.

3. Play with the software until you understand it.

4. Adjust the makefile templates to suit your preferences.

5. Rebuild the software tools from the provided source files to show that the source files are correct.

6. Permanently install the software by copying the CMTREE and CMHTREE to new locations.

7. Permanently readjust your environment variables in your *autoexec.bat* (on DOS) or shell initialization file (on UNIX).

The installation scripts on the disks don't install the software trees into their final locations because installing into the current directory is simpler and more reliable than installing into remote places that may require extended permissions (such as root permission on UNIX systems). It also allows you to try out the software (and to tune the makefile templates) before installing it permanently elsewhere. If something goes wrong, installing trees into the current directory makes it easier to start again from scratch.

Permanent installation is described at the end of this section.

System Requirements

Make sure that you have enough disk space. You'll need about three megabytes to unload the two floppy disks that come with the book, about eight megabytes of DOS disk space to hold the fully expanded source trees, and about one megabyte to hold the freshly compiled executable and object files for each platform (such as Borland C) that you decide to compile. If you use the *instdos cleanup* option to delete the source trees after installation on DOS systems, you can reduce the final disk space requirement to about two megabytes. All tools will easily run in 512K of memory on DOS systems.

TEAM and OWNER Modes of Installation

The tools included with this book have been initially configured to support multi-person, multi-platform development work in networked DOS-UNIX environments. In particular, the RCS tools have been specially modified to set the appropriate file permissions from both DOS and UNIX computers.

The reason for these modifications is the difference between DOS and UNIX file permissions. Under UNIX, if all members of a group have rwx permission on a directory, they can delete each other's read-only RCS files without having write permission on the files. (This is what RCS does whenever it modifies the RCS *,v* file.) The reason this works on UNIX is that RCS is modifying the directory entry itself in the filesystem, and not the file.

But under DOS, users must have write permission on a file in order to delete it. This means that DOS users who wish to check out a file stored on a UNIX server must have write permission on the file, in addition to having write permission on the directory. To get write permission, users must either use *chmod* to get write permission (which always fails on UNIX if the current user isn't the owner of the file), or they must already have write permission. Since users within a development group will not always own the files they try to check out, the only option is to leave files with read-write permissions by default.

The technical consequence of supporting this type of team development is that all RCS working files and RCS *,v* files are left with read-write permission for everyone in the UNIX group.

The code that implements this policy can be disabled by disabling the **TEAM** #ifdef and enabling the **OWNER** #ifdef in the code. Several tools are affected (in RCS: *v_rcs.h, co.c, vrepfile.c; cm_pd.lib/sun4gcc.plt/s/copyfile.c*).

If you won't be supporting teams of programmers on DOS-UNIX networks, and would prefer that RCS working files and RCS *,v* files have read-only permissions by default, enable the **OWNER** #ifdefs in the files named above and recompile the tools. Enabling the OWNER option causes RCS to set file permissions to read-only. (This behavior is more consistent with other "normal" RCS implementations.)

Installation on Networked DOS-UNIX Systems

The following installation process describes how to install the tools in a directory that's accessible to all machines on the network. Specifically, these instructions assume that:

1. There is a directory */local* on the UNIX server.

2. The */local* directory is exported by the server for mounting by other machines.

3. The DOS machines have drive L: linked to */local*.

4. Everyone will have read-write permisssions on all source files for the tools (as explained above). If you want to restrict access to the source trees later, you can reset file and directory permissions after the tools are installed.

Let's begin. If your network of UNIX and DOS machines meets the previous conditions, here's how to install the tools:

1. Perform the installation on the UNIX server.

2. Create a new directory to hold all the subdirectories for the tools. I recommend you use a directory such as */local/s/cm* on the server. This directory will hold the source files, makefile templates, and executables for the tools. Set permissions on the directory to 777. You may have to run as root to do this on your system.

3. Copy files from the distribution disks into */local/s/cm*. Copy all the files in the top level directory of the disks. Also copy the files from the UNIX and DOS subdirectories.

   If you're using another platform such as the Amiga, copy the files from the Amiga subdirectory, instead of those from the DOS and UNIX subdirectories.

4. Enable the execute permission bits on the UNIX installation scripts by typing **chmod 755 insts4***.

5. Type **insts4** to unpack the tools. Once this script has completed, the tools must be compiled and exported into the holding tree, where they can be used.

6. Set up your environment variables to point to the newly created directories.

   The CMTREE variable should point to */local/s/cm/cmtree*

   The CMHTREE variable should point to */local/s/cm/h*.

   The CMPCILOG variable should point to your log file. (I use *CMHTREE/pci.log*.)

7. Type **insts4_2** to compile the UNIX versions of the tools under the *sun4sh.plt* and *sun4gcc.plt* platforms (for Sun4 workstations equipped with the GNU C compiler).

If your UNIX machine isn't a Sun4 equipped with GNU *gcc*, you'll have to port the tools to your particular platform. Use the steps in the *insts4_2* script as a guide for manually compiling the tools.

8. Type **insts4_3** to copy the DOS executables into the holding tree.

9. Adjust filesystem permissions in the CMHTREE so that everyone can read and write to all directories in the CMHTREE. You can do this by changing to the parent directory above the CMHTREE and then typing **chmod -R 777 cmtree**.

At this point, executable versions of the tools for UNIX and DOS are available for use in the alpha test directories in the holding tree.

These directories are *CMHTREE/at/sun4gcc.plt* and *CMHTREE/h/at/sun4sh.plt* for UNIX.

For DOS, they are *CMHTREE/at/tbc.plt* and *CMHTREE/h/at/tdos.plt*.

The easiest way for people to access these tools is to add these directories to their **PATH** variable.

Installing UNIX Tools in /local/bin

You'll want to make the tools permanently available in the usual places on your network. To do this, you'll have to move or copy the tools from the alpha test directories named above to those customary directories.

To install the executable files for the tools into */local/bin*:

1. Login as root or bin to perform these steps, since files in */local/bin* aren't usually owned by non-privileged users.

2. Set read-write permissions on all the shell script files, since you're going to be modifying some of them. (You can look at the source code for *mvawkdir* for a precise list of files that will be modified.)

3. Copy the executable files from the alpha test directories (*CMHTREE/at/sun4sh.plt* and *CMHTREE/at/sun4gcc.plt*) into */local/bin*, maintaining your read-write permissions. Make sure you copy the *awk* files too.

4. Update the hardcoded pathnames of the *awkdir* variables in the tools that are implemented as batch file scripts, so they don't look in the alpha test directories to find their *awk* scripts (which they do by default).

   Use the *mvawkdir* script to update the pathnames, since it was written for this purpose. Invoke *mvawkdir* with no arguments to get instructions on how to run it. Invoke it with the new directory location (*/local/bin*) to modify the scripts.

5. Reset the ownership and file permissions on all scripts and relocated files to whatever is the standard for your site (we use ownership=root, permissions=755).

Installing DOS Tools on a Network Drive

Just as for UNIX, you'll probably want to make the DOS versions of the tools permanently available in the usual directories on your network. To do this, you'll have to move or copy the tools out of the alpha test directories into those customary directories.

To install the DOS executable files for the tools into */local/dos/bin* (or wherever you want them on your network drive):

1. Copy the DOS executable and script files from the alpha test directories into the new location (e.g., */local/dos/bin*).

2. Set read-write permissions on all the shell script files, since you're going to be modifying some of them. (You can look at the source code for *mvawkdir* for a precise list of files that will be modified.)

3. Update the hardcoded pathnames of the *awkdir* variables in the tools that are implemented as batch file scripts, so they don't look in the alpha test directories to find their *awk* scripts (which they do by default).

   Use the *mvawkdir* script to update the pathnames, since it was written for this purpose. Invoke *mvawkdir* with no arguments to get instructions on how to run it. Invoke it with the new directory location (*/local/bin*) to modify the scripts. (Warning: double backslashes are required in pathnames for DOS!)

4. Reset the ownership and file permissions on all scripts and relocated files to whatever is the standard for your site for DOS executables.

Now all people on the network (both DOS and UNIX users) should be able to use the tools without having the alpha test directories in their **PATH** variables. (People must still define **CMTREE**, **CMHTREE**, and **CMPCILOG** environment variables, and in addition **CMTREE_B**, **CMHTREE_B** for DOS.)

Users of Borland compilers should be careful to use the proper templates for their versions of Borland *make*. The *make* tool distributed with Borland C++ 2.0 treats a single dollar sign in a makefile as a dollar sign, so the following *sed* command from *CMTREE/plt/tbc.plt/makefile.llb* works fine:

```
$(SED) -e "s/^/+ /" -e "s/$/ \& /" -e "$s/\&//" $(TMPFILE) > $(OBJLIST)
```

But the *make* tool distributed with Borland C++ 4.0 needs two $$ in a makefile to create a $, so the *sed* line in the *makefile.llb* for *bc4.plt* must to be changed to:

```
$(SED) -e "s/^/+ /" -e "s/$/ \& /" -e "$$s/\&//" $(TMPFILE) > $(OBJLIST)
```

If you get an error message like "sed: unknown command" when you're compiling libraries with Borland tools, this is likely to be the underlying reason.

Installing Local Compiler Options

To complete the installation, you'll have to modify the compiler options in the make-file templates to match the conventions at your site. Then when the tools automatically generate makefiles, the makefiles will contain the appropriate compiler, linker, and library search path options for your site.

This set of instructions applies to all platforms, including UNIX and DOS.

1. Adjust the compiler and linker options in the platform template file for each plat-form you'll be using. (The platform file has the same name as the platform—*sun4gcc.plt* for the *sun4gcc.plt* platform, *tdos.plt* for the *tdos.plt* platform, and so on.)

2. Also adjust the location of the default logging file (or newsgroup) in the source code of the *pci* tool (located in the *cmtools/pci.scr* subtree). If you choose to use a newsgroup for logging on UNIX systems, be sure to create a newsgroup with a name that matches that in the *pci* source code.

   Individuals can override the default location of the log file by using the **CMPCILOG** environment variable.

Initializing Your Environment Variables

This discussion applies to all platforms.

It describes how to set up your **PATH**, **CMPCILOG**, **CMTREE**, **CMHTREE**, and **USER** environ-ment variables for the tools.

The **USER** variable should be set to the name you wish to appear in RCS version mes-sages. Normally, the **USER** variable is set to your network login name (for example, I have the statement **set user=jameson** in my *autoexec.bat* file.

The **CMPCILOG** variable should point to a file that will contain a copy of all RCS checkin messages.

The **CMTREE** and **CMHTREE** variables should point to the roots of their respective direc-tory trees (*cmt* and *h*).

PATH should contain the appropriate alpha test directories so that you can run exported executable files directly from the alpha test directories. For example, on my PC my **PATH** contains *\%cmhtree_b\%\at\tdos.plt* and *\%cmhtree_b\%\at\tbc.plt*. On UNIX, my path contains */$CMHTREE/at/sun4gcc.plt* and */$CMHTREE/at/sun4sh.plt*.

For DOS only: If your **PATH** variable doesn't have room to add these two directories, you might try using the DOS *subst* command to alias the directories to a drive name. Here's a sample sequence of commands from my *autoexec.bat* to do this. The com-mands let me use drives S and T to represent the two alpha test directories I named earlier. The commands also assume my *config.sys* file contains a **lastdrive=t** state-ment, which lets me access drives up to and including **t**.

```
lastdrive=t                      ;this line is in config.sys!

set cmhtree=j:/h                 ;these lines are in autoexec.bat
set cmhtree_b=j:\h
path=c:\dos                      ;so dos can find the subst command
...
subst s: %cmhtree_
subst t: %cmhtree_
...
PATH=s:;t:;%pat
```

Installation on UNIX-only Systems

If you're installing the tools on a UNIX system only, follow the steps for the DOS-UNIX network described above, but ignore all the steps that pertain to DOS.

Installation on DOS-only Systems

If you're installing the software for DOS system only, here's what you have to do. Some of the sections above may also be relevant to your situation, so you should read them if you haven't done so already.

1. Copy files from the distribution disks into a new directory. Copy all the files in the top level directory of each disk. In addition, copy all the files in the DOS subdirectory of each disk. The directory can be a temporary directory in your private hierarchy, or a permanent directory where the software will reside.

2. Type **instdos.bat** to unpack and install the software. This script has several options—one that installs only executable files (*instdos exe*), one that installs executable and source files (*instdos all*), and one that cleans up the source trees by deleting old object files (*instdos cleanup*).

3. There's no need to compile the software during installation (as is required for UNIX installations). This is because a full set of DOS executables is supplied on the distribution disks. But if you want to compile the software, use the *twalker* scripts at the top of the source trees to walk the platforms of interest. For example, you can walk and compile in all the *msc.plt* (Microsoft C) platforms by typing **walkmsc.bat nmake all**.

   If you're not working on a PC that's equipped with the Borland C 2.0 compiler or the Microsoft C 6.0 compiler, you'll have to manually port and compile the software to your particular platform. Create a set of new makefile templates for your platform (see the section called "Creating Makefile Templates for New Platforms" in Chapter 6, *Makefile Architectures*), and then use the steps in the *instdos.bat* script as a guide to proper installation. (It may help you to know there's a special section of code in *instdos.bat* that's enabled if **USER = jameson**. That special section of code automatically recompiles all the tools using tree walker scripts.)

4. Adjust the compiler and linker options in the appropriate makefile template files *CMTREE\plt\tbc.plt\tbc.plt* and *CMTREE\plt\tdos.plt\tdos.plt* (for Borland C compilers). Also adjust the options in any other platforms you intend to use, such as the *msc.plt* or *mdos.plt* platform files for Microsoft C compilers.

5. Adjust the default location of the *pci.log* file in the source code for *pci.bat*. It's located in the *cmtools\pci.scr* subtree (or in the *CMHTREE/at/tdos.plt* directory in the holding tree). If the environment variable $CMPCILOG isn't defined in a user's environment, the hardcoded value in *pci.bat* will be used. The log file collects a copy of all RCS checkin log entries in one file for convenience.

6. Relocate the CMTREE and the CMHTREE to permanent locations of your choice. This can be done by recursively copying the trees using *xcopy* (*mkdir newplace; xcopy oldtree newplace /s/e*). Be aware that the *xcopy* tool under DOS does not preserve file permissions, so all of the files in the new trees will be writable. (This isn't a really big deal, even for RCS files that are normally read-only.)

7. Set up your environment variables as described above.

Rebuilding the DOS Software from Scratch

DOS executable files are provided for all software tools that come with this book, so you don't have to rebuild the software from scratch on DOS systems if you don't want to. But if you're working on a UNIX system, you'll have to compile the tools before you can use them.

To rebuild the software on DOS, go into the root node of each of the *cmtools*, *cmpds*, and *cmdosexe* trees, and use the appropriate *twalker* script to traverse the platform directories of your choice.* The tree walker scripts are provided for your convenience. You can use them to walk the source trees, to rebuild the software programs therein, and to export the final programs into the alpha test directories that were mentioned earlier. (The generation and use of tree walker scripts is explained in Chapter 2. There's also more information later in the book. Use the index to find all the appropriate page references.)

For example, if you're working with the Borland C compiler, you could rebuild and export the software tool programs by typing **walktbc make all**. (But first, you'll have to modify the makefile templates in the CMTREE to specify the locations of the Borland link libraries on your machine before this command will work.) And if you understand

---

* *twalker* is a tool that produces batch scripts that "walk" (traverse) particular directories in source trees. Once you've generated such a script, you can use it to execute an arbitrary command in all the visited directories. It's common practice for me to generate and discard these scripts on an as-needed basis, since they're so easy to generate. The scripts provide the same generic kind of service as would the *find* command: *find . -type d -name '*.plt' -print -exec somecmd* in UNIX.

sed scripts, you can look in the *instdos.bat* file to see how *sed* is used to automatically modify the link library paths in the templates on my personal computer. For Microsoft C 6.0, you could type *walkmsc nmake all*. And so on.

Don't forget to rebuild the batch files too—*walktdos make all*, or *walkmdos nmake all*. Batch file products use a platform (e.g., *tdos.plt*) that is different that used by compiled products (e.g., *tbc.plt*) because batch file products require different treatment in the makefile templates than do compiled products (such as binary executables and libraries). For example, one difference is that you don't have to compile batch files.

To rebuild the software on a Sun workstation, you can use the *insts4*, *insts4_2*, and *insts4_3* scripts provided on the disks. They use the *sun4sh.plt* and *sun4gcc.plt* platforms.

Last, if you're on an operating system that's not already supported, you'll probably have to port some of the software tools before you can use the whole set. In that case, you should read the book to see how the whole code management system works, because it will save you porting time. In particular, read the hands-on tour chapters, because they explain the interactions of the tools and source trees you'll have to work with. Finally, once you understand how the system works, you might want to follow the steps that I used in the installation scripts to get the software up and running on your machine.

Installation on Other Systems

Directions for installing the software tools on other systems (such as for Amiga) are provided in files on the distribution disks. The OS/2 installation is identical to the DOS installation described above. The NeXT installation is identical to the UNIX installation described above.

Software Licensing Information

The following software copyright, licensing, and commercial support options are supposed to satisfactorily cover a range of common code management needs. However, despite my efforts, they might not satisfy your particular needs. If that's the case, please contact me and we'll try to work out something more suitable to you.

Kevin Jameson, 1994

Software Copyright

The software in this book is copyrighted ©1994, Realcase Software Research Corporation. All rights are reserved.

Single users

A single-user source code license is automatically included with the purchase of each book. The source license allows you to copy and modify the source code for your own individual use. The intent of the license is to allow book purchasers to modify the source code for the tools, to suit their particular needs and development environments.

Multiple users

Multiple users at a site can be supported by buying one book per user. However, this might not be convenient for all sites. If you would prefer to site license the software without purchasing a book for each user, multiply the number of users by $25.00 U.S. to calculate the site license fee.

Commercial support services

If you would like to receive commercial support services and upgrades to the book software, or if you are interested in an enhanced, fully commercial version of the tools in the future, please contact me at 403-265-0595 (the ISA Corp. offices) or via email at the address below.

Commercial payments

Site licensing fees can be paid by sending a bank note or postal money order directly to me at the following address:

Kevin Jameson
Realcase Software Research Corporation
Suite 506
2010 Ulster Road NW
Calgary AB
Canada T2N 4C2

My email address is *mpcm@realcase.com*.

1

Introduction

Multi-platform code management can be a real circus act, especially if you have to coordinate the *reliable* and *efficient* sharing of multiple source files and multiply-shared include and object library files, among multiple developers who work on multiple revisions of multiple configurations of multiple programs that form multiple product suites for use on multiple platforms.

When programming takes place on a large scale, the sheer number of dimensions can be surprising.

Calculating the "dimensionality" of code development environments is a useful (but extremely informal) way of quickly getting a feel for the complexity of an environment. (Compare Figure 1-1 and Figure 1-2, which show opposite extremes of complexity in code management environments.)

Just multiply all the relevant factors together. For example, one environment mentioned in this book has thousands of source files, hundreds of shared include files, tens of programmers, tens of programs in the product suite, several revisions and configurations of the products, and several platforms. Fortunately, most of us won't have to deal with that much complexity and dimensionality very often.

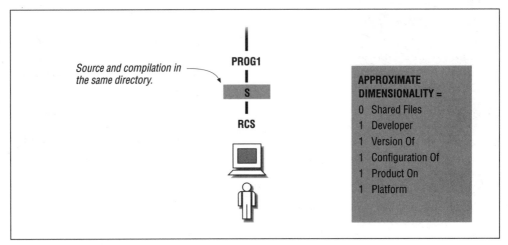

Figure 1-1. Single-person, single-platform development

This book describes an inexpensive, yet tested (and fully scalable) solution to many code management problems. Specifically, the book describes a set of policies, proce- dures, and automated software tools that will help you to improve your productivity in almost any kind of development environment. Complete source code for the tools is also provided, so that you can tune the tools to fit your particular environment if nec- essary.

The main purpose of this introductory chapter is to prepare you for understanding the solutions that are presented later on in the book. To do that, I'd like to start where you are (or should I say, where we all are? :-), probably in the code management trenches, and take you on a quick mental airplane ride so that you can get a bird's-eye view of the new ideas and concepts in the upcoming code management landscape.

Once I've explained my own perspective on familiar problems in code management, I'll show how the tools in this book can make your programming life a bit easier.

Here's an overview of what we'll cover in this chapter. First, we'll review a list of common software development problems. That'll give us both a common starting point and a firm understanding of the problems to be solved.

Second, we'll have a look at an important lesson that I once learned about problem solving. The lesson is that it's not always smart to divide a set of seemingly unrelated big problems into little problems that you think you can solve. Sometimes it's better to try to find a general *superproblem* that's shared by all of the little problems. That way you can walk around the whole forest, instead of spending a lot of time dodging indi- vidual trees.

Third, we'll use the superproblem technique to help us solve the list of code manage- ment subproblems that are commonly found "in the programming trenches."

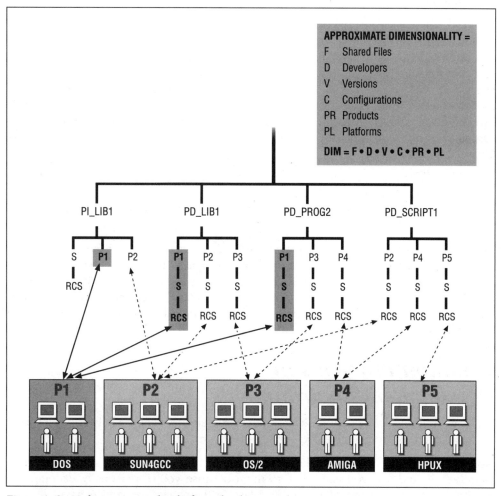

Figure 1-2. Multi-person, multi-platform development

Fourth, we'll take time out for a short overview of the main technical solutions used by the rest of the book. The overview is too short to tell the whole story, but you'll pick up more of the details later, as you work through the tutorial examples.

Definitions and Terminology

These are definitions for some common terms that I use throughout the book.

A *product* is a loose term that means "anything produced and exported by a source tree." For example, a product could be an executable program, a code library, or an include file that will be shared by other products.

A *product node* or *product source tree* is a place for storing product files. The structure of product nodes is described later in this chapter.

A *platform* is the name given to a particular computing environment. Usually, a platform is comprised of a particular compiler, with particular compilation options, for a particular operating system that runs on particular hardware. Other things can distinguish platforms too, such as particular versions of compilers, operating systems, and so on because different versions of software or hardware can require different treatment. Two of the common platform names used in this book are *tbc.plt* (for Borland's C compiler) and *sun4gcc.plt* (for the GNU C compiler running on SunOS on a Sun4 (Sparc) computer).

The abbreviations *pi*, *pd*, and *pid* mean "platform independent," "platform dependent," and "platform independent *and* dependent," respectively. The abbreviations help me to avoid long, throat-choking sentences that discuss pi and pd concepts.

When I use the word *standard* in this book, as in the phrases "standard directory structures" or "standard makefile structures," I don't mean to make you think of an ANSI or ISO standard with all of its attendant formality. Instead, I mean to describe something that has the same structure, purpose, or contents in a variety of different situations. For example, this book describes a few "standard" directory structures that can be effectively used on almost any project, and a "standard" six-part makefile structure that makes it easy to manage project makefiles.

Common Problems in Development Environments

This section lists some common development problems that can be solved (or substantially mitigated) by an effective code management system.

What you should get out of this list of problems is a familiar feeling that you've seen them before, and that you can relate to them because you've personally experienced them. (On the other hand, if you can't relate to them because you've never experienced them, then maybe *you* should be writing a book telling the rest of us how you've managed to avoid them for so long!)

I've divided the problems into three categories for convenience: problems with the code, problems with the makefiles, and problems with the project infrastructure.

Problems with Code

This section describes problems that are commonly associated with the source code itself or with its organization on the software project. These problems are usually tangible and obvious, since code is so concrete. We'll look at three subproblems here.

- How the use of conditional compilation statements (such as **#ifdefs** in the C language) can reduce code eadability and maintainability. I call this the *readability* problem. (The techniques in this book are valid for any programming language that uses an ASCII source representation, but we'll use C in the examples because it's so popular.)

- How the mixing of platform-independent (pi) and platform-dependent (pd) information in the same source file can reduce portability and maintainability. I call this the *multi-platform* problem.

- How poor file organization strategies reduce the ability of software projects to:

  - Efficiently store and share both source and binary files between multiple developers, for multiple platforms, over consecutive releases of the software

  - Efficiently isolate reusable software files

  - Efficiently organize (and reorganize) directory structures to better meet the needs of growing software projects

  I call this the *source code organization (and reorganization)* problem.

The readability problem

Are a couple of pictures worth a thousand words? Example 1-1 shows a freeware code sample that I received from the net. It comes from the popular *getopt.c* subroutine that's frequently used to parse command-line arguments in freeware programs.

Example 1-1: Code with Too Many #ifdefs

```
/* If compiled with GNU C, use the built-in alloca */
#ifdef __GNUC__
#define alloca __builtin_alloca
#else /* not __GNUC__ */
#ifdef sparc
#include <alloca.h>
#else
char *alloca ();
#endif
#endif /* not __GNUC__ */

#ifdef STDC_HEADERS || __GNU_LIBRARY__ || __STDC__
#include <stdlib.h>
#include <string.h>
#define bcopy(s, d, n) memcpy ((d), (s), (n))
#define index strchr
#else
#ifdef USG
#include <string.h>
#define bcopy(s, d, n) memcpy ((d), (s), (n))
#define index strchr
#else
#ifdef VMS
#include <string.h>
#else
```

Example 1–1: Code with Too Many #ifdef's (continued)

```
#include <strings.h>
#endif
void bcopy ();
#endif
```

Of course we know that most programmers could eventually parse and understand this code if they really wanted to. But I think you'd have a hard time convincing most people that this kind of code is easy to read, to understand, and to maintain. The truth is that almost all code requires some effort on the part of programmers to understand, especially if the code is poorly documented or if it uses lots of **#ifdefs**. But the point to remember is that there's a tradeoff between making the code easier to understand and wasting time and money. (Note that you can waste time and money by putting in either too much or too little documentation!)

Interestingly, the readability problem can compound geometrically as **#ifdefs** for new platforms are added. This is because the number of possible interactions between nested **#ifdefs** increases according to the powers of two.

The multi-platform problem

If your product supports multiple platforms, you probably have at least some platform-dependent code in your source files somewhere. The multi-platform problem has to do with how you represent and store that pd code. In particular, embedding sections of pd code into a large source file is usually a bad thing to do for several reasons:

- It makes the code harder to read and to maintain. (**#ifdefs** decrease readability, as discussed above.)

- It prevents the pd code from being reused in other programs. This is because the code is embedded inside a source file, where it can't easily be accessed, cloned, or reused in other programs.

- It's a technique that doesn't scale up well. This is because of the previous two problems.*

- It makes it more difficult to add support for new platforms, or to remove support for old platforms. Either way, programmers are forced to search out every platform-dependent **#ifdef** in the product and make the appropriate coding changes. This is often detailed work that requires a lot of concentration so the programmer understands the overlaps and interactions between the existing **#ifdefs** and the affected fragments of pi and pd code for multiple platforms. Also, it can force a lot of check-out and check-in activity in the source code control system. In other words, more work.

---

* For example, consider the many machine (*m-xxxxx.h*) and operating system (*s-xxxxx.h*) files used by the Free Software Foundation in the GNU Emacs editor. These include files don't use platform-dependent **#ifdefs**.

But consider what happens if all the pd code is isolated in separate files. Programmers then have it much easier. To add support for new platforms, they can clone and modify an existing set of pd files (sometimes the changes required are minimal). And to remove support for an existing platform, they just have to delete the appropriate pd files. No checkouts at all, and only a few checkins (one for each cloned file, to register the new pd files with the code control system).

Under this system, the "problem" of maintaining duplicate files does sometimes arise, because sometimes the pd code for two platforms will be identical. But the cost of maintaining such files is insignificant compared to normal code maintenance costs. I've found that making duplicate changes is either a matter of just copying the whole pd file, or of cutting and pasting the relevant piece of code. These are both cheap operations. And of course, when the duplicate files suddenly require *different* platform-dependent changes, having a code management system that supports separate files is a significant advantage.

For these reasons, this book recommends that you disallow platform-dependent `#ifdefs` in your code. (Other kinds of `#ifdefs` are okay, such as those for debugging, feature options, and so on. That's because they're platform-independent options.)

One of my co-workers used to say, "Platform-dependent code is the crabgrass in the lawn of life. It grows everywhere, and you never know how much there is until you try to get rid of it." Disallowing platform-dependent `#ifdefs` will help you to control this particular form of weed.

The source code organization problem

The problem of poor source code organization is widespread, and has no single, easily identified symptom. Instead, it has many symptoms.

One such symptom is the lack of a well-defined model for storing and accessing source files in a multi-person, multi-platform environment. For example, you can often recognize a poor file organization strategy by the presence of isolated pockets of source code among developers. (Instead, source code should be shared out of a central source tree.) Another symptom of a poor strategy is the difficulty of simultaneously supporting development, maintenance, and testing activities with the same set of source files. Or maybe it's difficult to create a private work environment to test *part* of the overall software product. Maybe it's difficult to add or remove support for new platforms, or to determine which files require porting in order to support a new computing environment. And so on.

A second big symptom of poor file organization is a difficulty in efficiently sharing files among products, programs, or co-workers, even within the same company. As a consequence, reuse is much less common than it should be.

For example, I once worked in a shop where there were six very expert C++ developers (with their own personal tools) working on a product that contained a very competent linked list package. There were also another two or three customer service programmers. And guess how many different linked list packages were on the filesystem? I'm sure you've already figured it out. I stopped counting at seven. What amazed me is that seven expert developers in a UNIX C++ environment (which is the epitome of a good development environment)—could end up with seven different linked list packages (which are generally acknowledged to be one of the simplest examples of reusable software in any language).

The source code reorganization problem

Another symptom of poor file organizations is that project *reorganizations* can badly disturb both the explicit (hardcoded) and implicit references that exist between current project files. The typical consequence of reorganizations in such environments is that the reorganized files and products fail to compile, to link, or to execute properly. Moreover, any auxiliary tools and script files that make explicit or implicit assumptions about the project directory structure may also fail to work properly.

However, reorganizations are a part of life in the trenches. They might be required to better support new, natural conceptual divisions in the product as it evolves. They might also be required because new files and interrelationships are added, because new sub-products are created, or for some other pressing reason. Whatever the cause, file reorganizations carried out in the presence of poor file organization strategies are often error-prone (and thus costly).

Problems with Makefiles

This section describes two problems that originate in the makefiles on software projects. There are many problems inherent in makefiles of course, such as *make*'s inability to track changes in filenames and its fragile sensitivity to clock synchronization problems in networked environments. But we're only going to consider two of them here, because they have to do with code management. The two problems are excessive makefile complexity and lack of makefile portability.

Excessive complexity

One of the most common makefile problems on software projects is excessive makefile complexity. This is especially true if you're working in a multi-platform environment. For example, different *make* tools for the different platforms often use different grammars, different built-in options and strategies, different macro symbols, and so on. This increases project complexity because programmers have to understand and use several different makefile languages.

Another source of complexity in makefiles is the practice of building multiple products from within one makefile. Multiple products often share files in the form of include files, libraries, and separate and special object files.

In some makefiles, the sometimes enormous number of macros are used to describe features and options for different machines, compiler options, linker options, and product feature options.

The use of recursive makefiles adds complexity, since the recursion is not always elegantly handled. (Recursion is rarely easy to understand the first few times you see it, even if it is elegantly done.)

As a project progresses, common development tasks tend to become encoded in special makefile targets, creating further complexity. Programmers don't want to keep repeating the same set of commands for commonly repeated development tasks. Instead, they encode the commands in a makefile target to easily reuse the encoded knowledge (simply by invoking *make* on the special makefile target). As a consequence, makefiles tend to collect all kinds of ad hoc, non-standard command sequences with a corresponding increase in complexity.

Lack of makefile portability

Another common problem with makefiles is that they are rarely portable across multiple platforms; sometimes even the default makefile filenames are different. (Some *make* tools use the *.mk* or *.mak* suffix, for example.) The lack of portability usually stems from two major sources: syntax and built-in features. The syntaxes of different *make* tools often differ in the use of special characters such as backslash (\), dollar ($), caret (^), and asterisk (*). Syntaxes also differ in the conventions for leading whitespace at the beginning of target rules (spaces or tabs) and for spacing around the colons that appear at the end of target names.

Many built-in features are very non-portable. For example, some *make* tools have special "conditional compilation" (`if/else`) features. Almost all *make* tools have special makefile macros for representing the current target name, target base name, target suffix, the current dependency name, the directory name part of the current dependency name, and so on. There are many special conventions in modern *make* tools that are not portable to other platforms. Some *make* tools even include special support for handling version control systems such as RCS (Revision Control System) and SCCS (Source Code Control System).

Recursion in makefiles is usually not a portable feature. The technique works fine on UNIX (where it was probably conceived), but it's very difficult to use on popular personal computer systems that don't have virtual memory.

Problems with Project Infrastructure

This section considers common development problems that arise from inadequacies in the project infrastructure. The term "infrastructure" refers to the set of basic facilities and services that supports any organization doing code development.

On a software project, infrastructure refers to the tools, procedures, and other systems that support the harmonious work of groups of managers and programmers. Typically, such systems include source code control, configuration management, mechanisms for promoting reuse of code through file sharing, and systems for supporting communication among project personnel.

Shortcomings in project infrastructures can give rise to several familiar development problems. We'll look at four here: source code control systems, inadequate file sharing systems, inadequate developer communication systems, and unstable private development environments.

Inadequate source code control

The hallmark symptoms of inadequate source code control systems are easy to recognize. They include baseline compilation or execution failures, software release failures, and software demonstration failures. (The **baseline** version of the software is the latest official version.) They are also indicated by various kinds of confusion and fumbling in the trenches—people aren't sure where to find the latest version of the source code, where to find a complete version of the source code, or what changes have been made to that code. The development, maintenance, and testing teams have trouble working from the same set of source files, and so on.

For example, the developers at one company where I worked had unofficially split the source code for the company's only product into three physically separated pieces—one piece for each of the three main developers on the project. The three pieces were the kernel (low-level communication and memory management software), the executive (the part that contained the core intelligence of the product), and the user interface (the part that the users saw). One or two other developers kind of hung around and worked on various non-core (but still important) parts of the product. The problem wasn't so much the dismemberment of the product into three pieces of personal turf—it was that there was so little coordination between the three pieces of turf. That is, there was no central, working repository of code. Instead, since all the developers (legitimately) wanted to work in their own stable development environments, they cloned the other 2/3 of the product that they needed from the personal source trees of the other two developers.

One day we were in a progress meeting, and someone described a bug that had just resurfaced in the software. One of the developers said with surprise, "I thought we fixed that two weeks ago." The problem occurred because he *had* fixed the defect—in his own cloned copy of a module that belonged to someone else's turf. So someone else, being the "owner" of that turf, had inadvertently clobbered the corrected version because he thought his copy was the most current copy.

This whole story took place in one of the sudden scrambles that usually occurred when a potential customer wanted a demonstration. There would be a mad rush to isolate the three major pieces of turf from their environments and then merge them into a single working copy of the product. It usually took a full week to do that, and then another full week to find and upgrade the latest copy of the test suites (which usually hadn't been used since the last demonstration).

Please don't think that these developers were just thumb-twiddlers who were fresh out of school, and who had never worked on a real software project of significant size. Some of them were fresh out of graduate school, for sure. But none of them were thumb-twiddlers. They were all consummate UNIX hackers, with a deep knowledge of C++, advanced shell script techniques, and UNIX internals. (They were also instrumental in constructing the first version of the ideas that motivated this book.) The point here is that that this kind of fumbling isn't just reserved for the inexperienced—it can happen to groups of experts, too. Unless a group is constantly on guard for it, this kind of behavior has a way of just sneaking up on your group while management has you concentrating on "more important" tasks.

After a story like this, is it really any surprise that a good code management system can save a company thousands of dollars, in a relatively short period of time?

Inadequate file sharing mechanisms

A second common project infrastructure problem is the inability to efficiently share files among programs, developers, or among teams of people within the same corporate environment.

The immediate consequence of poor file sharing mechanisms is the proliferation of personal copies of the files that couldn't be shared. I've already told one story about such proliferation—the seven personal linked-list packages that were owned by the seven expert developers. The main lesson of this story is that object oriented languages don't automatically promote code reuse; *efficacious file sharing mechanisms* do—regardless of the programming language used inside the shared files.

A second story about file sharing also comes to mind, this time illustrating the point that administrative (infrastructure) policies can play an important role in efficient file sharing. As I heard this story from a staff member at our local university, the university had a policy of not allowing computer games to be played on the mainframe. After all, the main purpose of the expensive computer was to service the legitimate computing needs of researchers, teachers, and students. And since resources were limited— particularly disk space—the administrative policy was to disallow all computer games. In particular, the policies disallowed one particular game (let's call it Astro Trek) that was popular at the time.

The administration eventually ended up in a computer war with the "gamesters," as they were sometimes affectionately called, in a fight for disk space. To recover disk space used for storing games files, the systems programmers wrote a script that deleted all recognizable computer games. The gamesters responded by recopying their games into files with non-standard names. The systems programmers started checking file sizes and binary file contents. And so it went.

Eventually the administration created a "Games" project to promote the sharing of one copy of each game. And what seemed even more clever to me was the small annual fee that was required to use the project—high enough for the university to offset administration costs, but low enough for everyone to afford. And—you guessed it—the systems programmers stopped finding hundreds of copies of the same computer games on the filesystem.

There are three other file sharing situations worth mentioning.

First, it's beneficial to an organization if the various development, maintenance, software testing, and software releasing teams can all work simultaneously from the same set of product source files.

For example, it makes little sense for the testing team to spend a lot of time testing one baseline version when the development team has made most of that version obsolete through the addition of new features. It's also a drag for the testing team to have to wait around for several days while the development team struggles to put together a working version of the baseline. Instead, it'd be much more efficient if the two teams could work independently from the same set of (evolving) source files.

Second, it would be beneficial if project file sharing mechanisms would track the use of shared include files, and automatically trigger recompilations of affected programs if the shared include files were changed. Current traditional methods of sharing include files (such as the **-Idirectory** method) won't do either of these things. This is one of the reasons that some development shops recompile all of their products on a periodic basis (such as once a week, once a month, or once a year). It is the only way they can make sure their products pick up new changes in include files referenced (shared) with the **-Idirectory** method.

And third, it's useful to be able to identify all the users of a shared file (regardless of whether it's an include file, a source file, or an object file). If the files are disorganized, you may have to search through thousands of source files and makefiles to find all the references to the filenames that interest you. And that can be time consuming, even with fully automated searches on fast machines.

Poor project communication mechanisms

The term "project communication mechanisms" is meant to describe the mechanisms that collect and store information about the project, and carry it to the developers. For example, RCS checkin logs, bug fix databases, lists of shared files, and even the programming notes that describe the latest baseline or official release of the software are all considered to be standard communication mechanisms on software projects. Inadequacies in any of these mechanisms can cause problems.

For example, suppose the baseline crashes when you rebuild it overnight after developers have been checking in code changes for a few days. If you have a comprehensive RCS checkin log available (one that lists all the RCS checkin messages in one place), then it's easy to read the last few days of the log to identify the source files and changes that are mostly likely responsible for the baseline failure.

If you don't have such a log, you're faced with a much less reliable process of holding meetings with the developers in hopes that their memories of the last few days can help to identify the offending code changes. And the situation without logs is far, far worse if the baseline defect isn't detected for a few extra days or weeks. By that time, it's likely that the developers will have made too many changes to remember them all.

Scale-up failure

Scale-up failures occur when the size of the project causes useful techniques to fail, and otherwise harmless problems to become intractable. Here's a story that illustrates the scale-up problem fairly well, and the feeling of helplessness that scales up along with the size of the problem.

My friend Andrew once worked at a company where they had about 20 big interrelated software products that were built from *thousands* of source files and about 750,000 lines of code. There was *lots* of file sharing going on, too—include files, code libraries, object files (which were members of multiple products), and even executable files. The sharing was necessary to both build and release the products because some files were part of several different products.

Andrew was asked to "ansify" (convert to ANSI standard) one of the products. This wasn't so bad, since the program files comprising that particular product were well isolated, and easy to identify. The include files were another story, however.

For historical reasons (which is a euphemism for "it just happened that way, and none of us could come up with a better idea until it was too late (expensive) to change our ways"), most of the include files in the company were in two include file directories. One directory contained include files that were released as parts of products, and the other directory contained include files that were intended for in-house use only (for compiling other files). Hundreds of include files were in each of the two directories.

The project had grown so large that no one knew anymore which products used which include files, or even if any particular include file was still useful to any program. (Really, who *could* know, when hundreds of include files and thousands of source files are involved?) Even worse, the include files were nested—many of them included a few other include files, too. The include file sharing relationships in this environment had become so complex that no human could understand them any more.

What were the main consequences of this situation? Here's what Andrew had to say about his experiences:

> It was difficult to find an appropriate place to store the new ANSI function prototypes. We wanted to put them inside the include files that were closely associated with the products that were going to use those include files. But we couldn't do that, because we didn't know which include files belonged to each product. The reality was that almost every program included almost every include file, directly or indirectly.

We eventually ended up with a small number of include files (say 10 or 20) that contained large numbers (hundreds) of prototypes. Now almost every program has to include some of these prototype files in order to compile, making the sharing relationships among files and include files even more complex.

Because we couldn't match include files with products, we didn't ansify the include files in any organized way at all. Instead, we just ansified the individual statements within include files as needed, just enough to fix compilation errors. As a consequence, some of our include files probably still aren't ansified, even though we spent several man-years on ansifying our code.

We learned not to put **typedefs** in the same include files as prototypes, because this forces you to include both sets of information when you only want to include one.

However, since the included prototypes often referenced other data types that weren't defined in that particular file, we were often forced to include even more include files to define the necessary data type definitions. That forced us to include more prototypes, which required more data type definitions, and so on.

The explosion in the number of included files (caused by the previous problems) indirectly coupled many source files to include files that they didn't directly use. As a result, many unwanted, unrelated recompilations are now triggered whenever we change almost any include file.

Recompilations are important to avoid on projects the size of ours because they typically consume many hours or even days of machine time. They also slow down turnaround times on test runs and product rebuilds.

You can easily imagine the overall effect—the progress of your team slows down to a crawl. And Kevin, be sure to note that the problem of triggering extra recompilations is *forever*, not just during ansification.

We also encountered the standard types of problems that are found in situations involving complex and unknown sharing relationships.

For instance, it was—and still is—too difficult to identify and delete obsolete definitions in the include files. This is because before you can delete a definition, you have to search all known source files for possible references to it, and this is very problematic.

One reason is that it's difficult to construct a search expression that matches only the token that you're interested in. Too general, and you a get a list of thousands of unwanted references; too specific, and you might miss some occurrences. So it's always hard to trust the results of your searches.

Not only that, but on a project as large as ours, the same token might have several different meanings in several different products. If that's the case, you have to manually examine every occurrence of the token.

It's usually too risky to delete things from include files anyway, because the consequences of being wrong are very high. For example, suppose the master software build operation fails because you made a mistake deleting a definition. Then you tend to get nasty electronic mail messages from the other developers because the current baseline rebuild is delayed for many hours or several days. No thank you, Kevin. I'd rather leave the obsolete definitions alone.

Andrew's most telling words on this subject will stay with me for a long, long time. Here they are.

> The biggest consequence [of the situation described above] is that the quality of your include files steadily degrades over time. And you're essentially powerless to stop it, unless you're prepared to devote large quantities of resources to solving the problem.

> And I do mean large—we spent several man-years ansifying our source files, and that still wasn't enough effort to overcome the problems in ansifying the shared include files.

I like this story because it's a good example of scale-up failure. The sobering part is, as Andrew once said, "It's difficult to justify short-term clean-up costs on projects of this size, especially when the corresponding benefits are long term and non-obvious to the customer. As a result, the code problems are usually never fixed, and your only option is to live with them—forever."

Unstable work environments

Unstable work environments are another potential infrastructure problem. It is very difficult for developers to track down and eliminate unwanted bugs in programs when their work environment (and maybe even the program being debugged) is changing underneath their feet. This can happen, for example, if the program being debugged uses subroutine libraries that are frequently updated by other programmers. In such cases, the programmers who are debugging programs inadvertently link in a new version of the library routines every time they recompile the program being debugged.

In practice, of course, programmers rarely put up with volatile work environments. Instead, they'll do almost anything to stabilize their work environment. They'll clone entire source trees, rebuild personal copies of entire libraries, work late at night to avoid other programmers, or even doctor the operating system defaults. You can't really blame them, either. Who wants to work in an office that's always moving up and down the hall?

Superproblem Analysis

The purpose of the previous section was to establish a common point of view by discussing some problems that are familiar to almost everyone. Now that we've done that, I can give you another perspective on those same problems by teaching you about superproblem analysis. (I'll teach you the same way that I was taught—by listening to another story!)

I once knew a man who was an acknowledged leader in his field of computer science research. He had both a wonderful clarity of thought and the ability to communicate those thoughts in a clear and cogent speaking style. One weekend when he was visiting our company (he was Co-founder and Chief Scientist or something like that), I had the opportunity to join him and several other people for lunch at a local Chinese restaurant.

During our conversation, I not-so-subtly queried him about his approach to problem solving, in the hopes that I could learn more about how he *thought*. So he and I carried on a question-and-answer session between ourselves for about five minutes. Here's what he said about superproblem analysis.

One of his very best problem-solving techniques was to take the time to look around in the problem space for *superproblems* instead of immediately focusing on the obvious symptoms (subproblems) right in front of him. This was a worthwhile approach because it was sometimes easier to solve the whole superproblem than it was to solve many interrelated subproblems. He continued by explaining that it was sometimes difficult to find clean solutions to subproblems, because the effects from other (related but unsolved) subproblems would get in the way.

I asked him, "How do you search for the superproblem, and how do you recognize it when you've found it?"

He laughed at my obvious expectation that *he* would have a perfectly clear answer. But then he said, "No one really knows—solving superproblems is a black art," and laughed some more. I continued to coax him for a few more words on the topic.

Our conversation started to break down then, mostly because he didn't have a well-defined answer to the question, but we did agree on several possible ways of generating or recognizing superproblems.

There were two general approaches. First, you could reason from the (specific) subproblems to the (general) superproblem. Or second, you could reason from the (general) superproblem to the (specific) subproblems. (The only tough thing about the second approach is that you have to guess at what the superproblem is before you can see if solving it will solve your subproblems.)

Here are two examples of the specific-to-general approach for finding superproblems. First, maybe the subproblems are unique and fit closely together like pieces in a jigsaw puzzle, thus forming a superproblem. Or second, maybe the subproblems all have similar characteristics from which you can abstract a common superproblem.

Unfortunately, I have no examples of how to guess at the superproblem using the general-to-specific approach. That's because he was probably right—guessing at possible superproblems *is* mostly a black art. All I know is that if you guess at (and solve) a superproblem that won't solve most of the subproblems, then the superproblem probably isn't the right one. (Of course, if there *isn't* a superproblem for your particular subproblems, then you'd be wasting your time trying to solve the subproblems with the superproblem approach.)

Let's try out the superproblem technique on the list of subproblems that we discussed earlier. In what follows, I'll show you how to use the specific-to-general approach to formulate three superproblems that will help us to solve most of the subproblems.

Common Symptoms and Failure Modes

To start the specific-to-general superproblem analysis, I listed all the subproblems and then searched for common characteristics among them. Table 1-1 summarizes the subproblems and their main consequences.

Table 1–1: Common Problems in Software Development Environments

Subproblem	Description
Problems with code:	
Too many `#ifdefs`	Reduces readability, maintainability
Mixed pi/pd info in same file	Increases ifdefs, reduces portability
Poor file organization	Discourages file sharing, code reuse
Problems with makefiles	
Excessive complexity	Increases development, maintenance costs
Lack of portability	Increases porting, maintenance costs
Problems with infrastructure	
Poor source code control	Increases dev/maint/test costs
Poor file sharing mechanisms	Increases dev/maint costs, reduces reuse
Poor communication mechanisms	Increases dev/maint/test costs
Unstable work environments	Increases dev/maint/test costs

When I analyzed these subproblems for common themes, I came up with the following idea. The subproblems all caused some type of failure in one of three ways—through *scale-up failure*, through *technical limitations*, or through *human limitations*.

Those are the superproblems that we have to solve. I'll describe each superproblem a little bit more before showing you the solutions in the next section.

Scale-up Failure

You can recognize a scale-up failure whenever something works well in small, specific situations, but then fails to work equally as well in larger, more general situations.

For example, techniques that work well on single-person, single-platform software projects often fail to work well in multi-person, multi-platform software projects. This is often because of the drastically increased number and complexity of interactions that can and do occur between the larger numbers of developers, source files, and platforms on multi-person, multi-platform development projects.

We can also see other examples in the subproblems that are shown in Table 1-1. First, having a few `#ifdefs` in the code isn't a big problem, but having too many of them severely increases the difficulty of reading and maintaining the code.

Second, mixing a little platform-dependent (pd) code in with the platform-independent (pi) code in the same file isn't a big problem on a single-platform project, but becomes a portability problem on a multi-platform project.

Third, promoting file sharing and code reuse on small single-person projects isn't hard, because one person knows about all the code on the project. But on big projects, not everyone knows about all the code on the project. Besides, even if they do find code to reuse, how can they easily isolate it and make it available for sharing?

For these reasons, most people will try to impose an appropriate amount of structure on a project right from the very beginning. (This is especially true if they think there's a chance of a scale-up failure in the future.) The trick is to pick an organizational structure that will handle projects of any size without being too much of a burden on small projects.

Technical Limitations

The second type of failure mode is due to technical limitations. By this I mean that a subproblem causes failure because of some technical limitation or incompatibility between the techniques that are being used and the goals that are to be achieved.

I see three levels of technical limitation. First, a technique could fail because it is technically limited in capability. For example, the goal of portability is completely thwarted by non-portable code, because non-portable code is (by definition) incapable of being portable. Similarly, other software development practices may be incapable of performing useful bulk RCS operations, or of tracking and displaying complex sharing relationships.

The second level of technical limitation was for reasons of *capacity*. In this type of limitation, the tool or technique is limited because it doesn't have the capacity to handle the large jobs that are demanded of it on large projects.

For example, the popular UNIX technique of performing recursive *make* operations is *possible* on MS-DOS platforms (since at least GNU *make* can do it), but it's usually not *feasible* on large projects because of the limited capacity of MS-DOS memory systems. (MS-DOS doesn't support virtual memory, so it's easy to run out of memory when performing recursive *make* operations.)

The third level of technical limitation was for reasons of awkwardness. That is, a technique could have the capability and capacity for the job, but could be limited because it is too awkward for humans to use the technique to accomplish the job.

For example, developers commonly try to avoid reorganizing source files and directories on large projects because it's too awkward. It takes time and tends to "break" makefiles, `#include` statements, and any other implicit assumptions that you've made about the location of the files and directories on your project.

Similarly, as mentioned before, sharing files and reusing code is often avoided for reasons of awkwardness. As a final example, it's often awkward to isolate just a small part of a large software product for testing, because the makefile for the product constructs all pieces of the product at once. You have to dissect the makefile in order to compile just the piece that you want to work on.

Human Limitations

The third type of failure mode is failure due to human limitations. This type of failure usually occurs because the task to be performed is beyond the ability of the average programmer.

A task can go beyond average human abilities in many ways. For example, it might be too complex to understand. It might be too tedious to do reliably many times in a row. It might require too much concentration or discipline over too long a period of time. The rewards of performing the task might not be high enough. The justification or need for the task might not be clear enough. And so on.

The examples that I associate with this kind of failure deal with coordinating the activities of several people on relatively complex tasks (such as multi-platform software development).

For example, two developers might fix the same bug, or they might clobber each other's bug fixes with unrelated modifications in the same file (because of poor source code control). As another example, a baseline compilation could fail, and no one would be able to figure out why. (Because no code modification logs were kept.) Or it might be impossible to tell which include files should be ansified when you ansify one product out of many.

You can probably think up your own examples of tasks that demanded more than the task performers were able to give. (You can often recognize such tasks because they're the ones that are simplified, bypassed, or simply ignored soon after they're announced.)

Solving the Superproblems

Now that we've identified the three superproblems/failure modes that drive the subproblems, it's time to propose possible solutions. After that, we'll validate the solutions against the original subproblems.

Imposing Structure

Working with large numbers of almost anything requires more discipline and logical structure than working with smaller quantities. Imposing structure on larger projects is a possible solution for solving scale-up failures.

We can impose a particular structure on directory trees to improve the organization of files and information on the software project. We can also impose rules on the types of files and the types of information that can be stored in those directories. Once we've defined a clear structural model, we can write tools to support the use of the new structures.

To validate this idea, let's check it against the "Problems with Code" subproblems in Table 1-1.

1. If we specify that all platform-dependent code (for any particular platform) is to be stored in a directory dedicated to that specific platform, then we wouldn't have a need for platform-specific `#ifdef` statements. Instead, platform-dependent code would be physically separated into different files for each platform. Source files would be easier to read because of the absence of platform specific `#ifdefs`.

2. If we specify that pd code is *not* to be stored in the same file as pi code, then porting source files to new platforms would be easier. With this specification, you'd always know which files had to be ported (the pd files), and which ones could be used without porting (the pi files). It would also be easier because you might be able to clone and modify the pd files from an existing platform. The pd code would be much more readable too, because it wouldn't have any platform specific `#ifdef` statements in it.

3. Last but not least, if we specify a directory structure that is general enough and convenient enough to support the isolation, development, and efficient sharing of *parts* of products, then file sharing and code reuse would be improved.

Defining Procedures

Defining procedures (and then automating them with tools) is one method for addressing troublesome tasks that fail for reasons of technical limitations.

We could define alternative procedures that wouldn't wouldn't suffer from the limitations. One possible way is to redefine the procedures to use simpler methods that are less likely to fail. And since this approach may force us to use more steps in the procedures, we should also try to automate the procedures with tools. Putting the necessary command sequences into standard makefile templates is one way of automating troublesome tasks. Writing specific tools to carry out the tasks is another approach.

To test the validity of this idea, let's check it against the "Problems with Makefiles" subproblems from Table 1-1.

1. Consider the problem of excessive makefile complexity. If we could define alternative methods of performing complex tasks, and then hide those command sequences in standard, unchanging makefile templates, then people could just include the template without having to deal with the complex internal command sequences.

    If a smart tool could be written to generate standard makefiles for building common software products such as libraries, executable programs, and so on, fewer people would have to struggle with manually creating makefiles.

And if we could define and support convenient procedures for creating *parts* of larger software products, there wouldn't be any need to write complex makefiles that generated multiple products from the same set of source files.

If we could do all these things, life would be much simpler for people who used makefiles.

2. Consider the lack of portability of makefiles between different platforms. The main problem here is that the special command sequences, tools, and *make* features that you use to build the product on one platform might not be available on other platforms. (For example, recursive *make* operations.)

   An alternative way of accomplishing the same result would be to define standard platform-specific makefile command sequences for each platform, and then put those commands into makefile templates. Then people wouldn't have to *port* their makefiles. Instead, they could quickly create new ones that accomplished the same results, simply by including the appropriate makefile templates. Or better yet, a tool could regenerate an appropriate makefile automatically.

   (The freeware *imake* tool offers a solution similar to this. It generates makefiles automatically (using the C preprocessor) from an input file containing C macro statements that describe the project. But in contrast to the approach taken in this book, *imake* doesn't avoid `#ifdef` complexity—instead, it welcomes and increases it.)

Simplify and Automate Human Task Interfaces

Simplifying and automating human task interfaces is one way to solve project infrastructure problems that fail for reasons of human limitations.

If we could define and automate troublesome development tasks, the demands placed on human programmers could be significantly reduced. As a consequence, the tasks would likely be completed more reliably with higher quality. A list of candidate tasks might include creating project subtrees, generating standard makefiles, and performing bulk RCS check-in and check-out operations.

To test the validity of this idea, let's check it against the "Problems with Project Infrastructure" subproblems from Table 1-1.

1. The problem of poor source code control can be addressed by writing tools that automatically perform common source code control tasks. Such tasks include checking files in, checking them out, assigning release labels, locking files for modification, and so on. Such tools tend to improve the frequency and reliability of source code control activities on a project because they make it more convenient for developers to use the source code control system in a meaningful way.

2. The problem of poor file sharing mechanisms and low code reuse can be addressed by writing tools for tracking and displaying file sharing relationships. In addition, conceptual models (supported by tools, of course) that help developers to

isolate and share reusable parts of existing products improve the likelihood of people creating and sharing reusable code. Again, the argument here is based on making it convenient for developers to take the desired actions.

3. The problem of poor project communication mechanisms (concerning source code modification logs and RCS checkin logs) can be partially addressed by the source code management tools mentioned earlier. Specifically, the tools could automatically collect a checkin log message from the developer at the time the file was checked in. Then the tool would make the message available to all developers through a public communication mechanism (such as a newsgroup or public log file). As a consequence, developers would find it easier to identify recent code changes that might have introduced bugs into newly modified products.

4. The problem of unstable personal work environments could be addressed by writing programs to help developers create their own private product trees. That way, developers could stabilize their personal environments while modifying or debugging existing products. Of course, policies and tools should also be created to make it easy for developers to check in files from their personal source trees. (The modified files should be available for everyone to use in the main source tree after they've been checked in.)

At this point, we have solutions to three superproblems which we found to comprise all our symptoms. It is useful here to distinguish solutions that are structural, such as standard directory trees, from those that are procedural, such as formal checkin procedures.

Structural Versus Procedural Solutions

The main strategy followed by the solutions in this book is to impose a conceptual *structure* on troublesome problems, so that well defined *procedures* can be created to solve them. Then the procedures can be supported with *automated tools*. A structural solution requires that files or code be in a certain order or place. A procedural solution tells you what to do with specific inputs.

This approach is illustrated by the relationship between programming languages and compilers. First, language grammars impose structure on the problem of expressing commands to computers. This makes it possible to define specific procedures for translating high-level language statements into executable binary code. Advanced compilers can then be created to automate the translation task.

This is a good approach because it produces workable solutions—perhaps not the best solutions on the first try, but certainly *useful* solutions. If you understand the main differences between structural and procedural solutions, you'll be more likely to use the right kind of approach in your time of need.

Structural solutions tend to be long lived and fairly uniform in their application, because they're usually applied to large problems (like huge trees of source code), and used by large numbers of people (such as all members on a team or everyone within a company). Structural solutions work best on large general problems, or problems that have a simple and stable underlying conceptual structure.

In this book, for example, a structural solution is used to solve the organizational problem of where to put source, object, executable, alpha test, and releasable files, for both platform independent and dependent file types.* A structural solution is appropriate because file storage locations are long lived, especially on large projects, and because many people (and software tools) might be required to understand and interact with the structural solution.

In contrast, procedural solutions have different characteristics. They tend to be short lived, easily changed, and very flexible, because people frequently change procedural solutions to suit the exact needs of their (possibly evolving) situation. Procedural solutions are best used to solve complex problems, or problems that naturally deal with a lot of special cases.

Consider the problem of how to tell the compiler where to find include files on a project. A structural solution is used for the most common include files from the standard C library—the `#include <stdio.h>` syntax. This is an effective technique for locating standard include files because this particular part of the problem has suitable characteristics for structural solutions—the problem is a large scale, conceptually simple problem that is faced by everyone who uses a C compiler. So the best solution—a standard place to look for all standard include files—has been structurally embodied in the C language.

However, for non-standard include files, procedural solutions are used instead. For example, many compilers take the **–Idirectory** control argument to define places where frequently used non-standard include files can be found. (This book provides an even more flexible procedural solution in the form of tools that import and export shared include files on an individual basis.)

Both types of solutions can be automated with software tools. Automated structural solutions tend to operate behind the scenes (driven by configuration files or software installation options), while automated procedural solutions tend to be more visible to the user (in the form of options or arguments on command lines). Scripts and batch files are also commonly used to carry out flexible procedural solutions.

In summary, keep these conceptual differences in mind when you're designing your own code management systems. Use structural solutions when long-lived uniformity is an advantage, and use procedural solutions when flexibility is an advantage. You'll save time during the design of your system, and you won't have to "refine" (a euphemism for "fix") your final system implementation quite so often.

---

* Alpha testing means "in-house testing," and usually means that the development team will test the software for a while before letting it out to friendly non-in-house testers (beta testing). After a successful beta test, products are usually released into the user community for unrestricted use.

Overview of Solutions Used by This Book

The following section gives an overview of the major code management solutions offered by this book. The overview section has three parts: one on structural solutions, one on procedural solutions, and one that summarizes how the solutions address the development problems described in the previous section.

Structural Solutions

Structural solutions can help to solve problems by imposing a conceptual (and also sometimes a physical) structure on the problems. The newly imposed structures often make it easier for both humans and software tools to work with the most salient features of the problems.

This book does just that—it imposes two major structural solutions on the overall code management problem. The first structural solution is a standard directory structure that consists of three types of directory trees and three types of source tree nodes. The second structural solution is a standard six-part makefile structure. Overviews of both structural solutions are provided below.

Three major trees (CMTREE, CMHTREE, source)

Standard directory structures are used to control the location of various types of files on a software project. Storing particular types of files in particular directories allows procedural solutions (in the form of makefiles, programs, or batch scripts) to make assumptions about where files are being stored on a software project. More uniform and more efficient procedures and tools can be constructed.

Three types of directory trees are used by the solutions in this book: the *CMTREE*, the *CMHTREE*, and any number of *source trees*. The CMTREE holds makefile templates and other information internal to the code management system. The CMHTREE holds product files that are available to users outside of the code management system (e.g., shared files, alpha test files, and released product files). Source trees hold files used to build software products (source and include files, documentation files, and so on). Chapter 5, *Directory Structures*, discusses the directory structure in detail.

Two environment variables (**$CMTREE** and **$CMHTREE**) are used to reference the locations of the CMTREE and CMHTREE.

CMTREE

The CMTREE holds makefile templates that are used by the makefile generation tools. This tree is named for "code management tree" and is probably the most important tree used by the solutions in this book. Tools can look inside of this tree (for the *$CMTREE/makefile.tre* file) to find out about the directory structure of the CMHTREE (defined below). In addition, the makefile generation tools also look in this tree to get the makefile templates that they need.

This tree contains a subdirectory for each platform supported by the code management system. Figure 1-3 shows the main components of a CMTREE.

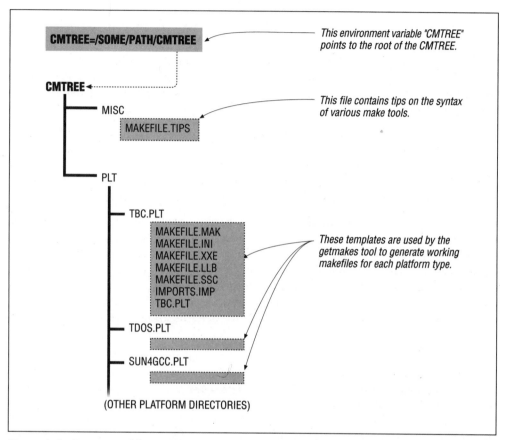

Figure 1–3. Structure of the CMTREE

Normally, only one CMTREE is defined for each workgroup within a company so that all people and all programs within the same workgroup can use the same default makefile templates. In fact, it's probably best if everyone in the company uses the same templates from the same CMTREE. However, you can switch to another CMTREE at any time if you want to, because its location is defined by the **$CMTREE** shell environment variable.

CMHTREE

The "code management holding tree" is a repository and holding area for various kinds of files in the code management system. Normally only one CMHTREE is defined for each workgroup so that everyone within the workgroup can use the same shared, alpha test, and released files. Figure 1-4 shows the contents of a CMHTREE.

The main purpose of the CMHTREE is to serve as a default location that is known to all the tools in the code management system. The tools in this book export and import files between the CMHTREE and the source trees, thereby implementing a file sharing mechanism.

The normal sharing mechanism operates as follows. Files that are to be shared are exported from their original source trees into the CMHTREE. Then the files are imported from the CMHTREE into the source trees where they are reused. Shared source files are typically version controlled (under RCS, for example) in the source tree that exports them. Shared object files are typically not version controlled.

The main advantage of implementing file sharing and reuse with a mechanism like this is that the exporting and importing source trees don't have to know anything about the other's location. And that makes it possible to reorganize one tree without impacting the others. This is an important advantage during code reorganizations, because you can reorganize your code without invalidating any absolute or relative pathnames that are required to reference shared files. This mechanism also makes other advantages possible (logging of all sharing operations, determination of all users (importers) of a shared file, and so on).

A second major use of the CMHTREE is to collect all the alpha test versions of the products that are under development. This mechanism works because the default action of the **exports** target in the makefile templates is to export compiled products into the alpha test directory of the CMHTREE. Having all the alpha test versions of programs in one place makes it easy for developers to add the appropriate CMHTREE directories to their search paths, so they can use the latest alpha test versions of all programs in their normal daily work.

The main advantages of implementing alpha testing in this way are that alpha test program installation costs are cheap (developers only have to type *make exports*), usage costs are cheap (developers only have to add the alpha test directories to their search paths), and organizational costs are cheap (the makefile templates and CMHTREE are preconfigured to implement this mechanism).

The CMHTREE also plays a small role in releasing software products. The default **release** targets in the makefile templates operate exactly like the **exports** targets, except that the destination directory in the CMHTREE is different. The **release** target exports into the *SHARE/release* directory instead of into the alpha test directory. Once all products are collected in the release directory, they can be moved or packaged according to the policies of the organization.

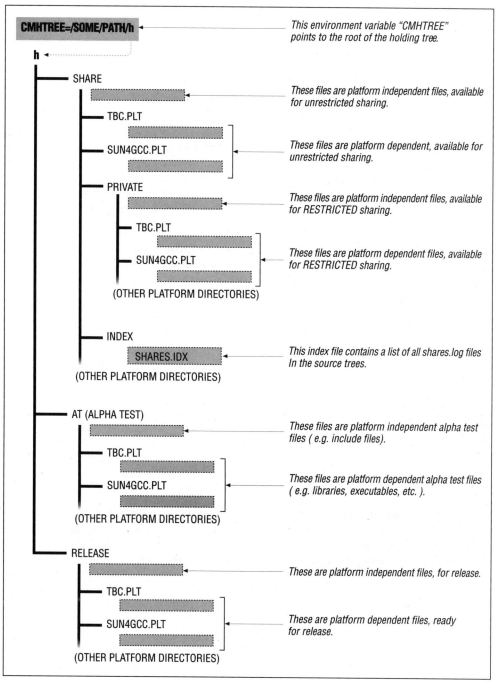

Figure 1–4. Structure of the CMHTREE (the holding tree)

The CMHTREE has platform subdirectories in all the right places to hold platform specific files of all kinds (source, binary, and script files).

The location of the CMHTREE is defined by an environment variable, so you can switch to another CMHTREE whenever you want to.

Source trees

There can be any number of source trees within the code management system, located in arbitrary positions within the computer filesystem. The positions of source trees can be arbitrary because all makefiles in the source trees reference the CMTREE and CMHTREE locations through the $CMTREE and $CMHTREE environment variables. This means that no fixed spatial relationships need to exist among the CMTREE, the CMHTREE, and the source trees. Each of the trees can be located anywhere in the filesystem. Figure 1-5 shows some of the variations that developers can choose from, just by changing environment variables.

Source trees can be small trees that just contain one small program such as *hello world* or they can be big trees containing many large programs. The internal directory structure of source trees is largely arbitrary, because the code management system described here imposes only a few restrictions on the structure of source trees.

Figure 1-6 shows a typical source tree.

I'll emphasize again that the high-level structure of source trees is almost arbitrary. Since the code management tools don't really care about the existence of directories that don't interest them, you can add any directories that you like to a source tree.

However, the tools do care about the internal structure of *product directories* (also called *product nodes*). These directories are subdivided into directories for various platforms.

Platform directories have names that end in *.plt*, such as *myproduct/sun4gcc.plt* and *myproduct/tbc.plt*. Platform directories (and their subtrees) store files that are in any way platform dependent.

Product directories are parents of platform directories. For example, *myproduct* is a parent directory of the platform directories *myproduct/sun4gcc.plt* and *myproduct/tbc.plt*. Product directories have special places for storing source files (in the *s* or *platform.plt/s* directories) and for storing makefiles (in the platform directories).

Product directories are usually associated with named software products such as object libraries, executable programs, or batch files. (I say "usually" because product directories can also be used to export collections of include files, too.)

In the tree shown by Figure 1-6, the directories *CMI, CMPWD,* and *GENDEP* are all product directories.

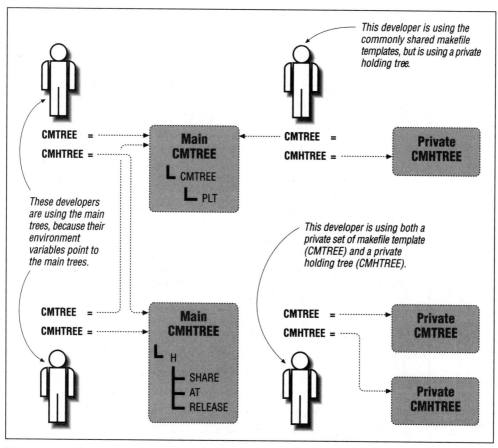

Figure 1–5. Private developer CMTREES and CMHTREES

Three types of source trees (pi, pd, pid)

Three types of source trees are used by this book as part of the standard directory structure: pi nodes (for platform-independent source files), pd nodes (for platform-dependent source files), and pid nodes (for both platform independent and dependent source files). A *node* is another name for *directory* or *subtree*. Figure 1-7 shows the structure of pi, pd, and pid nodes.

Pi nodes contain only platform *independent* code. As a consequence, files in the source directory of pi nodes can be used by all platform directories within the pi node.

Pd nodes contain only platform *dependent* source code. This means that files in the platform source directories of pd nodes usually can't be used by any other platforms. (However, sometimes the code for two or more platforms can be the same, even though the code is different for some of the other platforms within the product node.)

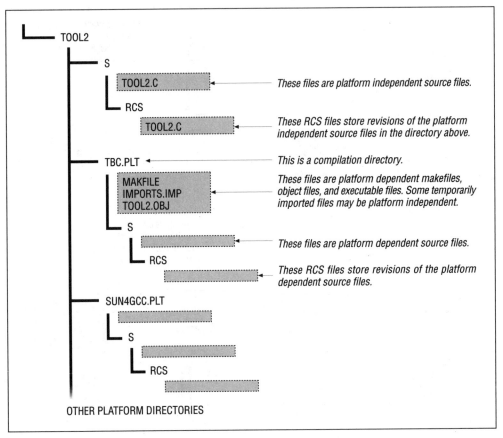

Figure 1–6. Structure of a source tree

Pid nodes can contain both pi and pd source code files. This means that pid nodes can be used to hold all the code for a project, period. Then why have pi and pd nodes, and when should they be used?

The main advantage of using pi and pd nodes in preference to pid nodes is that you can always (and easily) tell what kind of code is in a pi or pd node. It's either pi code or pd code, but never both. Knowing this information makes it easier to answer questions such as "What code do we have to port to support the new XYZ platform that marketing wants to support?" And it's easier for the tools to determine the node type as well.

In contrast, you can never easily tell what type of code is within a pid node. All that you know is that either, both, or none of the types of code can be stored in a pid

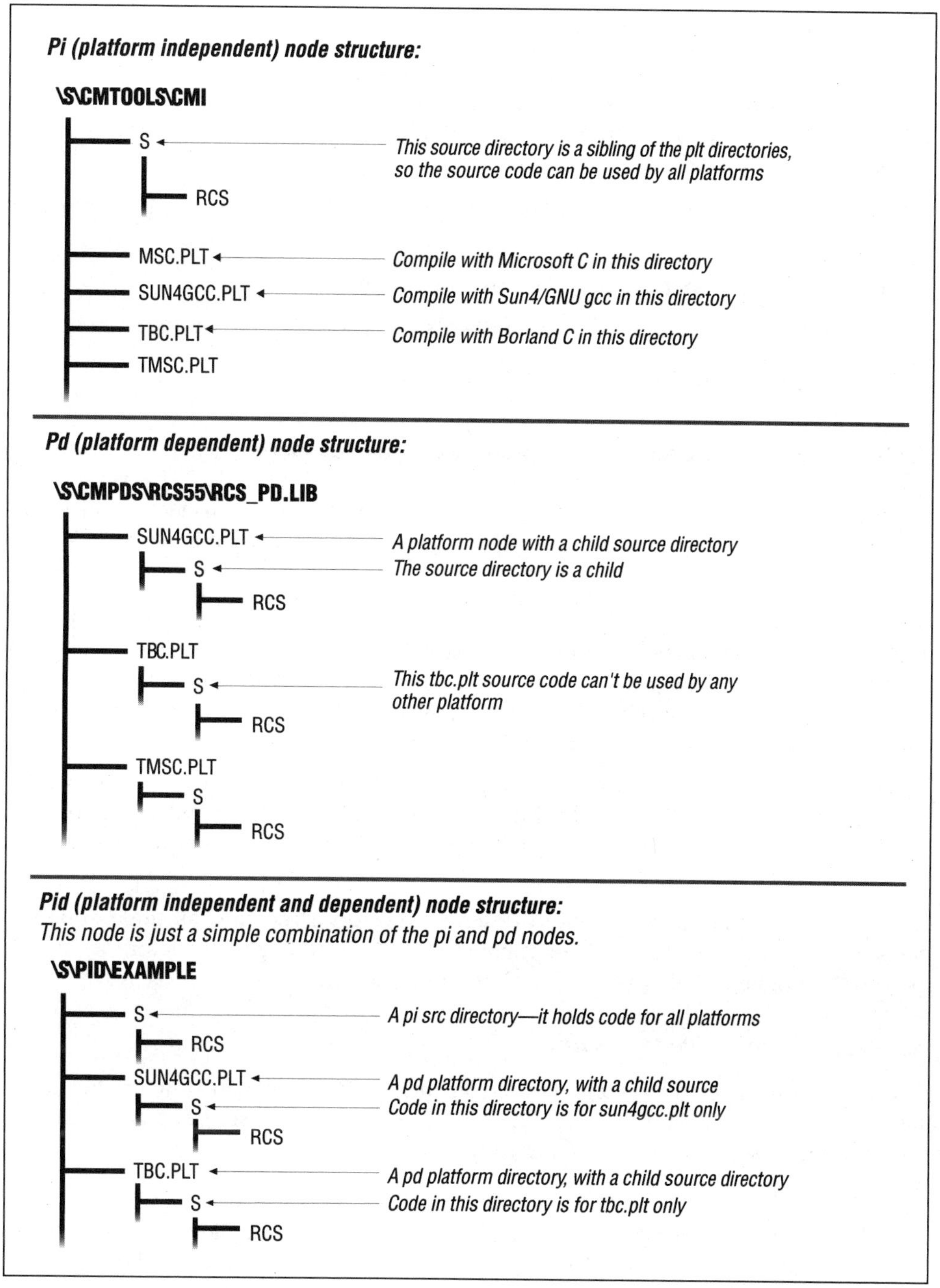

Pi (platform independent) node structure:

\S\CMTOOLS\CMI

```
├── S ◄──────────────────────── This source directory is a sibling of the plt directories,
│   └── RCS                      so the source code can be used by all platforms
│
├── MSC.PLT ◄─────────────────── Compile with Microsoft C in this directory
├── SUN4GCC.PLT ◄─────────────── Compile with Sun4/GNU gcc in this directory
├── TBC.PLT ◄─────────────────── Compile with Borland C in this directory
├── TMSC.PLT
```

Pd (platform dependent) node structure:

\S\CMPDS\RCS55\RCS_PD.LIB

```
├── SUN4GCC.PLT ◄────────────── A platform node with a child source directory
│   ├── S ◄──────────────────── The source directory is a child
│   │   └── RCS
│
├── TBC.PLT
│   ├── S ◄──────────────────── This tbc.plt source code can't be used by any
│   │   └── RCS                 other platform
│
├── TMSC.PLT
    ├── S
    │   └── RCS
```

Pid (platform independent and dependent) node structure:
This node is just a simple combination of the pi and pd nodes.

\S\PID\EXAMPLE

```
├── S ◄──────────────────────── A pi src directory—it holds code for all platforms
│   ├── RCS
│
├── SUN4GCC.PLT ◄────────────── A pd platform directory, with a child source
│   ├── S ◄──────────────────── Code in this directory is for sun4gcc.plt only
│   │   ├── RCS
│
├── TBC.PLT ◄────────────────── A pd platform directory, with a child source directory
    ├── S ◄──────────────────── Code in this directory is for tbc.plt only
    │   ├── RCS
```

Figure 1–7. Pi, pd, and pid node structures

node. And you can't resolve that question unless you physically inspect all of the pi and pd source directories inside the node.

The main advantage of using a pid node is that you can store *all* the source files—that is, both pi and pd files—for a single product within a single product node. And this can be a useful convenience from a code management point of view, since there are fewer source trees to maintain.

For these reasons, here are my personal conventions for using the three types of nodes.

1. If a product only contains pi code, I use a pi node.

2. If a product only contains pd code, I use a pd node.

3. If a product is reasonably small, and if it requires both pi and pd code, I use a pid node.

4. But if a product is large, or if the product is a suite of subproducts (like the tools in the RCS collection), I'll usually go back to using pi and pd nodes. This is because I find the product easier to manage if I have a pi library subproduct, a pd library subproduct, and a separate executable subproduct for each different tool in the program suite.

You can recognize the different types of nodes by inspecting the relative positions of the source directories and the platform directories in the nodes. Pi nodes always have exactly 1 source directory that's a *sibling* of the platform directories. Pd nodes can have many source directories (one for each platform) that are *children* of the platform directories. And pid nodes have both types of source directories.

I normally use the abbreviations to refer to files or to directory structures. When I'm using them to describe files, only the first two abbreviations (pi and pd) make any sense. There's no such thing as a "pid" file. A file is either platform independent or dependent, but it can't be both.

When I'm using the abbreviations to describe directory structures, all three abbreviations have distinct meanings. It is possible to design directory structures for the specific purpose of holding pi files, pd files, or both types of files.

Six standard makefile templates

The second major structural solution used by this book is a six-part structure for makefiles. Each of the six parts (or templates) has a specific purpose. Chapter 6, *Makefile Architectures* discusses their use more fully.

makefile

This is the top-level makefile. It includes the other five makefile parts and contains no program specific information itself. It contains a few default makefile targets: the default build target, the default export target, and the default release target.

There is only one *makefile* per platform directory. The makefile is normally generated by the *getmakes* tool (described in Chapter 2, *A Hands-on Tour: Part 1*) and can be automatically regenerated at any time. (This makes it possible for developers to easily and automatically update all makefiles in the filesystem after they make a change in a makefile template in the CMTREE.)

makefile.tre

This is the first included makefile. It defines makefile macros that point to various directories in the CMTREE and CMHTREE. The macros make it possible for the *make* tool to symbolically reference the directories when it's including, importing, or exporting files to and from the proper places. The *makefile.tre* file also defines temporary filenames that are used by commands in other makefile templates.

Normally, there is only one copy of *makefile.tre* per work environment because the directory macros must accurately reflect the true internal structure of the CMHTREE. Since there's normally only one CMHTREE per working environment, only one *makefile.tre* file is needed.

makefile.tre is never automatically regenerated, because only one copy of it exists—and that copy can be changed easily by hand. The *makefile.tre* file is stored in the CMTREE.

platform-name.plt

A platform file is usually the second included makefile.* It defines platform specific information such as the names of platform specific software tools, file suffixes, default compiler options, and implicit makefile rules.

The name of the platform file is always the same name as the platform directory that it represents. So the name of the platform file is *sun4gcc.plt* for the *sun4gcc.plt* platform, *sun4cc.plt* for the *sun4cc.plt* platform (it uses *cc* instead of *gcc*), *tbc.plt* for the Borland C platform *tbc.plt*, and so on.

There is only one copy of this file, since the standard information that it contains should be used by all makefiles running on the same platform. The *platform-name.plt* file is stored in the CMTREE.

imports.imp

This is the fourth included makefile template. It contains program specific information for the software product being constructed. For example, it contains the name of the product, any special importing, exporting, or release instructions, and the names of any libraries that the product should be linked with.

This file can't be automatically regenerated, since it contains so much program specific information. When makefiles are regenerated, all the other makefile

---

* It is third in Borland makefiles, because Borland's *make* (version 3.5) doesn't expand macros the same way as other *make* tools. This version of Borland's *make* has trouble expanding macros that reference other (temporarily undefined) macros.

templates in the directory are replaced except this one. One *imports.imp* file is stored in each platform directory.

makefile.pi, makefile.pd, makefile.pid

These files contain the makefile dependency rules for the software product being constructed. The suffixes tell the makefile generation tools where to look for the source code that's to be inspected for dependencies: if suffix is pi, look in *../s*; if suffix is pd, look in *s*; if suffix is pid, look in both places.

The pi (platform independent) suffix tells the tools to look for the source code in a normal source directory that is the *sibling* of the current platform directory. This is because *makefile.pi* files are found only in pi nodes. (Remember that all source code in pi nodes is platform independent and can be used by all platform directories.)

The pd (platform dependent) suffix tells the tools to look for the source code in a source directory that is the *child* of the current platform directory. This is because *makefile.pd* files are found only in pd nodes. All source code in pd nodes is platform dependent and can be used only by the parent platform directory.

The pid suffix is a combination of the pi and pd suffixes. It tells the makefile generation tools to look in both the *s* (sibling) and the *platform.plt/s* (child) source directories within the pid node.

makefile.pid files may be found in pi, pd, or pid nodes. This is because the makefile generation tools are modified to work correctly in pid nodes even if there are no source files in the pi or pd directories. But under normal circumstances, you'd only expect to find *makefile.pid* files in pid nodes.

makefile.llb, makefile.xxe, makefile.sse

These files contain *make* instructions for building libraries, executables, or script products. The files are different for each platform, as might be expected (as a general rule, all the makefile templates are platform dependent). *makefile.llb* tells how to build a library, *makefile.xxe* tells how to build an executable program, and *makefile.ssc* tells how to build a script.

There is only one copy of this file per platform, since the standard information it contains should be used by all makefiles that build that type of product on that particular platform. The *makefile.llb, makefile.xxe*, and *makefile.ssc* files are stored in the CMTREE with all the other makefile templates.

Under the rules advocated by this book, only one of these files (llb, xxe, or ssc) may be included in any top-level makefile. This means that each product node is allowed to generate exactly one named product—a library file, an executable file, or a script file.

The rules were designed this way to support the automatic generation and regeneration of makefiles. Automatically generating a set of makefiles to produce exactly one type of product is far less difficult than generating makefiles that can produce an arbitrary number of different types of products.

Even though this approach sometimes forces you to use more source nodes than with other code management approaches, the restriction isn't a very serious one. The uniform structure of the nodes makes them very easy to work with, using the advanced tools that have been provided with this book.

In summary, the six-part standard makefile structure advocated by this book isolates functionally different makefile information into separate template files:

- Tree structure macros are in *makefile.tre*

- Platform-dependent information is in *platform.plt*

- Program-specific information is in the *makefile.pi/pd/pid* files and *imports.imp*

- Product-construction information is in the *makefile.llb/xxe/ssc* files

Example 1-2 shows a standard top-level makefile.

Example 1–2: A Standard Top-level Makefile

```
# the makefile platform name, and the export platform name
MP=sun4gcc.plt
EP=sun4gcc.plt

# where to get the CMHTREE macros, and temporary filename definitions
TREE_DEFS=$(CMTREE)/makefile.tre

# the default thing to do when you just type 'make'
default: build

include $(TREE_DEFS)                    # tree structure information
include $(MDIR)/$(MP)/$(MP)             # platform information
include $(IMPORTS_IMP)                  # program information
include $(MAKEFILE_PI)                  # program target rule dependencies
include $(MDIR)/$(MP)/$(MAKEFILE_XXE)   # product type information

full: imports build

all: imports build exports

exports: exports.spe
    $(CMX) -nl $(PROG)$(X) -dd $(ALPHA_DIR)/$(EP)

release: release.spe
    $(CMX) -nl $(PROG)$(X) -dd $(RELEASE_DIR)/$(EP)
```

A standard makefile structure is important for code management systems because it allows you to isolate different kinds of knowledge into separate makefile template files. In turn, this allows you to automatically recombine the templates to suit the needs of a particular software product running on a particular platform.

Standard makefiles are also important because they embody and implement other structural and procedural solutions to code management problems. For example, the makefile structure shown here allows you to update all makefiles on a disk by changing a template in the CMTREE and traversing (walking) an arbitrary part of the filesystem to automatically update all affected makefiles. In other words, you can easily manipulate *entire trees* of software products, instead of having to treat each product node individually.

Makefile templates that are designed to carry out particular computational actions can be either as complex as or as simple as you want them to be. In fact, they might *have* to be significantly different on different platforms. However, my experience so far has been that you can usually reuse the templates on different platforms almost verbatim— they rarely require any complex changes.

Now you have seen (briefly) the three major structural solutions used in this book's code management system. In summary, they are listed here:

- A standard directory structure with three types of trees (CMTREE, CMHTREE, and source trees)

- Three subtypes of source nodes (pi, pd, and pid)

- A six-part standard makefile structure (*makefile, makefile.tre, imports.imp, make-file.plt, makefile.pi/pd/pid*, and *makefile.llb/xxe/ssc*)

Procedural Solutions

Procedural solutions can help to solve problems by imposing procedural conventions on problematic tasks. This book suggests several major procedural solutions to common code management problems. They can be loosely classified into product development procedures, RCS (Revision Control System) code management procedures, and software tools that automate those procedures.*

Product development procedures

Many product development procedures are suggested by this book. Since most of them are supported with tools, most of them are both convenient and efficient. Here is a sampling of the procedures that will be discussed in the rest of the book:

- How to install existing code into the code management system

- How to recognize and minimize platform-dependent code

- How to add new platforms to the code management system

- How to generate and use tree walker scripts

---

* Although RCS is used by this book, the tools and procedures can be adapted to other source code control systems.

- How to generate makefiles for a product

- How to fully recompile and export all products

- How to automatically update all the makefiles in your source trees from newly modified templates in the CMTREE

RCS code management procedures

In most code management systems, one or two dozen command procedures are heavily used by most developers. These procedures usually cover tasks such as checking files in and out of the source code control system, comparing files that may have changed, and inspecting code modification logs.

This book defines many such procedures and provides automated support in the form of software tools wherever possible. Here is a sampling of the RCS code management procedures that will be covered in later chapters:

- How to perform basic RCS check-in and check-out operations

- How to perform RCS operations on single files

- How to perform RCS operations on directories of files

- How to perform RCS operations on trees of files

- How to log all RCS transactions into a single log file

Automated tools

Most of the procedures described in this book are supported by automated tools. The tools all tend to increase productivity and stability within the development environment. A list of the tools included with the book can be found in the table of contents. Each tool is also listed in the index.

Which Solutions Solve Which Problems?

Here's a list that associates code management solutions with problems that were described earlier. The list should help you to see how the proposed solutions will solve the problems.

- To address the *source code readability problem*, this book advocates that platform-dependent `#ifdef` statements be disallowed from all source code. Instead, all platform-dependent code should be placed in pd or pid nodes, under the appropriate platform directory. Separating pi from pd code makes it easy for developers to identify pd code, which in turn helps them to clone and modify the pd code when new platforms are added to the code management system.

  Other kinds of `#ifdefs`, such as those that enable product features or debugging code, are allowed. These are irrelevant to the multi-platform problem.

- The same solution addresses the *multi-platform problem*. You put platform-dependent code into separate files which can be more easily managed by the code management system. Disallowing pd `#ifdefs` can also enhance the readability of your code.

- To address the *source code organization problem*, this book isolates different kinds of knowledge into three standard tree types (CMTREE, CMHTREE, and source trees), three source node subtypes (pi, pd, and pid), and six standard makefile templates. This division of knowledge makes it possible to efficiently support most software products in normal development environments.

- To address the *source code reorganization problem*, this book defines structural and procedural code management solutions that are almost totally independent of tree location. For example, tools typically use shell environment variables or dynamic tree searches to obtain the information that they require. The makefile templates are also independent of node location. As a result, product nodes can be relocated to arbitrary locations within the filesystem without disturbing the operation of the overall code management system.

  The makefile generation tools and the file sharing tools also address the code reorganization problem.

- To address the *makefile complexity problem*, this book provides several sets of predefined makefile templates that contain different kinds of makefile information supporting common development tasks. A functionally similar set of templates is provided for each supported platform. In practice, product makefiles include the templates to perform common development tasks (such as compiling programs or building code libraries). The use of templates helps to avoid the complexity problem because developers don't have to directly deal with the complex contents of the templates. Instead, developers can just use tools to generate complete makefiles, which in turn include the templates.

- To address the *makefile portability problem*, this book provides tools for automatically generating makefiles on supported platforms. The tools depend on the makefile templates that were described earlier. In practice, a new set of templates must be generated—once—for each newly supported platform. But once the initial set of templates has been created, the makefile generator tools can be used to completely bypass future makefile portability problems. That's because instead of porting existing makefiles, the tools can be used to generate completely new makefiles (for products and operations defined in the templates).

- To address the *source code control problem*, this book provides compilable source code for the freeware RCS (Revision Control System) for MS-DOS and UNIX platforms. In addition, the book both defines and automates many common RCS operations by providing the *rcsdo* tool. The *rcsdo* tool implements over a dozen common code management tasks, and can be used to perform RCS operations on entire trees of files when used with an appropriate tree walker script. Tools are also provided for logging all RCS transactions into a central log file.

- To address *poor project communication mechanisms*, this book provides tools for collecting all RCS checkin log messages into a central location (a file or a newsgroup). This makes it convenient for developers to keep aware of changes to project source files.

- To address the *file sharing problem*, this book provides file importing and exporting tools that understand the standard directory structures described earlier. As a consequence, the tools know where to look (by default) for files that are to be imported, exported, shared, or released. (The tools can also work with nonstandard import and export locations.) The tools are also capable of logging (and inspecting) all file sharing transactions.

- To address the *scale-up problem*, this book presents solutions that have been tested on medium-sized projects (100,000 lines of code, excluding comments).* As a result, the solutions presented in this book are likely to scale up well for you too, as your projects grow in size.

- To address the problem of *unstable work environments*, this book provides tools that help developers to create their own private source trees (on systems that support symbolic links). That way, developers can stabilize their own work environments, and isolate themselves as long as they want to from code changes checked in to the main source tree by other developers.

---

* Strictly speaking, not all of the newer ideas—such as the file sharing tools—have been tested on large projects. But since the file sharing ideas and tools form a small part of the overall solution, the "tested solutions" claim seems reasonable.

2

A Hands-on Tour:
Part 1

This chapter introduces you to the software provided with the book. Along the way, you can see the problems laid out in Chapter 1 and some of the solutions offered by the software.

If you're on an MS-DOS system, you should be able simply to load the binaries for the tools, set your environment variables as described in the software installation preface, and type away. On other systems, you'll have to do some compiling. Furthermore, you'll have to make some trivial changes when you enter the commands and filenames shown in this chapter (like using *cat* on UNIX systems instead of *type*).

All in all, this book offers seven examples. Three of them are in this chapter. I'll describe the examples soon—but first, some general things to be aware of.

Tips and Warnings About the Tour

In this section I want to give you some courtesy warnings about what you might encounter as you work through the tour.

The main thing to keep in mind is that this book addresses a very complex topic that can't always be hidden behind smooth presentations. Expect to have to concentrate on what's happening in the tour.

The following is a list of cautions to you, along with my suggestions for overcoming them:

- There's a lot of detailed technical material in this book, so be patient. It'll probably take you a significant amount of time to learn it all. You might even want to go through the entire book twice in order to catch up on the points that you missed the first time around. Two trips through will help you to build a deep understanding of what's going on.

For example, I introduce about 20 new software tools that you've probably never seen before in the tour, about six major code management concepts that might be completely new to you, and another six RCS tools (and associated RCS concepts) that you might also be unfamiliar with. And to top it off, the chapters right after the tour discuss about 50 detailed code management system design issues.

So this is not a light duty book. Instead it's a heavy duty book that tries to present a general solution to a very complex topic.

- The hands-on tour is a medium level tour, not a detailed tutorial. As a consequence, you'll probably have to concentrate on what's going on as you work through the tour examples.

  My purpose in writing the tour was to give you a general feeling for how the tools can be used to solve typical code management problems. I wanted to demonstrate overall workflow patterns and code porting strategies, rather than lead you through detailed exercises that demonstrated every possible option of every possible software tool.

  For these reasons, the tour isn't a slow-moving, low-level tutorial on each of the software tools included with the book. Instead, it's a medium level, medium-paced tour that shows you how to analyze and solve code management problems in an efficient way, one that works well on both large and small projects. So you may find it useful (or necessary) to read other parts of the book in order to find out detailed information about the tools and concepts that are introduced in the tour.

- Expect to retype the command sequences given in the tour examples. I've provided you with a complete list of my own commands for each example, under the belief that you'll learn more by retyping my commands than by just reading the tour.

  Retracing the command sequences that I've provided is also a good idea because I can't show you all of the output in a book of this size. If you follow the command sequences by typing them in yourself, you'll be able to see the output and to inspect the contents of all files, every step of the way. That will help you to learn about the code management system more quickly, for sure.

- Skim the rest of the book first, before working through the tour. Regardless of your experience level, I think you'll find the tour easier if you take the time to skim through the rest of the book first. The tour gets pretty deep in places, so it'll help if you already know something about the directory structures, makefiles, and file sharing techniques that are used.

- Draw yourself a picture of the final source trees to guide you. Since the examples contain many file creations, deletions, and movements, you'll probably find it easier to understand them if you have a picture of the directory trees on paper. That way you can draw lines on the diagram to represent file flows. Copy the final source directories that are shown in Chapter 8, *A Hands-on Tour: Part 3*. They'll serve you fairly well as an overall contextual guide to the examples.

How about when the tour is done? If you're an experienced developer who's familiar with multi-person, multi-platform development problems, then you can probably read the rest of the book from front to back without too much difficulty. Your own experience can be your guide.

If you're less experienced, you may find it easier to skip around and read the topics that are easiest for you first. That way you can experiment with the parts of your environment that are most important to you and try new ideas when you're ready.

The Tour Examples

The seven examples on the guided tour highlight the code management solutions that are described in this book. They're good examples because they *demonstrate*—and not just talk about—the usefulness of good code management practices.

The first six examples use MS-DOS commands. This publication decision was made because almost everyone can obtain access to a personal computer. Users on other systems shouldn't find it hard to substitute the proper commands and file names for those systems. The seventh example is presented using UNIX commands, because it shows how to support multi-person programming environments by using symbolic links.

Terminology: Platform Names

Platform names are heavily used throughout this book to represent the various particular combinations of software programs that comprise the development environment (not the target operating environment).

Each platform name used in this book has three components. The first component represents the particular *make* program that's used on the platform. The second component represents the particular compiler that's used on the platform. And the third component (the suffix) is always *.plt* so that the code management tools can recognize platform directories by that suffix. Table 2-1 shows a list of the platform names used in this book.

Of course, you can use any *make* tool and compiler combination that you want for this tour. And if for some reason none of the platforms provided in the CMTREE that came with this book is suitable for your needs, you can create your own platform names too. (Platform cloning is briefly demonstrated in Example 4 of the tour.)

Table 2-1: Platform Names

Make Tool	Compiler or Interpreter	Platform Name
Borland make	Borland C++ 2.0	*tbc.plt*
Borland make	DOS Command.com	*tdos.plt*
Microsoft nmake	Microsoft C 6.0	*msc.plt*
Microsoft nmake	DOS Command.com	*mdos.plt*
Sun 4 make	GNU C gcc	*sun4gcc.plt*
Sun 4 make	Sun 4 /bin/sh	*sun4sh.plt*
MKS make	Borland C++ 2.0	*mksbc2.plt*
MKS make	DOS Command.com	*mksdos.plt*

Overview of the Examples

Here is a short description of the examples, just to let you know what's on the tour. We build three tools and two subroutine libraries on the tour. The tools share both pi and pd data and code.

Example 1: A simple program

The *tool1* program in Example 1 is a simple program that contains eight different types of code and data. Eight different categories result from three independent factors (2 x 2 x 2) that affect the type of code or data from a code management point of view.

The three axes are pi or pd, local or shared, and code or data. The pi/pd axis refers to platform-independent or platform-dependent information. The local/shared axis refers to information that is shared or not shared between multiple source trees (also called product nodes). The code/data axis refers to executable code (code) or include file definitions (data).

Note that shared files are always shared *outside* their original product node, whereas local files stay *inside* their original product node even if they're shared among multiple platforms within the node.

The possible combinations of these factors define the eight possible types of code and data that good code management systems must be capable of storing and sharing. The eight types are shown in Table 2-2.

All the sample programs in this tour contain all eight types of code and data. The main goal of the tour is to show you how to manage all eight types of code and data with the tools and code management system described in this book.

Table 2-2: Eight Possible Types of Code and Data

Type	Pi/Pd	Local/Shared	Code/Data	Example
1	Pd	Local	Code	A program-dependent pd subroutine
2	Pd	Local	Data	A program-dependent pd include file
3	Pd	Shared	Code	A shareable, reusable pd subroutine
4	Pd	Shared	Data	A shareable, reusable pd include file
5	Pi	Local	Code	A program-dependent pi subroutine
6	Pi	Local	Data	A program-dependent pi include file
7	Pi	Shared	Code	A shareable, reusable pi subroutine
8	Pi	Shared	Data	A shareable, reusable pi include file

Even though the *tool1* program contains shareable data and code, we're never going to share any *tool1* files with any other example programs. That's because we're going to keep the *tool1* program around as an example of how *not* to manage code files.

Instead, we'll make our code management changes on *tool2* and *tool3*, which will start out as clones of *tool1*. That way, when we get to the end of the examples, you'll have working examples of both the right way (*tool2* and *tool3*) and the wrong way (*tool1*) to organize source files. This is an important advantage, because having both good and bad examples will make it much more convenient for you to investigate and understand the differences between the two.

As a consequence of the *tool1* program's simplicity and monolithic design, it won't be hard to set up in a code management sense. We'll just put all eight types of code in one file and be done with it. But you'll soon see when we start working with the two cloned programs, that they'll have to be changed quite a bit in order to share files between them. (That's why we need two clones, by the way—in order to demonstrate how to share files between them.)

We'll share an increasing amount of information between *tool2* and *tool3* as we progress through the examples. This will force us to separate out the eight types of code and data a little further each time.

This process of separation and isolation is worth learning because it's exactly what you'll need to know in order to port code to new platforms under this code management system. It's also worth learning how to do this on a guided tour such as this one, instead of immediately setting out on your own to treat big collections of large programs.

Here's a complete picture of the source code tree for *tool1*, complete with a listing of the various files that will eventually be stored in the tree after *tool1* is compiled.

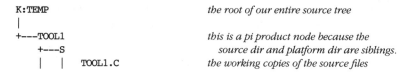

```
K:TEMP                          the root of our entire source tree
   |
   +---TOOL1                    this is a pi product node because the
        +---S                      source dir and platform dir are siblings.
        |   |   TOOL1.C          the working copies of the source files
```

```
|   |   TOOL1.H                     pi+pd local data
|   |   TOOLS.H                     pi+pd shared data
|   |
|   \---RCS                         rcs files are stored in a subdir of s.
|           TOOL1.C                 an rcs version-controlled file
|           TOOL1.H                 an rcs version-controlled file
|           TOOLS.H                 an rcs version-controlled file
|
\-------TBC.PLT                     the tbc.plt platform is for Borland C
        MAKEFILE                    the top-level main makefile
        MAKEFILE.PI                 makefile dependency rules
        IMPORTS.IMP                 custom makefile targets
        TOOL1.OBJ                   the compiled object file
        TOOL1.EXE                   the final executable file
```

To see where we're going to end up after completing all the examples, look at the sequence of directory structures shown in Example 5 in Chapter 8. As you can see, the original *tool1* tree has grown into a collection of several trees, including pi and pd library nodes, pi and pd initialization nodes (explained during the tour), and a pi product node.

Example 2: Sharing data files

In this example, we'll start separating the eight types of information that were all mixed together in the *tool1* program. In particular, this example shows how to share data files between multiple programs. We'll create two new example programs for this purpose, *tool2* and *tool3*.

This example also shows how to upgrade existing programs by the addition of new source files. We'll add two new subroutine files and two new include files to the *tool2* program, so we can demonstrate how to work with products that are built from multiple source files.

Example 3: Sharing code files

In this example, we create a subroutine library to hold the subroutines that we want to share between *tool2* and *tool3*. We put both the pi and pd subroutines into a single library at first to demonstrate how to share code through a library. But of course, putting both pi and pd code into one library is a mistake because the two types of code and data must be separated later when you port the programs to multiple platforms (because you need two different copies of the pd information). Later we'll undo our deliberate mistakes to more clearly emphasize the separation of pi and pd code.

Example 4: Multiple platforms

This example adds a second platform to all programs and forces us to separate the pi code and data from the pd code and data (throughout all source trees). As a consequence, this is a very long example, because we have both local and shared, pi and pd, code and data to separate. But it's also an important example to read, since you'll run into similar problems when you port your own code to multiple platforms.

Specifically, we have to separate the pi and pd *data* in both the local and shared include files for each of the tools. Then we have to separate the pi and pd *code* in the both the local programs and shared libraries.

Example 5: Managing shell script products

This short example shows you how to build pd scripts and batch file products (instead of compilable programs and libraries).

The most interesting thing about this example is that it contains a complete graphical picture of all source trees, complete with the files that you should expect to find in the trees. You'll find it easier to keep yourself oriented through the examples if you refer to this picture frequently.

Example 6: Bulk operations

This example shows you how to perform various kinds of bulk operations on the source trees using the code management tools provided with this book. We'll replace all the existing makefiles with brand new ones, modify all the *imports.imp* files in the sample source trees, and then rebuild all products from scratch to demonstrate that the system still works.

I'll also introduce the idea of cloning source trees, and show you that under DOS, cloning trees is mostly pointless (at least for the purposes of this book). This is because DOS doesn't support symbolic links, which in turn means that cloned trees can't share the same set of RCS files under this code management system. The next example—which is intended to be run on a UNIX system—does demonstrate meaningful tree cloning in multi-developer work environments.

Example 7: Multiple developers

This example shows you how to use the code management tools to support multiple developers. Specifically, we'll clone the main source tree, check out the latest version of all source files into the cloned tree, regenerate new makefiles in the cloned tree, and recompile all the sample programs. Then we'll modify and check in a source file in the cloned tree to show that the modifications can be accessed from within the main source tree (or from within other cloned trees). We can do this because the RCS directories in the cloned tree are symbolic links that point back to the RCS directories in the main tree. As a consequence, RCS operations performed in the cloned tree actually operate on the RCS files in the main tree.

I'll also show you how to create custom tree walker scripts that visit an arbitrary set of directories.

Standard Development Steps

There are five basic steps that we'll use for building the first few sample programs and libraries on our tour of the code management system:

> **Step 1.** Create a directory tree using *makenode* or *makeplt.*
> **Step 2.** Create the source code, usually with an editor, but sometimes by cloning.
> **Step 3.** Generate the makefiles with *getmakes.*
> **Step 4.** Compile, export, and test the product with *make.*
> **Step 5.** Update the RCS files with the *rcsdo* program.

These steps will be highlighted at each point that they occur in the examples. The point of using these five steps is to add more structure to the development process to make it easier for you at the beginning of the tour.

In Example 4, I'll abandon this strict five step sequence and start intermixing various steps as appropriate to the task at hand. I do this because the intermixed approach is a more efficient development process, and because I wanted to show you the best development techniques that I knew of. (By the time you reach Example 4, you'll be familiar enough with the tools and the five steps to follow along without difficulty.)

Example 1: A Simple Program

This example shows how to use the code management tools to compile a simple program (*tool1.c*) on a single platform (*tbc.plt*, for Borland C).

If you're working on a UNIX machine, or prefer to use a different platform (compiler), you'll have to substitute the name of your platform in the following examples. Look in the *CMTREE/plt* directory to find a list of platforms currently supported by the tools. If you want to make up a brand new platform, the section called "Creating a New Platform" in Chapter 3, *A Hands-on Tour: Part 2*, shows you how.

Constructing the Program

Step 1. Create the directory tree. The first thing we have to do is create a directory tree to hold the source and binary files for our example.

Create a single directory named *main* (for "main source tree") to hold the source trees for all the example programs we'll be constructing. Doing it this way will allow you to easily delete, move, or store the whole set of examples after the tour.

```
K:\> mkdir main
K:\> cd main
```

Creating pi nodes

Now we're going to use the first code management tool included on the disks. The name of the tool is *makenode*, and its purpose is to create a particular type of directory subtree that's in accordance with the code management principles advocated by this book.

There is nothing particularly fancy about either the *makenode* tool or the subtree that it creates. The tool is a simple batch file containing a few *mkdir* commands, and the tree structure has only four subdirectories. The purpose of the *makenode* tool is to help you create these common code management subtrees quickly and correctly.

Don't worry about the arguments to *makenode* right now. *makenode* is described in the reference section in the back of the book, and you can look it up there if you want more information. (Or if you're really keen, you can read the code for the batch file.) For now, it's enough to tell you what the arguments mean. The first argument, *tool1*, is the name of the software product that we want to build (our example program, *tool1.c*). The second argument, *pi*, tells *makenode* to create a directory structure that's good for storing platform-independent programs. The third argument, *tbc.plt*, is my standard platform name for storing Borland C makefiles.

```
K:\MAIN> makenode tool1 pi tbc.plt
```

Let's have a look at the tree that *makenode* has created. Use the standard MS-DOS *tree* command to print out the tree using only ASCII (*/a*) characters. (You might want to drop the */a* to get more readable output.)

```
K:\MAIN> tree /a tool1
K:TOOL1                    the name of our product tree "node"
+---S                      a place for pi source files
|   \---RCS                a place for RCS files
\---TBC.PLT                a place for makefiles, object, and exe files
```

As you can see, *makenode* creates a source directory with the ultra-simple name *s* for holding our *.c* and *.h* files. A subdirectory was created to store the corresponding RCS files. We also have a platform directory named *tbc.plt* where the makefiles will go.

If the project supported many different platforms, we'd create a directory for each with *makenode* and store customized makefiles for each platform in each platform directory. For example, here's how I'd build a product node for three platforms all at once, using *makenode*. (I can do this because *makenode* can accept an arbitrary number of platform arguments on the command line.)

```
K:\MAIN> makenode manyplts pi tbc.plt msc.plt sun4gcc.plt
K:\MAIN> tree /a manyplts
K:MANYPLTS                 a product node with "many platforms"
+---S                      a place to pi source files
|   \---RCS                a place for the corresponding RCS files
+---TBC.PLT                makefiles + objs + exes for platform 1 (Borland C)
+---MSC.PLT                makefiles + objs + exes for platform 2 (Microsoft C)
\---SUN4GCC.PLT            makefiles + objs + exes for platform 3 (Sun4 GNU gcc)
```

But we don't need this subtree for our examples, so let's delete it. You can do this with the freeware *rm* program included on the disk.

```
K:\MAIN> rm -rf manyplts
```

I usually call the tree structures that are created by *makenode* "product trees," "product nodes," or just "nodes" for short. You'll see all three terms in this book.

Note that in pi nodes (which store platform-independent source files), the source directory is a *sibling* of the platform directory, because pi source files are shared by all platforms. (Some people prefer to distinguish pi and pd nodes by the following rule: Anything below a *.plt* directory is pd; anything else is pi.)

Creating pd nodes

In pd nodes (which store platform-dependent source files), the source directories are in a different location. They're *children* of the platform directories, not siblings. This is because the pd source files are different for each platform. Thus it makes sense to store the platform-dependent source files somewhere in the subtree below the platform directory. Here's an example of a pd node:

```
K:\MAIN> makenode pd_node1 pd tbc.plt msc.plt sun4gcc.plt
K:\MAIN> tree /a pd_node1
K:PD_NODE1                    the name of this node
+---TBC.PLT                   a place for pd (Borland) makefiles, objs, exes
|   \---S                     a place for pd (Borland-dependent) source files
|       \---RCS
+---MSC.PLT                   a place for pd (Microsoft) makefiles, objs, exes
|   \---S                     a place for pd (Microsoft-dependent) source files
|       \---RCS
\---SUN4GCC.PLT               a place for pd (Sun4/GNU gcc) makefiles, objs, exes
    \---S                     a place for pd (Sun4/GNU gcc) source files
        \---RCS
```

Storing the source files for a particular platform underneath the platform directory makes it easier to support multiple platforms. You can easily add new platform directories (or delete old ones) at will, without affecting the proper compilation of other platforms. The platform-dependent files for any product are always very easy to find, too.

We don't need this node for our examples, so let's get rid of it.

```
K:\MAIN> rm -rf pd_node1
```

Creating pid nodes

Now let's have a brief look at the third and final type of node—a pid node. This node type is a combination of the previous two, because it can hold both pi and pd source files. It looks like a pd node, but with an extra *sibling* (pi) source directory added.

```
K:\MAIN> makenode pid_node1 pid tbc.plt msc.plt sun4gcc.plt
K:\MAIN> tree /a pid_node1
K:PID_NODE1                          the name of our pid product node
+---S                                a place for pi source files (used by all platforms)
|   \---RCS
+---TBC.PLT                          a place for pd (Borland) makefiles, objs, exes
|   \---S                            a place for pd (Borland-dependent) source files
|       \---RCS
+---MSC.PLT                          a place for pd (Microsoft) makefiles, objs, exes
|   \---S                            a place for pd (Microsoft-dependent) source files
|       \---RCS
\---SUN4GCC.PLT                      a place for pd (Sun4/GNU gcc) makefiles, objs, exes
    \---S                            a place for pd (Sun4/GNU gcc) source files
        \---RCS
```

We don't need this node for our examples either, so let's get rid of it.

```
K:\MAIN> rm -rf pid_node1
```

Now that you've seen the three types of trees that *makenode* can create, we can get back to the task at hand—creating a node to hold our first example program, *tool1.c*.

You'll soon see that *tool1.c* is a pd program because it contains hardcoded platform names. This means that we shouldn't really be storing *tool1.c* in a pi node. But since the *tool1* example is supposed to be an example of how *not* to do things, using an inappropriate directory structure doesn't really matter.

Portability and pi, pd, pid nodes

The main purpose of using pi, pd, and pid nodes is to help separate platform-independent from platform-dependent code. Knowing which is which is important, because platform-independent code is usually easier to handle and requires less effort to port and maintain. (Since platform-independent code has no platform-dependent quirks, it's usually easier to understand, easier to port, and easier to share among multiple products.)

Probably most of us would like to believe that "pi code equals portable code," because that way we can make ourselves feel good about writing portable code. Unfortunately, that definition of portability isn't quite correct.

In fact, portability is a concept that can only be defined for a specific set of platforms. Someone once observed that "there's no such thing as portable code, only code that's been ported." So it is precise and correct to say, "This code is portable among platforms X, Y, and Z." But it's not very precise or correct to say, "This code is portable," since the code might fail to run on the very next machine that you try to run it on.

The definitions of pi, pd, and pid are similar to the definition of "portable"—they make sense only when they're accompanied by a list of platforms. For example, if you write a program that only runs on one platform, is it pi code, pd code, or pid code? The answer depends on the list of platforms being considered.

To make things more precise in this book, we'll always use the platforms within a product node as the list of platforms to be considered. Then, for any source files within a product node, the following definitions will hold for pi, pd, and pid code:

- Pi code is code that can be shared by all platforms within a node.

- Pd code is code that can't be shared by all platforms within a node.

- There's no such thing as pid code, because code is either pi or pd, according to the previous definitions.

These definitions leave us open to some funny situations. For instance, suppose some pi include files from one product node are reused by some other code in a second product node. Then, according our definitions, it's possible for the include files to be pi files in the first node, but pd files in the second node (or vice versa). The classification just depends on the particular combination of platforms that are present in the product node where the code is being classified.

Here's a list of the corresponding definitions for pi, pd, pid product nodes (source trees):

- Pi nodes contain only pi code.

- Pd nodes contain only pd code.

- Pid nodes can contain pi code, pd code, or both pi and pd code.

There's one more situation in which we use the pi, pd, and pid labels, and that's to help control some of the code management tools provided with the book. Specifically, a few of the tools require you to specify pi, pd, or pid as a command line argument. They take slightly different actions depending on whether you use them to create (or operate on) a pi node, pd node, or pid node. For example, the tools might create different directory structures, look in different places for source code, or generate different output files. (These different behaviors are described later in the tour.)

The main advantage of using pi, pd, and pid nodes from a human point of view is that the three node types make it easier for programmers to remember what's inside of the product node. For example, suppose you wanted to port several products to a new platform. How could you answer the question, "What code must be ported?"

As a first guess, you could correctly answer, "at least everything in pd nodes and everything in the platform directories of pid nodes." This much is fairly obvious. What might not be immediately obvious is that our definitions of pi and pd code leave us open to another possibility. That is, some of the previously pi code could become pd code when the new platform is added. (Fortunately, this is fairly rare once you've ported your code to a few platforms.)

I use pi or pd nodes in preference to pid nodes whenever it is feasible. It is easier to locate the pd code when the need arises.

Step 2. Create the source code. Now that the pi node has been created, we'll create the source code for our *tool1.c* program.

At several points during the tour, we have to edit files. I'm not going to show you the whole file all the time, because that would be wasteful. But I'll show you the crucial parts so that you can make sure your own files are correct as we go along. Sometimes I'll just show you the key lines that I've inserted or edited, and sometimes I'll show you a difference output between the original and the edited file. (Difference outputs can be produced from either the *diff* or *rcsdiff* tools.)

I'll also show you my editor command in all cases, right at the point where you have to edit each file. My editor is *emacs*. You should use whatever editor you're comfortable with.

Let's create the *tool1* program. Change directories to the source directory. If you've unpacked my *tourchap.tar* file from the diskettes, you can just copy all the source files for *tool1.c*, *tool1.h*, and *tools.h* from the directory *main1/tool1/s*.

The source code created for *tool1.c* is shown right below the editor command.

```
K:\MAIN> cd tool1\s
K:\MAIN\TOOL1\S> emacs tool1.c              use your favorite editor
K:\MAIN\TOOL1\S> type tool1.c
/* $Id$ */
#include <stdio.h>
#include "tool1.h"             /* pi and pd local  data */
#include "tools.h"             /* pi and pd shared data */
void main ()
{
    printf("0  This is tool1 compiled on platform (tbc.plt).\n");
    printf("1  (tbc.plt) This is pd local  code from tool1/s/tool1.c.\n");
    printf("2  %s\n",T1_PD_DATA);       /* print pd local  data */
    printf("3  (tbc.plt) This is pd shared code from tool1/s/tool1.c.\n");
    printf("4  %s\n",TN_PD_DATA);       /* print pd shared data */
    printf("5  (pi)      This is pi local  code from tool1/s/tool1.c.\n");
    printf("6  %s\n",T1_PI_DATA);       /* print pi local  data */
    printf("7  (pi)      This is pi shared code from tool1/s/tool1.c.\n");
    printf("8  %s\n",TN_PI_DATA);       /* print pi shared data */
}
```

The *tool1* program contains nine lines (numbered 0-8) of output in total. The first line identifies the tool name, and the platform that it was compiled on. (Hardcoding the platform name into line 0 makes it a pd code line.) The other eight lines are each an example of one of the eight possible types of information that were shown earlier in Table 2-2.

Furthermore, each of the eight numbered lines in *tool1.c* contains a hardcoded pathname to show you where the information in that line has been stored within the source tree. That way, the output of each sample program can visually "explain" how that particular program was assembled from a collection of the eight types of information. This is an important advantage because it allows you to directly "see" the underlying directory node structures and file sharing relationships in the output of each program.

The *tool1.c* program also contains two include files. I've created these files to show you how to work with include files in the code management system. Each file contains both pi and pd data.

The first include file, *tool1.h*, contains local data—data that's used only by *tool1.c*. The second include file, *tools.h*, contains shared data that's going to be shared among several programs during the tour. Using two include files this way allows me to represent all four of the possible types of data information (out of the eight types of information shown in Table 2-2).

tool1.h contains local pi and pd data for the exclusive use of *tool1.c*.

```
K:\MAIN\TOOL1\S> emacs tool1.h
K:\MAIN\TOOL1\S> type tool1.h
/* $Id: tool1.h 1.1 1993/07/09 13:36:58 jameson Exp jameson $ */
#define T1_PD_DATA "(tbc.plt) This is pd local  data from tool1/s/tool1.h."
#define T1_PI_DATA "(pi)     This is pi local  data from tool1/s/tool1.h."
```

tools.h contains shared pi and pd data for the use of all sample programs (we'll eventually share this file between *tool2.c* and *tool3.c*).

```
K:\MAIN\TOOL1\S> emacs tools.h
K:\MAIN\TOOL1\S> type tools.h
/* $Id: tools.h 1.1 1993/07/09 13:36:58 jameson Exp jameson $ */
#define TN_PD_DATA "(tbc.plt) This is pd shared data from tool1/s/tools.h."
#define TN_PI_DATA "(pi)     This is pi shared data from tool1/s/tools.h".
```

Why are we using this particular tool1.c program?

tool1.c is a contrived program. My main design goals were to illustrate important code management principles, while keeping everything as simple as possible. *tool1.c* has eight types of information contained within a single source file (*tool1.c*) that is being compiled on a single platform (*tbc.plt*).

The eight types of information are a result of two kinds of information for each of three "axes": local/shared, pi/pd, and code/data.

Local means "shared within the product node." Local code can actually be shared by files within one node, but it has to stay within the node.

Shared means "shared through the CMHTREE." This kind of information isn't local, because it has to be exported outside of the product node in order to be shared.

Having all eight types of information in one file is bad code management practice. During the tour, one of our main goals will be to separate the eight types of information into separate files so that the information can be easily shared among multiple programs running on multiple platforms.

Step 3. Generate the makefiles. Now that the source code is ready, we'll use the makefile generation tools to generate the makefiles. The commands to do this are shown below. The arguments to *getmakes* tell it to generate makefiles on a platform named *tbc.plt* for a platform-independent program called *tool1*.

```
K:\MAIN\TOOL1\S> cd ..\tbc.plt
K:\MAIN\TOOL1\TBC.PLT> getmakes tbc.plt pi program tool1
```

Now would be a good time to peek inside the generated makefiles, if you're so inclined. The top-level *makefile* is a simple makefile that includes other makefiles, as shown in Figure 2-1. *makefile.pi* is one of the files included—it contains makefile dependency rules for pi source files.

Chapter 6, *Makefile Architectures*, discusses the contents of makefiles in detail, so I won't discuss them here. I will say that the makefile strategy of this code management system is based on two ideas.

The first idea is to separate particular types of makefile knowledge into separate template makefiles. For example, the templates in the platform directories of the CMTREE describe how to compile and link executable programs, how to compile and construct subroutine libraries, and so on.

The second idea is to use *getmakes* to assemble complete, functional makefiles from the various template files. Here's an approximate description of what the *getmakes* tool does when you invoke it to generate makefiles:

1. It determines the platform type (e.g., *tbc.plt*) from the arguments.

2. It determines the product type (program, library, script) from the arguments.

3. It copies *makefile.mak* from the CMTREE into the current directory.

4. It edits *makefile.mak* to include the appropriate templates for the program type. Two template names are normally added: one for the program type (e.g., *makefile.xxe*) and one for the dependency rules (e.g., *makefile.pi*).

5. It renames the edited makefile from *makefile.mak* to *makefile*.

6. It calls *gendep* to generate makefile dependency rules from the source code, if necessary. The dependency rules are generated in the file whose name was edited into the makefile above (e.g., *makefile.pi*).

Now that *getmakes* has generated a set of standard makefiles for us, we must still customize two of the makefile targets in the *imports.imp* file. Specifically, we have to tell *make* to copy (import) the two include files *tool1.h* and *tools.h* from the source directory into the platform directory, so the compiler can access them. We do that by adding import statements to the *imports.imp* file.

This type of copy operation is called "importing" because it brings a copy of a file into a place where you can use it. Similarly, when I copy a file *from* a place where you've

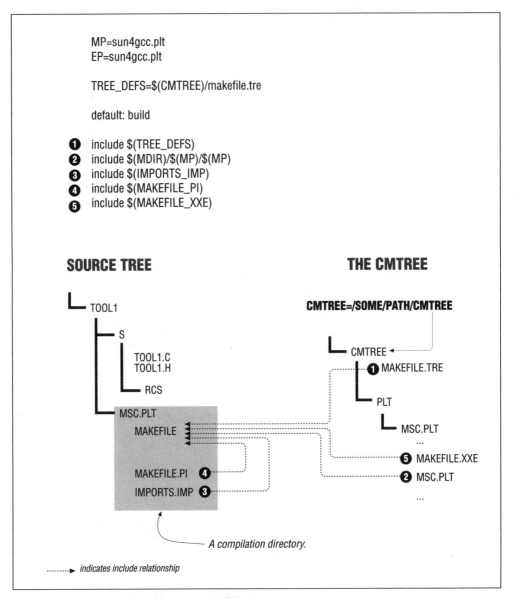

Figure 2–1. Include relationships in makefiles

created it *to* another place where others can use it (into the CMHTREE, for example), that operation is called "exporting."

There are several other ways of helping the compiler find the include files, of course. Some compilers are smart enough to look for include files in the same directory that contains the source files. Other compilers accept **–Idirectory** control arguments that specify directories for the compiler to search. All of these mechanisms have their limitations, and none of them is as general as the file sharing technique shown here. Moreover, none of them allow you to track which programs use which include files.

File sharing is a more complex topic than first impressions might indicate. File sharing issues are discussed at length in Chapter 4, *Designing a Code Management System*, and Chapter 7, *File Sharing*.

Getting back to the task at hand, which is to customize our *imports.imp* file, we need to make two custom changes to the file. First, under the **imports** target, use the *cmi* program (described in detail in Chapter 7) to import the two include files required to compile *tool1.c.*

Normally, important file sharing operations are logged by both the *cmi* and *cmx* tools (for importing and exporting files, respectively). These log messages provide useful documentation when files come from far away on the system. But since both of the include files come from the local source directory, we'll inhibit import logging with the *-nl* ("no log") control argument. That's because we don't want to clutter up our share logs with relatively unimportant file sharing operations that occur within a single product node. (I use a literal *-nl* in the makefile command line instead of a macro, such as **$CMIFLAGS**, because I often won't use the *-nl* argument. If I were using a macro, then I'd have to define another macro for the opposite case, and so on. I've found it easier to just type in *-nl* when I need it.)

The second change to *imports.imp*, this time under the **imports.rev** target, will be to delete every file imported under the **imports** target. This is so that you can easily "reverse" your importing operations by typing **make imports.rev** or **make empty**.

So let's do it. Note that I'll always show you the crucial code changes in the lines just below the line where I invoke my editor. That way you can check your editing changes against mine.

```
K:\MAIN\TOOL1\TBC.PLT> emacs imports.imp
imports:
        $(CMI) -nl ../s/tool1.h
        $(CMI) -nl ../s/tools.h

imports.rev:
        $(RM) tool1.h
        $(RM) tools.h
```

Step 4. Compile, export, and test the products. Everything is ready now, so we can compile and test the program. But first let's have a look at the contents of our platform directory, before we import any files, or create any object files.

```
K:\MAIN\TOOL1\TBC.PLT> ls
imports.imp makefile    makefile.pi
```

Type **make imports** to import the include files, and then **ls** to list the two imported include files.

```
K:\MAIN\TOOL1\TBC.PLT> make imports
        cmi  -nl ../s/tool1.h
        1 file(s) copied
Imported k:/main/tool1/s/tool1.h to k:/main/tool1/tbc.plt/tool1.h.
        cmi  -nl ../s/tools.h
        1 file(s) copied
Imported k:/main/tool1/s/tools.h to k:/main/tool1/tbc.plt/tools.h.

K:\MAIN\TOOL1\TBC.PLT> ls
  imports.imp makefile      makefile.pi tool1.h      tools.h
```

Type **make build** to compile the program, and then **ls** to list the new executable file.

```
K:\MAIN\TOOL1\TBC.PLT> make build
        bcc -c -Qe- -Qx=,1024 -g1 -j1 -A -ml ../s/tool1.c
        1 file(s) copied
        1 file(s) copied
        tlink /yx/x/d/Ld:\bc\l;j:\h\at\tbc.plt;h:\mks\lib c01 @o.tmp,tool1,,emu math1 cl

K:\MAIN\TOOL1\TBC.PLT> ls
  imports.imp makefile.pi tool1.h      tools.h
  makefile    tool1.exe   tool1.obj
```

Type **make exports** to export the executable file into the alpha test directory in the CMHTREE.

```
K:\MAIN\TOOL1\TBC.PLT> make exports
        cmx  -nl tool1.exe -dd j:/h/at/tbc.plt
        1 file(s) copied
Exported k:/main/tool1/tbc.plt/tool1.exe to j:/h/at/tbc.plt/tool1.exe.
```

Now you've seen how to perform the three separate operations of importing, compiling, and exporting. Separately performing three such common operations isn't very convenient however, so I've provided several other makefile targets for convenience:

- *make imports* imports precursor files (usually include files).

- *make build* builds the final product files in the appropriate way.

- *make exports* exports the final products to the proper destinations.

- *make full* imports and builds.

- *make all* imports, builds, and exports.

- *make clean* deletes imported, temporary, and object files.

- *make empty* runs *make clean* and then deletes final product files.

Try these various targets out long enough to get a feeling for what they do. I'm only going to demonstrate two of the targets below, since I rarely use any of the targets except **empty**, **full**, and **all**.

Type **make empty** to start over from scratch, then **make all** to completely rebuild and export the program.

```
K:\MAIN\TOOL1\TBC.PLT> make empty                delete everything
K:\MAIN\TOOL1\TBC.PLT> ls
 imports.imp  makefile     makefile.pi

K:\MAIN\TOOL1\TBC.PLT> make all                  rebuild everything
K:\MAIN\TOOL1\TBC.PLT> ls
 imports.imp  makefile.pi  tool1.h      tools.h
 makefile     tool1.exe    tool1.obj
```

Now let's have a look at the output of the *tool1* program:

```
K:\MAIN\TOOL1\TBC.PLT> tool1
0  This is tool1 compiled on platform (tbc.plt).
1  (tbc.plt) This is pd local  code from tool1/s/tool1.c.
2  (tbc.plt) This is pd local  data from tool1/s/tool1.h.
3  (tbc.plt) This is pd shared code from tool1/s/tool1.c.
4  (tbc.plt) This is pd shared data from tool1/s/tools.h.
5  (pi)      This is pi local  code from tool1/s/tool1.c.
6  (pi)      This is pi local  data from tool1/s/tool1.h.
7  (pi)      This is pi shared code from tool1/s/tool1.c.
8  (pi)      This is pi shared data from tool1/s/tools.h.
```

Everything looks good. All we have left to do is to check all these files into the RCS source code control system. After that, we'll analyze the output of this program to see what's wrong with it from a code management point of view.

Step 5. Update the RCS files. Now we'll use the *rcsdo* command to perform some bulk RCS operations. (To avoid confusion, let me explain that the *rcsdo* tool isn't part of the standard RCS distribution, even though its name starts with "rcs." Instead, it's one of the code management tools that I wrote.)

For those of you who aren't familiar with RCS, it's a Revision Control System that allows you to recreate previous versions of a file. Of course, you have to register the versions that you want to preserve by "checking them in," which is what we're about to do here. You can also associate log messages with each check-in operation to help you remember the unique features of the files you're checking in.

To begin this bulk check-in of several files, create a simple log message using the *echo* command. (I normally create the *msg* file in the editor at the same time I'm modifying the source files, but using the *echo* command is easier for simple messages.) Since we want to check in the *original* source files in the source directory—not the include files that we imported into the platform directory—we have to change directories.

```
K:\MAIN\TOOL1\TBC.PLT> cd ..\s
K:\MAIN\TOOL1\S> echo This is the source code for example 1. > msg
```

Next, check in all the new files with the *ci_u_initial* option of *rcsdo*. This option checks in all locked files in the current directory into RCS, except for the file named as the message file on the command line. (In standard RCS language, this operation is equivalent to performing a *ci -u filename $<$ msg* operation on each locked file in the current directory.) The *ci_u_initial* option is the most appropriate one to use in this situation, because all of our source files are new. Later on we'll have to use other *rcsdo* options to check in modified files that have already had RCS files created for them.

The next option on the *rcsdo* command line specifies the name of the RCS check-in message file (*msg*). The *-log default* argument specifies that the check-ins are to be logged into the default RCS check-in log file. The location of the default RCS log file is controlled by the environment variable $CMPCILOG, or by the hardcoded value in the *pci* tool if the environment variable doesn't exist. Figure 2-2 shows the relationship between an RCS check-in and the log file.

(By way of an early warning, if this next command generates "File creation error" messages on your machine, you probably haven't properly set the $CMPCILOG variable. It overrides the default pathname for the RCS check-in log message file in the *pci* tool. To permanently define the location of the log file without using an environment variable, you can edit the source code for the *pci* tool.)

```
K:\MAIN\TOOL1\S> rcsdo ci_u_initial msg -log default
rcs\tools.h  <-  tools.h
initial revision: 1.1
done
rcs\tool1.h  <-  tool1.h
initial revision: 1.1
done
rcs\tool1.c  <-  tool1.c
initial revision: 1.1
done

Files checked in:

k:/main/tool1/s
        tools.h
        tool1.h
        tool1.c

This is the source code for example 1.
K:\MAIN\TOOL1\S> del msg
```

Now let's add a symbolic name to all of the files in this version of the *tool1* software so that we can later check them out as a group. The *rcsdo* options for this are self explanatory.

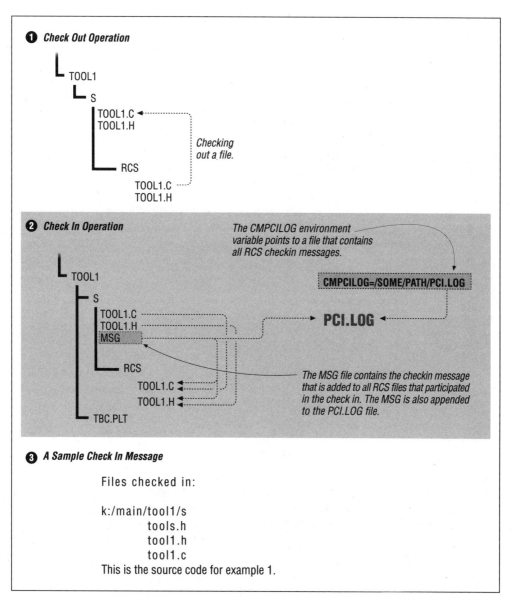

Figure 2–2. Information flow in RCS operations

Note: you can't use periods in the RCS version names (the RCS tools don't like it).

```
K:\MAIN\TOOL1\S> rcsdo add_name ex_1          ex_1 stands for "example 1"
RCS file: rcs\tool1.c
done
RCS file: rcs\tool1.h
```

```
done
RCS file: rcs\tools.h
done
K:\MAIN\TOOL1\S> rcsdo ls_names
ex_1
K:\MAIN\TOOL1\S> rcsdo ls_name ex_1
tool1.c      1.1 is part of symbolic name ex_1
tool1.h      1.1 is part of symbolic name ex_1
tools.h      1.1 is part of symbolic name ex_1
```

RCS assigns a version number to each file that's checked in. The first version number is always 1.1, which is why all the version numbers above are the same. The version numbers are automatically increased by one each time the file is modified and checked in again.

The symbolic name **ex_1** is never incremented by RCS, since RCS just treats **ex_1** as a text string label. And this is the right thing for RCS to do, too, because the label is a string, not an integer. For example, I could have picked the label "foobar." And how would RCS increment that? I just picked **ex_1** to stand for "example 1," because this is the first example in this tour.

Recall that I put an *$Id* symbol on the first line of all source files. Now that the files have been checked into RCS, RCS has replaced the symbol with an RCS identification string. The string can be seen by looking at the first line in the file. It can also be shown with the help of the RCS *ident* command.

```
K:\MAIN\TOOL1\S> type tool1.c
/* $Id: tool1.c 1.1 1993/07/09 13:36:58 jameson Exp jameson $ */
... etc.

K:\MAIN\TOOL1\S> ident tool1.c
tool1.c:
     $Id: tool1.c 1.1 1993/07/09 13:36:58 jameson Exp jameson $
```

I've used the *ident* tool on a source file here just to demonstrate its use. The real strength of the *ident* tool is to identify the version information in executable files (if the version information was ever stored in the files). You can store RCS version information in binary files (in C) by defining a static character string whose value is the RCS **$Id** string, as shown below. Then you can use *ident* to print out the version of the compiled object file.

```
static char rcs_info [] = "$Id$";   /* store rcs info in object file */
```

This is the end of Example 1. Now you know how to install simple programs under the code management system described in this book.

It might be a good idea for you to poke around a little bit in the *tool1* directory tree before we continue with more examples. It'll probably help you better understand how, where, and why the various files in the system are stored in, and moved around among, the various directories.

For example, you could look in the CMHTREE (the holding tree) to see where the tools put the exported copy of the final *tool1.exe* product. You might also look in the default check-in log file to verify that the *rcsdo* tool installed the log message properly. Or you might want to poke around in the contents of the makefile templates in the CMTREE to see how all this makefile magic is happening (the makefile architecture is explained in Chapter 6, in case you need more help.)

What's Wrong with This Program?

Before we proceed with the rest of the examples, I'm going to take some time out to analyze the *tool1* program from a code management point of view. I'll point out what's good about it, what's bad about it, and give you an overview of how we'll solve its problems.

The Current Situation

Now you've seen some benefits of the code management system described in this book. For instance, it provides tools that create tree structures, generate makefiles, and perform bulk RCS check-ins. These are all meaningful advantages over traditional, unsupported development environments. We still haven't covered all of the advantages of the code management system because the current program examples haven't given us the necessary opportunities. (They still don't properly separate the eight different types of information.)

This situation (of improperly separated types of information) sometimes also occurs when you inherit programs from other people—they compile, but they're organizational nightmares. They're filled with all manner of **#ifdef** statements, with pi and pd code and data—both local and shared—all mixed together. Sometimes parts of the code are even duplicated.

Specifically, the *tool1* program contains a monolithic mix of all possible types of pi and pd, local and shared, code and data.* This kind of a code management strategy makes code maintenance more difficult, and it fails miserably when small, single-program projects (such as *tool1*) are scaled up into collections of larger software products that run on multiple platforms.

The consequence of using a bad code management strategy such as the one above is that you have to change strategies in midstream when your project grows. And that, euphemistically expressed, can be "technically and managerially challenging."

---

* Mixing pi and pd information, or local and shared information, is what usually causes most code management problems. In fewer cases, treating data as code—that is, hardcoding it in programs instead of storing it in include files—also causes maintenance and sharing problems.

Specific Problems

Several problems arise if we try to share information between *tool1* and other tools, or when we port the tools to multiple platforms. We'll deal with the following two problems first:

1. There is pd code in the pi *tool1\s* directory.

    Lines 1 through 4 of the *tool1* output are a problem because they are pd code lines, and so will be different for different platforms. (Lines 1 through 4 would probably be surrounded with pd **#ifdefs** in other code management systems.)

    In the system described here, lines 1 through 4 should be stored in a pd file in a pd location. Specifically, the proper place for them is in a source directory underneath a platform directory (such as *tool1\tbc.plt\s\tool1.b*), instead of being stored where they are, in a pi file in a pi source directory.

    The main problem with the traditional **#ifdef** approach is that as you add more platforms, you have to add more and more **#ifdef** statements, often nesting them. After a while there are so many **#ifdef** statements in the code that it is difficult to understand what any particular version of the code is supposed to be doing. Moreover, it's equally difficult to remove the appropriate **#ifdef** statements when you want to remove support for an obsolete platform.

    In contrast, the strategy taken here—to isolate pd information in separate files and directories—completely avoids the **#ifdef** problem by disallowing platform-dependent **#ifdef** statements in the code. This strategy also makes adding new platforms straightforward, and removing platforms trivial—just delete the relevant platform directories.

2. There is non-locally shared code in the *tool1\s* directory.

    Lines 3, 4, 7, and 8 are a problem because there's no good way of properly sharing these items of information while they're stored within the *tool1* directory tree.

    The way we'll solve this problem is to put the shared information in special initialization and library nodes. Then we'll export the shared information (as include files and code libraries) to an appropriate location in the holding tree (the CMHTREE) so other programs can access the shared information.

    (For the record, lines 5 and 6 are okay—they are pi local code lines in pi files in a pi source directory.)

The rest of the examples in this tour have been designed to highlight these organizational faults in the *tool1* program. Each successive example will force us to fix one or more of the faults by separating and reorganizing some of the code. By the end of the tour, we'll have all the code and data properly stored in directory structures that can be used to manage many products (of arbitrary size) on multiple platforms.

Example 2: Sharing Data Files

This example is more complex than the previous one, because it shows you how to share data files between multiple programs. First we'll create two new programs, *tool2* and *tool3*, by cloning the source files that we used for *tool1*. Then we'll demonstrate file sharing by sharing the old *tools.h* include file between the two new programs.

The output of our programs wil reflect the new file sharing in line 4 and line 8. The pathname displayed in these lines will be that of the shared *tools.h* file.

We'll change the other six lines of the program output in later examples.

Initialization Nodes

To fix lines 4 and 8, we'll have to set up a non-local share of the include file *tools.h* between programs *tool2* and *tool3*. Here's how we'll do it.

First, we'll create a special new product node called *temp\tool_pi.ini* to store and export the shared include file. This node is an *initialization node*—a node whose main purpose is to store (and export) shared include files so that other products can eventually import them.

These nodes initialize the contents of the *$CMHTREE\share* directory. That is, they export shared files in the *share* directory *before* other programs import them. Figure 2-3 shows how file sharing is carried out by exporting and importing operations.

Normally, the code management tools ensure that initialization nodes are processed before other nodes. This ensures that shared files from initialization nodes will always be exported before other nodes try to import them.

An Overview of Example 2

Here's a list of the things that we'll do in this example:

1. Build an initialization node for shared include files.

2. Generate makefiles for programs with multiple source files.

3. Automatically update makefile dependency rules.

4. Check out, modify, and update source files and RCS files.

5. Generate batch files that can walk entire source trees.

6. Apply arbitrary commands to entire source trees.

Because there's so much to accomplish in this example, I've divided it into four parts.

First, we'll build initial versions of *tool2* and *tool3* by cloning and modifying the source code from *tool1*. From that point on, we won't touch *tool1* again. Instead, we'll leave it alone as an example of how *not* to organize source code.

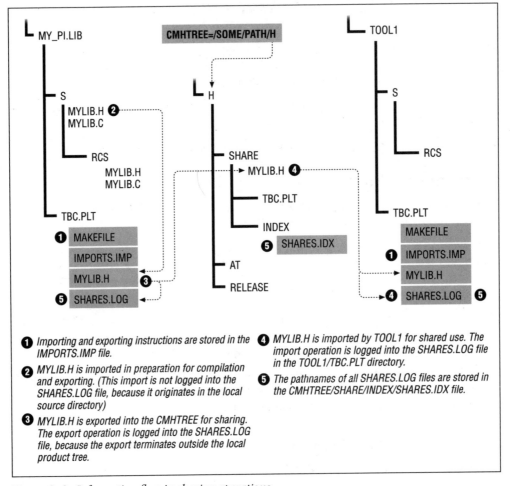

Figure 2-3. Information flow in sharing operations

Second, we'll share the *tools.h* include file between programs *tool2* and *tool3* by creating an initialization node (*tool_pi.ini*) to export *tools.h* into the *$CMHTREE\share* directory.

Third, we'll add several subroutines to *tool2* to show how to work with multiple source files within one product.

And fourth, we'll investigate the *twalker* tool, and introduce a few more options to the *rcsdo* command.

I'll warn you ahead of time that the new pi node *tool_pi.ini* node is going to contain both pi and pd information. This is because the old *tools.h* include file—which we're going to put into the *tool_pi.ini* node for sharing—contains both pi and pd information. Normally I wouldn't store both pi and pd code in a pi node that's named *tool_pi.ini*, since I certainly know better. But we don't want to fix everything at once; let's take it step by step.

You can expect that we'll be changing the pi *tool_pi.ini* node to a pd node when we add a new platform in Example 4. At that time, we'll have to properly separate the pi and pd information in all the source trees.

Building tool2 and tool3 by Cloning tool1

First let's get the initial versions of *tool2* and *tool3* working by cloning and modifying the source files from the *tool1\s* directory. We'll continue to follow the five step construction procedure that we established in Example 1.

Step 1. Create the directory tree. We'll create this directory tree (or product node) the same way we created the tree for *tool1*. We'll create it as a pi tree, too, even though we'll end up changing it later. You'll learn more about the tree structures if you have to change them. Besides, it's the normal way to port software—assume that the software is platform independent first, and then extract the platform-dependent software later.

The arguments to the *makenode* command tell *makenode* to create a node named *tool2* for storing pi files for a single platform named *tbc.plt*.

```
K:\MAIN\TOOL1\S> cd ..\..
K:\MAIN> makenode tool2 pi tbc.plt
```

Here's a picture of the created node—it looks exactly like the pi node that we created for *tool1*.

```
K:\MAIN> tree /a tool2
K:TOOL2                   the name of the pi node
+---S                     a place for pi source files
|   \---RCS               a place for the corresponding RCS files
\---TBC.PLT               a place for tbc.plt makefiles, obj, and exe files
```

Step 2. Create the source code. We can do this by cloning the source files from program *tool1*. That is, we'll copy, rename, and modify the relevant source files.

The required modifications to the files are very simple: change all "tool1" strings to "tool2," and all "T1" strings to "T2."

```
K:\MAIN> cd tool2\s
K:\MAIN\TOOL2\S> copy ..\..\tool1\s\*.*       three files copied

K:\MAIN\TOOL2\S> ren tool1.c tool2.c          change the external filename
K:\MAIN\TOOL2\S> emacs tool2.c                change tool1->tool2, T1->T2

K:\MAIN\TOOL2\S> ren tool1.h tool2.h          change the external filename
K:\MAIN\TOOL2\S> emacs tool2.h                change tool1->tool2, T1->T2
```

```
K:\MAIN\TOOL2\S> type tool2.h
/* $Id: tool2.h 1.1 1993/07/09 13:36:58 jameson Exp jameson $ */
#define T2_PD_DATA "(tbc.plt) This is pd local  data from tool2/s/tool2.h."
#define T2_PI_DATA "(pi)     This is pi local  data from tool2/s/tool2.h."
```

```
K:\MAIN\TOOL2\S> emacs tools.h              change tool1->tool2
K:\MAIN\TOOL1\S> type tools.h
/* $Id: tools.h 1.1 1993/07/09 13:36:58 jameson Exp jameson $ */
#define TN_PD_DATA "(tbc.plt) This is pd shared data from tool2/s/tools.h."
#define TN_PI_DATA "(pi)     This is pi shared data from tool2/s/tools.h."
```

Step 3. Generate the makefiles. I'm going to take another little shortcut here, by copying in the existing *imports.imp* file from *tool1\tbc.plt* instead of editing the default one in *tool2\tbc.plt* that was just produced by *getmakes*. I have two reasons for doing this.

First, it introduces you to the idea of reusing *imports.imp* files. I do this sort of thing frequently when I'm adding new platforms to existing product nodes, since the *imports.imp* files for the various platforms are almost always identical. This saves me the effort of customizing the default *imports.imp* file with import statements on each newly added platform. (It works for me because all the *make* tools on all the platforms that I use accept the same syntax for the *imports.imp* file.)

Second, it requires less typing. We only have to change the string "tool1" to "tool2" throughout the copied file, instead of having to retype all the (possibly many) import statements.

```
K:\MAIN\TOOL2\S> cd ..\tbc.plt
K:\MAIN\TOOL2\TBC.PLT> getmakes tbc.plt pi program tool2
K:\MAIN\TOOL2\TBC.PLT> type imports.imp     this file has no import statements

K:\MAIN\TOOL2\TBC.PLT> copy ..\..\tool1\tbc.plt\imports.imp
K:\MAIN\TOOL2\TBC.PLT> emacs imports.imp    change tool1->tool2
```

These are the important lines in the *imports.imp* file that you just copied and edited. These statements import the required include files into the compilation directory, and delete them when we type *make empty*.

```
PROG=tool2

imports:
        $(CMI) -nl ../s/tool2.h         this line used to say tool1
        $(CMI) -nl ../s/tools.h

imports.rev:
        $(RM) tool2.h                   and this one too
        $(RM) tools.h
```

Step 4. Compile, export, and test the product. The remaining tasks are straightforward, since the makefiles have been generated. Just type **make all** to compile the program.

```
K:\MAIN\TOOL2\TBC.PLT> make all
```

Let's see what the output of the program looks like. If we did everything right, we should see the string "tool2" instead of "tool1" everywhere in the output.

```
K:\MAIN\TOOL2\TBC.PLT> tool2
0  This is tool2 compiled on platform (tbc.plt).
1  (tbc.plt) This is pd local  code from tool2/s/tool2.c.
2  (tbc.plt) This is pd local  data from tool2/s/tool2.h.
3  (tbc.plt) This is pd shared code from tool2/s/tool2.c.
4  (tbc.plt) This is pd shared data from tool2/s/tools.h.
5  (pi)      This is pi local  code from tool2/s/tool2.c.
6  (pi)      This is pi local  data from tool2/s/tool2.h.
7  (pi)      This is pi shared code from tool2/s/tool2.c.
8  (pi)      This is pi shared data from tool2/s/tools.h.
```

Everything looks fine here, so our cloning operation (of *tool1* to *tool2*) has been successful. (The original code management problems aren't fixed in *tool2.c* yet, of course, but we'll start fixing them soon.)

Now let's go back and repeat these same steps (1 to 4) for *tool3*. Create the product tree, create the source code by cloning the files in the *tool1\s* directory, generate the makefiles, and then compile and test the program.

Create the node for program *tool3*.

```
K:\MAIN\TOOL2\TBC.PLT> cd ..\..
K:\MAIN> makenode tool3 pi tbc.plt
```

Create the source files for program *tool3* by cloning and modifying the source files from *tool1*.

```
K:\MAIN> cd tool3\s
K:\MAIN\TOOL3\S> copy ..\..\tool1\s\*.*
K:\MAIN\TOOL3\S> ren tool1.c tool3.c
K:\MAIN\TOOL3\S> emacs tool3.c          change tool1->tool3, T1->T3
K:\MAIN\TOOL3\S> ren tool1.h tool3.h
K:\MAIN\TOOL3\S> emacs tool3.h          change tool1->tool3, T1->T3
K:\MAIN\TOOL3\S> emacs tools.h          change tool1->tool3
```

Generate the makefiles, and then clone and modify the old *imports.imp* file from the *tool1\s* directory to save typing.

```
K:\MAIN\TOOL3\S> cd ..\tbc.plt
K:\MAIN\TOOL3\TBC.PLT> getmakes tbc.plt pi program tool3
K:\MAIN\TOOL3\TBC.PLT> copy ..\..\tool1\tbc.plt\imports.imp   get import stmts
K:\MAIN\TOOL3\TBC.PLT> emacs imports.imp      change tool1->tool3
```

```
PROG=tool3
imports:
        $(CMI) -nl ../s/tool3.h
        $(CMI) -nl ../s/tools.h
```

```
imports.rev:
        $(RM) tool3.h
        $(RM) tools.h
```

Now compile and test program *tool3*.

```
K:\MAIN\TOOL3\TBC.PLT> make all
K:\MAIN\TOOL3\TBC.PLT> tool3
0  This is tool3 compiled on platform (tbc.plt).
1  (tbc.plt) This is pd local   code from tool3/s/tool3.c.
2  (tbc.plt) This is pd local   data from tool3/s/tool3.h.
3  (tbc.plt) This is pd shared code from tool3/s/tool3.c.
4  (tbc.plt) This is pd shared data from tool3/s/tools.h.
5  (pi)      This is pi local   code from tool3/s/tool3.c.
6  (pi)      This is pi local   data from tool3/s/tool3.h.
7  (pi)      This is pi shared code from tool3/s/tool3.c.
8  (pi)      This is pi shared data from tool3/s/tools.h.
```

The outputs of the two programs shown above are correct. However, there is a small code management problem here. We have two copies of the *tools.h* file—one in each of the *tool2\s* and *tool3\s* source directories. (Actually, we have three copies, including the copy in the *tool1\s* directory. But I won't talk about the *tool1* files any more, since we're leaving them alone.)

What's worse is that the contents of the two files are different—compare lines 4 and 8 from the output of *tool2* with the same lines in the output of *tool3*. The fact that the two files are different is a deliberate coincidence—it helps us to see that we're working with two different copies of the "same" file.

Normally we'd perform the fifth step of our standard process now—update the RCS files. But instead we'll fix this sharing problem first.

Managing Shared Include Files

Now that we've created programs *tool2* and *tool3*, we can start to work on solving the "pi and pd shared data" problems associated with lines 4 and 8 of the program output.

Recall that I stated in the example overview that we'd solve this problem by creating a special initialization node (*tool_pi.ini*) to store and export the old *tools.h* file. In our case, the *tool_pi.ini* node will export the *tools.h* file to the *CMHTREE\share* directory so that programs *tool2* and *tool3* can import the file for compilation purposes.

Be aware that we'll have to repeat the first four steps of our sequence in order to set up the new initialization node and export the *tools.h* file for sharing. We'll also have to update the import commands in the files *tool2\tbc.plt\imports.imp* and *tool3\tbc.plt\imports.imp*.

To emphasize the four repeated steps while we create the **tool_pi.ini** product, I've added the name of the *tools.h* file to the bold face paragraph labels that identify the four steps.

The fifth step, updating RCS files, has its own subsection. That's because we're going to use bulk *rcsdo* operations and tree walker scripts to update the RCS files this time around.

Step 1. (tools.h) Create the directory tree. As before, we're deliberately going to create this tree as a pi tree, even though we know that it contains pd data too.

Create the node and show its internal structure with the DOS *tree* command.

```
K:\MAIN\TOOL2\TBC.PLT> cd ..\..
K:\MAIN> makenode tool_pi.ini pi tbc.plt
K:\MAIN> tree /a tool_pi.ini
K:TOOL_PI.INI
+---S
|   \---RCS
\---TBC.PLT
```

Step 2. (tools.h) Create the source code. Do this by copying the original *tool1\s\tools.h* file (and it's corresponding RCS file *tool1\s\rcs\tools.h*) into the new initialization tree. (It's important to copy the RCS file too, since we want to preserve the revision history that's stored within the RCS file.)

```
K:\MAIN> copy tool1\s\tools.h tool_pi.ini\s
K:\MAIN> copy tool1\s\rcs\tools.h tool_pi.ini\s\rcs
```

We won't delete the *tools.h* file in the *tool1\s* directory. Instead, we'll save the entire *tool1* node in its original state so you can compare it with the *tool2* and *tool3* programs at the end of the tour. But do delete the *tools.h* files that are still in the *tool2\s* and *tool3\s* directories. We won't need them any more after we create a shared version of the old *tools.h* file.

```
K:\MAIN> del tool2\s\tools.h
K:\MAIN> del tool3\s\tools.h
```

Now let's check the *tools.h* file out from the copied RCS file, so that we can modify it for sharing. (We have to update the pathname inside the include file to show where the file is now stored).

We'll use the RCS *co* (check out) command and specify that RCS should lock the file so we can modify it, and that the check out should be forced. In the command below, the *-l* argument tells RCS to lock the file so that no one else can check it out while we own the lock, and the *-f* specifies that the check-out should be forced (the checked out version of the file replaces the working copy of the file with no questions asked.)

As an aside, we don't really need the *-f* argument in this case, because there's no checked out, writeable copy of the file in the current directory. If there were, RCS would protest and prompt you for a confirmation before it overwrote the existing writeable version with the checked out version. I usually force check-outs because I don't like answering such questions. You may prefer not to use the *-f* argument.

```
K:\MAIN> cd tool_pi.ini\s
K:\MAIN\TOOL_PI.INI\S> co -l -f tools.h
```

Now update the checked out file with the pathname of its new location in the *tool_pi.ini* tree.

```
K:\MAIN\TOOL_PI.INI\S> emacs tools.h
K:\MAIN\TOOL_PI.INI\S> type tools.h
/* $Id: tools.h 1.1 1993/07/09 13:37:46 jameson Exp jameson $ */
#define TN_PD_DATA "(tbc.plt) This is pd shared data from tool_pi.ini/s/tools.h."
#define TN_PI_DATA "(pi)     This is pi shared data from tool_pi.ini/s/tools.h."
```

The outputs of the programs will now show (correctly) where the shared data has been stored.

Step 3. (tools.h) Generate the makefiles. This can be done by telling *getmakes* to generate makefiles for an initialization node. (You won't see a *makefile.pi* in the directory this time, since no compiling is performed for initialization nodes. No makefile dependency rules are required.)

```
K:\MAIN\TOOL_PI.INI\S> cd ..\tbc.plt
K:\MAIN\TOOL_PI.INI\TBC.PLT> getmakes tbc.plt pi ini tool_pi.ini
```

After you've generated the makefiles, edit the *imports.imp* file to export the *tools.h* file into the *CMHTREE\share* directory. Since we're pretending that the *tools.h* file is platform independent for now, we'll export it to the pi directory *CMHTREE\share* instead of to the pd directory *CMHTREE\share\tbc.plt*.

Also, note that the default action of the *cmx* tool is to export the named file to the *CMHTREE\share* directory and to log the transaction. Since that's exactly what we want to do, we don't give the *cmx* command any arguments to change the default behavior. The only other argument that I've provided below is a comment that describes the reason for the export. This comment is written into the share logs to make it easier to understand why the file is being shared.

```
K:\MAIN\TOOL_PI.INI\TBC.PLT> emacs imports.imp
exports.spe:
        $(CMX) ../s/tools.h -c for all tools
```

Because we did *not* specify the *-nl* argument to the *cmx* tool, it'll log the exporting operation when it does the export. This will all take place when we type *make all* below. Then we'll be able to inspect the share logs with the *cmlsr* (list sharing relationships) tool.

Step 4. (tools.h) Compile, export, and test. You can export the *tools.h* file now by typing **make all**.

```
K:\MAIN\TOOL_PI.INI\TBC.PLT> make all
```

The *tools.h* file is available for sharing now, in the directory *CMHTREE\share*.

Let's see what the file sharing tools recorded in their log files. We can do this by asking the *cmlsr* tool. The argument to *cmlsr* is a match string that is used to match log entries.

```
K:\MAIN\TOOL_PI.INI\TBC.PLT> cmlsr tools.h
export k:/main/tool_pi.ini/tbc.plt/tools.h -> j:/h/share/tools.h (for all tools)
```

The next step is to modify the import statements in *tool2\tbc.plt\imports.imp* and *tool3\tbc.plt\imports.imp* to pick up *tools.h* from its new location in *CMHTREE\share*. Since we want to log this sharing relationship, we'll omit the *-nl* argument in the *cmi* command.

```
K:\MAIN\TOOL_PI.INI\TBC.PLT> cd ..\..\tool2\tbc.plt
K:\MAIN\TOOL2\TBC.PLT> emacs imports.imp
imports:
        $(CMI) -nl ../s/tool2.h
        $(CMI) tools.h
```

Now we should rebuild the *tool2* program to make sure that everything still works with the shared *tools.h* file. We'll use the *make empty* command to delete everything but our makefiles. Then we'll use *make all* to rebuild everything again.

```
K:\MAIN\TOOL2\TBC.PLT> make empty
K:\MAIN\TOOL2\TBC.PLT> make all
K:\MAIN\TOOL2\TBC.PLT> tool2
0  This is tool2 compiled on platform (tbc.plt).
1  (tbc.plt) This is pd local  code from tool2/s/tool2.c.
2  (tbc.plt) This is pd local  data from tool2/s/tool2.h.
3  (tbc.plt) This is pd shared code from tool2/s/tool2.c.
4  (tbc.plt) This is pd shared data from tool_pi.ini/s/tools.h.
5  (pi)      This is pi local  code from tool2/s/tool2.c.
6  (pi)      This is pi local  data from tool2/s/tool2.h.
7  (pi)      This is pi shared code from tool2/s/tool2.c.
8  (pi)      This is pi shared data from tool_pi.ini/s/tools.h.
```

Since this output is correct, we can say that the "pi and pd local shared data" problem has been solved for now. Lines 4 and 8 correctly show that the pi and pd data for tools 1, 2, and 3 is stored in *tool_pi.ini\s\tools.h*.

Be sure to understand how the new *tools.h* file arrived in our *k:\main\tool2\tbc.plt* compilation directory. The file was exported from *tool_pi.ini\s\tools.h* (where it is stored under RCS for version control) into *$CMHTREE\share*. Then we imported it from *$CMHTREE\share* into *k:\main\tool2\tbc.plt*. This path—from source directory, to share directory, to source directory—demonstrates how the sharing mechanism works.

At this point, let's review the travels of the original *tools.h* file. Its original location was *tool1\s\tools.h*, but then we cloned it twice to build *tool2* and *tool3*. At this point there were three similar copies of *tools.h*. Then we cloned it one more time, and put the new copy in *tool_pi.ini\s\tools.h*, so we could share it between *tool2.c* and *tool3.c*. We deleted the private copies in *tool2\s\tools.h* and *tool2\s\tools.h* because we didn't need them any more. And now we've just rebuilt *tool2* to show that we have successfully imported the shared copy of *tools.h* from the holding tree.

Now let's update and rebuild *tool3* too, to complete the sharing operation. We have to change the *tool3\tbc.plt\imports.imp* file to import the *tools.h* file from the *CMHTREE\share* directory.

```
K:\MAIN\TOOL2\TBC.PLT> cd ..\..\tool3\tbc.plt
K:\MAIN\TOOL3\TBC.PLT> emacs imports.imp
imports:
        $(CMI) -nl ../s/tool3.h
        $(CMI) tools.h
```

Rebuild *tool3* from scratch to pick up the shared *tools.h* file. Use the **empty** target in the makefile to delete all unwanted files before performing a full rebuild.

```
K:\MAIN\TOOL3\TBC.PLT> make empty all              do both targets sequentially

K:\MAIN\TOOL3\TBC.PLT> tool3
0  This is tool3 compiled on platform (tbc.plt).
1  (tbc.plt) This is pd local  code from tool3/s/tool3.c.
2  (tbc.plt) This is pd local  data from tool3/s/tool3.h.
3  (tbc.plt) This is pd shared code from tool3/s/tool3.c.
4  (tbc.plt) This is pd shared data from tool_pi.ini/s/tools.h.
5  (pi)      This is pi local  code from tool3/s/tool3.c.
6  (pi)      This is pi local  data from tool3/s/tool3.h.
7  (pi)      This is pi shared code from tool3/s/tool3.c.
8  (pi)      This is pi shared data from tool_pi.ini/s/tools.h.
```

This output is also correct. It completes the part of the example that deals with sharing data files.

Managing Multiple Source Files

As you'll see in this part of the example, working with multiple source files in this code management system is no different from working with one source file. You can use the tools exactly the same way in both cases.

To show you how to work with multiple source files, we're going to change lines 3 and 7 of the example programs into subroutines. That'll give us two extra source files to work with. We'll also give each subroutine an include file, so we will also have multiple include files to work with.

Creating the subroutines will also be our first step toward solving the code management problems expressed by lines 3 and 7 of the sample program output. The particular problem is that we've got two copies of the supposedly shared code—one in *tool2\s\tool2.c* and another in *tool3\s\tool3.c*. Instead, we should only have one shared copy of each line (3 and 7).

Eventually, we'll solve this problem by putting the shared code in shared subroutine libraries so that the libraries can be shared between programs *tool2* and *tool3*. But we won't do that until Example 3, when I'll show you how to work with shared code files.

Right now, let's create the subroutines. We'll make two of them, *pd_sub.c* and *pi_sub.c*, by extracting lines 3 and 7 from *tool2\s\tool2.c*. (Recall that we didn't check *tool2\s\tool2.c* into RCS when we copied it. Normally we should have, but in this case I knew in advance that we'd soon be making this modification.)

```
K:\MAIN\TOOL3\TBC.PLT> cd ..\..\tool2\s
K:\MAIN\TOOL2\S> copy tool2.c original          so we can use diff below
K:\MAIN\TOOL2\S> emacs tool2.c                  make subroutines

K:\MAIN\TOOL2\S> diff original tool2.c          show the differences
10c10
<        printf("3  (tbc.plt) This is pd shared code from tool2/s/tool2.c.\n");
---
>        pd_sub();                              /* call  pd shared code */
14c14
<        printf("7  (pi)      This is pi shared code from tool2/s/tool2.c.\n");
---
>        pi_sub();                              /* call  pi shared code */
```

Here's the pd subroutine and its associated include file:

```
K:\MAIN\TOOL2\S> type pd_sub.c
/* $Id: pd_sub.c 1.1 1993/07/09 13:37:46 jameson Exp jameson $ */
#include <stdio.h>
#include "pd_sub.h"                            /* holds local pd_sub data */
void pd_sub ()
{
    printf("3  (tbc.plt) This is pd shared code from %s.\n",PD_SHARE_LOCATION);
}


K:\MAIN\TOOL2\S> type pd_sub.h
/* $Id: pd_sub.h 1.1 1993/07/09 13:37:46 jameson Exp jameson $ */
#define PD_SHARE_LOCATION "tool2/s/pd_sub.c"
```

This is the pi subroutine and its include file:

```
K:\MAIN\TOOL2\S> type pi_sub.c
/* $Id: pi_sub.c 1.1 1993/07/09 13:37:46 jameson Exp jameson $ */
#include <stdio.h>
#include "pi_sub.h"                            /* holds local pi_sub data */
void pi_sub ()
{
    printf("7  (pi)      This is pi shared code from %s.\n",PI_SHARE_LOCATION);
}


K:\MAIN\TOOL2\S> type pi_sub.h
/* $Id: pi_sub.h 1.1 1993/07/09 13:37:46 jameson Exp jameson $ */
#define PI_SHARE_LOCATION "tool2/s/pi_sub.c"
```

We've added several new files to the *tool2* subtree, so it's a good idea to stop here and look at the big picture. Here is a listing of the entire *tool2* subtree and the files that it currently contains. The */f* argument to the tree command causes filenames to appear in the output.

```
K:\MAIN\TOOL2\S> tree /a/f \main\tool2
```

```
K:TEMP\TOOL2
+---S
|   |   TOOL2.C          the main program
|   |   PD_SUB.C         this pd subroutine contains line 3
|   |   PD_SUB.H         the include file for the pd subroutine
|   |   PI_SUB.C         this pi subroutine contains line 7
|   |   PI_SUB.H         the include file for the pi subroutine
|   |   TOOL2.H          the original pi+pd local data file
|   |   ORIGINAL         the original tool2.c that we copied above
|   |
|   \---RCS              nothing has been checked in yet
|
\---TBC.PLT              these old files are from the previous compilation
        MAKEFILE         the original makefile
        MAKEFILE.PI      the original dependencies file
        IMPORTS.IMP      the original imports.imp file
        TOOL2.H          imported from ../s
        TOOLS.H          imported from CMHTREE/share
        TOOL2.OBJ        compiled here
        TOOL2.EXE        the final executable product file
        SHARES.LOG       log file, from omitting the -nl arg to cmi
```

We still have to update the makefiles and the *imports.imp* file to pick up the new subroutines and include files before we can rebuild and test the program.

I'll use a new tool called *gendep* (for "generate dependencies") to update the makefile dependencies this time, rather than using *getmakes* to rebuild the whole set of makefiles (which would also work correctly). The *getmakes* tool automatically calls *gendep* to generate the dependencies, as part of the normal makefile generation process. The only difference here is that we're invoking it directly from the command line ourselves instead of getting *getmakes* to do it for us.

The defaults of the *gendep* tool are set up to do the right thing under normal circumstances if you just specify *pi*, *pd*, or *pid* on the command line. It'll figure out what the new makefile dependencies are for our modified software and will regenerate the existing *makefile.pi* file.

```
K:\MAIN\TOOL2\S> cd ..\tbc.plt
K:\MAIN\TOOL2\TBC.PLT> gendep pi
```

Now we have to update the *imports.imp* file to import the two new include files from the source directory into the compilation (platform) directory. (I've disabled logging again, since I don't want to clutter the share logs with imports of local include files.)

```
K:\MAIN\TOOL2\TBC.PLT> emacs imports.imp
imports:
        $(CMI) -nl ../s/tool2.h
        $(CMI) -nl tools.h
        $(CMI) -nl ../s/pi_sub.h
        $(CMI) -nl ../s/pd_sub.h

imports.rev:
        $(RM) tool2.h
        $(RM) tools.h
        $(RM) pi_sub.h
        $(RM) pd_sub.h
```

Compile and test the new *tool2* program. It's composed from six different source files now, but note that it didn't require any extra effort on our part to regenerate and run the makefiles. That was the point of this part of the example—multiple source files don't require any special treatment from the makefile tools. (Multiple include files require a bit of extra effort though, since you have to add more statements to the *imports.imp* file.)

```
K:\MAIN\TOOL2\TBC.PLT> make all
K:\MAIN\TOOL2\TBC.PLT> tool2
0  This is tool2 compiled on platform (tbc.plt).
1  (tbc.plt) This is pd local  code from tool2/s/tool2.c.
2  (tbc.plt) This is pd local  data from tool2/s/tool2.h.
3  (tbc.plt) This is pd shared code from tool2/s/pd_sub.c.
4  (tbc.plt) This is pd shared data from tool_pi.ini/s/tools.h.
5  (pi)      This is pi local  code from tool2/s/tool2.c.
6  (pi)      This is pi local  data from tool2/s/tool2.h.
7  (pi)      This is pi shared code from tool2/s/pi_sub.c.
8  (pi)      This is pi shared data from tool_pi.ini/s/tools.h.
```

This ends this part of the example. Now we're ready to update the RCS files.

Performing Bulk RCS Operations with Tree Walker Scripts

Updating the RCS files this time around will be a little different from the previous example because we have both old and new source files to check into RCS. Since the *rcsdo* tool needs different control arguments to check in the two types of files, we'll process the files in two separate groups.

Processing a directory full of new files is easy—we did it before in Example 1 using the *ci_u_initial* option of the *rcsdo* command. Similarly, processing a directory of old files is also easy—the *ci_u_locked* option will find and check in any files that were checked out with a lock. The only awkward situations occur when directories contain both new and old files.

Let's begin by cleaning up the source directories to remove any unnecessary *msg* or other temporary files that were used for other operations. This clean up operation will introduce you to the *twalker* tool.

The *twalker* tool creates a batch file that visits subdirectories in the subtree below the point where *twalker* is invoked. The set of directories visited by the batch file is controlled by the second argument to the *twalker* tool, a match string that matches the last name in a directory pathname. The batch file produced by *twalker* will visit every directory whose pathname ends in the match string. For instance, if you provide *tbc.plt* as an argument, *twalker* will act on all directories named *tbc.plt*. See Figure 2-4.

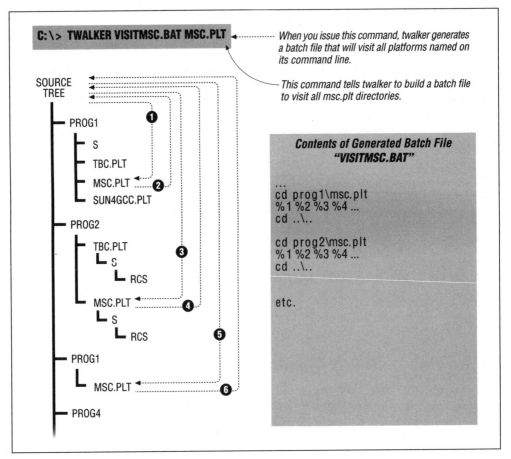

Figure 2–4. Operation of the twalker tool

Let's make a batch file to visit all the source directories in our subtrees. The first argument to *twalker* is the name of the batch file. The second argument is the name of the directories to visit within the subtree. We want to visit all the source directories, so we'll give *twalker* a single match string of "s." (The *twalker* tool is capable of taking several match strings at once.)

```
K:\MAIN\TOOL2\TBC.PLT> cd ..\..
K:\MAIN> twalker walksrc.bat s                    generate the batch file
```

I've shown a sample of the output batch file below so that you can see how a tree walker script works. It just changes to a particular directory within the subtree, executes an arbitrary command in that directory, and then changes back to the starting directory. A simple approach to be sure, but reliable, convenient, and effective.

```
K:\MAIN> type walksrc.bat                    look inside of the batch file
. . .
cd tool_pi.ini\s                             go to the next directory
echo *********************                    print a marker for the user
cmpwd unix                                   print the current working dir
echo %1 %2 %3 %4 %5 %6 %7 %8
cd k:\main                                   change back to starting dir

cd tool2\s                                   go to the next directory
echo *********************                    print a marker for the user
cmpwd unix                                   print the current working dir
echo %1 %2 %3 %4 %5 %6 %7 %8
cd k:\main                                   change back to starting dir
. . .
```

These are the commands for removing unnecessary *msg* files from the source directories, using the batch file.

```
K:\MAIN> walksrc ls
*********************
k:/main/tool_pi.ini/s
ls
  msg          rcs          tools.h
*********************
k:/main/tool1/s
ls
  msg          rcs          tool1.c      tool1.h
*********************
k:/main/tool2/s
ls
  msg          pd_sub.c     pi_sub.c     rcs          tool2.h
  original     pd_sub.h     pi_sub.h     tool2.c
  pd_sub.h     pi_sub.h     tool2.c
*********************
k:/main/tool3/s
ls
rcs          tool3.c      tool3.h
```

We have two filenames to delete to clean up our source directories—*msg* and *original*. (Recall that *original* was a saved copy of *tool2.c* that we used in a *diff* command.) To delete them, you can use either the standard DOS *del* command, or the *rm -f* command on the disks (the *-f* suppresses "File not found" error messages from *rm*).

```
K:\MAIN> walksrc del msg
K:\MAIN> walksrc rm -f original
K:\MAIN> walksrc ls
```

Now let's try to determine which files in the trees have corresponding RCS files, and which files do not have RCS files. Then we can create RCS files for those that don't have them. We'll do this by walking the RCS subdirectories and listing the RCS files that have already been created.

```
K:\MAIN> twalker walkrcs.bat rcs        generate a file to visit rcs directories
K:\MAIN> walkrcs ls                     now pass the ls cmd to the batch file
*********************
k:/main/tool_pi.ini/s/rcs
ls
  tools.h
*********************
k:/main/tool1/s/rcs
ls
  tool1.c      tool1.h      tools.h
*********************
k:/main/tool2/s/rcs
ls
*********************
k:/main/tool3/s/rcs
ls
```

A comparison of this listing with the one that we obtained earlier from the command *walksrc.bat ls*), shows that two of our four source directories contain RCS files (*tool1\s* and *tool_pi.ini\s*), and two others do not (*tool2\s* and *tool3\s*). We'll have to create new RCS files in at least two directories. (We may also have to update some old RCS files in the other two directories if the source files have been checked out and changed.)

The read-only file permissions technique

We have to identify the source files that actually need updating under RCS so that we can check them all in properly with minimum effort. This section explains a simple, but effective method for identifying files that have been checked out of RCS for modification but haven't been checked back in. The method is based on read-only file permissions.

The read-only file permission technique will work very well if you installed the tools in OWNER (standalone) mode. (TEAM and OWNER installation modes are explained in the software installation preface, if you want to review them.)

The read-only permission technique won't work at all if you installed the tools in TEAM (network) mode. This is because all source files that are shared by a group on UNIX must have read-write permission for everyone on the team. As a consequence, this section will have limited value to those working in team situations.

Here's how the read-only file permission technique works for spotting modified source files.

First, the technique assumes that all source files are always checked in through *rcsdo* with either the *ci_u_initial* or *ci_u_locked* options. The assumption is required because the *ci_u_initial* and *ci_u_locked* options always leave working source files unlocked (read-only) immediately after they've been checked in. (The "u" in the option names means "unlocked.") This implies that read-only files haven't been changed since their last check-in.

The assumption is valid in our case, because we've only once checked in source files (in Example 1), and that was with the *ci_u_initial* option.

Second, since files that are checked out for modification must be writeable, it follows that source files with read-write have probably been modified. (I say "probably" because sometimes I've checked out files thinking that I want to modify them, but not actually modifying them. I normally correct such situations by forcing another check out without a lock: *co -u -f myfile.c*, which resets the file permissions to read-only.)

So we can spot the files that *don't* need updating because they'll still be read-only files. Let's find them using the tree walker script that we created earlier for walking all the source directories in the source tree.

```
K:\MAIN> walksrc ls -l
*********************
k:/main/tool_pi.ini/s
ls -l
  -d----   1993 Jul  7  18:07              rcs
  a-----   1993 Jul  7  18:14      232    tools.h
*********************
k:/main/tool1/s
ls -l
  -d----   1993 Jul  7  17:26              rcs
  a----r   1993 Jul  7  17:28      756    tool1.c
  a----r   1993 Jul  7  17:28      212    tool1.h
  a----r   1993 Jul  7  17:28      212    tools.h
*********************
k:/main/tool2/s
ls -l
  a-----   1993 Jul  7  19:17      205    pd_sub.c
  a-----   1993 Jul  7  19:16       58    pd_sub.h
  a-----   1993 Jul  7  19:17      205    pi_sub.c
  a-----   1993 Jul  7  19:16       58    pi_sub.h
  -d----   1993 Jul  7  17:29              rcs
  a-----   1993 Jul  7  19:17      740    tool2.c
  a-----   1993 Jul  7  17:31      212    tool2.h
*********************
k:/main/tool3/s
ls -l
  -d----   1993 Jul  7  17:30              rcs
  a-----   1993 Jul  7  18:10      880    tool3.c
  a-----   1993 Jul  7  18:10      212    tool3.h
```

As you can see, the source files in directories *tool_pi.ini\s, tool2\s,* and *tool3\s* need to be updated (they are all writeable files).

We'll update the indicated files with an *rcsdo ci_u_initial* command. Starting with the *tool_pi.ini\s* directory, we'll use the *rcsdo ci_u_locked* option, because we locked the *tools.h* file when we checked it out to update the pathnames for sharing.

```
K:\MAIN> cd tool_pi.ini\s
K:\MAIN\TOOL_PI.INI\S> echo Updated pathnames for shared tools.h.> msg
K:\MAIN\TOOL_PI.INI\S> rcsdo ci_u_locked msg -log default
K:\MAIN\TOOL_PI.INI\S> del msg

K:\MAIN> cd ..\..\tool2\s
K:\MAIN\TOOL2\S> echo These files are the original tool2 source files. > msg
K:\MAIN\TOOL2\S> rcsdo ci_u_initial msg -log default
K:\MAIN\TOOL2\S> del msg
```

We need to rebuild program *tool2* since the executable is out of date. Checking files into RCS always changes the timestamps on the source files, which puts them out-of-date with respect to the timestamps on the object and executable files.

```
K:\MAIN\TOOL2\S> cd ..\tbc.plt
K:\MAIN\TOOL2\TBC.PLT> make all
```

Do the same for the *tool3* program: create the RCS files and then rebuild the program.

```
K:\MAIN\TOOL2\S> cd ..\..\tool3\s

K:\MAIN\TOOL3\S> echo These files are the original tool3 source files. >msg
K:\MAIN\TOOL3\S> rcsdo ci_u_initial msg -log default
K:\MAIN\TOOL3\S> del msg

K:\MAIN\TOOL3\S> cd ..\tbc.plt
K:\MAIN\TOOL3\TBC.PLT> make all
```

We've updated all RCS files now. Let's go back and check our work using the read-only file permission technique. First, we'll delete any leftover *msg* files. Then, we'll check that all source files have read-only permissions. (On UNIX, or in team mode, use *rcsdo ls_locked* instead.)

```
K:\MAIN\TOOL3\TBC.PLT> cd ..\..
K:\MAIN> twalker walksrc.bat s
K:\MAIN> walksrc.bat rm -f msg
K:\MAIN> walksrc.bat ls -l
```

All that's left to do in this example is assign a new version label to all the files in the source trees. We want to do this because we created some new files and modified some others.

Step 5. Update all RCS files To assign a new version label to all the files in all the source trees, we'll use a *twalker* batch file and an *rcsdo add_name* command, just like we did in Example 1. Don't forget that we have to use the *call* keyword on the command line, since we're calling one batch file from another under DOS. The *call* keyword makes sure that the called batch file returns execution control back to its caller when it's done, instead of exiting back to DOS. Other platforms such as UNIX don't require the *call* keyword.

Note that the label is being applied to all the source files in all four product nodes (*tool1, tool2, tool3, tool_pi.ini*), regardless of whether the files are new or old. This is the right thing to do, since we want to assign the new label to all files in our example.

I've included a few extra *rcsdo* commands in the sequence below to better illustrate the current (and newly added) labels in the source files.

Remember that the *tools.h* file was moved from *tool1\s* to *tool_pi.ini* when we made it shareable. That's why it's part of the **ex_1** version label. Also, recall that the labels **ex_1** and **ex_2** refer to the two successive times that RCS labels were assigned to RCS files, and not to the programs *tool1* and *tool2.*

```
K:\MAIN> walksrc call rcsdo ls_names        list all labels ever assigned
K:\MAIN> walksrc call rcsdo ls_name ex_1    list all files in group ex_1
```

Now add the new symbolic name. It will be assigned to all files, even the ones in the *tool1* source tree. But that's okay, because they're part of this snapshot of the source trees.

```
K:\MAIN> walksrc call rcsdo add_name ex_2   add the new label ex_2

K:\MAIN> walksrc call rcsdo ls_names        list all the labels again
K:\MAIN> walksrc call rcsdo ls_name ex_1    list all files in group ex_1
K:\MAIN> walksrc call rcsdo ls_name ex_2    list all files in group ex_2
```

The last thing that I'll show you in this example is how to check out the group of files that corresponds to a particular symbolic RCS label.

First, I'd like to empty out the source directories so that you can see which files get checked out when we issue the check-out command. To perform this emptying, I could use a tree walker script to apply a *rm -f *.** command to the source files in all directories. But because I want to demonstrate another useful *rcsdo* option, I'll use the *dl_unchanged* option to delete all the source files that are unchanged with respect to their RCS files. (All of our source files are unchanged, of course, since we've just finished updating all of them.) I'll use a tree walker script to issue the *rcsdo dl_unchanged* command in the source directories of all four of our current product nodes.

As an aside, I still worry about issuing global deletion commands, even years after a colleague of mine accidentally deleted an entire disk pack on a big mainframe. (One that took the operators two days to restore from backup tapes.) They nicknamed him "The Volume Deleter" after that. Or was it that other colleague who accidentally deleted another developer's entire (large) subtree on a UNIX system early one morning, right while the guy was working on it? Fortunately for us, the flakey backup system had successfully run to completion the night before.

Recall that the tree walker batch file *walksrc.bat* will visit all the source directories in the entire subtree below the current directory. Specifically, it will visit the following source directories: *tool1\s, tool2\s, tool3\s,* and *tool_pi.ini\s.*

```
K:\MAIN> walksrc ls -1              is everything checked in?
K:\MAIN> walksrc rm -f msg          no extra files should be seen
K:\MAIN> walksrc call rcsdo dl_unchanged   bang! delete unchanged files
K:\MAIN> walksrc ls -1              source files are gone
```

The *dl_unchanged* option is useful when you want to use the *ci_u_initial* option to check in large numbers of new files in a directory that contains both old and new source files. The presence of the old files prevents you from using *ci_u_initial.* (Recall that *ci_u_initial* tries to create RCS files for all files in the working directory, regardless of whether the files already have RCS files.)

The proper strategy in such cases is to use the following sequence of *rcsdo* options: *ci_u_locked, dl_unchanged, ci_u_initial,* and *co_u_f.* This sequence checks in the old modified (locked) files, then deletes all the old files because they're now unchanged with respect to their RCS files. (All the RCS files are preserved, of course.) This leaves only new files in the directory, which makes it possible to check them all in at once with the *ci_u_initial* option. Last, all the files are checked back out again with *co_u_f,* which leaves a full set of source files in the source directory.

To more clearly show what occurs when you check out the group of files associated with a particular RCS label, let's do a before-and-after experiment. The three commands shown below will list the contents of all source directories, check out all source files that were labeled with the symbolic label **ex_1** in Example 1, and then list the contents of the source directories again.

We expect the source directories to be empty for the first *ls* command and to be stocked with the appropriate files for the second *ls* command (after the *rcsdo co_u_f* has been run).

```
K:\MAIN> walksrc ls                      verify that source dirs are empty
K:\MAIN> walksrc call rcsdo co_u_f ex_1  ignore co errs for missing ex_1
K:\MAIN> walksrc ls                      visible files should be from Ex.1
```

Ignore the "Symbolic number ex_1 is undefined" error messages; they're harmless. But notice that revision 1.1 of the *tool_pi.ini\s\tools.h* file was checked out. This happens because we copied over the *tool1\s\rcs\tools.h* RCS file from the *tool1* directory when we made *tools.h* shareable.

Will the checked out program *tool1.c* compile successfully? The easy way to answer this question would be type **make empty all** in the *tool1\tbc.plt* platform directory. But that wouldn't teach you very much, so we'll find out the answer using a more general technique. Construct a tree walker script for visiting all *tbc.plt* platform directories, then modify it to delete all the visits to the *tool2, tool3,* and *tool_pi.ini* directories. This will demonstrate the technique of creating a tree walker script and editing it to customize it to your specific needs.

Generating and editing a tree walker script is more work than is really required in our particular case because we only have one directory to visit. All we really want to do is to rebuild one newly-checked-out program from scratch, so that we can be sure that it will compile successfully.

What if you had 200 directories to visit, and 200 programs to rebuild from scratch? Then, if your only other alternative was to manually type **make empty all** in each directory, the tree walker script editing technique would probably be much more appealing, wouldn't it?

```
K:\MAIN> twalker walkex1.bat tbc.plt
K:\MAIN> emacs walkex1.bat                 delete trips to all dirs but tool1

K:\MAIN> walkex1 make empty all            rebuild everything from scratch
K:\MAIN> tool1                             verify that the output is from ex_1
```

Now let's extract version **ex_2** and rebuild it.

We can't use the *dl_unchanged* option here because some of the files that were checked out under label **ex_1** (e.g., RCS version 1.1 of *tools.h*) are different from the latest checked-in versions (e.g., version 1.2 of *tools.h*). *dl_unchanged* won't delete such files.

It looks like the fastest way to empty out the source trees is just to issue a global delete command such as *rm -f* in all the source directories in the tree. (Why is it that you're always in a hurry when you find out that the best solution to your current problem is a global deletion command?) Anyhow, we can always get those source files back from RCS files or from your backup tapes, right?

```
K:\MAIN> walksrc ls                        are we visiting the right directories?
K:\MAIN> walksrc rm -f *.c *.h             yes, so globally delete everything
```

Now that we've emptied out the source directories, we can check out all the files that were assigned the label **ex_2**.

```
K:\MAIN> walksrc call rcsdo co_u_f ex_2    check out files in group ex_2
```

Now rebuild all three tools from scratch to verify that the global check out was successful.

```
K:\MAIN> twalker walktbc.bat tbc.plt       generate a new tree walker script
K:\MAIN> walktbc make empty                first get rid of all old files
K:\MAIN> walktbc make all                  then rebuild everything from scratch

K:\MAIN> tool1                             try out the recompiled programs
K:\MAIN> tool2
K:\MAIN> tool3
```

Notice that *tool2* is using the pi and pd subroutines that we created, whereas *tool3* is not. We'll make the include files and the pi and pd subroutines shareable in later examples.

Example 3: Sharing Code Files

In this example, I'll show you how to share multiple output files among multiple application programs, product groups, or developers. (By output files I mean compiled files, either libraries or executable programs.)

Sharing files is very important because it helps everyone reuse previously constructed software. For maintenance purposes, it's useful to have a list of all the source and destination directories that participate in a particular sharing relationship. This example will cover all of these topics.

The compiled code file that we'll be sharing in this example is a subroutine library we will create from the two subroutines added to *tool2* in the last example (*pi_sub.c* and *pd_sub.c*). Once we've made the library available for sharing in the CMHTREE, we'll update and rebuild the *tool2* and *tool3* programs so that they both use the subroutines in the new library.

Here's how we'll proceed in the example:

1. Create the subroutine library according to the standard five steps that we've been using so far: create the tree, create the source, generate the makefiles, compile and test, and update RCS files.

   Remember that this library won't contain purely pi code because we're going to put both pi and pd subroutines into it. Later, in Example 4, we'll split the library into two separate pi and pd libraries when we add another platform to our source trees.

2. Go back and modify the *tool3.c* program so that it uses the subroutines. (The *tool2* program was already modified to use the subroutines in the previous example.)

3. Update both the *imports.imp* files for *tool2* and *tool3* to link in the new subroutine library.

4. Update all the RCS files using tree walker scripts to perform bulk *rcsdo ci_u_initial* check-in operations on entire source trees.

Create the Subroutine Library

The first thing we have to do is create the subroutine library by moving the relevant files from the *tool2\s* directory into the new *tool_pi.lib\s* directory. Let's go through our standard five development steps.

Step 1. Create a directory tree. Here's the command that I used to create the pi tree node for the new library:

```
K:\MAIN> makenode tool_pi.lib pi tbc.plt
K:\MAIN> tree /a tool_pi.lib
```

```
K:TOOL_PI.LIB              the name of the node
+---S                      a place for pi source files
|   \---RCS                a place for the corresponding RCS files
\---TBC.PLT                a place to compile, and for makefiles, objs, etc
```

It's important to use the `.lib` suffix on libraries, because one of the other code management tools (*newmakes*) uses it to determine what kind of makefiles should go in the platform directories. (For example, makefiles for a code library, an executable, a script, or initialization files.)

Step 2. Create the source code. To do this, move the relevant source code and RCS files from the *tool2\s* directory to the new *tool_pi.lib\s* directory.

```
K:\MAIN> copy tool2\s\p*.* tool_pi.lib\s
TOOL2\S\PD_SUB.C
TOOL2\S\PD_SUB.H
TOOL2\S\PI_SUB.C
TOOL2\S\PI_SUB.H
        4 file(s) copied


K:\MAIN> copy tool2\s\rcs\p*.* tool_pi.lib\s\rcs   4 rcs files copied
K:\MAIN> attrib -r tool2\s\p*.*         enable write access
K:\MAIN> del tool2\s\p*.*               delete the old source files
K:\MAIN> attrib -r tool2\s\rcs\p*.*     enable write access
K:\MAIN> del tool2\s\rcs\p*.*           delete the old rcs files
```

Let's have another quick look at our source tree now that we've got some source files in the source directory.

```
K:\MAIN> tree /a/f tool_pi.lib          /f shows files too
K:\MAIN\TOOL_PI.LIB                      the name of our node
+---S
|   |   PI_SUB.C                         we just copied in these files
|   |   PI_SUB.H
|   |   PD_SUB.C
|   |   PD_SUB.H
|   |
|   \---RCS
|           PI_SUB.C                     and these rcs files
|           PI_SUB.H
|           PD_SUB.C
|           PD_SUB.H
|
\---TBC.PLT                              nothing here yet
```

Now we'll modify the contents of the relocated subroutines and include files in preparation for sharing, and to reflect their new locations in the source trees.

```
K:\MAIN> cd tool_pi.lib\s
K:\MAIN\TOOL_PI.LIB\S> co -l -f pi_sub.h pd_sub.h
K:\MAIN\TOOL_PI.LIB\S> emacs pi_sub.h    change tool2 to tool_pi.lib
K:\MAIN\TOOL_PI.LIB\S> emacs pd_sub.h    change tool2 to tool_pi.lib
```

Step 3. Generate the makefiles. You've seen the *getmakes* command a couple of times already. This time the arguments tell *getmakes* to create *tbc.plt* platform makefiles for a pi library that's named **tool_pi**.

```
K:\MAIN\TOOL_PI.LIB\S> cd ..\tbc.plt
K:\MAIN\TOOL_PI.LIB\TBC.PLT> getmakes tbc.plt pi lib tool_pi
```

As always, we have to customize the *imports.imp* file to import include files from the local source directory into the compilation directory. (Recall that I never use logging on these particular kinds of imports because I don't think this type of sharing is important enough to record in a global log. But you can follow your own policy, of course.)

```
K:\MAIN\TOOL_PI.LIB\TBC.PLT> emacs imports.imp          import include files
imports:
        $(CMI) -nl ../s/pi_sub.h
        $(CMI) -nl ../s/pd_sub.h

imports.rev:
        $(RM) pi_sub.h
        $(RM) pd_sub.h
```

Step 4. Compile, export, and test the product. There's nothing left to do but compile and export the library. If you watch the commands printed out by your *make* tool as it runs, you'll see that the makefiles generated by *getmakes* just do the regular things that are required to build code libraries.

Notice that we can't test the library right now by running it like an executable program. We'll have to wait until we rebuild *tool2* to see if the library file actually works.

```
K:\MAIN\TOOL_PI.LIB\TBC.PLT> make all
```

Update tool2 to Use the Library

Now the library is ready to be used by the *tool2* and *tool3* programs. We'll begin to modify *tool2* by modifying the *tool2\tbc.plt\imports.imp* file to pick up the new library.

```
K:\MAIN\TOOL_PI.LIB\TBC.PLT> cd ..\..\tool2\tbc.plt
K:\MAIN\TOOL2\TBC.PLT> make empty          delete old files
```

Notice that I'm issuing a *make empty* command before I modify the *imports.imp* file. This is because I know that the modifications I'm about to make in the *imports.imp* file will remove the old file deletion statements that I had under the **imports.rev** target. Once they're gone, it means that I can't type *make empty* to delete the old existing subroutine object and include files that are currently in the platform directory. I'd have to manually delete them myself. So to save myself effort, I've issued a *make empty* command to delete the files while I still have the appropriate *make* commands to help me.

This is a handy trick to remember—type **make empty** or **make imports.rev** before you remove statements from the **imports** and **imports.rev** targets in an existing *imports.imp* file.

Now back to the task at hand. We're about to modify the *tool2\tbc.plt\imports.imp* file to pick up the new subroutine library.

The only new kind of editing change in this example is that we have to put the name of the library in the **lb3** makefile macro. The purpose of this macro is to hold the names of the object libraries that will appear in the linker command line in the makefile template. This macro is named **lb3** because it's the third of three macros that specify libraries in the linker command line. (Search for "lb3" in the makefile template file *CMTREE\plt\tbc.plt\tbc.plt* if you want to see where the **lb3** macro appears in the linker command line.)

On UNIX, prepend **–l** to the name of each library in the **lb3** macro, so that the line reads *lb3=-ltool_pi*. The *-l* is required as a command-line argument by the UNIX linker.

```
K:\MAIN\TOOL2\TBC.PLT> emacs imports.imp
lb3=tool_pi                             tell the linker to use the library
imports:
        $(CMI) -nl ../s/tool2.h
        $(CMI) -nl tools.h
                    delete the pi/pd_sub.h stmts
imports.rev:
        $(RM) tool2.h
        $(RM) tools.h
                    delete the pi/pd_sub.h stmts
```

We have to update the makefile dependencies before we rebuild the program. They're out of date now because we moved the subroutine source files to another location.

```
K:\MAIN\TOOL_PI.LIB\TBC.PLT> gendep pi   update makefile dependencies,
```

Now we can rebuild and test *tool2*. We'll add the **empty** target to the command line to force a rebuild from scratch.

```
K:\MAIN\TOOL_PI.LIB\TBC.PLT> make empty all   since subroutines have been moved
```

```
K:\MAIN\TOOL2\TBC.PLT> tool2
0  This is tool2 compiled on platform (tbc.plt).
1  (tbc.plt) This is pd local  code from tool2/s/tool2.c.
2  (tbc.plt) This is pd local  data from tool2/s/tool2.h.
3  (tbc.plt) This is pd shared code from tool_pi.lib/s/pd_sub.c.
4  (tbc.plt) This is pd shared data from tool_pi.ini/s/tools.h.
5  (pi)      This is pi local  code from tool2/s/tool2.c.
6  (pi)      This is pi local  data from tool2/s/tool2.h.
7  (pi)      This is pi shared code from tool_pi.lib/s/pi_sub.c.
8  (pi)      This is pi shared data from tool_pi.ini/s/tools.h.
```

The pathnames in lines 3 and 7 are correct now because they reflect the new location of the shared code files.

There are still several problems in the output that will surface when we add a second platform directory to the source trees in Example 4. Specifically, lines 1, 2, 3, and 4 are all pd lines, and yet they're all stored in pi source directories. The problems are the same for *tool3*, of course, because it's a direct clone of *tool2*.

I'll show you more about pd nodes and how to fix these particular problems when we get to Example 4. Right now, we've got to press on and rebuild *tool3* to complete the demonstration of how to share code files.

Update tool3 to Use the Library

Recall that the source files *tool3.c* and *tool3.h* are still clones of the original *tool1* files in *tool1\s* directory. We didn't modify *tool3.c* to use subroutines when we modified *tool2.c*. Instead, the only change we ever made in the entire *tool3* node was to modify the *imports.imp* file to import the shared *tools.h* file from its new location in the *CMHTREE\share* directory. So the original *tool3.c* hasn't been changed at all.

To upgrade *tool3*, we'll have to change *tool3.c* to be similar to *tool2\s\tool2.c* (*tool3.h* doesn't need changing). Here's how we'll upgrade *tool3.c*. We'll check it out from RCS, and then "modify" it by copying in *tool2\s\tool2.c* and renaming it. After changing a few text strings we'll be done. Doing it this way will save us time and keystrokes. So let's begin.

Check out *tool3.c* with a lock so the checked-out file will be writeable. Delete the checked-out file in preparation for copying in the *tool2.c* file from *tool2\s*.

```
K:\MAIN\TOOL2\TBC.PLT> cd ..\..\tool3\s
K:\MAIN\TOOL3\S> co -l -f tool3.c              check out old file
K:\MAIN\TOOL3\S> rm tool3.c                    and get rid of it
```

Copy in *tool2\s\tool2.c* and edit it to change all the 2s to 3s.

```
K:\MAIN\TOOL3\S> copy ..\..\tool2\s\tool2.c tool3.c   copy and rename the file
K:\MAIN\TOOL3\S> attrib -r tool3.c                    chmod +w tool3
K:\MAIN\TOOL3\S> emacs tool3.c                        change tool2->tool3, T2->T3
```

Update the *tool3\tbc.plt\imports.imp* file to link in the new subroutine library.

```
K:\MAIN\TOOL3\S> cd ..\tbc.plt
K:\MAIN\TOOL3\TBC.PLT> emacs imports.imp
lb3=tool_pi                                    link with this library
```

Compile and test *tool3*.

```
K:\MAIN\TOOL3\TBC.PLT> make empty all
K:\MAIN\TOOL3\TBC.PLT> tool3
0  This is tool3 compiled on platform (tbc.plt).
1  (tbc.plt) This is pd local   code from tool3/s/tool3.c.
2  (tbc.plt) This is pd local   data from tool3/s/tool3.h.
3  (tbc.plt) This is pd shared  code from tool_pi.lib/s/pd_sub.c.
4  (tbc.plt) This is pd shared  data from tool_pi.ini/s/tools.h.
5  (pi)      This is pi local   code from tool3/s/tool3.c.
```

```
6  (pi)        This is pi local  data from tool3/s/tool3.h.
7  (pi)        This is pi shared code from tool_pi.lib/s/pi_sub.c.
8  (pi)        This is pi shared data from tool_pi.ini/s/tools.h.
```

All three programs should be working properly. *tool2* and *tool3* are now sharing a data file (*tool_pi.h*) and a subroutine library (*tool_pi.lib*). Compare the outputs of all three tools.

```
K:\MAIN\TOOL3\TBC.PLT> tool1        compare the outputs of
K:\MAIN\TOOL3\TBC.PLT> tool2        all three programs
K:\MAIN\TOOL3\TBC.PLT> tool3
```

Since all three programs are working once again, it's time to update the RCS files.

Step 5. Update the RCS files. Let's analyze the situation before we jump in and start to update RCS files. Taking a minute to think before performing bulk RCS check-ins is a good practice to develop for many reasons, not the least of which is that it can save you some embarrassment among your co-workers. After all, RCS has a tendency to lock in your mistakes for everyone to see. And everyone else *will* see them, too, if they're working with the same RCS files that you are, or if they try to use a baseline (official) version of the software that's built from your botched RCS check-ins.

Speaking of botched check-ins, I remember when we first put in a code management system like this at one company where I once worked (in fact, the code management system there was the inspiration for this book). Time after time, the baseline check-out and compilation would crash because developers either checked in changes that didn't work, or "forgot" to check in all the files they modified. Eventually though, with the help of little bits of peer pressure, self-flagellation, and continued effort on the part of the developers, the problems were solved.

We eventually determined that our code management tools were also at fault much of the time because they couldn't detect improper RCS check-in operations that failed due to NFS timestamp caching problems over our network. Specifically, the NFS/cache timestamp problems that we were experiencing would fool our *make* tools into randomly ignoring RCS operations that should have taken place. Unsynchronized clocks on networked computers also caused similar problems.

The solution that we eventually adopted was not to trust the status codes returned by troublesome RCS operations in our UNIX tool scripts. Instead, we modified the scripts to ignore the status codes. After each suspect RCS operation, we would issue enough successive commands in the script to make sure that the RCS operation was actually successful. This technique may help you catch errors in any code management scripts that you have to write in the future, too.

Let's focus again on our situation here. We were about to analyze the source trees to figure out the most efficient way of updating the RCS files. Which of our files have changed, and which files are new?

Recall that my previous approach to answering this question was to walk the source directories looking for read-only permissions on source files. This is a reasonable technique because read-only permissions on a file usually mean that it hasn't been modified since it was last checked in. (This rule of thumb is valid only for files that have RCS files, of course.) I've found that the read-only technique is also the quickest way to answer the question too, so I use it all the time.

But you can also do the job by using the *ls_changed* option of *rcsdo*. I'll use it this time, just to show you how it works.

To find out which files have changed in the *tool3\s* directory, we'll just go there and issue the appropriate *rcsdo ls_changed* command.

```
K:\MAIN\TOOL3\TBC.PLT> cd ..\s
K:\MAIN\TOOL3\S> ls
 rcs           tool3.c       tool3.h
K:\MAIN\TOOL3\S> rcsdo ls_changed
tool3.c       has changed.
```

You can use the same *ls_changed* technique with *twalker* to inspect entire subtrees, but it's slow compared to the file permissions technique. This is because the *ls_changed* operation, for each file in the RCS directory, checks out a temporary copy of the latest version that's stored in the RCS file. Then the *ls_changed* uses *diff* to detect differences between the two files, and prints out a message based on the value of the status code returned by *diff*.

One situation in which the *rcsdo ls_changed* option is useful is when your file permissions are invalidated for some reason. For example, DOS sets the permissions on all copied files to read-only, preventing the effective use of the read-only technique shown earlier.

Let's continue on, but with the read-only file permission technique. As I recall, the subroutine library files are new, the *tool3\s* files are changed, and the *tool2\s* files are unchanged.

We'll have to build a new *twalker* script to walk the source directories, since we've added a new product node (*tool_pi.lib*) since the last *twalker* files were generated. (It's worth noting here that if we'd been using recursive makefiles to walk these product trees, they'd be out of date, just like our current *twalker* scripts. But updating the *twalker* scripts is trivial in comparison to the manual editing that would be required to update a series of recursive makefiles.)

```
K:\MAIN\TOOL3\S> cd ..\..
K:\MAIN> twalker walksrc.bat s        generate a new twalker file
```

Use the tree walker script to list all the files in the source directories. Use it to delete leftover *msg* files, and then use it again to check for read-only file permissions.

```
K:\MAIN> walksrc ls               check for non-source files
K:\MAIN> walksrc rm -f msg        clean up by deleting all non-source files
K:\MAIN> walksrc ls -l *.c *.h    only show *.c and *.h files, no rcs dirs
```

As expected, the listings show writeable files in the *tool_pi.lib\s* and *tool3\s* directories (meaning that those files must be checked in to RCS). Now let's figure out which of those files are new and which are modified. We can do this by examining the contents of the relevant RCS directories using either this:

```
K:\MAIN> walksrc ls rcs          see who doesn't have rcs files
```

or this:

```
K:\MAIN> twalker walkrcs.bat rcs     see who doesn't have rcs files
K:\MAIN> walkrcs ls
```

A surprise, yes? The listings show RCS files in the *tool_pi.lib\s* directory too. This is because when we created the new subroutine library, we moved both the source files *and* the RCS files out of the the *tool2* subtree. The reason we have writeable permissions on the source files in *tool_pi.lib\s* is because DOS reset the permissions when it copied the files.

Since the file permissions have been invalidated, let's use the *ls_changed* option to make sure that the writeable files haven't been modified.

```
K:\MAIN> cd tool_pi.lib\s
K:\MAIN\TOOL_PI.LIB\S> rcsdo ls_changed
pd_sub.h      has changed.
pi_sub.h      has changed.
```

As you can see, some of the files have changed, and some haven't.

So what's our best *rcsdo* strategy for updating all the files, now that we know all files that have to be updated are modified files and not new files? (There are no new files.)

The best strategy—at least for teaching you how to walk trees—is to issue an *rcsdo ci_u_locked* command in all directories. That's how we'll do it, too, so that you can learn about the advantages and disadvantages of using tree walker scripts to perform bulk RCS check-ins.

It's worth pointing out that I rarely use bulk RCS check-ins across multiple subtrees. This is because I haven't had to check files into RCS in more than one or two directories at a time—ever—and because the cost of manually visiting one or two directories is cheap. The next section offers some more philosophy on bulk check-ins.

Let's try it. We'll use a tree walker script to visit all source directories and let *rcsdo* figure out which files to check in.

Remember that you have to use an absolute pathname for the log message file when you're checking in files with *rcsdo* from a twalker script. This is because the *rcsdo* tool references the *msg* file from many different directories in the source tree. Also, under DOS (for nested batch files), don't forget that you must use the *call* keyword, too.

```
K:\MAIN\TOOL_PI.LIB\S> cd ..\..
K:\MAIN> echo Updated these files to share the tool_pi.lib library. > \main\msg
K:\MAIN> walksrc call rcsdo ci_u_locked \main\msg -log default
```

```
K:\MAIN> walksrc ls -l      verify check-ins with read-only permission technique
K:\MAIN> del \main\msg
```

Notice that there are still two files in the *tool_pi.lib\s* directory (*pi_sub.c* and *pd_sub.c*) that still have write permissions. According to the read-only file permission technique, this would normally indicate that the files have been checked out and modified, but in this case we know that they aren't modified for two reasons. First, the *rcsdo ls_changed* command didn't list them a few minutes ago, and second, we know that DOS removes read-only file permissions on copied files.

We'll fix this by forcibly checking out the files with no lock. Resetting read-only file permissions would be equivalent.

Let's make one last check of file permissions before we start any RCS operations, because once we start with RCS, the writeable file permissions will change. We'll use *rcsdiff* to compare the writeable working files in the source directories with the latest checked in copies that are stored in the RCS files.

```
K:\MAIN> cd tool_pi.lib\s                   let's fix those permissions
K:\MAIN\TOOL_PI.LIB\S> rcsdiff pi_sub.c     be very sure files haven't changed
K:\MAIN\TOOL_PI.LIB\S> rcsdiff pd_sub.c
K:\MAIN\TOOL_PI.LIB\S> co -u -f pi_sub.c pd_sub.c   reset the permissions
```

Assign RCS Labels

There's only one more thing to do—assign a new symbolic label (RCS calls them symbolic *names*) to all the files in the source trees. After we've done that, we'll inspect the list of files that were marked with the label.

```
K:\MAIN\TOOL_PI.LIB\S> cd ..\..
K:\MAIN> walksrc call rcsdo add_name ex_3
K:\MAIN> walksrc call rcsdo ls_names       make sure that labels stuck
K:\MAIN> walksrc call rcsdo ls_name ex_3   are the version numbers correct?
```

This ends Example 3.

Some Philosophy on Bulk RCS Operations

Example 3 showed you how to perform some bulk RCS operations by using a tree walker script to walk the source tree.

Not all people approve of the bulk RCS approach because they feel that it can leave modified code "unprotected" for too long a period of time. Instead, they are much more comfortable with checking in each small code change as they proceed, thereby generally avoiding the need for bulk operations.

I agree with them about the overall value of checking in small changes and recommend the practice later on in the book. But I've also found that bulk operations are so useful in some situations that I'm willing to override the general principle of small check-ins.

One situation where bulk check-ins are useful is when you're checking in the initial version of some freeware code that you've received from the net (or from some other repository). In this case, your first goal is to check in the code just as you received it, before you start modifying or porting anything for your system, and the bulk check-in operation *rcsdo ci_u_initial msg* is exactly what you need. It saves you from having to check in each individual file.

A second situation where bulk check-ins are useful is when you've had to modify several files to fix one defect in the code. In this case, you might want to check in all of the modified the files as a group using the same RCS log message. This is logical since the modified files were all participants in the same bug fix.

A special case can occur when the bug fix is associated with a formal problem report number. The presence of a formal bug tracking system is a good hint that the organization wants to formally track the resolution of problem reports. In these cases, it's usual to somehow associate the problem report number with the names of all of the files that you had to modify to fix the problem. That way, people can answer the question "Which files had to be modified to fix this bug?"

The *rcsdo* tool is preconfigured to help you out with this kind of grouping, associating, and logging. All you have to do is put the problem number in the check-in message, along with the descriptions of the file modifications that you made. Then you invoke *rcsdo* with one of the bulk check-in operations (*ci_l_locked, ci_u_locked, ci_u_initial*). The *rcsdo* tool will generate a list of files to be checked in, check them in using your original log message, add the list of filenames to your log message, and file the composite log message to the default *pci* log file.

The practice of including the pathnames of modified files in your public check-in messages is a good way to promote awareness of system changes among a group of developers. Then developers who read the check-in messages in the "check-ins" newsgroup (or in the public log file) have a chance to respond to changes in any system files that might affect their current tasks.

3

A Hands-on Tour: Part 2

In this chapter, I'll show you how to work with multiple platforms.

Example 4: Multiple Platforms

In this example we'll separate all the platform-independent code and data from the platform-dependent code and data in our sample programs. This means that there will be a lot of editing to do and that the example will be very long. But take heart—once we're finished with this example, you'll have a beautifully separated, fully automated set of programs that demonstrate good code management principles. And even better, you'll have concrete examples of both an unsatisfactory way (*tool1*) and a better way (*tool2, tool3, tool_pi.ini,* etc.) to manage your source trees.

An Overview of Example 4

The main goal in this example is to show you how to work with multiple platforms. Here's what we'll do.

First, since we need a second platform, we'll add a new platform to the CMTREE by cloning the existing *tbc.plt* platform and giving the clone a new name. This will allow us to work with two platforms on one computer.

Next, we'll start separating the pi and pd code in the source trees. We will split the existing subroutine library into separate pi and pd libraries (*tool_pi.lib* and *tool_pd.lib*) and the existing *tools.h* file into separate pi and pd include files (*tool_pi.h* and *tool_pd.h*). Then, we'll even split the *tool2.c* and *tool3.c* files into their pi and pd parts.

Last, we'll create two new *pid nodes* to store the pi and pd parts of the *tool2* and *tool3* programs. (A pid node is a combined pi and pd node, since it has both pi and pd source directories.)

To refresh your memory, here's a picture of a pid node. Notice that it has a pi (sibling) source directory that can be shared by all platform directories, as well as a pd (child) source directory for every platform.

```
K:\MAIN> makenode tool_pid pid tbc.plt msc.plt sun4gcc.plt
K:\MAIN> tree /a tool_pid
K:TOOL_PID
+---S                                source for all platforms
|   \---RCS
+---TBC.PLT
|   \---S                            source for the tbc.plt platform only
|       \---RCS
+---MSC.PLT
|   \---S                            source for the msc.plt platform only
|       \---RCS
\---SUN4GCC.PLT                      source for the sun4gcc.plt platform only
    \---S
        \---RCS

K:\MAIN> rm -rf tool_pid
```

Creating a New Platform

Since not everyone who reads this book will have a true heterogeneous multi-platform computer system to work on, we are going to create a multiple platform environment using only one machine and one compiler.

We'll do this by cloning and renaming the makefile templates for our current *tbc.plt* platform and by naming the new platform *tb2.plt*. This is a good approach to take, because we'll be able to use the same compiler, the same *make* tool, and the same computer for all of our work. (Note that if we changed something in the cloned templates, the new platform would truly be a new and distinct platform.)

To create a new platform, we have to add a new set of templates to the CMTREE and a new set of corresponding directories to the CMHTREE. (My CMTREE is on drive **d:**, but yours might not be. Adjust the pathnames in the example to suit your environment.)

First, let's create the new makefile templates in the CMTREE.

```
K:\MAIN> cd d:\cmt\plt                     go to your cmtree
D:\CMT\PLT> mkdir tb2.plt                  the name of our new platform
D:\CMT\PLT> copy tbc.plt\*.* tb2.plt       clone the platform templates
D:\CMT\PLT> cd tb2.plt
D:\CMT\PLT\TB2.PLT> ren tbc.plt tb2.plt    rename the platform file

D:\CMT\PLT\TB2.PLT> emacs makefile.mak              change tbc.plt to tb2.plt inside
D:\CMT\PLT\TB2.PLT> diff ..\tbc.plt\makefile.mak makefile.mak
4,5c4,5
< MP=tbc.plt
< EP=tbc.plt
---
> MP=tb2.plt
> EP=tb2.plt

D:\CMT\PLT\TB2.PLT> emacs makefile.ini              change tbc.plt to tb2.plt inside
```

The two makefile macros **MP** and **EP** stand for "makefile platform" and "export platform." **MP** tells *make* where to get makefile templates, and **EP** tells *make* where to export files. For example, if **MP=tbc.plt**, *make* will get any needed makefile templates from the *CMTREE/tbc.plt* directory. And if **EP=tbc.plt**, *make* will export completed product files into the *CMHTREE/at/tbc.plt* directory in the CMHTREE.

Although it might seem like it at first, one macro isn't enough. Sometimes it's convenient to have the ability to build products under two platforms, but to export the products to the same destination directory. For example, sometimes while I'm investigating new *make* tools, I'll build the same DOS script or program under several platforms that differ only in their *make* tool and compiler combinations.*

Notice that I modified the *makefile.ini* file in addition to the *makefile.mak* file.

Now create the required new directories in the CMHTREE. (Note that I didn't have to create these directories for the *tbc.plt* platform because they were created as part of the software installation process.) Again, when you create these directories, you'll have to adjust the pathnames to suit the filesystem on your computer.

```
D:\CMT\PLT\TB2.PLT> cd j:\h          go to the holding tree
J:\H> mkdir at\tb2.plt               a place for alpha test executables
J:\H> mkdir share\tb2.plt            a place for shared pd files
J:\H> mkdir release\tb2.plt          a place for released pd files
```

This completes the addition of the new *tb2.plt* platform to our code management environment.

Using the New Platform

Now let's start to port *tool2* to the new platform and see what difficulties arise. This initial "port" will be easy, because *tool2* is a pi node (meaning that there's no troublesome pd code to mess with), and because the port is going to produce the wrong result. But that's how it normally goes with porting, isn't it? Compile, find a problem, edit, compile, test, and so on. It's no different here.

The first step in porting is to create a new platform directory to hold the *tb2.plt* platform files. To help us along with this task, we'll use the *makeplt* tool. This tool is similar to *makenode*, but it creates only the platform subtrees instead of whole product nodes.

You have to be inside the top directory of a product node before invoking *makeplt*. The arguments in the command line below tell *makeplt* to create a pi platform directory for the *tb2.plt* platform.

---

* I once built a C program under *tbc.plt* (Borland make, Borland C), *msc.plt* (Microsoft nmake, Microsoft C), *mksbc.plt* (MKS make, Borland C), *tmsc.plt* (Borland make, Microsoft C), and so on. I set **EP** to *tbc.plt* in all cases, so the products all ended up in the same directory. (Since the product name was the same in each case, the successive exports actually overwrote each other.)

```
J:\H> cd k:\main
K:\MAIN> cd tool2
K:\MAIN\TOOL2> makeplt pi tb2.plt
```

Let's have a look at the structure of the *temp\tool2* product node now that we've added another platform.

```
K:\MAIN\TOOL2> tree /a \main\tool2
K:MAIN\TOOL2
+---S
|   \---RCS
+---TB2.PLT                              here's the new platform directory
|   \---S
|       \---RCS
\---TBC.PLT
    \---S
        \---RCS
```

As you can see, *makeplt* just created another platform directory beside the existing *tbc.plt* platform directory.

Now let's generate some makefiles from the new *tb2.plt* makefile templates. Nothing new here. We just change into the new platform directory and ask *getmakes* to make a set of *tb2.plt* makefiles for a pi program named *tool2*.

```
K:\MAIN\TOOL2> cd tb2.plt
K:\MAIN\TOOL2\TB2.PLT> getmakes tb2.plt pi program tool2
```

And, as is usual after generating a set of makefiles, we'll copy in an *imports.imp* file from somewhere else if we can, to save typing. This time we have an ideal file to copy, from *..\tbc.plt\imports.imp*. It doesn't require any changes at all.

After the copy, compile and test the program under the new *tb2.plt* platform.

```
K:\MAIN\TOOL2\TB2.PLT> copy ..\tbc.plt\imports.imp    save typing
K:\MAIN\TOOL2\TB2.PLT> make all                       and build the program

=> Fatal: Unable to open file 'tool_pi.lib'           the linker error
```

As you can see from the error message, the linker can't find the subroutine library for the *tb2.plt* platform. This isn't surprising because we haven't ported the library to the *tb2.plt* platform yet. So we'll have to go and port the shared include files and libraries for the *tb2.plt* platform before we can continue here.

First, let's port the shared data file to the *tb2.plt* platform, and then do the shared libraries. Then we'll come back to *tool2* and try to rebuild it again.

To port the shared data file *tool_pi.h*, we'll have to go through the same steps as we did for *tool2*. That is, create a new platform with *makeplt*, generate makefiles, and build the product.

```
K:\MAIN\TOOL2\TB2.PLT> cd ..\..\tool_pi.ini
K:\MAIN\TOOL_PI.INI> makeplt pi tb2.plt
K:\MAIN\TOOL_PI.INI> cd tb2.plt
K:\MAIN\TOOL_PI.INI> getmakes tb2.plt pi ini tool_pi
K:\MAIN\TOOL_PI.INI> copy ..\tbc.plt\imports.imp          lazy edit technique
K:\MAIN\TOOL_PI.INI> make all
```

Everything worked fine. But as you could tell—if you were observant—a subtle thing occurred (or didn't occur, to be exact). During the make operation, the *cmx* tool did not print an exporting message. That means the *tools.h* file wasn't physically copied to the *CMHTREE\share* directory.

This is because the importing and exporting tools will only perform a copy if the timestamps on the source and destination files are out of date. And since, in this particular case, both platforms (*tbc.plt* and *tb2.plt*) are exporting the same ..\s\tools.h file to the same destination in the *CMHTREE\share* directory, the timestamps were already up to date. No copy was required, and no copy was performed.

Using timestamps to optimize importing and exporting operations is a smart thing to do because it reduces product construction time.

Now let's port the subroutine library *tool_pi.lib* to the *tb2.plt* platform. After that, we should be able to get *tool2* to compile on the *tb2.plt* platform.

The porting steps are the same as they were for the shared data file *tool_pi.h*. Create the platform, generate the makefiles, customize the *imports.imp* (by copying one in to save typing), and then compile and export the final result.

```
K:\MAIN\TOOL_PI.INI> cd ..\..\tool_pi.lib
K:\MAIN\TOOL_PI.LIB> makeplt pi tb2.plt                       make a new platform dir
K:\MAIN\TOOL_PI.LIB> cd tb2.plt
K:\MAIN\TOOL_PI.LIB\TB2.PLT> getmakes tb2.plt pi lib tool_pi  get makefiles
K:\MAIN\TOOL_PI.LIB\TB2.PLT> copy ..\tbc.plt\imports.imp      customize imports.imp
K:\MAIN\TOOL_PI.LIB\TB2.PLT> make all                         build and export the product
```

The library is now available for sharing in the *tb2.plt* alpha test directory. We shouldn't get any more linker error messages when we rebuild *tool2* on the *tb2.plt* platform. Let's try it and see what happens.

```
K:\MAIN\TOOL_PI.LIB\TB2.PLT> cd ..\..\tool2\tb2.plt
K:\MAIN\TOOL2\TB2.PLT> make all          rebuild and test
K:\MAIN\TOOL2\TB2.PLT> tool2
0  This is tool2 compiled on platform (tbc.plt).
1  (tbc.plt) This is pd local  code from tool2/s/tool2.c.
2  (tbc.plt) This is pd local  data from tool2/s/tool2.h.
3  (tbc.plt) This is pd shared code from tool_pi.lib/s/pd_sub.c.
4  (tbc.plt) This is pd shared data from tool_pi.ini/s/tools.h.
5  (pi)      This is pi local  code from tool2/s/tool2.c.
6  (pi)      This is pi local  data from tool2/s/tool2.h.
7  (pi)      This is pi shared code from tool_pi.lib/s/pi_sub.c.
8  (pi)      This is pi shared data from tool_pi.ini/s/tools.h.
```

The *tool2* program is now compiling successfully under the new *tb2.plt* platform. But from a code management perspective, it's still a long way from being perfect. I'll analyze it in depth in the next section, since this is where we actually start to separate pi and pd code and data into separate files.

What's Wrong with This Code?

The first thing I want to emphasize is that since the word "tbc.pl" is hardcoded in the *.c* source files, the word is pd *code*, and not pd *data*. (In contrast, data is something that you usually find #define'd in include files.) I've chosen to use hardcoded text to represent platform-dependent code, because it's obvious in the code, obvious in the output, and simple to understand.

Now let's begin the analysis. The *tool2* program compiles without error on the *tb2.plt* platform, but the output contains several multi-platform problems. For example, everywhere that *tbc.plt* appears in the output, *tb2.plt* should appear, since the program was compiled on the *tb2.plt* platform. This problem occurs in five places, on lines 0-4. This is no surprise, since lines 0-4 are the pd lines in the program.

So we'll have to port all five lines to the *tb2.plt* platform in order to complete this example.

An Overview of Our Porting Strategy

To resolve these problems, we'll have to clone and modify the four files *tool2.c*, *tool2.h*, *pd_sub.c*, and *tools.h* (the files that contain pd lines).

We'll also have to create a new pd node (or a pid node) for each of the four cases so that we can properly store the newly cloned and modified pd files in separate pd source directories. We need to do this because the modified files for the new *tb2.plt* platform will have the same filenames as the files for the original *tbc.plt* platform.

We'll treat the four sub-problems as follows:

Shared pi and pd code—*pd_sub.c*
>   Separate the pi and pd subroutines into two separate libraries called *tool_pi.lib* and *tool_pd.lib*, respectively.

Shared pi and pd data—*tools.h*
>   Split the *tools.h* file into two new files named *tools_pi.h* and *tools_pd.h*.

Local pi and pd code—*tool2.c*
>   Clone and modify the original *tool2.c* program for the *tb2.plt* platform. We'll have to convert the existing pi *tool2* node to a new pid node to hold the platform-dependent files.

Local pi and pd data—*tool2.h*

> Separate the local pi and pd data into two new files named *tool2_pi.h* and *tool2_pd.h*, and store them in the appropriate directories of the newly converted *tool2* pid node.

That will complete the conversion of our examples to multiple platforms.

Checking in RCS Files as You Go

I'm going to abandon the strict order of our five "traditional" development steps now, since they are too restrictive. I want to show you how I normally work with the tools, and besides, by now you've seen the concepts and used the tools enough times to be comfortable with them.

The main difference in procedure is that we're going to update the RCS files as we go along, being confident that we won't have to back out the changes. This improves work efficiency because you don't have to go back at the end of a development cycle and try to determine what you changed and why you changed it. Here, I recommend two things.

First, make small changes to your code and test them incrementally. Small changes are easier to understand. They're easier to get right because they're easier to install, to test, and so on. If you follow this approach, it's more likely that your program will always work. Or if it doesn't, you'll be able to determine immediately exactly what made it fail, and what to do to get the program working again (back out your changes). These two pieces of knowledge are very valuable because they can save you much time and effort.

Second, make it a standard practice to check in your changed files as soon as you're confident that your changes will work. This will help you to lock in a series of small successful changes and thereby make it easier for you to back up to a working program in case a new change fails. (You back up by checking out the most recent working version of the file that failed, using the RCS *co -l -f myfile.c* command.)

The main point here is that if you follow this practice, the "modification distance" between successive locked-in changes will be small. If you ever have to back up to an earlier working version of your code, you won't have to take a giant step backwards. Instead, you can take a very small step backwards, and thus preserve as much of your earlier work as possible.

These two practices (small changes and frequent check-ins of working changes) can have an important effect on your productivity because they tend to lock in your good work-in-progress.

In addition, you'll always look good in front of management and customers because you'll never be caught with a program that isn't working—especially during demos. Instead, your programs will always be improving, and your progress will become more predictable—slow, but steady. And you'll be able to fix almost any problem that arises almost immediately, simply by backing up to the most recent working version. These kinds of things all help to make a programmer's workday a little bit easier.

Managing Shared Pi and Pd Code with Libraries

The process of creating a second (pd) library from our existing mixed pi and pd code library is fairly straightforward. We'll do it in the following five steps:

1. Create a pd library node called *tool_pd.lib*.

2. Relocate the pd source files and RCS files in *tool_pi.lib\s* into the new *tool_pd.lib* node.

3. Generate makefiles in both platform directories of the old pi node *tool_pi.lib*, and export the two products. No source code modifications are necessary because the original pi source files haven't been relocated.

4. Build the *tb2.plt* version of the new pd *tool_pd.lib* library. Do this by updating pathnames in the relocated pd source files, check in the RCS files, generate the makefiles, and export the resulting pd *tool_pd.lib* library for the *tbc.plt* platform.

5. Build the *tbc.plt* version of the new pd *tool_pd.lib* library. Do this by updating pathnames in the relocated pd source files. Check in the RCS files, generate the makefiles, and export the resulting pd *tool_pd.lib* library for the *tbc.plt* platform.

The original pi source code in *tool_pi.lib\s* won't require modification, of course. But we'll have to modify the relocated pd source code in *tool_pd.lib\tbc.plt\s* and *tool_pd.lib\tb2.plt\s* to update the pathnames in the relocated files. Taken together, these actions will fix line 3 in the output.

Step 1. Create the directory tree (both platforms). First, we'll use *makenode* to create a new pd library node called *tool_pd.lib* to hold the pd subroutine *pd_sub.c*.

Notice that I've given two platform names to the *makenode* tool in the command below. You can give *makenode* an arbitrary number of platform names, if necessary.

```
K:\MAIN\TOOL2\TB2.PLT> cd ..\..
K:\MAIN> makenode tool_pd.lib pd tbc.plt tb2.plt
```

Here's a picture of the tree that *makenode* created.

```
K:\MAIN> tree /a tool_pd.lib
K:TOOL_PD.LIB
+---TB2.PLT              the second platform
|   \---S                pd_sub.c and pd_sub.h for tb2.plt will go here
|       \---RCS
\---TBC.PLT              the first platform
    \---S          .     pd_sub.c and pd_sub.h for tbc.plt will go here
        \---RCS
```

Step 2. Relocate the source files (both platforms). Now let's move *only* the pd source code out of the *tool_pi.lib* tree and into the *tool_pd.lib* tree. We'll need to put two copies of the original pi code into the new *tool_pd.lib* tree, since each of the *tbc.plt* and *tb2.plt* source directories will require its own version of the code.

```
K:\MAIN> copy tool_pi.lib\s\pd_sub.* tool_pd.lib\tbc.plt\s
K:\MAIN> copy tool_pi.lib\s\pd_sub.* tool_pd.lib\tb2.plt\s
K:\MAIN> copy tool_pi.lib\s\rcs\pd_sub.* tool_pd.lib\tbc.plt\s\rcs
K:\MAIN> copy tool_pi.lib\s\rcs\pd_sub.* tool_pd.lib\tb2.plt\s\rcs
```

Delete only the pd source files in the old *tool_pi.lib\s* directory once the copy is complete.

```
K:\MAIN> attrib -r tool_pi.lib\s\pd_sub.*        remove read-only permission
K:\MAIN> del tool_pi.lib\s\pd_sub.*
K:\MAIN> attrib -r tool_pi.lib\s\rcs\pd_sub.*    remove read-only permission
K:\MAIN> del tool_pi.lib\s\rcs\pd_sub.*
```

Step 3a. Generate makefiles and export the pi library (*tbc.plt*). Now that we've relocated the pd code files out of the *tool_pi.lib* tree, we'll rebuild the (shrunken) pi library on both platforms. Let's rebuild the *tool_pi.lib* product for the *tbc.plt* platform first.

Regenerate the makefile dependencies.

```
K:\MAIN> cd tool_pi.lib\tbc.plt
K:\MAIN\TOOL_PI.LIB\TBC.PLT> make empty         delete old files
K:\MAIN\TOOL_PI.LIB\TBC.PLT> gendep pi          regenerate dependencies
```

Update the *imports.imp* file so that it does *not* import the *pd_sub.h* include file (which has been relocated).

```
K:\MAIN\TOOL_PI.LIB\TBC.PLT> emacs imports.imp   delete pd_sub stuff
imports:
        $(CMI) -nl ../s/pi_sub.h

imports.rev:
        $(RM) pi_sub.h
```

Now rebuild and export the *tool_pi.lib* library for the *tbc.plt* platform.

```
K:\MAIN\TOOL_PI.LIB\TBC.PLT> make all
```

Step 3b. Generate makefiles and export the pi library (*tb2.plt*). Now we have to complete the port to the *tb2.plt* platform. Start by regenerating the makefile dependencies. Then update the *imports.imp* file so that it does not import the *pd_sub.h* include file (which has been relocated). You can do this by copying in the *..\tbc.plt\imports.imp* file, since it's exactly what we need.

```
K:\MAIN\TOOL_PI.LIB\TBC.PLT> cd ..\tb2.plt
K:\MAIN\TOOL_PI.LIB\TB2.PLT> make empty          delete old files
K:\MAIN\TOOL_PI.LIB\TB2.PLT> gendep pi           regenerate dependencies
K:\MAIN\TOOL_PI.LIB\TB2.PLT> copy ..\tbc.plt\imports.imp  update imports.imp
```

Now rebuild and export the *tool_pi.lib* library for the *tb2.plt* platform.

```
K:\MAIN\TOOL_PI.LIB\TB2.PLT> make all
```

The port of the pi library *tool_pi.lib* is now complete, both to the *tbc.plt* and to the *tb2.plt* platforms.

Step 4. Build the pd library *tool_pd.lib* (*tb2.plt*). Now we'll do almost exactly the same thing for the two platforms in the pd library tree (*tool_pd.lib*), but this time we'll port the code for the *tb2.plt* platform before we build and export it. We'll port it by modifying the platform names and pathnames that are hardcoded in the source files.

We'll also have to update the pathnames in both the *tbc.plt* and the *tb2.plt* copies of the *pd_sub.h* include files, since we've moved both of those pd source files to new directory locations.

```
K:\MAIN\TOOL_PI.LIB\TB2.PLT> cd ..\..\tool_pd.lib\tb2.plt\s
K:\MAIN\TOOL_PD.LIB\TB2.PLT\S> co -l -f pd_sub.c pd_sub.h
K:\MAIN\TOOL_PD.LIB\TB2.PLT\S> emacs pd_sub.c          change tbc.plt to tb2.plt

K:\MAIN\TOOL_PD.LIB\TB2.PLT\S> emacs pd_sub.h          change pathname
#define PD_SHARE_LOCATION "tool_pd.lib/tb2.plt/s/pd_sub.c"
```

Now we should check in the modifications we just made to the two pd files *pd_sub.c* and *pd_sub.h*.

Before we get started, you might want to make up a command-line abbreviation or a batch file to save you typing the command *rcsdo ci_u_locked msg -log default* over and over again. I call my abbreviation *rcsup*, for "rcs update." It saves me time and effort because I don't have to type in the full *rcsdo* command each time I update RCS files.

On UNIX, you can make an alias. On DOS, you can either use an alias (if you have a resident command-line editor), or you can make up a batch file that contains the single line *call rcsdo ci_u_locked msg -log default*. Doing this will probably be worth your time, because we'll be checking in a lot of files in the rest of this example.

First, let's try out the *rcsdo ls_locked* option on the two files that we're about to check in, just to see if we locked them. (Of course, you and I both know that the files are already checked out and locked, because we checked them out that way not too long ago. But you might not always know.)

```
K:\MAIN\TOOL_PD.LIB\TB2.PLT\S> rcsdo ls_locked
pd_sub.c      1.1 is locked by jameson
pd_sub.h      1.2 is locked by jameson
```

Sure enough, we've already locked the two files for modification, and now you know how to use the *rcsdo ls_locked* option.

Finish up the check-in operation in the normal way, using the *rcsdo ci_u_locked* option (or better yet, using your new abbreviation for the long *rcsdo ci_u_locked msg -log default* command).

```
K:\MAIN\TOOL_PD.LIB\TB2.PLT\S> echo Ported code to tb2.plt from tbc.plt.>msg
K:\MAIN\TOOL_PD.LIB\TB2.PLT\S> rcsdo ci_u_locked msg -log default
K:\MAIN\TOOL_PD.LIB\TB2.PLT\S> del msg
```

We don't have to come back to this platform later to check in our modified files. Instead, we made up a log message while the modifications were fresh in our mind and locked in our work. This is an important point because it's easy to forget the details of why modifications were made, especially if you've made more than a few modifications in one working session.

Now generate the makefiles and export the resulting library for the *tool_pd.lib* library for the *tb2.plt* platform.

```
K:\MAIN\TOOL_PD.LIB\TB2.PLT\S> cd ..
K:\MAIN\TOOL_PD.LIB\TB2.PLT> getmakes tb2.plt pd lib tool_pd
```

Import the *pd_sub.h* include file.

```
K:\MAIN\TOOL_PD.LIB\TB2.PLT> emacs imports.imp
imports:
        $(CMI) -nl s/pd_sub.h

imports.rev:
        $(RM) pd_sub.h
```

Rebuild and export the ported *tool_pd.lib* library for the *tb2.plt* platform.

```
K:\MAIN\TOOL_PD.LIB\TB2.PLT> make all
```

This completes the port of the *tool_pd.lib* library to the *tb2.plt* platform.

Step 5. Build the pd library *tool_pd.lib* for *tbc.plt*. Begin by modifying the pathname in the pd source file *pd_sub.h* to reflect the new location of the file, below the *tbc.plt* platform directory. No changes are required for *pd_sub.c*, since it still contains the appropriate platform name (*tbc.plt*) in its internal code.

```
K:\MAIN\TOOL_PD.LIB\TB2.PLT> cd ..\tbc.plt\s
K:\MAIN\TOOL_PD.LIB\TB2.PLT\S> co -l -f pd_sub.h          check out with a lock
K:\MAIN\TOOL_PD.LIB\TB2.PLT\S> emacs pd_sub.h            update the pathname
#define PD_SHARE_LOCATION "tool_pd.lib/tbc.plt/s/pd_sub.c"
```

Now check in the modified source files, since we're confident that the pathname changes were made correctly.

```
K:\MAIN\TOOL_PD.LIB\TB2.PLT\S> echo Updated pathnames for new directory location.> msg
K:\MAIN\TOOL_PD.LIB\TB2.PLT\S> rcsdo ci_u_locked msg -log default
K:\MAIN\TOOL_PD.LIB\TB2.PLT\S> del msg
```

Now generate *tbc.plt* makefiles for the pd library *tool_pd.lib* and customize *imports.imp* by copying in the *..\tb2.plt\imports.imp* file. Then we can rebuild and export the *tool_pd.lib* library for the *tbc.plt* platform.

```
K:\MAIN\TOOL_PD.LIB\TB2.PLT\S> cd ..
K:\MAIN\TOOL_PD.LIB\TB2.PLT> getmakes tbc.plt pd lib tool_pd
K:\MAIN\TOOL_PD.LIB\TBC.PLT> copy ..\tb2.plt\imports.imp
K:\MAIN\TOOL_PD.LIB\TBC.PLT> make all
```

The shared pi and pd code libraries *tool_pi.lib* and *tool_pd.lib* have now been ported to both the *tbc.plt* and *tb2.plt* platforms.

We've also fixed the earlier problem with line 3 in the output too, although you won't be able to see that until we recompile *tool2* and *tool3*.

Managing Shared Pi and Pd Data with Include Files

The next thing we'll do is split *tools.h* into two separate pi and pd include files called *tool_pi.h* and *tool_pd.h*. Here's how we'll proceed:

1. Create a *tool_pd.ini* node with two platforms to export the pd include files.

2. Create a *tool_pd.h* file in each of the platform source directories in the new *tool_pd.ini* node. Do this by cloning the original *tools.h* file twice.

3. Create a *tool_pi.h* file in the old *tool_pi.ini* node. (Do this by renaming the old *tools.h* file to *tool_pi.h* and by stripping out unwanted pd information.)

4. Generate makefiles for *tool_pi.h* for both platforms, and then export the pi file to the *CMHTREE\share* directory.

5. Update the pathnames in *tool_pd.ini\tbc.plt\tool_pd.h* and export the pd file to the *CMHTREE\share\tbc.plt* directory.

6. Update the pathnames in *tool_pd.ini\tb2.plt\tool_pd.h* and export the pd file to the *CMHTREE\share\tb2.plt* directory.

These actions will fix line 4 in the output.

Step 1. Create a *tool_pd.ini* node. The first thing we need is a new node to hold the new pd *tool_pd.h* files that we're going to create.

```
K:\MAIN\TOOL_PD.LIB\TBC.PLT> cd ..\..
K:\MAIN> makenode tool_pd.ini pd tbc.plt tb2.plt
```

Here's a picture of the node that we just created:

```
K:\MAIN> tree /a tool_pd.ini
K:TOOL_PD.INI                    the node name
+---TB2.PLT                      the second platform
|   \---S                        a place for the tb2.plt version of tool_pd.h
|       \---RCS
\---TBC.PLT                      the first platform
    \---S                        a place for the tbc.plt version of tool_pd.h
        \---RCS
```

Step 2. Create two *tool_pd.h* files in platform source directories. **Now we'll create the two *tool_pd.h* files that we need by cloning the original *tools.h* file twice.** Later on, we'll strip the unwanted pi information out of the cloned files.

Notice that I'm not cloning the original *tools.h* RCS file too, even though it wouldn't hurt to do so. Instead, I'd rather make new RCS files in this case, because the cloned files are completely new and deserve RCS files of their own. In addition, I don't think I'll ever need to back up to the original mixed pi and pd version of the file.

Let's clone the original *tools.h* file twice to create the *tool_pd.h* files that we want.

```
K:\MAIN> copy tool_pi.ini\s\tools.h tool_pd.ini\tbc.plt\s\tool_pd.h      clone it
K:\MAIN> copy tool_pi.ini\s\tools.h tool_pd.ini\tb2.plt\s\tool_pd.h      clone it again
```

Step 3. Create *tool_pi.h* in the old *tool_pi.ini* node. Now we're going to do something that might worry you a bit—we're going to rename some RCS files. But don't worry— the external name of the file isn't permanently stored inside the RCS files. Instead, RCS loads the external filename of the RCS file into the working file when the working file is checked out. So what we're going to do here won't cause any trouble.

```
K:\MAIN> cd tool_pi.ini\s
K:\MAIN\TOOL_PI.INI\S> ren tools.h tool_pi.h      rename the working file
K:\MAIN\TOOL_PI.INI\S> ren rcs\tools.h tool_pi.h  rename the rcs file, too
```

(On UNIX, use the command *mv rcs/tools.h rcs/tool_pi.h*.) Now check out the *tool_pi.h* file and strip out the unwanted pd information.

```
K:\MAIN\TOOL_PI.INI\S> co -l -f tool_pi.h          check out a working file
K:\MAIN\TOOL_PI.INI\S> emacs tool_pi.h             delete pd info, update pathname
#define TN_PI_DATA "(pi)      This is pi shared data from tool_pi.ini/s/tool_pi.h."
```

Check the changes back into RCS.

```
K:\MAIN\TOOL_PI.INI\S> echo Removed pd data for port to tb2.plt. > msg
K:\MAIN\TOOL_PI.INI\S> rcsdo ci_u_locked msg -log default
K:\MAIN\TOOL_PI.INI\S> del msg
```

Step 4. Generate makefiles for *tool_pi.h* (both platforms). **Update the two *imports.imp* files in the *tbc.plt* and *tb2.plt* directories since we changed the name of the *tools.h* file to *tool_pi.h*.** Then export the new (and pure) pi file.

```
K:\MAIN\TOOL_PI.INI\S> cd ..\tbc.plt
K:\MAIN\TOOL_PI.INI\TBC.PLT> emacs imports.imp                    save typing
imports:
     $(CMI) -nl ../s/tool_pi.h

imports.rev:
     $(RM) tool_pi.h

exports.spe:
     $(CMX) ../s/tool_pi.h -for to share with other tools

K:\MAIN\TOOL_PI.INI\TBC.PLT> make all                            export tool_pi.h for tbc.plt
```

```
K:\MAIN\TOOL_PI.INI\TBC.PLT> cd ..\tb2.plt              do tb2.plt too
K:\MAIN\TOOL_PI.INI\TB2.PLT> copy ..\tbc.plt\imports.imp    save typing
K:\MAIN\TOOL_PI.INI\TB2.PLT> make all                   export tool_pi.h for tb2.plt
```

This completes the port of the new *tool_pi.h* file to both platforms.

Step 5a. Update pathnames in *tool_pd.h* for *tbc.plt*. Recall that *tool_pd.h* is the pd part of the old *tools.h* file. We'll port it by stripping out the unwanted pi information and modifying the pathnames to reflect the new location of the file.

```
K:\MAIN\TOOL_PI.INI\TB2.PLT> cd ..\..\tool_pd.ini\tbc.plt\s
K:\MAIN\TOOL_PD.INI\TBC.PLT\S> attrib -r tool_pd.h   unix= chmod +w tool_pd.h
K:\MAIN\TOOL_PD.INI\TBC.PLT\S> emacs tool_pd.h       strip pi info, update paths
#define TN_PD_DATA "(tbc.plt) This is pd shared data from tool_pd.ini/tbc.plt/s/tool_pd.h."
```

Check the modified file into RCS with *rcsdo ci_u_initial*.

```
K:\MAIN\TOOL_PD.INI\TBC.PLT\S> echo Ported old tools.h to pd tbc.plt > msg
K:\MAIN\TOOL_PD.INI\TBC.PLT\S> rcsdo ci_u_initial msg -log default
K:\MAIN\TOOL_PD.INI\TBC.PLT\S> del msg
```

Generate the makefiles, customize the *imports.imp* file, and export *tool_pd.h* for *tbc.plt* into the *CMHTREE\share\tbc.plt* directory.

```
K:\MAIN\TOOL_PD.INI\TBC.PLT\S> cd ..
K:\MAIN\TOOL_PD.INI\TBC.PLT> getmakes tbc.plt pd ini tool_pd.ini
K:\MAIN\TOOL_PD.INI\TBC.PLT> emacs imports.imp
imports:
    $(CMI) -nl s/tool_pd.h

imports.rev:
    $(RM) tool_pd.h

exports.spe:
    $(CMX) tool_pd.h -p $(EP)
```

Notice that for the first time ever we typed a command into the *imports.imp* file that explicitly exports a file into a platform directory under the *CMHTREE\share* directory. (The macro **$(EP)** in the *cmx* export command means "export platform," and has a value such as **tbc.plt** or **tb2.plt**.) We're doing this because exported pd files must be separated according to their platform, just like the source files.

Finish the job by running *make* to export the file. Watch for the export message, and be sure that the exported pd file goes into the *CMHTREE\share\tbc.plt* directory.

```
K:\MAIN\TOOL_PD.INI\TBC.PLT\S> make all
```

Step 5b. Update pathnames in *tool_pd.h* for *tb2.plt*. Now we'll port the pd part of the old *tools.h* file for *tbc.plt*. The steps are identical to those used to port *tool_pd.h* for *tbc.plt*.

Strip the unwanted pi information from the file.

```
K:\MAIN\TOOL_PI.INI\TBC.PLT> cd ..\tb2.plt\s
K:\MAIN\TOOL_PD.INI\TB2.PLT\S> attrib -r tool_pd.h    unix= chmod +w tool_pd.h
K:\MAIN\TOOL_PD.INI\TB2.PLT\S> emacs tool_pd.h        delete pi info, update pd
#define TN_PD_DATA "(tb2.plt) This is pd shared data from tool_pd.ini/tb2.plt/s/tool_pd.h."
```

Check in the modified *tool_pd.h* file for *tbc.plt* using the *rcsdo ci_u_initial* option.

```
K:\MAIN\TOOL_PD.INI\TB2.PLT\S> echo Ported old tools.h to pd tb2.plt > msg
K:\MAIN\TOOL_PD.INI\TB2.PLT\S> rcsdo ci_u_initial msg -log default
K:\MAIN\TOOL_PD.INI\TB2.PLT\S> del msg
```

Generate the makefiles, copy in the *..\tbc.plt\imports.imp* file, and export the *tool_pd.h* for *tb2.plt* to the *CMHTREE\share\tb2.plt* directory.

```
K:\MAIN\TOOL_PD.INI\TB2.PLT\S> cd ..
K:\MAIN\TOOL_PD.INI\TB2.PLT> getmakes tb2.plt pd ini tool_pd.ini
K:\MAIN\TOOL_PD.INI\TB2.PLT> copy ..\tbc.plt\imports.imp        save editing
K:\MAIN\TOOL_PD.INI\TB2.PLT\S> make all
```

This completes the separation of the old *tools.h* file into its separate pi and pd parts (one copy of *tool_pi.h* and two copies of *tool_pd.h*). This also fixes the problem in line 4 of the output.

Let's rebuild the *tool2* program again to get a visible check on our fixes for lines 3 and 4.

Managing Local Pi and Pd Data with Pid Nodes

Recall that the last time we ran *tool2*, we could see pd portability problems in lines 0-4 (platform names and pathnames were incorrect for the *tb2.plt* platform). Two of those problems are fixed. Line 3 was fixed earlier by creating a *tool_pd.lib* library for both platforms, and line 4 was fixed by creating a *tool_pd.h* include file for both platforms.

This part of Example 4 will fix the problems in lines 2 and 6 by separating the old *tool2.h* file into separate pi and pd files (*tool2_pi.h* and two copies of *tool2_pd.h*).

Here's a list of the steps that we'll follow:

1. Get *tool2* working again on both platforms to demonstrate our previous fixes for lines 3 and 4.

2. Replace the current *tool2* pi node with a new pid node so that we can store pi and pd local data within the same tree node.

3. Split the old *tool2.h* file into separate pi and pd files. We'll make one copy of *tool2_pi.h* and two copies of *tool2_pd.h* (one for each platform). Then we'll update the pathnames in all three files.

4. Modify the *tool2.c* program to use the two new include files *tool2_pi.h* and *tool2_pd.h* in place of the old *tool2.h* file.

5. Update the makefiles for *tool2* on the *tbc.plt* platform, then rebuild and test the program. This will help to verify our fix for lines 2 and 6.

6. Update the makefiles for *tool2* on the *tb2.plt* platform, then rebuild and test the program. This will help to verify our fix for lines 2 and 6.

After we've fixed lines 2 and 6, lines 0, 1 and 5 will be the only problems left to resolve in the *tool2* program. After those lines are fixed, we can clone *tool2* to update *tool3* the easy way, and complete this entire multi-platform code development example.

Get tool2 working again on both platforms

To rebuild *tool2*, we have to modify its *imports.imp* file to use (or import) the two new libraries and the two new include files that we've created. We must also install the new include file names in the source code of the *tool2.c* program.

First, modify the *tool2.c* source code to use the two new include files.

```
K:\MAIN\TOOL_PD.INI\TB2.PLT\S> cd ..\..\tool2\s
K:\MAIN\TOOL2\S> co -l -f tool2.c                 check out locked, for modification
K:\MAIN\TOOL2\S> emacs tool2.c                    change #include statements
K:\MAIN\TOOL2\S> rcsdiff tool2.c                  here are my changes
4c4,5
< #include "tools.h"                /* pi and pd data, all tools */
---
> #include "tool_pi.h"              /* pi data, all tools */
> #include "tool_pd.h"              /* pd data, all tools */
```

Next, update the makefiles. Change to the *tb2.plt* directory, rebuild the makefile dependencies with *gendep*, and update the *imports.imp* file with the appropriate new library names and import statements.

We'll work with the *tb2.plt* platform first (instead of the *tbc.plt* platform) because it will be easier to see the effects of our porting changes in the output of the *tb2.plt* version. Any *tb2.plt* platform names that we modify will stand out from the original background of *tbc.plt* names.

```
K:\MAIN\TOOL2\S> cd ..\tb2.plt
K:\MAIN\TOOL2\TB2.PLT> make empty             delete old files
K:\MAIN\TOOL2\TB2.PLT> gendep pi              gen dependencies from new tool2.c
K:\MAIN\TOOL2\TB2.PLT> emacs imports.imp      link to new libs, import include files
lb3=tool_pi tool_pd                           link to these libraries
imports:
        $(CMI) -nl ../s/tool2.h               from local ../s dir
        $(CMI) tool_pi.h                      from CMHTREE/share dir
        $(CMI) -p $(EP) tool_pd.h             from CMHTREE/share/tbc.plt

imports.rev:
        $(RM) tool2.h
        $(RM) tool_pi.h
        $(RM) tool_pd.h
```

Now recompile and test the *tool2* executable to see if our fixes for lines 3 and 4 had the desired effect.

On UNIX, be sure that you invoke the right executable for *tool2*. This is the first time we reference an executable that might not be on your search paths out of the alpha test directory. If you have trouble, try using *./tool2* to pick up the executable from the current directory. It'll be the same as the exported version in the alpha test directory for the *tb2.plt* platform.

```
K:\MAIN\TOOL2\TB2.PLT> make all
K:\MAIN\TOOL2\TB2.PLT> tool2
0  This is tool2 compiled on platform (tbc.plt).
1  (tbc.plt) This is pd local  code from tool2/s/tool2.c.
2  (tbc.plt) This is pd local  data from tool2/s/tool2.h.
3  (tb2.plt) This is pd shared code from tool_pd.lib/tb2.plt/s/pd_sub.c.
4  (tb2.plt) This is pd shared data from tool_pd.ini/tb2.plt/s/tool_pd.h.
5  (pi)      This is pi local  code from tool2/s/tool2.c.
6  (pi)      This is pi local  data from tool2/s/tool2.h.
7  (pi)      This is pi shared code from tool_pi.lib/s/pi_sub.c.
8  (pi)      This is pi shared data from tool_pi.ini/s/tool_pi.h.
```

As you can see, the original portability problems on lines 3 and 4 have been solved. That's because we corrected both the platform names and the pathnames in lines 3 and 4 when we split the old *tools.h* file (line 4) and the old *tool_pi.lib* library (line 3) into separate pi and pd products.

Similarly, if we rebuild *tool2* for the *tbc.plt* platform, we'll see that the same lines have been corrected there too. This is because we put separate copies of the relevant pd source code in the pd source code directories in *tool_pd.ini* and *tool_pd.lib*. Let's verify that by rebuilding *tool2* for *tbc.plt*.

```
K:\MAIN\TOOL2\TB2.PLT> cd ..\tbc.plt            go there
K:\MAIN\TOOL2\TBC.PLT> make empty               delete old files
K:\MAIN\TOOL2\TBC.PLT> copy ..\tb2.plt\imports.imp   customize the easy way
K:\MAIN\TOOL2\TBC.PLT> gendep pi                regenerate deps from new tool2.c
K:\MAIN\TOOL2\TBC.PLT> make all                 compile
K:\MAIN\TOOL2\TBC.PLT> tool2                    and test
0  This is tool2 compiled on platform (tbc.plt).
1  (tbc.plt) This is pd local  code from tool2/s/tool2.c.
2  (tbc.plt) This is pd local  data from tool2/s/tool2.h.
3  (tbc.plt) This is pd shared code from tool_pd.lib/tbc.plt/s/pd_sub.c.
4  (tbc.plt) This is pd shared data from tool_pd.ini/tbc.plt/s/tool_pd.h.
5  (pi)      This is pi local  code from tool2/s/tool2.c.
6  (pi)      This is pi local  data from tool2/s/tool2.h.
7  (pi)      This is pi shared code from tool_pi.lib/s/pi_sub.c.
8  (pi)      This is pi shared data from tool_pi.ini/s/tool_pi.h.
```

As you can see, lines 3 and 4 are correct in this output too. This verifies the correctness of our previous fixes for lines 3 (*tool_pd.lib*) and 4 (*tool_pd.ini*).

It also means that we've completed the first step in our process for solving the portability problems in lines 2 and 6. Now we can move on to the next step of replacing the current pi *tool2* node with a new pid node.

Replace the tool2 pi node with a new pid node

Before we create the new pid node, I want to explain to you why we need it. The short explanation is that we need a pid node because it's the only kind of node that can properly store both pi and pd information. But you probably already knew that. The deep explanation is quite a bit longer, because it requires a good understanding of the two remaining problems that we have yet to solve: lines 1 and 5, and 2 and 6.

The main problem with lines 1 and 2 is that they're local *pd* code and data lines that are being stored in source files shared by different platforms. Lines 1 and 2 should really be different for each of the *tbc.plt* and *tb2.plt* versions of the *tool2* program, but they aren't (yet). Instead, you can see that they're identical in each of the last two outputs of the *tool2* program.

The problem with lines 5 and 6 is almost the opposite of the previous problem. Lines 5 and 6 are local *pi* code and data lines that are being stored in *pd* source files (*tool2.c* and *tool2.h*). To solve this problem, we'll have to move lines 5 and 6 out of the pd source files and into pi source files. If we don't move them into pi files, we'll end up with two copies of each line when we make two copies of the pd files *tool2.c* and *tool2.h* in the platform source directories. We should have only one copy of pi source lines. (We have to make two copies of the pd source files so that we can customize them for our two different platforms.)

Line 0 under the *tb2.plt* platform is also technically a problem since it's a pd code line in the same way that line 1 is a pd code line. But since line 0 is in the same source file as line 1, line 0 isn't a different *type* of problem. Rather, it can be viewed as a second *instance* of the same type of local pd code problem as exemplified by line 1.

Why is a pid node is the best solution? Our goal is to separate the pi and pd information in *tool2.c*, which contains lines 1 and 5, and in *tool2.h*, which contains lines 2 and 6. But all four lines contain *local* information, so it would be nice if we could store all four lines of information somewhere within the *tool2* directory node. Our previous solutions for pi information—which involve separate libraries, initialization nodes, and file sharing—seem inappropriate in this case.

A pid node is a good solution for our current situation because it's capable of storing both pi and pd information within the same node. Let's apply this solution to the problems of lines 2 and 6 (which are pd and pi local data lines, respectively.)

We'll create a new pid node so that we can separate the local *pd* data line (line 2 in *tool2.h*) from the local *pi* data line (line 6 in the same file). We'll end up with two local include files—one that holds pd data and one that holds pi data.

There are two ways to create a pid node to replace the existing *tool2* subtree: manually or automatically. Either way, we'll have to issue several commands. I've chosen to use the automatic method so that I can continue to demonstrate code management techniques that will work for bigger software systems than the ones used in the examples. (I also make fewer errors when I let the tools do most of the work.)

We face a small problem when we're working on an MS-DOS system. The problem is that the normal MS-DOS *ren* command isn't capable of renaming directories. To get around this limitation, we'll convert the existing pi *tool2* node to a pid node according to the following steps:

1. Create a temporary pid node named *temper* to temporarily store the source files that are currently stored in the existing *tool2* node.

2. Copy the source files in the original *tool2* node into the temporary pid node.

3. Delete the existing pi *tool2* node, because we don't need it any more.

4. Create a new pid *tool2* node in place of the old pi *tool2* node.

5. Move the source files from the temporary pid node into the new pid *tool2* node.

6. Delete the temporary pid node.

Let's begin. First, create a temporary pid node.

```
K:\MAIN\TOOL2\TB2.PLT> cd ..\..
K:\MAIN> makenode temper pid tbc.plt tb2.plt          make the new node
```

Here's what the temporary node looks like. The new pid *tool2* node that we create will have exactly the same structure.

```
K:\MAIN> tree /a temper
K:TEMPER
+---S                                a place for pi source files
|   \---RCS
+---TBC.PLT
|   \---S                            a place for pd tbc.plt source files
|       \---RCS
\---TB2.PLT
    \---S                            a place for pd tb2.plt source files
        \---RCS
```

Now, copy the source files out of the old pi *tool2* node into the new pid temporary node. Copy out the RCS files too.

```
K:\MAIN> copy tool2\s\*.* temper\tbc.plt\s            two files copied
K:\MAIN> copy tool2\s\*.* temper\tb2.plt\s
K:\MAIN> copy tool2\s\rcs\*.* temper\tbc.plt\s\rcs
K:\MAIN> copy tool2\s\rcs\*.* temper\tb2.plt\s\rcs
```

Delete the original pi *tool2* node now, since we've copied all the good files out of it into the temporary node.

```
K:\MAIN> rm -rf tool2                                 delete old tree
```

Now we have to create a new pid node and copy all the good files back from the temporary node into the newly created pid node. (The new pid node has exactly the same tree structure as the temporary pid node shown above.) On UNIX, you can just rename the temporary node (*mv temper tool2*).

```
K:\MAIN> makenode tool2 pid tbc.plt tb2.plt          create new tree
K:\MAIN> xcopy temper tool2 /s/e                     recover the files
K:\MAIN> rm -rf temper                               delete the temp tree
```

Split tool2.h into separate pi and pd files

Now that we've created a pid node, we're ready to start splitting the old *tool2.h* file into three separate pi and pd files (one copy of *tool2_pi.h* and two copies of *tool2_pd.h*).

Note that the file permissions on *tool2.c* and *tool2.h* are writeable. Why? Is it because the files are locked and modified, or is it because MS-DOS reset the read-only permissions when we copied the files between nodes?

```
K:\MAIN> cd tool2\tbc.plt\s
K:\MAIN\TOOL2\TBC.PLT\S> ls -l              all files have write permission
K:\MAIN\TOOL2\TBC.PLT\S> rcsdo ls_changed   find out if they've been changed
tool2.c has changed.                        we changed some include file names
```

These are the changes that we've made to program *tbc.plt\tool2.c* so far:

```
K:\MAIN\TOOL2\TBC.PLT\S> rcsdiff tool2.c
< #include "tools.h"                   /* pi and pd data, all tools */
---
> #include "tool_pi.h"                 /* pi data, all tools */
> #include "tool_pd.h"                 /* pd data, all tools */
```

Split the original *tool2.h* file into two files called *tool2_pi.h* and *tool2_pd.h*.

```
K:\MAIN\TOOL2\TBC.PLT\S> copy tool2.h ..\..\s\tool2_pi.h          create tool_pi.h
K:\MAIN\TOOL2\TBC.PLT\S> copy rcs\tool2.h ..\..\s\rcs\tool2_pi.h
K:\MAIN\TOOL2\TBC.PLT\S> ren tool2.h tool2_pd.h                   create tool_pd.h
K:\MAIN\TOOL2\TBC.PLT\S> ren rcs\tool2.h tool2_pd.h
```

We can now update the source files for the *tbc.plt* platform, and then rebuild the *tool2* program to check our progress.

First, let's update the contents of the new *tool_pd.h* file for the *tbc.plt* platform. We have to modify each of the two include files to be purely pi or pd by deleting unwanted information. Update the pathname strings, too.

```
K:\MAIN\TOOL2\TBC.PLT\S> co -l -f tool2_pd.h      check out for modification
K:\MAIN\TOOL2\TBC.PLT\S> emacs tool2_pd.h         strip pi info, update path
#define T2_PD_DATA "(tbc.plt) This is pd local data from tool2/tbc.plt/s/tool2_pd.h."
```

Update the *tool2_pi.h* file.

```
K:\MAIN\TOOL2\TBC.PLT\S> cd ..\..\s               go to tool2/s dir
K:\MAIN\TOOL2\S> co -l -f tool2_pi.h              check out for modification
K:\MAIN\TOOL2\S> emacs tool2_pi.h                 strip pd info, update path
#define T2_PI_DATA "(pi) This is pi local data from tool2/s/tool2_pi.h."
```

Compose an RCS log message and check the changes into RCS while they're fresh in our mind.

```
K:\MAIN\TOOL2\S> echo Ported tool2_pi.h to the new pid node.>  msg
K:\MAIN\TOOL2\S> rcsdo ci_u_locked msg -log default
K:\MAIN\TOOL2\S> del msg
```

This completes the splitting of *tool2.h* into two separate pi and pd parts. We'll check the *tool2_pd.h* file in later, once we've finished modifying *tool2.c* (which is in the same directory).

Modify tool2.c to use the two new include files

Let's update the *tool2.c* program to use the two new include files that we've just created (*tool2_pi.h* and *tool2_pd.h*). While we're editing *tool2.c*, we'll also update the pathnames in lines 1 and 5 to reflect the new location of the *tool2.c* file.

```
K:\MAIN\TOOL2\S> cd ..\tbc.plt\s
K:\MAIN\TOOL2\TBC.PLT\S> emacs tool2.c                update include file names for tool2.h
K:\MAIN\TOOL2\TBC.PLT\S> rcsdiff tool2.c              here's what I changed
3,4c3,6
< #include "tool2.h"                      /* pi and pd data, tool2 */
< #include "tools.h"                      /* pi and pd data, all tools */
---
> #include "tool2_pi.h"                   /* pi local data */
> #include "tool2_pd.h"                   /* pd local data */
> #include "tool_pi.h"                    /* pi data, all tools */
> #include "tool_pd.h"                    /* pd data, all tools */
8c10
<     printf("1  (tbc.plt) This is pd local  code from tool2/s/tool2.c.\n");
---
>     printf("1  (tbc.plt) This is pd local  code from tool2/tbc.plt/s/tool2.c.\n");
12c14
<     printf("5  (pi)   . This is pi local  code from tool2/s/tool2.c.\n");
---
>     printf("5  (pi)     This is pi local  code from tool2/tbc.plt/s/tool2.c.\n");
```

Can you see that we exchanged one problem for another by changing lines 1 and 5? We fixed line 1 because we moved the pd source file *tool2.c* into a pd source directory. But we broke line 5 because we moved a pi source line into a pd source directory. (We'll fix line 5 later by making it into a pi subroutine.)

Finally, check the *tool2.c* and *tool2_pd.h* changes into RCS while they're fresh in our minds.

```
K:\MAIN\TOOL2\TBC.PLT\S> echo Ported tool2.c tool2_pd.h to tbc.plt in a pid node.> msg
K:\MAIN\TOOL2\TBC.PLT\S> rcsdo ci_u_locked msg -log default
K:\MAIN\TOOL2\TBC.PLT\S> del msg
```

This completes the port of the *tool2_pd.h* file for the *tbc.plt* platform.

Update and rebuild tool2 on tbc.plt

Now we can rebuild *tool2* to get a visual check on our progress in fixing the problems in line 2 and 6. I expect them to be solved because we split the old *tool2.h* include file into separate pi and pd parts.

To rebuild *tool2*, generate makefiles and customize the *imports.imp* file in the normal ways. We'll have to generate the makefiles from scratch, since we destroyed our old makefiles when we replaced the old pi *tool2* node with the new pid node. On UNIX, remember you have to prepend a *-l* to each library named in the **lb3** macro.

```
K:\MAIN\TOOL2\TBC.PLT\S> cd ..
K:\MAIN\TOOL2\TBC.PLT> getmakes tbc.plt pid program tool2
K:\MAIN\TOOL2\TBC.PLT> emacs imports.imp
lb3=tool_pi tool_pd                        we need these libraries
   (-ltool_pi -ltool_pd on unix)


imports:
        $(CMI) -nl s/tool2_pd.h            imported from local s
        $(CMI) -nl ../s/tool2_pi.h         imported from local ..\s
        $(CMI) tool_pi.h                   imported from CMHTREE\share
        $(CMI) -p $(EP) tool_pd.h          imported from CMHTREE\share\tbc.plt


imports.rev:
        $(RM) tool2_pi.h
        $(RM) tool2_pd.h
        $(RM) tool_pi.h
        $(RM) tool_pd.h
```

Now for the big test, let's see if we fixed lines 2 and 6 by splitting the old *tool2.h* file into two separate parts. Recompile the program and test it.

```
K:\MAIN\TOOL2\TBC.PLT> make all
K:\MAIN\TOOL2\TBC.PLT> tool2
0  This is tool2 compiled on platform (tbc.plt).
1  (tbc.plt) This is pd local  code from tool2/tbc.plt/s/tool2.c.
2  (tbc.plt) This is pd local  data from tool2/tbc.plt/s/tool2_pd.h.
3  (tbc.plt) This is pd shared code from tool_pd.lib/tbc.plt/s/pd_sub.c.
4  (tbc.plt) This is pd shared data from tool_pd.ini/tbc.plt/s/tool_pd.h.
5  (pi)      This is pi local  code from tool2/tbc.plt/s/tool2.c.
6  (pi)      This is pi local  data from tool2/s/tool2_pi.h.
7  (pi)      This is pi shared code from tool_pi.lib/s/pi_sub.c.
8  (pi)      This is pi shared data from tool_pi.ini/s/tool_pi.h.
```

As expected, lines 2 and 6 in the *tool2* program on the *tbc.plt* platform are now correct.

Update and rebuild tool2 on tb2.plt

Let's finish up this part of the example by verifying that lines 2 and 6 are also correct in the *tb2.plt* version of the *tool2* program.

To do this we'll have to update the pd source files in the *tb2.plt\s* directory, regenerate the makefiles, and customize the *imports.imp* files. Since we just went through this process in detail (in steps 3, 4, and 5), I won't bother to explain each step in detail a second time.

Update the source files in the *tb2.plt\s* directory. First, do the *tb2.plt\s\tool_pd.h* include file.

```
K:\MAIN\TOOL2\TBC.PLT> cd ..\tb2.plt\s          go there
K:\MAIN\TOOL2\TB2.PLT\S> ren tool2.h tool2_pd.h          create tool_pd.h
K:\MAIN\TOOL2\TB2.PLT\S> ren rcs\tool2.h tool2_pd.h   and its rcs file
K:\MAIN\TOOL2\TB2.PLT\S> co -l -f tool2_pd.h          check out to modify
K:\MAIN\TOOL2\TB2.PLT\S> emacs tool2_pd.h          strip pi info, update path
#define T2_PD_DATA "(tb2.plt) This is pd local data from tool2/tb2.plt/s/tool2_pd.h."
```

Then do the *tb2.plt\s\tool2.c* program file.

```
K:\MAIN\TOOL2\TB2.PLT\S> emacs tool2.c          update include file names for tool2.h
K:\MAIN\TOOL2\TB2.PLT\S> rcsdiff tool2.c          here's what I changed
3,4c3,6
< #include "tool2.h"                /* pi and pd data, tool2 */
< #include "tools.h"                /* pi and pd data, all tools */
---
> #include "tool2_pi.h"             /* pi data, tool2 */
> #include "tool2_pd.h"             /* pd data, tool2 */
> #include "tool_pi.h"              /* pi data, all tools */
> #include "tool_pd.h"              /* pd data, all tools */
8c10
<     printf("1 (tbc.plt) This is pd local code from tool2/s/tool2.c.\n");
---
>     printf("1 (tb2.plt) This is pd local code from tool2/tb2.plt/s/tool2.c.\n");
12c14
<     printf("5 (pi)     This is pi local code from tool2/s/tool2.c.\n");
---
>     printf("5 (pi)     This is pi local code from tool2/tb2.plt/s/tool2.c.\n");
```

Update the RCS files.

```
K:\MAIN\TOOL2\TB2.PLT\S> echo Ported tool2.c tool2_pd.h to tb2.plt in a pid node.> msg
K:\MAIN\TOOL2\TB2.PLT\S> rcsdo ci_u_locked msg -log default
K:\MAIN\TOOL2\TB2.PLT\S> del msg
```

Regenerate the makefiles and customize the *imports.imp* file for *tb2.plt* by copying in the *tbc.plt* version of the same file.

```
K:\MAIN\TOOL2\TB2.PLT\S> cd ..
K:\MAIN\TOOL2\TB2.PLT> getmakes tb2.plt pid program tool2
K:\MAIN\TOOL2\TB2.PLT> copy ..\tbc.plt\imports.imp
```

Now rebuild and test the *tb2.plt* version of *tool2*.

```
K:\MAIN\TOOL2\TB2.PLT> make all
K:\MAIN\TOOL2\TB2.PLT> tool2
0  This is tool2 compiled on platform (tb2.plt).
```

```
1  (tb2.plt)  This is pd local   code from tool2/tb2.plt/s/tool2.c.
2  (tb2.plt)  This is pd local   data from tool2/tb2.plt/s/tool2_pd.h.
3  (tb2.plt)  This is pd shared  code from tool_pd.lib/tb2.plt/s/pd_sub.c.
4  (tb2.plt)  This is pd shared  data from tool_pd.ini/tb2.plt/s/tool_pd.h.
5  (pi)       This is pi local   code from tool2/tb2.plt/s/tool2.c.
6  (pi)       This is pi local   data from tool2/s/tool2_pi.h.
7  (pi)       This is pi shared  code from tool_pi.lib/s/pi_sub.c.
8  (pi)       This is pi shared  data from tool_pi.ini/s/tool_pi.h.
```

As expected, lines 2 and 6 are correct because we successfully separated the old *tool2.h* file into two distinct pi and pd parts (*tool2_pd.h* for line 2, and *tool2_pi.h* for line 6.)

Lines 2, 3, 4, 6, 7, and 8 are now correct. Only the inconsistencies between lines 0, 1, and 5 still need to be reconciled. I'll explain the inconsistencies in the next part of this example and then resolve them by moving line 5 into a separate pi subroutine.

Managing Local Pi and Pd Code with Pid Nodes

The one remaining puzzle in the output is line 5. Why are we storing pi code in a pd source directory? There is no clear answer to this question. It's a matter of personal taste. If you store *tool2.c* in the pd directory as I've done, you'll get a pi code line (line 5) stored in a pd directory. But if you store *tool2.c* in the pi directory to make line 5 correct, then line 1 will be wrong—it'll be a pd code line stored in a pi directory.

The proper technical solution is to make line 5 a local pi subroutine, and then store it in the local pi source directory of the pid *tool2* node. So that's what I'll do, because I want to show you a complete and proper technical solution for the purposes of this book.

But it's easy to see that the complete and proper technical solution—making subroutines out of single lines of code—is a very tedious solution. Who wants to strip every common line of code out of "identical" programs (such as *tool2.c*), just because they're stored in two different platform directories? (Not me, that's for sure.)

Instead, we'd be smarter to realize that making subroutines out of common local code lines can be more work than maintaining two copies of the shared code. The crossover point, of course, depends on the particular case.

For teaching purposes, I'm going to treat the entire file *tool2.c* as a pd program, and isolate and share line 5 as a pi subroutine, but I'd probably do it the other way with a real program. That is, I'd treat the entire file *tool2.c* as a pi program and make line 0 a pd subroutine because most programs have far more pi code than they do pd code.

So let's make a pi subroutine out of line 5, and then share the subroutine between the two platforms. Name the subroutine *t2_sub.c* and store it in the pi source directory. The contents of the subroutine are shown below.

```
K:\MAIN\TOOL2\TB2.PLT> cd s
K:\MAIN\TOOL2\TB2.PLT\S> co -l -f tool2.c          check out with lock, for modifications
K:\MAIN\TOOL2\TB2.PLT\S> emacs tool2.c             put line 5 in ..\..\s\t2_sub.c
K:\MAIN\TOOL2\TB2.PLT\S> rcsdiff tool2.c           and put it in t2_sub.c
14c14
<    printf("5 (pi)    This is pi local  code from tool2/tbc.plt/s/tool2.c.\n");
---
>    t2_sub();                         /* call pi local shared code */
```

Here's the new subroutine *t2_sub.c*:

```
K:\MAIN\TOOL2\TB2.PLT\S> cd ..\..\s          go to pi directory
K:\MAIN\TOOL2\S> type t2_sub.c               show the new subroutine
/* $rcs_id$ */
#include <stdio.h>
void t2_sub ()
{
    printf("5 (pi)    This is pi local  code from tool2/s/t2_sub.c.\n");
}
```

Check in the *tbc.plt\s\tool2.c* code changes while they're fresh in your mind. The *t2_sub.c* subroutine file should be moved to the pi source directory (*..\..\s*) before you check in the *tool2.c* changes with *rcsdo ci_u_locked*.

```
K:\MAIN\TOOL2\S> cd ..\tb2.plt\si
K:\MAIN\TOOL2\TB2.PLT\S> echo Moved line 5 into a local pi subroutine.> msg
K:\MAIN\TOOL2\TB2.PLT\S> rcsdo ci_u_locked msg -log default
K:\MAIN\TOOL2\TB2.PLT\S> del msg
```

We're going to check the new *t2_sub.c* subroutine into RCS now. I'm going to use a new *rcsdo* option that you haven't seen before (*rcsdo dl_unchanged*). Here's why.

We want to check *t2_sub.c* into RCS using *rcsdo ci_u_initial msg -log default* so that we can create a new RCS file for it and record a standard log message, as usual. But since the pi directory already contains a checked-in file (*tool2_pi.h*), *ci_u_initial* will get confused. This is because the *ci_u_initial* option always tries to check in *all* files in the source directory, regardless of whether any of them already have RCS files. (In such cases, *rcsdo* usually aborts the check-ins of files that already have RCS files, but blithely records the names of the aborted files in the log message anyway.)

To get around this small problem, I'm going to use the *rcsdo dl_unchanged* option to delete all the unchanged files from the directory. This will leave only new files and changed files in the directory.

To treat changed files, first identify them with with *rcsdo ls_changed*, and then check them in—with deletion—by using *rcsdo ci_d_locked*. An equally valid technique would be to use the sequence *rcsdo ci_u_locked* to check them in, and *rcsdo dl_unchanged* to delete them immediately afterward. Either command sequence would leave only new files in the source directory, which is what we need for the *ci_u_initial* option.

We happen to know that there won't be any changed files in this case, however, because we've only got two files in the directory (*t2_sub.c* and *tool2_pi.h*).

Since there will only be new files in the source directory, we can check them in with *rcsdo ci_u_initial*. After that, we'll restore all the files with *rcsdo co_u_f* so that we have a full set of source files once again.

Delete all files that are unchanged since their last check-in.

```
K:\MAIN\TOOL2\TB2.PLT\S> cd ..\..\s
K:\MAIN\TOOL2\S> ls                          list them
  rcs         t2_sub.c         tool2_pi.h
K:\MAIN\TOOL2\S> rcsdo dl_unchanged          dl_unchanged
K:\MAIN\TOOL2\S> ls                          list again
  rcs         t2_sub.c
```

We'll skip the *rcsdo ls_changed* test, since we know that *t2_sub.c* is the only remaining file and that it's new.

Check in the new files with *rcsdo ci_u_initial*, and then use *rcsdo co_u_f* to restore a full set of working files.

```
K:\MAIN\TOOL2\S> echo Created a pi subroutine from line 5 of tool2.c.> msg
K:\MAIN\TOOL2\S> rcsdo ci_u_initial msg -log default
K:\MAIN\TOOL2\S> del msg
K:\MAIN\TOOL2\S> rcsdo co_u_f
```

Now both the modified *tool2.c* program (for *tb2.plt*) and the new pi subroutine *t2_sub.c* have been checked in, so we're ready to rebuild *tool2* for *tb2.plt* to check our progress.

Update the dependencies for the *tool2* program on the *tbc.plt* platform, and then rebuild and test *tool2*. All lines in the output should be correct this time.

```
K:\MAIN\TOOL2\S> cd ..\tb2.plt             go there
K:\MAIN\TOOL2\TB2.PLT> gendep pid          update dependencies
K:\MAIN\TOOL2\TB2.PLT> make all            rebuild it
K:\MAIN\TOOL2\TB2.PLT> tool2               and test it
0   This is tool2 compiled on platform (tb2.plt).
1   (tb2.plt) This is pd local  code from tool2/tb2.plt/s/tool2.c.
2   (tb2.plt) This is pd local  data from tool2/tb2.plt/s/tool2_pd.h.
3   (tb2.plt) This is pd shared code from tool_pd.lib/tb2.plt/s/pd_sub.c.
4   (tb2.plt) This is pd shared data from tool_pd.ini/tb2.plt/s/tool_pd.h.
5   (pi)      This is pi local  code from tool2/s/t2_sub.c.
6   (pi)      This is pi local  data from tool2/s/tool2_pi.h.
7   (pi)      This is pi shared code from tool_pi.lib/s/pi_sub.c.
8   (pi)      This is pi shared data from tool_pi.ini/s/tool_pi.h.
```

Yes, everything is correct. Each element of code is in its proper place.

- Pd code and pd data are stored in pd source directories.

- Pi code and pi data are stored in pi source directories.

- Local code and data are stored inside the *tool2* tree.

- Locally shared (between platforms) pi code files are stored inside the *tool2* tree and are accessed as local pi subroutines.

- Locally shared (between platforms) data is stored locally and is accessed as locally imported include files.

- Globally shared (between nodes) code and data are stored outside the *tool2* tree.

- Globally shared (between nodes) code files are stored and accessed as shared subroutine libraries.

- Globally shared (between nodes) data is stored and accessed in the form of include files.

Now you've seen the first high point of the tour—a complete example of how to manage the code for a multi-platform program.

But right now we've got to finish the job at hand. We've ported *tool2* to the *tb2.plt* platform, but we still have to finish the port of *tool2* to the *tbc.plt* platform. Specifically, we have to update the pd source files and the makefiles in the *tool2\tbc.plt* subtree.

Let's begin by calling the new pi subroutine *t2_sub.c* in place of line 5.

```
K:\MAIN\TOOL2\TB2.PLT> cd ..\tbc.plt\s
K:\MAIN\TOOL2\TBC.PLT\S> co -l -f tool2.c
K:\MAIN\TOOL2\TBC.PLT\S> emacs tool2.c                 update tool2.c
K:\MAIN\TOOL2\TBC.PLT\S> rcsdiff tool2.c               here are my changes
12c14
<      printf("5  (pi)      This is pi local  code from tool2/s/tool2.c.\n");
---
>      t2_sub ();                        /* call pi local shared code */
```

Update the RCS files while the changes are fresh in your mind.

```
K:\MAIN\TOOL2\TBC.PLT\S> echo Called t2_sub instead of line 5.> msg
K:\MAIN\TOOL2\TBC.PLT\S> rcsdo ci_u_locked msg -log default
K:\MAIN\TOOL2\TBC.PLT\S> del msg
```

Regenerate the makefiles.

```
K:\MAIN\TOOL2\TBC.PLT\S> cd ..
K:\MAIN\TOOL2\TBC.PLT> getmakes tbc.plt pid program tool2
K:\MAIN\TOOL2\TBC.PLT> copy ..\tb2.plt\imports.imp          save those keystrokes!
```

Now rebuild and test the *tb2.plt* version of *tool2*.

```
K:\MAIN\TOOL2\TBC.PLT> make all
K:\MAIN\TOOL2\TBC.PLT> tool2
0  This is tool2 compiled on platform (tbc.plt).
1  (tbc.plt) This is pd local  code from tool2/tbc.plt/s/tool2.c.
2  (tbc.plt) This is pd local  data from tool2/tbc.plt/s/tool2_pd.h.
3  (tbc.plt) This is pd shared code from tool_pd.lib/tbc.plt/s/pd_sub.c.
```

```
4  (tbc.plt) This is pd shared data from tool_pd.ini/tbc.plt/s/tool_pd.h.
5  (pi)      This is pi local  code from tool2/s/t2_sub.c.
6  (pi)      This is pi local  data from tool2/s/tool2_pi.h.
7  (pi)      This is pi shared code from tool_pi.lib/s/pi_sub.c.
8  (pi)      This is pi shared data from tool_pi.ini/s/tool_pi.h.
```

As you can see, the output for the *tool2* program on *tbc.plt* is also correct. This completes all of our work on the *tool2* program for Example 4.

We only have to port *tool3*, clean up the source directories, and assign a new RCS symbolic name to the source files, and then we'll be completely done this example.

Porting tool3

Normally, to port *tool3* to the two platforms, we should go through the same porting process that we did for *tool2*. (The process would be the same because *tool3* is supposed to be a clone of *tool2*.) But you've already been through that process once, so there's no point in repeating it.

So instead of upgrading *tool3* in small steps, let's just replace the entire *tool3* node (which is a pi node, by the way) with a straight clone of the new *tool2* tree (which is a pid node). Then we can rename and edit a few files to make the appropriate name changes, producing the same results and saving a lot of time.

(If you want to give yourself practice by upgrading *tool3* with the steps that we used to upgrade *tool2*, now would be a good time to start. You can rejoin us at the point where we start cleaning up the directories with tree walker scripts.)

Let's begin. Delete the old *tool3* node, create a new *tool3* directory, and use the DOS *xcopy* command to clone the entire *tool2* node. On UNIX, use *cp -Rp tool2 tool3* instead of the DOS *xcopy* sequence.

```
K:\MAIN\TOOL2\TBC.PLT> cd ..\..
K:\MAIN> rm -rf tool3                    delete the old node
K:\MAIN> mkdir tool3                     xcopy needs this
K:\MAIN> xcopy tool2 tool3 /s/e          35 files copied
```

Port the source files in the pi source directory by renaming them and by changing all the 2's to 3's inside of them.

```
K:\MAIN> cd tool3\s
K:\MAIN\TOOL3\S> ren t2_sub.c t3_sub.c           rename files from 2's to 3's
K:\MAIN\TOOL3\S> ren rcs\t2_sub.c t3_sub.c
K:\MAIN\TOOL3\S> ren tool2_pi.h tool3_pi.h
K:\MAIN\TOOL3\S> ren rcs\tool2_pi.h tool3_pi.h

K:\MAIN\TOOL3\S> co -l -f t3_sub.c tool3_pi.h    check out with lock, for modification

K:\MAIN\TOOL3\S> emacs t3_sub.c                  change 2's to 3's
K:\MAIN\TOOL3\S> emacs tool3_pi.h                change 2's to 3's
```

Check the two modified pi source files back into RCS.

```
K:\MAIN\TOOL3\S> echo Ported copied tool2 pi source files to tool3.> msg
K:\MAIN\TOOL3\S> rcsdo ci_u_locked msg -log default
K:\MAIN\TOOL3\S> del msg
```

Port the pd source files in the *tbc.plt* platform source directory in the same way: rename them, check them out, edit them, and check them back in to RCS.

```
K:\MAIN\TOOL3\S> cd ..\tbc.plt\s
K:\MAIN\TOOL3\TBC.PLT\S> ren tool2.c tool3.c            rename
K:\MAIN\TOOL3\TBC.PLT\S> ren rcs\tool2.c tool3.c
K:\MAIN\TOOL3\TBC.PLT\S> ren tool2_pd.h tool3_pd.h
K:\MAIN\TOOL3\TBC.PLT\S> ren rcs\tool2_pd.h tool3_pd.h
K:\MAIN\TOOL3\TBC.PLT\S> co -l -f tool3.c tool3_pd.h    check out
K:\MAIN\TOOL3\TBC.PLT\S> emacs tool3.c                  change 2's to 3's
K:\MAIN\TOOL3\TBC.PLT\S> emacs tool3_pd.h               change 2's to 3's
```

Don't forget to call **t3_sub** in the modified *tool3.c*. Check the files in when you're done.

```
K:\MAIN\TOOL3\TBC.PLT\S> echo Ported copied tool2 files to tool3.> msg
K:\MAIN\TOOL3\TBC.PLT\S> rcsdo ci_u_locked msg -log default
K:\MAIN\TOOL3\TBC.PLT\S> del msg
```

Now port the source files in the *tb2.plt* platform source directory: rename, check out, edit, and check in.

```
K:\MAIN\TOOL3\TBC.PLT\S> cd ..\..\tb2.plt\s
K:\MAIN\TOOL3\TB2.PLT\S> ren tool2.c tool3.c            rename
K:\MAIN\TOOL3\TB2.PLT\S> ren rcs\tool2.c tool3.c
K:\MAIN\TOOL3\TB2.PLT\S> ren tool2_pd.h tool3_pd.h
K:\MAIN\TOOL3\TB2.PLT\S> ren rcs\tool2_pd.h tool3_pd.h
K:\MAIN\TOOL3\TB2.PLT\S> co -l -f tool3.c tool3_pd.h    check out
K:\MAIN\TOOL3\TB2.PLT\S> emacs tool3.c                  change 2's to 3's
K:\MAIN\TOOL3\TB2.PLT\S> emacs tool3_pd.h               change 2's to 3's
```

Don't forget to call **t3_sub** in the modified *tool3.c*. Check the files in when you're done.

```
K:\MAIN\TOOL3\TB2.PLT\S> echo Ported copied tool2 files to tool3.> msg
K:\MAIN\TOOL3\TB2.PLT\S> rcsdo ci_u_locked msg -log default
K:\MAIN\TOOL3\TB2.PLT\S> del msg
```

This completes the source code modifications for *tool3*.

Let's build *tool3* under the *tb2.plt* platform. Regenerate the makefile dependencies, change some 2's to 3's in the *imports.imp* file, and build and test the *tool3* program.

```
K:\MAIN\TOOL3\TB2.PLT\S> cd ..
K:\MAIN\TOOL3\TB2.PLT> make empty          delete old tool2 files
K:\MAIN\TOOL3\TB2.PLT> gendep pid          regenerate dependencies
K:\MAIN\TOOL3\TB2.PLT> emacs imports.imp   change some 2's to 3's

PROG=tool3
```

```
imports:
        $(CMI) -nl s/tool3_pd.h              imported from local s
        $(CMI) -nl ../s/tool3_pi.h           imported from local ..\s
        $(CMI) tool_pi.h                     imported from CMHTREE\share
        $(CMI) -p $(EP) tool_pd.h            imported from CMHTREE\share\tbc.plt


imports.rev:
        $(RM) tool3_pi.h
        $(RM) tool3_pd.h
        $(RM) tool_pi.h
        $(RM) tool_pd.h
```

Compile and run the finished program.

```
K:\MAIN\TOOL3\TB2.PLT> make all             build tool3 for tb2.plt
K:\MAIN\TOOL3\TB2.PLT> tool3                and test it
0  This is tool3 compiled on platform (tb2.plt).
1  (tb2.plt) This is pd local  code from tool3/tb2.plt/s/tool3.c.
2  (tb2.plt) This is pd local  data from tool3/tb2.plt/s/tool3_pd.h.
3  (tb2.plt) This is pd shared code from tool_pd.lib/tb2.plt/s/pd_sub.c.
4  (tb2.plt) This is pd shared data from tool_pd.ini/tb2.plt/s/tool_pd.h.
5  (pi)      This is pi local  code from tool3/s/t3_sub.c.
6  (pi)      This is pi local  data from tool3/s/tool3_pi.h.
7  (pi)      This is pi shared code from tool_pi.lib/s/pi_sub.c.
8  (pi)      This is pi shared data from tool_pi.ini/s/tool_pi.h.
```

As you can see, the output of the *tb2.plt* version of the *tool3* program is correct.

Now build the *tbc.plt* of the *tool3* program. Regenerate the makefile dependencies, update the *imports.imp* file by copying in the *tbc.plt* version, and then rebuild and test the *tbc.plt* version of the *tool3* program.

```
K:\MAIN\TOOL3\TB2.PLT> cd ..\tbc.plt
K:\MAIN\TOOL3\TBC.PLT> make empty            delete old tool2 files
K:\MAIN\TOOL3\TBC.PLT> gendep pid            regenerate dependencies
K:\MAIN\TOOL3\TBC.PLT> copy ..\tb2.plt\imports.imp    save typing


K:\MAIN\TOOL3\TBC.PLT> make all              build tool3 for tbc.plt
K:\MAIN\TOOL3\TBC.PLT> tool3
0  This is tool3 compiled on platform (tbc.plt).
1  (tbc.plt) This is pd local  code from tool3/tbc.plt/s/tool3.c.
2  (tbc.plt) This is pd local  data from tool3/tbc.plt/s/tool3_pd.h.
3  (tbc.plt) This is pd shared code from tool_pd.lib/tbc.plt/s/pd_sub.c.
4  (tbc.plt) This is pd shared data from tool_pd.ini/tbc.plt/s/tool_pd.h.
5  (pi)      This is pi local  code from tool3/s/t3_sub.c.
6  (pi)      This is pi local  data from tool3/s/tool3_pi.h.
7  (pi)      This is pi shared code from tool_pi.lib/s/pi_sub.c.
8  (pi)      This is pi shared data from tool_pi.ini/s/tool_pi.h.
```

The output of the *tbc.plt* version of the *tool3* program is correct too.

The tour is almost over. Run the *tool1* program once more.

```
K:\MAIN\TOOL3\TBC.PLT> tool1
0  This is tool1 compiled on platform (tbc.plt).
1  (tbc.plt) This is pd local  code from tool1/s/tool1.c.
2  (tbc.plt) This is pd local  data from tool1/s/tool1.h.
3  (tbc.plt) This is pd shared code from tool1/s/tool1.c.
4  (tbc.plt) This is pd shared data from tool1/s/tools.h.
5  (pi)      This is pi local  code from tool1/s/tool1.c.
6  (pi)      This is pi local  data from tool1/s/tool1.h.
7  (pi)      This is pi shared code from tool1/s/tool1.c.
8  (pi)      This is pi shared data from tool1/s/tools.h.
```

Compare the output of *tool1* with the outputs of *tool2* and *tool3*. From a code management viewpoint, these are very different programs, aren't they?

This is a good place for you to take a break and think about what you've learned on the tour so far, because we've come to end of an important set of ideas. Before continuing, make sure that you understand both the original code management problems and the solutions that we've used to solve them.

To help you to orient yourself in this task, check the complete picture of what our source trees will look like at the end of Example 5, in Chapter 8, *A Hands-on Tour: Part 3*.

Cleaning Up with Tree Walker Scripts

We will finish Example 4 by looking around with the tree walker tools and cleaning up any messy source trees.

The first thing we'll do is delete the old tree walker scripts because they don't know about all the new directories we've added to the source trees. (It's also because I don't know what's in them. I'll just delete them and regenerate them as I need them, since regenerating tree walker scripts is a quick and easy thing to do.)

```
K:\MAIN\TOOL3\TBC.PLT> cd ..\..
K:\MAIN> del *.bat                    delete obsolete tree walker scripts
```

Let's make up a tree walker script to walk the source directories and delete any *msg* files that we forgot to delete. I've used the **if** statement from the DOS batch file language on the command line, to show you how to avoid error messages when using DOS commands. The technique works only because the **if** statement is being called from within the *walksrc.bat* batch file.

```
K:\MAIN> twalker walksrc.bat s          walk all the s directories
K:\MAIN> walksrc if exist msg del msg   pass in an MS-DOS batch language statement
```

Updating the RCS Files

Let's walk the trees and check for any locked source files that we forgot to check into RCS. We shouldn't find too many of them because we've been following the new practice of checking in our files immediately after we modify them.

We can check for locked RCS files in two ways: manually, using the read-only permissions technique, or automatically, using the *rcsdo ls_changed* or *rcsdo ls_locked* options. Try it both ways to see which one you like the best.

You'll find that the read-only permission technique is much faster than the *ls_locked* method, but occasionally less truthful. The read-only permission technique—which expects files to be either read-only and unchanged, or writeable and changed—can sometimes be confused by files that are read-only but changed, or writeable but unchanged.

The read-only technique works well for me because my normal work habits tend not to generate the two troublesome cases. For example, I rarely manually set read-only permissions on source files, so read-only (but changed) files are rarely a problem for me.

Writeable (but unchanged) source files aren't a problem either, because I always check files out with locks before I modify them. And even if I do happen to find a writeable (but unchanged) file, it's trivial to check it with *rcsdo ls_changed* or *rcsdiff* to determine the true state of the file.

Let's search for modified files in our source tree by using both techniques. First, we'll list the file permissions, and then look around with *rcsdo ls_changed*. After we're done, we'll assign a new symbolic RCS name to all source files.

```
K:\MAIN> walksrc ls -l *.c *.h            look for read-only permissions
K:\MAIN> walksrc call rcsdo ls_changed    look for changed files

K:\MAIN> walksrc call rcsdo add_name ex_4  add a new symbolic name
K:\MAIN> walksrc call rcsdo ls_name ex_4   list files that were labeled
```

This completes Example 4. In this example, you learned how to create and use multiple platforms, and how to separate, store, and share the eight types of information that are commonly found in computer programs.

Finally, if you haven't done it already, look at the final source tree diagrams shown at the end of Example 5 in Chapter 8. They show where we will be after our examples, and exemplify a solid setup for code management.

4

Designing a Code Management System

Some readers of this book will be developing or upgrading their own code management systems. Others will use the system that is on the diskettes included with the book. But the diskettes contain just a set of tools—they don't organize source code and set policy. So both types of readers have to think about the reasons for their systems and how they want them to be used.

This chapter discusses the requirements and choices involved in developing a good code management system and begins the "theory" section of the book. If you want to understand the underlying design issues of code management systems, then this chapter is for you. But if you don't really care about the theoretical issues, and just want to get on with using the system described here, feel free to skip ahead to Chapter 5, *Directory Structures*.

If you're still with us, the current chapter has two parts. The first discusses the requirements of a code management system. The second talks about its design: alternative ways of meeting the requirements.

Desirable Features

First, let's state our requirements—all the things we'd love to have as part of a code management system. This section has three parts.

The first part discusses general system requirements such as usability, generality, portability, and so on. Some people call these requirements the "abilities."

The second part discusses some fundamental technical requirements that form the foundation of all code management systems. These include the need to work with large numbers of files, to effectively organize and group those files, and to manage the evolution of complete software releases.

The third part discusses the importance of supporting a variety of common human activities in software development environments. Specifically, it argues that software developers, testers, and maintainers each have different needs, and that good code management systems should support all sets of needs.

General Requirements

This section lists several general requirements that are desirable in code management systems. The first four requirements deal with the *present usability* of the system; it should be useful, usable, general, and complete.

The next three requirements deal with the *future usability* of the system; it should adapt well to change, growth, and the addition of new platforms.

Just before we start, it's worth pointing out that even though these requirements might seem to be obvious, designing a code management system to satisfy them is not so obvious. In fact, it's usually *more* difficult to design a system that satisfies certain general requirements than a system that satisfies a similar number of specific requirements.

General requirements usually demand broader and more flexible solutions, which are difficult to design. They can assume almost nothing, they have to work almost anywhere, and they must do almost everything. In contrast, almost anyone can design a system to satisfy a few specific requirements that don't conflict with each other.

I think the general requirements listed here are the most important ones—and the most difficult ones—to satisfy in the design of a code management system.

- **The code management system should support a team's daily activities**. For example, it should prevent people from overwriting someone else's code changes, help them stabilize their work environments, and help them smoothly develop and release software products.

- **The code management system should be usable**. This means that the system should be as user-friendly as possible, and that it shouldn't interfere with the normal work flow of the development team. Specifically, this means that the principles and use of the system should be well documented, and that the tools should have reasonable user interfaces.

- **The code management system should be general**. This is desirable because a code management system should support a wide variety of different projects within an organization. For example, it should support big and small projects, single and multiple platform projects, and executable, library, and script products. It should also have a good chance of supporting normal and hypertext databases, images, sound clips, and third party products too. Ideally, one general, broad-scope code management approach should be used as the standard for the entire organization.

- **The code management system should be complete**. This is because you want the code management system to support the whole project, not just part of it. It should support all the file types: source, include, binary, library, script, documentation, test suites, and make files. It should support all the platforms used within an organization. And it should support all the members of the software team: developers, testers, releasers, and maintainers.

- **The code management system should be flexible.** This requirement means that the code management system should be easy to customize to fit the future needs of particular organizations. That is, it shouldn't be so rigid that it blocks or discourages the use of existing, non-crucial conventions in the working environment.

- **The code management system should be scalable.** This requirement provides for the future growth of an organization's software products. It means that a code management system should have the capacity to support small projects that eventually grow large. It should have the capacity to manage single platform projects that become multi-platform projects. The code management system shouldn't break down halfway through a project just because the software products have increased in size and complexity.

- **The code management system should be easy to port.** This requirement provides for the future addition of new platforms to a software environment. A code management system shouldn't break down just because the industry moves to new computing platforms. Instead, it should be possible for an organization to move the code management system to new platforms as they become available. This means that the organization must either have the code management source code so they can port it themselves, or that they can easily have changes made by the original code management system development team.

  As one reviewer pointed out, there is a quote that says, "There's no such thing as portable code, only code that's been ported." This is an excellent thought to keep in mind, because code that's "portable" across several platforms (because it has already been ported to those platforms) might suddenly become "non-portable" on a new platform (because it won't port smoothly to that platform).

  Portability, then, is an attribute that has meaning only when it's accompanied by a list of platforms to which the code has been ported.

Basic Technical Requirements

This section describes three fundamental requirements that should be satified by any competent code management system: the ability to store large numbers of files, the ability to effectively organize, group, and share those files, and the ability to coordinate the construction and release of software products that are composed from those files.

Handling large numbers of files

The first requirement for any competent code management system is that it be able to competently store and manage large numbers of files. Furthermore, it should be able to handle the many different file types that are found on software projects (source files, include files, binary files, and so on).

Code management systems usually handle large numbers of files by storing them in different directories, according to their type. For example, binary files and source files are stored in different directories, and files for different platforms are stored in different directories. That way, files of different types (and for different platforms) won't interfere with each other.

A second reason for separating files of different types into different directories is to avoid filename collisions, which are quite common on large projects that have hundreds or thousands of files. Filename collisions are almost inevitable on multi-platform projects too, regardless of the project size, because the object files for the different platforms often have the same name.

A third reason that code management systems separate files into different directories is so that they can isolate multiple developers from each other. That way, changes being made by one developer won't interfere with work being done by other developers. They each get to work independently in their own private source trees.

Organizing and managing groups of files

The code management system should also be able to associate individual files with larger groups of files. For example, the code management system should be able to effectively associate include files with the products that use them. Furthermore, the code management system should make it easier for developers to create, inspect, and manage such associations.

This isn't as simple as it seems, especially on large projects that have thousands of files. For example, do you remember the "ansification" story that I told in the first chapter? There were tens of developers working on thousands of source files in that situation. And hundreds of files were being widely shared among many products. The associations between individual files and products were so complex that no one could figure them out any more.

And the association (or "group membership") problem is even more complex on multi-platform projects, since many platform-dependent files (both source and object files) have identical names.

The main point to understand here is that code management systems should offer some disciplined way of managing and tracking the associations that exist among files on large projects, because the alternative can be pretty messy. Recall the words of my friend: "The most noticeable effect that you see is a steady degradation in the quality of your include files . . . and you're powerless to prevent it."

Coordinating and managing software releases

The code management system should help to coordinate the construction and release of software products that involve many files.

One important feature to look for in code management systems is some kind of source code control facility. Source code control systems manage the evolution of software files by storing successive versions of the files in a safe place. (Efficient storage techniques are usually used to save disk space.) These systems allow you to "back up" to an earlier version of a file if the need arises (such as when a bug fix breaks something else that's even more important than the problem that was fixed).

A second feature that's useful is the ability to symbolically label all the files that are part of a particular release. For example, you might want to label all files in Release 1 with the tag "release_1_0." That way, if you ever want to regenerate the release at a later date, you can ask the code management system to regenerate all the files that were labelled "release_1_0."

A third useful feature is the ability to perform code management operations on large groups of files, or on entire subtrees of files. This can save you a lot of time if your release is made up of many files.

Support for Common Project Activities

The main purpose of all code management systems is to promote the orderly construction and release of software products. And since many different activities are involved in the production of software, many different activities must be supported by code management systems.

This section describes four of the most important activities that should be supported by good code management systems: development, maintenance, porting, and quality assurance.

Support for development activities

Code management systems should aid or automate as many common development tasks as possible. These include the common activities of compiling, sharing, linking, exporting, testing, and releasing software files. Furthermore, code management systems should log source code changes, file sharing relationships, and the names and versions of all files that are part of a formal software release. The list of what a good code management system should do to support development activities can be a surprisingly long one (this chapter, for example).

Support for maintenance activities

One of the main differences between maintenance and development activities is that maintenance activities are easier to perform in uniform working environments. By this I mean that maintenance activities are easier to accomplish in environments that have effective, uniform directory structures, well defined operating conventions, and good tool support.

This difference arises from the different types of work that are performed by developers and maintainers. For example, developers usually work on one project (or sometimes even one module) for long periods of time. This means that they become intimately familiar with everything about that part of the project, no matter how non-uniform that part is.

In contrast, software maintainers normally touch many software products. And instead of working for long periods of time on one module or product, they tend to work for short amounts of time on many different modules or products. That's why it's unreasonable to expect maintainers to learn the intimate quirks of each different product that they have to work on. It's also the reason why a maintainer's job is made easier if all products are organized in the same way, if all makefiles behave in the same way, and so on. Then maintainers can use the same set of mental models and procedural habits on all the products that they maintain.

Good support for maintenance activities is an important issue in code management systems, because the literature suggests that something like 60% of the total lifecycle cost of software is generated by maintenance activities. That's why code management systems should support the daily activities of software maintainers. For example, they should make it easy for maintainers to create and recompile clones of the main source tree. They should make it easy to identify products that produce or use shared files. They should make it easy to reorganize source trees. And they should make it easy to upgrade or install new features into the makefiles for all products in the code management system.

Support for code porting

For several good economic reasons, the need for code management systems to support multi-platform environments is becoming a more popular requirement in the software industry.

Code management systems can primarily support code porting activities by isolating platform-dependent code in separate files. Probably no other technique (other than disallowing platform-dependent code totally) is as useful for supporting code porting.

Isolating platform-dependent code in separate files is important for two reasons. First, it helps developers to estimate the amount of code that has to be ported to new platforms. (Any or all of the code might still have to be ported to a new platform, of course. This is because you don't know how much of your existing code will be affected by a new, unknown platform.) Second, isolation of platform-dependent code usually provides developers with convenient examples of previously ported code.

Isolated code is also easier to access than code that's embedded in other programs. At the very least, it means that you don't have to rip the "reusable" code out of the guts of some other program before you can reuse it.

Support for quality assurance activities

Code management systems should also support software quality assurance (SQA) activities. (Since the usefulness of quality assurance activities is generally accepted within the software community, it needs no justification here.)

One way of supporting SQA activities is to support the construction and maintenance of an "official" baseline version of the source code for all software products. Having an official baseline makes it possible for all developers to use the same official copy of the source files in their work.

Having an official or "main" source tree also helps to isolate SQA activities from ongoing development and maintenance activities. This is because good code management systems will allow all three teams (SQA, development, maintenance) to use the main source tree independently of the other teams. As a consequence, each of the three teams can proceed with their work at a pace that's convenient for them.

Related Software Engineering Procedures

Writing and building programs are only a couple of the many activities that a software organization has to perform. Practical software engineering also involves administrative and follow-up activities, such as change control, baseline testing, and software releases. While these are not the subject of this book, you'll probably want to know how they fit in with code management. Therefore, this section briefly describes some procedures that have been successfully used with the code management system described so far.

Although the procedures are completely independent of the code management system, and vice versa, it seems worthwhile to offer these tested solutions as a possible model for your own environment.

Change control procedures

Change control and *change management* are names that refer to the management of the *forces of change* that arise against software products. These forces come from many sources, and include requests for bug fixes, requests for new features, requests for marketing demonstrations, and so on.

The simple change control system described here has three conceptual parts: the developers, the change control board (CCB) members, and the change control system (CCS) itself. The example below explains the operation of the CCS by describing typical scenarios.

Suppose that someone discovers a defect in the software product. They would report the defect by completing an online change request (CR) that describes the problem. The CR would be sent to the change request administrator (cradmin) for processing. The administrator, after checking the CR for obvious formatting errors, would then enter the CR into the CCS database, where it would await review at the next CCB meeting. New CRs could also be posted to a newsgroup, so that developers could see them immediately, without waiting for the next CCB meeting.

At the weekly CCB meeting, knowledgeable developers and managers would gather to participate in the administration of all known change requests.

In phase one of the CCB meeting, all new CRs would be reviewed and discussed to determine an appropriate response to each one. New CRs could be rejected, accepted, or could be marked as "waiting," pending further information from the person who originally submitted them. If they're rejected, no futher work on them is required. And if they're accepted, they would be assigned a priority (low, normal, high, or critical).

In phase two of the CCB meeting, past progress on existing CRs is reviewed. That is, developers discuss how their work over the past week has affected the states of the CRs to which they were assigned.

In phase three of the CCB meeting, new assignments of developers to CRs are made. Developers may be asked to stop work on some CRs, to start work on other CRs, or to change their daily work priorities to spend more or less of their time working on CRs or other non-CR projects.

This cycle would be repeated each week.

Baseline testing

Baseline testing is another large topic in itself, much like change control. So the following discussion is only a summary of one possible baseline testing approach that is known to work with the code management system described in this book.

Three general types of testing are recommended by this book: developer testing, regular baseline testing, and full scale release testing. Each of the three types has a different purpose, quality, and cost.

The first type of testing is developer testing. This type should be performed by developers on any code that they change, before they check the code into the main RCS source tree. The purpose is to ensure that the new code works acceptably well on all supported platforms before being checked into the main RCS source tree. The quality of this testing should be high, if possible. This is because the developer who originally changes the code is probably the person that best knows how to evaluate the code. This type of testing is usually costly because it's detailed, it's not automated, and it can take a long time.

The second type of testing is regular baseline "monitoring" testing. The main purpose of this type of testing is to prove that the complete software product is still working, despite any new code check-ins. The quality of this type of checking is usually limited by economic factors, such as the time and cost of performing the tests. For example, if the products being tested can be conveniently and completely recompiled and fully tested overnight, then the costs of a comprehensive, high quality baseline test are not a problem. However, for large products, the costs of recompilations and baseline tests can be so high that even superficial baseline tests can be performed only once a week.

The third type of testing is full-scale release testing. This type of testing is required if the regular baseline test isn't comprehensive enough. The purpose of release testing is to ensure that the released software meets the expectations of everyone concerned: the developers, the management, and the customers. The quality of release testing should be appropriately high. And the costs of release testing should be at least as high as baseline testing. (Probably they should be higher, since good release tests will comprehensively test all parts of the software product.)

One possible way of organizing the three types of testing is as follows:

1. Developers should test their code changes on all platforms before checking the changes into the main RCS source tree.

2. The baseline test manager should check out the latest copies of all files in the main source tree, and build a set of baseline products from those files. Then automated baseline testing should be performed on the baseline product files.

    Developers should not check in new changes while the baseline test manager is checking out the latest copies of the source files. This is because synchronization differences between new developer check-ins and baseline manager check-outs might cause the baseline manager to get some, but not all, of a developers most recent check-ins. And if this happened, it would cause inconsistencies between source files in the baseline test manager's source tree.

3. The release test manager should check out the latest copies of all files in the main source tree, just as in baseline testing. The main difference is that the release test suite may be more comprehensive. Other smaller administrative differences also exist too, such as the need to record RCS version numbers for all files that appear in the release.

A major advantage of these simple testing procedures is that the testing team can perform their duties almost independently of the development team. The two teams only have to coordinate with each other while the test team is checking files out of the main source tree. And even for large systems, this usually takes only a few hours.

Release procedures

This section describes a simple release procedure that works well with the change control and baseline procedures described earlier. The main phases of this release procedure are planning, releasing, and performing administrative work.

In the first phase of the release process, the contents of the next release should be planned—well in advance of the release date. The list of the proposed contents should specify all the files and features that should be in the next release. This includes documentation files, software product files and features, and auxiliary files such as release notes, installation notes, and so on. The purpose of the release contents list is to help people plan their work so that they can complete their assigned tasks before the release date. (Release plans can be discussed and monitored during weekly CCB meetings.)

In the second phase of the release process, the software products should be released. Most of this procedure was discussed above. The release personnel check out the latest copies of the source files for release testing, and then test them. Then, if some products fail the release tests, it may be necessary to correct the defects before proceeding with the release. (We usually handled this type of problem by manually checking out the fixed files from the main source tree after the developers had made the necessary corrections. This was to avoid the cost of restarting the whole release testing procedure, which would involve a new plan, completely new check-outs, and other such costs.)

In the third phase of the release process, the RCS version numbers of all files in the release should be recorded for future administrative purposes. Documentation files, release notes, and installation notes should also be added to the collection of released files. This completes the release.

Key Issues in the Design

This section identifies and describes most of the policy decisions that you'll have to face in setting up your code management system. It also tries to characterize the possible consequences of making particular decisions on various policy issues. You might want to think of this section as a reference manual that enumerates possible code management policy decisions, but without recommending any particular decisions.

After reading this section, you should have a good understanding of the major decisions that must be made in the design of a code management system. This should help you customize a system to fit the needs of any reasonable working environment.

In what follows, policy decisions are divided into seemingly independent subgroups for presentation purposes, even though some policy decisions from one group may affect issues and decisions in other groups. Issues and decisions are presented in approximate order of most significant to least significant, most far-reaching to most local, and most difficult to change to least difficult to change. This order means that the issues and decisions in the first subgroups tend to be computing environment issues (such as platform and corporate issues), while issues in the later subgroups tend to be implementation issues (directory structure and makefile issues). The former tend to determine the latter.

Finally, the chapter concludes with several checklists that summarize the issues. Glance over the end of the chapter now if you want a quick overview of the issues that we'll be discussing.

Platform Issues

Since the characteristics of computing platforms are usually either difficult or impossible to change, platform issues usually impose the most fundamental constraints on code management systems. For example, all MS-DOS code management systems are constrained by the lack of support for symbolic links. Similar constraints exist for filename syntax, file formats, and native character sets on other platforms.

Multiple development platforms

The first platform issue to be decided is the number and identity of the development and target platforms that will be supported by the code management system. This decision will have a large effect on the complexity of the system, especially if the platforms are significantly different or if there are many software products to be maintained.

The key requirements that make multi-platform environments more complex are the needs to identify, separate, and maintain multiple platform-dependent files that have the same filenames. These requirements usually force the creation of many sibling platform directories within the project directory structure. They also force more complexity in the source files, makefiles, and development procedures that are used to construct and maintain the platform-dependent products and directories.

What are the limitations of each development platform?

The limitations of your development platforms are the next issues that should be considered. The characteristics of the development platform cannot usually be changed or easily bypassed without special efforts and tools.

Moreover, if you're considering a multi-platform environment, you should consider the interactions *between* the limitations of all your development platforms. This may require you to adopt a "least common denominator" approach to resolving conflicts between the limitations of different platforms. Or it may encourage you to write a software layer whose purpose is to separate the main application code from the vagaries of the supported platforms.

For instance, my makefiles use just the basic capabilities that almost every platform supports. Although it's tempting to use the advanced features in some tools such as GNU *make*, I haven't done so because I'll just have to revert to simpler solutions on the platforms where I can't use GNU *make*.

There are plenty of other examples of platform limitations. They include filename length restrictions, filename character restrictions, the number of simultaneous computational processes available, the amount of virtual memory available, the power of the shell script programming language, the presence or absence of symbolic links, and so on.

If you intend to develop software on a heterogeneous set of hardware platforms, it may be the case that the platforms can't reference the same set of source files across a common network connection. If this is the case, then a few of the solutions described in this book won't apply to your situation. That's because those few solutions assume the presence of a common network filesystem (such as NFS) between platforms.

Symbolic links versus file copy operations

If the platform has no links, then all sharing and releasing of files must be done by physical copy operations. If links are available, either copy operations or links can be used for sharing and releasing operations.

Using links instead of copy operations may save a significant amount of disk space on large projects or on projects with very limited disk space. It may also save a few seconds of file copying time in some circumstances, such as if the copy operations aren't under the control of a time-stamp comparison mechanism as that used in *make* tools.

However, because links are structural (and not procedural) solutions to the sharing problems, they may cause minor maintenance problems after directory reorganizations. Also, the linking mechanism may break down if links cannot be used where file copies can be used (such as across shared file systems on different platforms).

Newsgroups versus flat files for log messages

This issue affects how notices of code modifications are distributed to the development team. It's useful for the whole development team to be aware of the evolution of the product(s) that they work on. They can watch for changes in product behavior after major changes and can organize their work schedules to minimize attempts to work on the same sections of code.

If your development platform has newsgroups, then it's possible to post all code modification notices to a newsgroup so that all developers can read them. If no newsgroups are available, then a distribution solution that uses ASCII files must be used.

Electronic mailing lists can also be used to distribute such information, but they're poorer solutions for several reasons. First, developers have no control over when they look at the notices—the notices just show up in their mailboxes. And second, multiple developers may end up saving the notices if no central archive is available, thus duplicating storage.

Corporate Issues

Corporate policy decisions are the next issues to be considered after platform issues. Decisions made on these issues can have large scale, wide reaching effects on the design of your code management system.

Maintenance by replacement or maintenance by repair?

The choice of maintenance policy has a profound effect on the form of a CM system, so be sure to spend enough time on this issue to make a good decision. The bottom line is that maintenance by replacement is much more efficient and much less trouble for the development organization if the product line and the customers allow it.

Under a policy of maintenance by replacement, defects in released versions of the software are never fixed. Rather, defective versions of the software are "maintained" by replacing the defective release with a newer release. Thus software problems are resolved by fixing defects in the main source tree and releasing an updated version.

Maintenance by replacement works best for rapidly evolving software products whose successive releases are upwardly compatible with each other. Maintenance by replacement is the approach used for most personal computer software products. A defect found in release 2.0 might be detected and corrected in release 4.0. Then all customers running 2.0 would have to upgrade to release 4.0 if they wanted to avoid the defect. Under maintenance by replacement, the vendor would never put out a corrected version of release 2.0.

However, the problem with maintenance by replacement is that customers may not want to upgrade to new releases if their current product software is satisfactorily performing a critical function in their business. They may also want to avoid upgrades if such acts will force them to re-certify the reliability and quality of any in-house applications that are based on the vendor's software.

To avoid such unnecessary costs, customers might just want the vendor to fix the minor irritations that are present in the release that they're using. So if you want happy customers, forcing them along major upgrade paths using a maintenance by replacement policy is probably inappropriate.

In contrast, under a policy of maintenance by repair, defects in released software are corrected for that release, as well as for successive releases. Defects are resolved by fixing the defect in all (still supported) previous releases of the software, fixing the defect in the baseline release of the software, and then re-releasing all corrected releases of the software. This means that customers don't have to upgrade to a new (and possibly incompatible) release of the software in order to get a defect fixed in their current release.

Maintenance by repair is the approach used for some large mainframe software products. A defect found in release 2.0 would normally be fixed in release 2.0, even if the current release was 4.0. Then once corrected, release 2.0 would be re-released as a maintenance release (perhaps as release 2.0.1). Similarly, release 3.0 would be corrected and re-released (perhaps as release 3.0.1). Customers then have a choice of upgrading to a minor maintenance release (2.0.1) instead of to the latest release (4.0), as they see fit.

Maintenance by repair works best for large software products whose successive releases are not always upwardly compatible with each other because customers may be faced with massive upgrading costs for each new release. As a case in point, suppose customers write hundreds of thousands of lines of application code to work with release 2.0 of the software product. Then imagine that the software interfaces undergo a large reorganization and cleanup between releases 2.0 and 3.0. This means that customers will be faced with potentially huge costs to upgrade to the next release. Not only will they have to pay for the upgrade itself, but they'll have to pay to convert their application code to the new release.

A policy of maintenance by repair requires that at least some of the previous releases of the software be maintained, corrected, and re-released. Maintenance by repair also requires a more complex code management system than does maintenance by replacement.

In contrast, a policy of maintenance by replacement requires only that the next version of the software be maintained, corrected, and released. And because only one version of the software needs to be managed in a source tree, the surrounding code management system can be simpler than for maintenance by repair.

For these reasons, you'll probably save a lot of time and effort if you can adopt a corporate policy of maintenance by replacement.

Multiple developers

The decision to use multiple developers on a project is another decision that has a profound effect on the complexity of a code management system. Multiple developers force code management systems to provide mechanisms that isolate developers from each other, from the main source tree, and from the latest baseline versions of the products.

This is a list of some issues that must be considered in a multi-person development environment:

- Since multiple developers cannot all simultaneously compile code in the one and only directory that holds the source code, a main source tree must be created for everyone to use. Then developers can check out the files that they need from the main source tree into their own private workspace. When they're done modifying the checked-out code, they can check the changed files back into the main source tree.

- But this requires the code management system to provide bulk tree cloning support, since now each developer needs a private tree that's a mirror image of the main source tree.

- Developers on multi-person projects are far more likely to inadvertently destroy each other's source code changes than are single developers on single person projects. (Individuals working by themselves are less likely to forget their own code changes.) To protect against the mutual clobbering of each other's code changes, source files in the main source tree should be protected with some kind of version control system (such as RCS).

• Since tens or hundreds of files might have to be checked out from the main source tree in order to compile a product, the code management system should provide some kind of bulk check-in and check-out support for the version control system.

• Since it's reasonable to assume that developers will want to stay aware of the evolution of the main source tree, the code management system should provide a means of sharing source code change summaries between developers.

• Since many changes from multiple developers will be involved in the evolution of the software product, it makes sense to construct an official baseline version of the products on a regular (e.g., weekly) basis. This makes maintenance easier because everyone will be using the same baseline version for testing.

And so on. This is not a comprehensive list of all the effects of the multiple-developer policy decision. Instead, the list is only intended to show the large effect that multiple developers can have on a software project. (See Example 7 in Chapter 8, *A Hands-on Tour: Part 3*, for a description of a multiple-developer environment under the system used in this book.)

File sharing support

Many kinds of files are shared among programmers—tools, libraries of commonly-used code, etc. Many kinds of files are also shared among different software products—include files, source files, object files, code libraries, and even executable files.

All these shared files have to be maintained just like source code and kept in a usable state while someone is working on new versions. This can be a complicated thing to do, as you probably already know. Simply put, sharing should be managed with just as much rigor as all the other aspects of software development.

It's true that some sharing mechanisms already exist for include files (such as include statements and **-Idirectory** or **-Ldirectory** compiler command-line arguments). But if you want to share arbitrary source, binary, or library files among the products in a code management system, more sophisticated sharing mechanisms are required.

When designing a sharing mechanism, it's best to begin by identifying the types of sharing that you want to support. For example, the sharing mechanisms in this book support both public (unrestricted) and private (restricted) sharing of arbitrary files between software products within the code management system. Public sharing occurs when you make a file available for sharing by anyone who cares to use the file. Private sharing occurs when you only want to share a file among a limited group of people or products.

One important issue that must be considered in the design of a sharing mechanism is how to keep shared files up-to-date. If you copy a file to share it, how do you ensure that updates made to the original copy of the file are propagated to all the places where the file is shared?

Using symbolic links is one way to solve this problem. Recopying the file prior to each build operation is another way (but relatively expensive). Yet another possibility is to use a timestamp-comparison mechanism (such as the one found in *make* tools) to force an update copy operation only when appropriate.

A second issue to consider is how to manage the sharing relationships within a project. For example, how can you design sharing mechanisms to help you answer the questions "Where is this file used?" or "Where did this shared file come from?" or "What product owns this shared file?"

One solution to this problem is to log all sharing operations when they occur. Another solution is to constrain sharing operations so that only certain types of sharing are possible (such as child directories exporting sharable files into parent directories). Then you'd always know where a shared file came from.

A third issue to consider is how to ensure that particular *sets* of files are up-to-date with each other. For example, how will you ensure consistency between shared applications and their default startup files, or between new compilers and their associated runtime libraries?

Usually this type of consistency is ensured by a formal application installation process. But if the application is being used by other developers as it evolves, the best way of maintaining consistency is with a procedural solution that's automated within a makefile. Specifically, the makefile commands should update the shared startup file whenever the application is updated.

File releasing support

The term *releasing* means making files officially available for public use. In this book, releasing refers only to the process of placing files in a defined directory location that is intended to hold released files. It doesn't refer to the idea of putting the software through some sort of formal evaluation or software quality assurance process.

Probably the most significant issue in this area is how to support both alpha test releases and formal public releases. Alpha test releases are for people within the company or group releasing the software. Beta test releases are for small groups of people outside of the company releasing the software. Normal product releases are for general public use by all people, inside or outside of the vending company.

It is useful to have different physical locations in the filesystem for officially released and alpha test (or experimental) software products. That way, the two types of software won't get confused whenever simultaneous releases are being made.

You should provide a special place in the filesystem for alpha test software. Developers often like to make their new or updated software products available for use by the development team or others within the company before officially releasing them for public use.

Now that we've discussed the desirability of having separate alpha test and release directories, let's ask the next question: How can such a policy be carried out?

Candidate solutions should provide a way to keep shared alpha test files up-to-date with respect to changes made to the original copies of the alpha test files. (Recall that alpha test files are always exported from a source tree somewhere.) In addition, how will alpha test sharing and releasing mechanisms be affected by directory reorganizations? Will makefiles need updating if the alpha test directory is moved, or if the exporting source tree is moved, or if the exporting makefile is moved? Specialized tool support is probably the best solution for these problems.

Support for testing

Code management systems can support testing activities in at least three significant ways.

First, code management systems should allow both development and test teams to use the same source code in their daily tasks. The test team can then use the latest stable baseline copy of the code for their test cases and not some ancient version of the code that no one uses any more.

It's important to keep the "modification distance" as small as possible between the current development version and the testing version of the code. If the modification distance gets too large, new software features can be added to the development version, *on top of* defects that haven't yet been found by the testing team.

This situation can be costly, because it forces the development team to do more work when defects are reported by the testing team. Specifically, when the testing team discovers a defect, the development team has to do three things: undo the new features that depended on the defective code, correct the defect, and then redo the new features again. Code management systems that allow the same code to be used for both development and testing help to minimize this effect.

Second, from a convenience point of view, the code management system should make it easy for the testing team to obtain the latest source code from the main source tree *independently* of the development team. That way both development and testing teams can operate independently of each other, each at its own speed.

Third, the code management system should be able to produce a list of the RCS version numbers of all software components that comprise a release of the software product. The testing team needs the version numbers in order to report faults to the development team. The development team needs the version numbers in order to recreate the faulty configuration of the software.

Directory Structure Issues

Now that we've been through some of the platform and corporate issues, you can see that lots of decisions implicitly require the definition of a formal directory structure. For instance, building files for multiple platforms suggests the need for a subdirectory for each different platform. The need to store and share files efficiently also suggests the need for special sharing directories.

This section addresses such dirctory structure issues. In particular, it discusses how to implement the corporate policy issues that were discussed earlier.

Basic tree structures

First, an overall strategy is required for organizing files into a manageable directory structure. The structure should provide specific places for at least the following items or actions:

- **Source files for each software product.** And for large products, it may be desirable to split the source files into groups and store them in subdirectories under the main source directory for the product.

- **Include files.** There are two main strategies for storing include files.

  First, all include files can be stored in a single include directory. This strategy makes it easier to compile the (possibly many) products that use the include files because no file copying is required. Instead, the **-Idirectory** compiler argument can be used to reference the include files.

  However, this strategy makes it difficult to determine which product originally owned the include file. This is because file ownership is usually defined by a file's physical location rather than by information contained inside the file. So once you move a heavily used include file out of the subtree of the product where the file was originally created, it becomes difficult to tell which product still conceptually "owns" it. (Remember the large ansification project that my friend worked on? They had hundreds of orphaned include files that were each used by many products, but owned by none.)

  A second approach is to store include files with the source code of the product. This strategy makes it easy to identify the owner of an include file because the physical location is obvious. But it also requires some kind of sharing mechanism to make include files available for reuse by other products.

- **Version control files.** The directory structure should probably provide a distinct location for version control files for projects of all sizes. There are several ways of doing this, depending on the capabilities of the version control tool and the limitations of the development platforms. Here are three possible options, illustrated in Figure 4-1:

  - Put the version control files in the same directory that holds the original working files.

- Put the version control files into a separate subdirectory below the original working files.

- Put the version control files into a separate source tree located a long way away from the original working files, a remote repository of some kind.

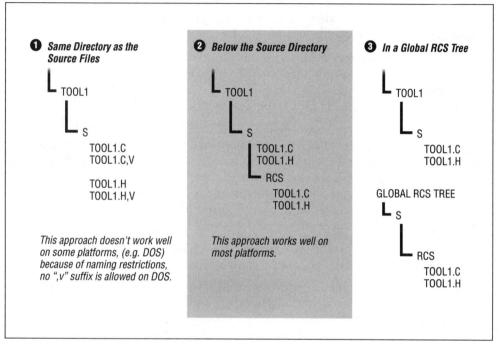

Figure 4-1. Options for storing version control files

The following discussion assumes that you're using RCS (Tichy's Revision Control System) as your source code control system. RCS is included on the disks that accompany this book. If you're not using RCS, you'll probably find that most of the following comments are general enough to apply to any similar source code control system.

The system in this book uses a subdirectory to store RCS files for single person development environments (such as those found on non-networked personal computers), and a remote repository for multi-person environments (such as those found on UNIX systems that support symbolic links).

I don't suggest storing them in the same directory as the originals because it will be very awkward; the RCS files clutter up the directory containing the source files. Furthermore, it can be difficult to work around RCS filenames when performing bulk file deletions with filename wildcard characters such as "*" and "?". On DOS systems, it's difficult to avoid name clashes when working with filenames that have a three-character suffix. It is difficult to think up an RCS naming convention that works for files with three character suffixes. For example, if the convention is to create an RCS filename by appending a "v" or ",v" to the suffix of the checked-in filename, what should the RCS names be for three files (in the same directory) named *foo.ccv, foo.cc,* and *foo.ccp?*

A separate RCS subdirectory is a better solution because it avoids all of these problems. In particular, you can use the same filenames (but in different directories) for both the original working file and the RCS file.

A separate RCS repository is also a reasonable solution. It permits many people to share the same version-controlled source files, facilitates easy backups (back up everything in the repository), and easy control of file and directory permissions (so people can't easily wipe out files in the repository).

In some cases, a separate RCS repository can completely hide its internal structure and location from users. This forces developers to treat the version control repository as a black box—they can't look inside it to figure out how it works. For all they know, the version-controlled files might be stored in one directory, several directories, or in directories all over the filesystem. It would make no difference to them anyway, because they could access stored files only through the interfaces provided by the revision control system.

- **Makefiles.** There are two main options: store makefiles in product subtrees, or store them all in one directory. Both options are used in practice.

There are clear advantages to storing makefiles within product subtrees. First, it's easy to see which makefiles belong to which products (and to which platforms). Second, makefiles that are stored within product nodes are easy to use. They're also easy to modify, should the dependency rules require updating due to source code changes. And third, if makefiles are stored inside product subtrees, it's easy to reorganize them along with the source files; when you relocate or delete a product subtree, you don't have to separately move, change, or delete the corresponding makefile. Instead, the makefiles conveniently travel with the source code.

There are also advantages to storing all makefiles in one big directory. It is easy to inspect the makefiles to determine which makefiles reference a particular source file, or which makefiles use or produce particular software products. You can just do a text search on all makefiles (perhaps with *fgrep*) to find the filenames that you're interested in.

- **Compilations.** The structure should provide an area where compilations can be performed for each product. There are three main options: compile within the original product subtree, compile in a separate compilation directory, or clone the original source tree and compile within the cloned copy of the subtree.

Compiling in the original product tree is most useful for small, single-person, single-platform projects. The source code can be configured for only one platform at a time, and the compilation directory can only hold object files for one platform at a time. The simultaneous existence of different source code and object files for more than one platform is impossible.

Compiling in a separate compilation directory is a more useful technique because it supports the simultaneous existence of object files for multiple platforms. Also, if the pi and pd source code for the product is configured to allow it, this method can support the simultaneous existence of source files for different platforms. This method is useful for single-person, multi-platform projects.

Compiling within a cloned source tree is the most flexible of the three methods, but it also requires the most support from the code management system. Tools are needed to manage the main source tree, to create private developer trees by cloning the structure of the main source tree, and to check modified files into and out of the version control files in the main source tree (or repository). This method will support multi-person, multi-platform development projects.

- **Object files.** There are two main strategies for storing object files. Either leave them in the compilation directory, or somehow direct them to a separate object file directory (perhaps with a compiler command-line argument).

  If the source directory is not the compilation directory, it's easiest to leave the object files in the compilation directory.

  If the source directory *is* the compilation directory, the object files may clutter up the directory to the point of being inconvenient. In that case, it may be better to redirect the object files to some other directory. A more serious problem is that if you keep the object files in the source directory, you can't maintain multiple platforms simultaneously—only one set of object files can exist at a time.

  The solutions described in this book always use separate compilation and source directories, and always leave the object files in the compilation directory.

- **Alpha test product files.** If it agrees with your corporate policy, the directory structure should provide a place to store alpha test files. Usually this directory is in a public place on the filesystem, where everyone can easily access it. In this book, the default alpha test directory is called *CMHTREE/at.*

- **Officially released product files.** The directory structure should provide a place to collect released files *before* they are put through the testing or quality assurance process. In this book, the default release directory is called *CMHTREE/release.*

- **Current baseline product files.** If it's your corporate policy to construct a baseline (or "latest official") version of the software, the directory structure should provide a location for storing these files.

  The main advantages of storing the binary baseline files is that everyone can use the same set of files as the latest official version of the product software. This means that all developers can use the same files when they investigate the behavior of the official products.

- **Current baseline source files.** It is sometimes useful to store a copy of the baseline source code beside the baseline products so the testing team can easily access it. This makes it much more convenient for the testing team to identify and inspect the versions of the source files that are in the baseline product they are currently testing. Since you have to check out a copy of all source files from the version control system anyway (in order to compile the baseline), why not leave them around until the next time the baseline is rebuilt?

  A second reason for keeping a copy of the current baseline files in a known place is to reduce your dependence on the source code control system. For example, developers at some sites aren't comfortable with trusting RCS to correctly and accurately reconstruct complex software products that customers have paid thousands of dollars for. So to increase their sense of security, developers at these sites "keep backups out their wazoos" (as one such developer quipped).

  The practice of storing a current copy of the baseline source code won't desynchronize the checked out source code and the baseline executables, because the executables were constructed from the checked out source. Nor will it desynchronize the baseline from the source in the main source tree. Only checking new source code changes into the main source tree can desynchronize the main source tree from the baseline.

  (As an aside, what if it was possible to have a system in which the baseline was always in perfect synchronization with the code in the main source tree? This would imply that a new baseline executable would be created immediately after any new code changes were checked in to the main source tree. I don't think such a system would have a large advantage over a compiling up a new baseline once or twice a week, especially if defective code was ever checked in. That's because the baseline would immediately crash, and prevent the test team from working in a stable baseline testing environment. Probably check-ins would have to be batched up and restricted to certain time periods so that the testing team could count on having a stable baseline to test for some pre-determined length of time.)

- **Old released product and source files.** If your corporate policy is one of maintenance-by-repair, the directory structure must provide places for old released product files, and for updated released versions of the old product files. This requires a "main source tree" (a release tree) for each old release of the software, since the files in each release tree will evolve independently of their counterparts in other release trees.

  There is a tradeoff to be made here between maintenance convenience and resource costs (time and disk space). For very small products, regenerating old released versions when needed is not expensive. However, for larger projects, the cost of checking out and compiling old releases can easily stretch into several hours or days. Therefore, it is usually more effective to keep checked-out and pre-compiled copies of the old releases around (especially if daily maintenance is being performed on the old releases).

From the list above, it's easy to see that even simple code management systems must satisfy many basic directory structure requirements. Complex code management systems must satisfy even more requirements, as shown in the following sections.

Multiple developers

Putting multiple developers to work simultaneously on a software product makes several major demands on a code management system. These demands, listed below, primarily have to do with isolating the developers from each other and from the main source tree.

1. **How do you isolate and stabilize developer trees?** When several developers are working on the same source code, they must have separate workspaces so their work activities don't conflict with each other.

   This means that the code management system must support three things. First, it must support the creation of separate developer workspaces. This is usually done by cloning the main source tree and checking out the latest baseline source code into the cloned tree. Second, the system should support bulk source code control system operations (check-ins, check-outs, and so on) to make the creation of cloned trees as convenient as possible. And third, it should allow developers to check code into the main source tree directly from their developer trees.

   Cloned source trees should *not* automatically pick up new changes that are made to the main source tree. The reason is that developers require a stable working environment when they're investigating defects in the software in their private developer trees. (However, it's convenient to have the *option* of automatically updating a private tree.)

2. **How do you control conflicting source modifications?** When multiple developers are working on the same source code, their modifications may conflict with one another. This means that the code management system must provide a source code control service (such as RCS).

   The source code control service prevents inadvertent destruction of uncoordinated changes by saving a copy of each change as it is checked into the version control system. This means that no changes will be lost, if the conventions of the source code control system are properly followed.

   However, saving a copy of each incoming change does *not* mean that sequential changes are compatible with each other. For example, two developers may change the same line of code, and check them into the version control system sequentially. Then only the last change would survive.

   To avoid this problem, source code control systems usually allow developers to lock a file when they check it out, thereby letting other developers know that the file is being changed. Then (if possible) the other developers can leave the file alone until it's unlocked, indicating that it's their turn to check out (and lock) the file so they can make their own modifications. The locking mechanism serializes source code changes to avoid simultaneous (parallel) modifications.

There are two popular coordination policies. Under the first policy, developers check out (and lock) files while modifications are being made. (Modification periods typically stretch anywhere from a few minutes to a few days, or even weeks in extreme cases.) Locks implement coordination between developers at the time of locking, and are released when files are checked back in. The advantage of this approach is that only two files are ever involved in the change process—the locked file and the modified file. The disadvantage of this approach is that locked files can be tied up for days, for the exclusive use of the developer who owns the lock.

Under the second policy, files are not locked while modifications are being made. Instead, any developer can check out a file and modify it at any time. However, in order to check the file in, the developer must take four actions. First, obtain a lock on the file; second, reconcile any differences between the file that was originally checked out and the newly locked file (it might have been changed since the developer's working copy was checked out); third, reconcile the changes with the newly locked file; and fourth, check the newly locked, modified, and reconciled file back in. The main advantage of this concurrent approach is that files aren't tied up for long periods of time. Instead, they're only tied up for as long as it takes to reconcile the changes between the locked file, the original working file, and the modifications that were made to the working file. The main disadvantage of this approach is that it can require a lot of reconcilations between multiple developers, multiple files, and multiple modifications.

3. **How do you log and communicate changes among developers?** When multiple developers are working on a software product, it's useful to keep them all aware of changes being made to the source code. They can plan their work activities around the changes being made, and thus avoid schedule and source code conflicts with each other. (Since log messages are only as good as the people who write them, it's probably a good idea to use style and content guidelines in multi-person development environments.)

Logs also help developers identify and explain changes in the product's behavior. For example, if all the developers know that the product's input/output system was just re-written and checked in, they'll all be more sensitive to changes in the I/O system behavior.

Global product logs can also show everything that has happened to a product in chronological order. For example, logs make it easy to find out when a particular change was made to a product. They can also help you to reconstruct a list of all changes that have been made to the code since the last official release (this is useful when you're describing new product changes in the release notes).

4. **How do you support multiple developers with tools?** There are several reasons why you should support multiple developers with automated software tools. These reasons include supporting uniformity and consistency in common development tasks,

supporting efficiency on common tree cloning tasks, and supporting communication among members of the development team.

Multiple platforms

The policy choice to support multiple platforms is much like the choice to support multiple developers—it has a major effect on the directory structures of the code management system. The issue, again, is one of separating files into separate directories for organizational convenience. But this time, platform-dependent files are being separated, not developers. There can be many platform-dependent files on a project—source files, object files, library files, executable files, makefiles, and even utility tools such as *make*, compilers, and linkers that run on different platforms.

The need to support multiple platforms requires two things of the code management system. First, it must help identify and isolate all platform-dependent code in the original single-platform product. For example, disallowing platform-dependent **#ifdefs** can help force pd code into separate files, where it can be more easily identified and manipulated.

Second, it must provide separate directories for storing and compiling the pd code for all supported platforms. This usually provides a solution to the classic multi-platform problem of different files that have the same filename.

1. **How do you represent platform-dependent code?** There are two main approaches.

   The first approach is to use a conditional compilation technique, such as the **#ifdef** facility in the C programming language. This method has the advantage of being simple, efficient, and readable for small code changes for a limited number of platforms.

   The main drawback of this technique is that it doesn't scale up well. It can make source code difficult to read (and thus to maintain) when many changes for many platforms are involved. In particular, nested **#ifdefs** are notorious for being difficult to maintain.

   Another drawback of this technique is that many simple tools can't understand the conditional compilation mechanism and can't screen out unwanted sections of conditionally compiled code. As a consequence, the tools sometimes protest statements that are illegal on one platform, but legal on another.

   For example, generating makefile dependency rules directly from the source code is usually awkward when include statements for many platforms appear in the source file. Since most tools can't screen out the include statements for other platforms, they end up generating makefile dependency rules for all include statements for all platforms.

   The second approach is to place all platform-dependent code in separate files, in separate platform-dependent directories. The most visible characteristic of this approach is that it usually results in the creation of significantly more files and directories.

But fortunately, separate files and directories usually don't require more work when compared to other multi-platform techniques such as embedded **#ifdefs**. The separate files and directories are highly visible and can be easily manipulated by humans and tools. In contrast, embedded **#ifdefs** are hidden inside of files and cannot be easily manipulated by tools. Human attention is almost always required.

For these reasons, the solutions in this book disallow the use of **#ifdef** statements for the purposes of isolating platform-dependent code, and require that pd code be placed in separate pd files in separate platform directories. (**#ifdefs** are allowed for other reasons, such as for debugging, product feature inclusion, etc.)

2. **How do you isolate platform-dependent source files?** There are two ways of separating pd source files.

    The first solution is to give each platform-dependent source file a different name and store them all in the same directory. The second solution is to give all the files the same name and store them in different directories.

    The first solution usually requires some special preparations before compilation can take place. That's because the makefiles usually expect to use a particular "generic" filename for the platform-dependent information. So before you compile, you must somehow associate the generic name with the actual pd file. This is usually done by linking the generic name to the platform-dependent file, by copying and renaming the platform-dependent file, or by editing a generic file to include the platform-dependent file. This method is used for some of the include files in the GNU Emacs distribution.

    The main advantage of this approach (different names, same directory) is that it can efficiently store files for many, many platforms in a single directory (see the GNU Emacs distribution). However, software configured this way can usually be compiled for only one platform at a time.

    The second solution (same names, different directories) is more flexible since no linking, copying, or renaming is required. Compilation can proceed normally for all platforms in the platform-dependent compilation directories. It has several important advantages:

    – The source code is readable (fewer **#ifdefs**).

    – Platform-dependent files are easily recognized by their physical locations in platform directories.

    – Developers have only to consider one platform when they're reading or modifying any particular source file, not many platforms.

    – All code in a pd file can be designed and optimized to operate as efficiently as possible on just one platform.

- The technique scales-up very well and can be used on projects of any size. Arbitrary numbers of platforms and files can be added, managed, or deleted from the code management system with a minimum of effort.

3. **How do you isolate platform-dependent binary files?** Platform-dependent binary files are usually stored in three places: in the compilation directory, in the *share* directory (when platform-dependent binary files are shared), and in the library and executable product (alpha test and release) directories. The code management system must keep the files separated in all three places.

Filename clashes in all three places are most easily avoided by using separate subdirectories for each platform. For example, imagine a platform-dependent library product called *mylib_pd.lib*. Then the name of the main product node directory would be *mylib_pd.lib*, and the platform directories would be subdirectories of *mylib_pd.lib*, as shown in the pd node here:

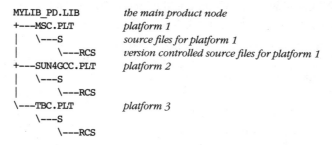

```
MYLIB_PD.LIB          the main product node
+---MSC.PLT           platform 1
|    \---S            source files for platform 1
|        \---RCS      version controlled source files for platform 1
+---SUN4GCC.PLT       platform 2
|    \---S
|        \---RCS
\---TBC.PLT           platform 3
     \---S
         \---RCS
```

Scripts and makefiles are stored in separate pd directories too, because scripts are usually written in a platform-dependent interpreted language (such as */bin/sh* on UNIX or *command.com* on MS-DOS). Makefiles are also usually platform dependent since the different *make* tools for different platforms often have slightly different syntaxes and almost always contain platform-dependent compilation arguments.

Avoiding filename clashes among platform-dependent scripts and makefiles is usually done in the same way as for source and binary files—with separate directories for each platform. For example, in this book, pd makefiles are kept in pd compilation directories.

4. **How do you support porting source code to multiple platforms?** There are two central questions that must be answered when a company considers the support of a new platform. First, "What files in the software product have to be ported to the new platform?" And second, "How much will it cost to port those files?"

These are interesting questions because in most cases the cost of the port is roughly proportional to the number and complexity of the platform-dependent files that have to be physically modified to work on the new platform. (That is, all platform-dependent files will have to be ported, but perhaps some of them won't have to be modified. This can happen if a platform-dependent file can be reused without modification on a new platform.)

They are also important questions because bad estimates result in schedule overruns, cost overruns, and stress overloads for everyone involved. So a good code management system should, as much as possible, help reduce the cost of answering this question, and increase the accuracy of the final answer.

One way a code management system can help answer this question is to separate platform-dependent files from platform-independent files. Then the identity of most (if not all) files that have to be ported is obvious. If the costs of an earlier port were recorded or remembered, a reasonably accurate answer to the second question can be provided as well.

Beware of thinking that the second question is sufficient by itself just because it describes the cost of earlier ports. In practice, the new platform might be very different from previous platforms. It may require that more "platform-independent" files be moved into platform-dependent directories.

5. **How do you support multi-platform development with tools?** This question can be posed in several different ways. For example, you might ask, "What multi-platform development tasks would most benefit from automated tool support?" Or you might ask, "What costly multi-platform development activities are performed in routine, predictable ways?"

    There are several areas where you should support multi-platform development with automated software tools. These include supporting uniformity and consistency in common development tasks, supporting efficiency on common platform subtree-creation tasks, and supporting bulk operations on all the platforms of a particular type within a set of product source trees.

Include files

The issues surrounding pd include files are much like those that surround pd source files, but with one major difference. Source file names are only referenced from outside the source files—usually by makefiles. This means that directory reorganizations don't usually affect source files or makefiles if they are located within the same product subtree.

However, include file names are referenced by statements inside the source files. This has many effects, especially if the include statements in the source files use absolute or relative pathnames to specify the location of the include file.

The two main issues that concern include files are discussed below: how to store the files, and how to reference (share) them.

1. **How do you store include files?** There are two aspects to consider. The first concerns the relation between the include file and the (product) owner of the include file. Storing include files within their product subtrees preserves the ownership relationship, and storing them in a central include directory does not.

The second aspect concerns the ease of sharing the include files. Storing the include files within their product subtrees makes it difficult to share the files with other products, and storing them in central include directory makes it easier.

As you can see, the ownership and sharing issues favor different storage solutions. Either you lose ownership relationships, or you make it difficult to share include files.

Most organizations that I've seen favor ease of sharing over loss of ownership relationships, because the ownership of most include files can usually be figured out by manual inspection of the filename or file contents. However, this approach becomes less satisfying in large organizations that have hundreds or thousands of include files in a central directory because of the cost and accuracy of manual inspection techniques.

The solutions in this book preserve both ownership relationships and ease of sharing by explicitly exporting and importing files to and from a central *share* directory.

2. **What forms of #include references are allowed?** The form of the pathname or filename in include statements is interrelated with the storage techniques that were discussed above. Obviously, the pathname in the include statement and the location of the file must agree with each other if the compiler is to find the file. There are several ways of referencing shared include files.

The first, and least desirable way is to use a hardcoded pathname (relative or absolute) in the include statement. This is not a good practice because it makes the source code very sensitive to directory reorganizations. It also makes the code more difficult to port to other platforms because the other platforms may not be able to recreate a directory structure that will make the include pathnames valid. For example, MS-DOS and UNIX use the backslash and forward slash characters (respectively) as pathname separators. And while most modern MS-DOS compilers will now accept forward slashes for UNIX code compatibility, the reverse is rarely true. Most people agree that using absolute or relative pathnames in include statements is something to be avoided wherever possible.

The second technique for referencing include files is to make the compiler decode the reference. That is, place include files in one or more central include directories, and then configure the compiler defaults so that the compiler will look in the appropriate places. Alternatively, most modern compilers now accept command-line arguments for specifying include file search paths (such as the `-Idirectory` option on some UNIX compilers, for example).

A third technique—the one that's used by the solutions in this book—is to import sharable include files from the *$CMHTREE/share* directory into the current compilation directory. (Recall that files located in the *$CMHTREE/share* directory were all originally exported to there from within version-controlled source trees.) This approach preserves ownership relationships, makes it easy to share files, and is not sensitive to directory structure reorganizations. Moreover, it allows all sharing relationships to be logged and inspected.

Documentation files

There are several forms of documentation commonly associated with software products. These include user documentation, technical design documentation, test program documentation, maintenance documentation, and so on.

The code management techniques described here are also appropriate for managing these types of documentation files.

How do you store documentation files? There are two main principles that guide the selection of a storage technique.

The first principle is that documentation files stored close to the source code they describe have a greater likelihood of being kept up-to-date. It is more convenient—and thus more likely, in practice—for programmers to update documentation if it's stored near the code that they've just modified.

The second principle is that documentation files for word processors are much easier to work with if they're all in one directory.* In contrast, ASCII documentation files can be stored almost anywhere, without loss of convenience or efficiency.

These principles suggest that documentation files for user and tutorial manuals should be stored together near the top of the product tree because they have little direct relationship to the internal structure of the source code. That way, the documentation files will move with the product files during a directory reorganization, yet won't clutter up the code and platform subtrees.

The principles also suggest that the "distributed storage" technique is best suited to self-contained ASCII files that aren't part of a larger document. This is because it's easy to use any editor to work on an ASCII file. However, it might not be so easy to use a word processor program on documentation files that are distributed throughout the main source tree.

Test program files

Test program files are usually small programs or scripts that are used to test or evaluate particular features of the software product for which they were designed. For some software products, there may be tens or hundreds of these separate test files or scripts. In these cases, the set of test programs is usually called a test suite.

1. **How do you store test program files?** Many factors can affect the answer. For example, there may be one, or tens, or even hundreds of them. They may be invoked as a set of tests by one or more large test driver scripts. In that case, should they be stored separately in the fashion of other software products, or as a group, in one directory?

---

* In many cases, the documentation is on a completely different machine, such as a Macintosh. This is because it is easier for documentation personnel to create documentation on a platform that's more familiar to them, is easier to use, or has more powerful word processing and documentation capabilities.

2. **Should test programs be treated as individual software products?** The main issue to be decided here is the amount of code management support that you should give to your test programs.

   Should each test program be put under source code control and treated as a separate "product?" This approach makes the most sense if each test program represents a significant amount of development effort or if the programs are part of a formal acceptance test suite.

   But is it worth the extra trouble if most of the programs are just simple "thrown together" test programs? Hundreds of platform-dependent test programs will force the creation of several times that many directories and makefiles if the test programs are maintained as fully separate products.

   You'll have to decide what the best tradeoff is within your environment. I've found that I use both approaches, depending on the complexity and seriousness of the test programs.

   One other thing to keep in mind is that test programs can often be dependent on the version of the tested product. This means that you'll require a different version of the test program for each different version of the tested product. If that's the case, you'll almost certainly want to treat the test program just like any other normal version-controlled product.

3. **Who should maintain test programs?** Should the programs be stored and maintained by the development team or by the testing and quality assurance team? Both developers and test personnel will probably use the programs.

There are no absolute answers to these questions. Different situations will motivate different answers. Nonetheless, some suggested rules of thumb are offered below.

- **Official test programs should be under source code control.** This improves the stability of the test programs and also provides an audit trail for the testing team. However, this suggestion doesn't mean that each program should have its own product node, since it may be more efficient and effective to store them all in a single directory.

  The main consequence of not storing programs according to the standard code management system methods is that non-standard storage may prevent the use of standard, automated code management tools. Which is easier—manual maintenance on a few directories and hundreds of programs, or automated maintenance on hundreds of directories and hundreds of programs? Only you can decide for your situation.

- **Large test programs or test scripts should be stored as separate products.** They represent a significant amount of development and maintenance work, and so should be protected and controlled by the normal conventions of the code management system.

- **Source files for test programs are usually platform dependent.** Most top-level test programs usually aren't programs at all—they're usually scripts that perform various functional tests on the tested product. Since scripts are always platform-dependent, top-level test suites are usually platform dependent, too. (Unless, of course, the script language is identical on all test platforms.)

  The only time test program source files are *not* platform dependent is when the test program is a compilable program that contains no platform dependent code. (Even so, the binaries are platform dependent.)

  It is usually easiest to store single small test programs in or below the compilation directories, under source code control. The test programs are stored in a platform-dependent location, yet are immediately available to the developer just after compilation.

- **Large official test suites should be stored in separate trees.** If a test suite has its own development and maintenance staff, then it should be stored as a completely separate set of software products.

  Figure 4-2 shows an example of how you might structure a directory tree to store a suite of official test programs for several products.

Software products with special needs

Non-standard software products aren't stored in the code management system in the normal ways for a variety of reasons. For example, the product might be public domain or copylefted software whose distribution tree structure might not be under your control. You may want to leave it unchanged so that you can easily upgrade to future versions of the product. As a second example, you might have a suite of test programs that you don't want to store in the standard ways as discussed earlier. But whatever the reason, it's likely that you'll eventually want to store some non-standard software products in your code management system at some time.

1. **How should non-standard software products be stored?** The main issue to consider is how much of the standard code management system functionality you should give up, and why.

2. **What costs are acceptable for converting non-standard programs?** Will you only have to convert the program once, or will you have to do it every time there's a new release? Probably you'll have to pay a large cost the first time, and smaller, more standard costs for each upgrade to a new release because there's more work to do for the initial conversion—new tree structures and makefiles have to be created, and so on.

   Surprisingly, I've found that the largest costs of converting non-standard products to conform with standard code management systems are the costs of identifying the code that is platform dependent, the code that is shared among various files within the product, and the location of the natural conceptual boundaries in the product. The "technical" costs of setting up new directories and makefiles is trivial in

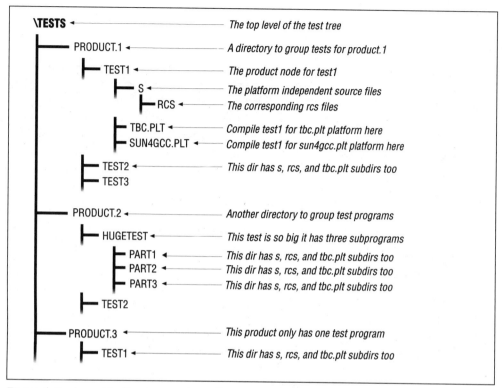

Figure 4–2. A sample directory structure for test suite programs

comparison to the "knowledge" costs associated with learning about the internal structure and operation of the new product.

The main reason for this is that most freeware tools aren't well organized from a code management perspective. Instead, it's more usual to find source files, include files, and makefiles—for all supported platforms—all lumped together in one directory. It's also common to find a lack of documentation on any platform-dependent files in the distribution. So it's easy to spend a lot of time looking through source files and makefiles to make these identifications.

I usually make the effort to convert freeware programs to my standard code management style for two reasons. The most important reason is that I usually want to port the program to MS-DOS, with minimal effort. And second, it's easier to share and reuse code among programs once they've been converted because both the platform dependent and platform independent files are easier to identify and export for sharing under a good code management system.

Sharing and releasing

The remaining issues to be discussed in this section concern sharing and releasing files.

1. **How do you share platform-independent files with platform-dependent files?** The main difference between sharing platform independent and platform-dependent files is simple. You need only one directory to store all platform-independent files but many directories to share all platform-dependent files (one directory for each platform).

   The solutions in this book assume that shareable platform independent files are stored in the parent directory of the platform-dependent share directories. The name of that parent directory in this book is *CMHTREE/share*. Figure 4-3 shows the structure of the *CMHTREE/share* directory on my DOS computer.

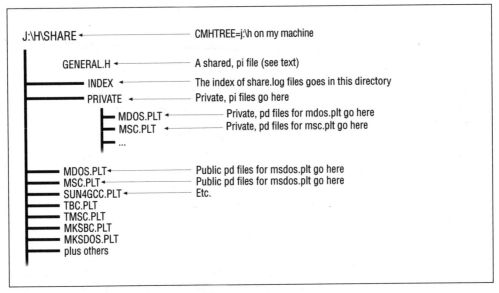

Figure 4-3. The share directory on my DOS computer

   For example, suppose that you want to share a platform-independent file named *general.h*. You'd export it from the product tree that owns the file into the *CMHTREE/share* directory. That would make it available for public sharing—any person could reuse the file for any reason. Now suppose that you wanted to reuse the file in another product that's being compiled on the *sun4gcc.plt* platform. To do this, you would add an import command to the makefile in the *sun4gcc.plt* platform directory and import *general.h* from the *CMHTREE/share* directory.

2. **How do you share platform-dependent files?** The code management system must provide a mechanism for sharing platform-dependent files. One approach is to

copy the shared files directly from the owner's directory to the user's compilation directory. But as noted before, this approach is sensitive to directory reorganizations.

A better approach is always to export to a central *share* directory when you want to make a file available for sharing, and import from the same directory in order to reuse the file. Of course, this approach requires a set of separate, platform-dependent *share/platform.plt* directories if simultaneous multi-platform sharing is to be supported.

The solutions in this book use a separate sharing directory for each platform. For example, the platform-dependent sharing directories for the two platforms *tbc.plt* and *sun4gcc.plt* would be *share/tbc.plt* and *share/sun4gcc.plt*, respectively. Shared files are first exported into an appropriate platform-dependent share directory, and then imported into the platform-dependent compilation directories where they will be reused.

3. **How do you support releasing?** In this book, the technical process used for releasing a file is identical to the process that's used for sharing files. Files are exported by physically copying them to new locations. The only difference is the target directories. Shared files are usually exported into the *CMHTREE/share* subtree, and released files are usually exported into the *CMHTREE/release* subtree. However, some conceptual differences between sharing and releasing are worthy of mention.

One significant issue to consider when releasing products concerns the identity of the releasing personnel. That is, should the developers construct the releasable products from the main source tree, or should the testing or quality assurance team construct and release the products? And if the quality assurance team does construct the releasable products, will their activities block the developers from using the main source tree while the release is being prepared?

Ideally, the development, testing, and release teams should all be able to simultaneously use the main source tree. That way, each team is independent of all other teams. However, to support such simultaneous use, the code management system must provide support for multiple developers.

Makefile Architecture Issues

This section identifies and discusses many important makefile architecture issues. For the most part, the issues described here implement, rather than decide, the corporate policy decisions made earlier.

This section has been written to include comments and issues that concern the automated generation of makefiles. This is because automated makefile generation is a more efficient, more uniform way of generating makefiles than manual methods.

But because these comments have been included, some statements below may seem trivial in the context of small, manually generated makefiles. The comments may seem more appropriate if you adopt the perspective of a developer who has 100 different multi-platform software products to maintain. Then the advantages of makefile uniformity, information isolation, and automated processing will seem much more meaningful. Automated techniques can drastically affect the productivity of an individual developer who has to create or modify tens or hundreds of makefiles on multiple platforms. You'll find that the discussions below heavily emphasize standard makefiles and automated support.

Makefile content and operational issues

This section is concerned with the informational content and operational behavior of makefiles. It asks two questions: "What should be inside the makefiles of a code management system?" and "How do code management system makefiles support code management system policies and other desirable makefile behaviors?" The content issues appear first, followed by the behavioral issues.

1. **What standard makefile targets should be used?** This question can be answered in a general way by saying that makefiles should include standard makefile targets for all common development needs. Typically, this includes targets for constructing, installing, and cleaning up the software products and directories that are managed by the makefile. Some makefiles contain targets for archiving and testing the software as well.

2. **How do you support different types of products (exe, lib, script)?** Since different types of products require different sets of targets and commands in the makefile, the code management system must define makefile conventions to satisfy these needs. One approach is to use monolithic, manually created makefiles. Then developers can use any targets and commands that they think are appropriate for the different product types. However, such an approach would be difficult to support with automated tools.

   A second approach is to define enough standard makefile conventions to make it possible to generate makefiles automatically. Then developers would have to manually generate extra makefile commands only in special cases. Of course, the major drawback of this approach is the effort that it takes to define workable makefile conventions for different product types, different platforms, and different development environments.

3. **How do you support multiple platforms?** There are four major difficulties in supporting makefiles on multiple platforms:

   – The syntax of the *make* tool may change with each platform.

   – The names and locations of software tools will probably change with each platform. For example, if the platforms had different binary file formats, you'd have to use different versions of software tools. Even if the platforms didn't have different binary formats, they might still require different software tools.

   – The compilation, linking, and library construction processes will probably be different on each platform. This will require different command sequences in each of the makefiles, even if the same tools with the same names and locations are used for all platforms. For example, the compiler, linker, and library tools might use different command-line options and might search different directories for each of the platforms.

- Filename collisions will probably occur between makefiles and object files for the different platforms. For example, collisions would likely occur if all the makefiles and object files for all platforms were stored in the same compilation directory.

There is no solution to the first problem of different makefile syntaxes for different platforms, except to find another *make* tool that offers a more acceptable syntax. (But this book helps to bypass the problem because it provides tools and templates for some of the common tasks that are usually implemented with special syntax features. For example, recursive *make* operations are avoided by using tree walking batch files.)

There are two solutions to the second problem of accessing different tools for different platforms. The first approach is to change the search paths in the PATH environment variable whenever you begin work on a different platform. However, this is tedious if you switch platforms often. A better solution is to hardcode the pathnames for platform-dependent tools into makefile macros. Then the makefile directly invokes the correct tools for the platform, regardless of the user's search paths in the PATH variable. The main drawback with this approach is that it's sensitive to relocations of the tools. But this usually isn't a problem, because the tools are rarely moved.

The third problem can be addressed by grouping and isolating platform-dependent makefile information into separate include files. Theses files have the same name as the platform directories (e.g., *sun4gcc.plt*, *tbc.plt*). Then the appropriate include file is included when the top-level makefile is generated for any particular platform. For an example, see the source code and makefiles that are used to build the multi-platform products that accompany this book.

The fourth problem can be addressed by providing separate compilation directories for all platforms in a product node.

4. **How do you support special targets for individual products?** Probably there will always be a need for special processing commands in any set of standard makefile conventions. This is because truly special cases do arise from time to time, despite our best efforts to make software development as predictable and uniform as possible.

The main implication of such special cases in this context is that they usually require human intervention. This leads to two difficulties in standard, automated code management systems. First, a special place must be defined in the standard makefile templates for custom makefile targets and operating-system commands.

And second, the custom information must be preserved (if possible) whenever the makefile is automatically regenerated.

5. **How do you support default sharing and releasing operations?** The normal way to support standard operations is to include the appropriate targets and commands within the makefile template that's used to construct standard makefiles. Then new makefiles are created by cloning and modifying the standard template.

One refinement to this technique is to define a macro to hold the name of the software product. Then the commands for default operations don't have to be modified after they're cloned. Instead, they can all be written to use the macro name. This saves time because neither tools nor humans have to modify the template commands to hold hardcoded product names.

6. **How do you support automated traversals of product trees?** Tree walking mechanisms are a major issue in code management systems for two main reasons. First, all tree walking mechanisms are usually very sensitive to directory structure reorganizations. Second, recursive tree walking mechanisms place especially heavy demands on both *make* tools and operating systems.

The reason that most tree walking mechanisms are sensitive to directory reorganizations is that they contain hardcoded directory names and pathnames. This means that the tree walking mechanisms must be updated every time the directories are relocated. Perhaps the updating costs will be expensive, and perhaps not. It depends on the frequency and costs of individual reorganizations and the associated tree walker upgrading costs.

One popular technique is to put the tree walking mechanism into the makefile. Then the makefile walks the named subdirectories and recursively invokes *make* in each of them. Often a new child shell is used for each recursive *make* invocation for error control purposes. A common implementation of this technique is shown in Example 4-1.

Example 4-1: Compiling Subtrees with the Recursive Make For-loop Technique

```
# These targets are in the parent directory's makefile
SUBDIRS= subdir1 subdir2

compile_all:
    for dir in ${SUBDIRS}; do \
        (cd $$dir; \                  # go there, using a new child subshell
        $(MAKE) compile; \            # run this target on all subdirs
        cd ..; \                      # not really needed, since the ()
        ) \                           # is a child process. The parent
    done                              # process never changes dirs.
    $(MAKE) compile                   # then do this dir too (if need be)
```

Unfortunately, this technique places heavy memory demands on both the *make* tool and the operating system. As a consequence, the technique is not a good one for multi-platform development work unless all the platforms can support the demands. For example, MS-DOS platforms have difficulty because they don't have enough memory to support two invocations of both the command shell interpreter and the *make* tool.

A better technique is to use regular shell scripts to walk the necessary directories because they demand less from the *make* tool and operating system. The *make* tool doesn't have to support recursion, and the operating system only has to support one invocation of the command interpreter and *make* tool. (The initial invocation of the command shell is always present in memory.) As an added benefit, the tree walker scripts can accept and invoke arbitrary commands in each directory; they aren't just limited to *make* commands, as the makefile technique is.

One bothersome drawback still remains. Now it's the script that requires updating after reorganizations, because now it contains the hardcoded directory names.

To solve the script updating problem, the solutions in this book automatically generate tree walker scripts. The directory names that appear in any script are controlled by a pattern-matching expression that's given as a command-line argument to the tree walker generator tool. The scripts can execute an arbitrary command in each directory named in the script.

As a consequence of this approach, updating tree walker scripts after reorganizations is both simple, efficient, and very inexpensive. In seconds, users can easily generate, or regenerate, scripts that will walk entire product trees.

Minimizing sensitivity to change

This section describes how to make standard makefile systems less sensitive to changes in filenames, directory structures, and platforms.

1. **How do you minimize sensitivity to filename changes?** One good (and traditional) technique is to use makefile macros to reference all software tool names and filenames of temporary files (such as *junk1.tmp*) used in various target command sequences. That way, only the macros will require changing if a tool or filename requires changing. For example, imagine that a makefile is being ported from MS-DOS to UNIX. Then at least some of the software tool names are likely to change: *type* on MS-DOS becomes *cat* on UNIX, and *bcc* (the Borland C compiler) might become *cc* or *gcc* (the GNU C compiler) on UNIX. Using macros allows you to make each change only in one place.

   An even better approach is to isolate all common tool and file name macro definitions in a single platform-dependent file. Then you can include that file in all of the top-level makefiles for that platform. All makefiles in the product tree can use a single set of tool and file name definitions.

   This useful approach reduces the cost of porting existing makefiles to new platforms. To create new makefiles for the new platform, just clone the old makefiles and modify the tool and file names. (Other minor modifications may be required to accomodate the possibly different makefile syntax on the new platform.)

2. **How do you accomodate different commands for different platforms?** This issue is also concerned with differences between platforms. But in this case we're concerned with differences in dynamic software-construction procedures instead of differences in static filenames and tool names. The filename issue could be solved with macros. This issue cannot.

   There are at least three main construction processes to consider: the compilation process, the linking process, and the library creation process. All three processes can have different forms on different platforms.

   The solutions in this book take an "information encapsulation" approach that places makefile commands for each of the processes into a separate file. The appropriate process for each different type of software product (an executable program, an object library, or a shell script) can be included into the top-level makefile simply by including the appropriate process template file.

   This approach also makes it easier for the makefile generation tools to generate an appropriate makefile for the various product types. The tools only have to include a particular file, rather than generate a potentially complex series of makefile macros, targets, and commands.

3. **How do you minimize sensitivity to directory reorganizations?** There are three main types of reorganizations to consider in makefile sensitivity studies. These are reorganizations of the directories within the product subtrees, directories outside the product subtrees but within the main source tree, and directories outside the main source tree such as the share, alpha test, and release directories.

   The main problem is that makefiles that refer to any of these directories will fail if those directories are relocated. So the most obvious solution is to minimize (or remove) as many directory references from the makefiles as is feasible.

   Makefiles that change directories and then recursively invoke *make* in the new directories are particularly sensitive to directory reorganizations. There are two factors at work in such files, and it's important to distinguish between the two.

   The first factor is that of tree walking. The top-level makefile traverses several subdirectories and recursively invokes *make* to build the subproducts. This means that if some other tree walking method could be used, the makefile sensitivity could be avoided.

   The second factor is that hardcoded relative pathnames are being used for the subdirectory names. This is a difficult sensitivity to totally avoid if tree walking is the responsibility of the makefile. The most you can do is to use either a macro or some other makefile technique to minimize the number of occurences of the hardcoded names. Then if you have to change them, you have to change them only once.

   The solutions in this book use shell scripts to walk the product tree, and thereby avoid the makefile sensitivity described above. And since the tree walking scripts can be automatically generated, it's easy to update them after arbitrarily complex directory reorganizations.

The solutions in this book also use macros in a special makefile include file to define the locations of the *share, alpha test,* and *release* directories. This means that all makefiles in the code management system can be updated simultaneously by making a single change in a global makefile.

Automatic generation of makefiles

It is an advantage to be able to automatically generate makefiles in multi-platform environments for several reasons. First, it frees developers from having to remember the syntactic quirks of different *make* tools on different platforms. Second, it's faster and less error prone than generating makefiles with manual methods. And third, it results in more standard, more uniform working environments—all the makefiles for all the products on all the platforms behave in the same way.

However, it's not that easy to do. For instance, it's easy to fall into the trap of making too many restrictive assumptions on the working environment. Then your generator tool won't be general enough to be used in many existing work environments.

It's also easy to fall into the trap of not making *enough* assumptions about the working environment. Then you'll probably be faced with having to write a very complex makefile generator, which will probably be difficult to use in multi-platform environments because your non-restrictive assumptions will allow environments to be vastly different from each other.

The following discussion uses the C programming language for examples because of its popularity. (Some of the issues below don't arise with other languages.)

1. **How do you automatically generate makefile dependency rules?** This is not too difficult for simple programs. For example, there are several available freeware tools that have this capability.

   However, the main drawback of such tools is that they can be confused by several common situations. Suppose the source code uses different sets of include files for different platforms. Then the code will contain different sets of **#include** statements bracketed by platform-dependent **#ifdef/endif** statements. Since simple tools might not be smart enough to understand the **#ifdef** statements, they may generate incorrect dependency rules.

   As a second example, consider the original RCS 5.5 code distribution that was used to construct the tools that accompany this book. Many tools (such as *ci, co, rcsdiff,* etc.) were constructed by the (solitary) makefile, which contained different dependency rules for each tool. Even smart dependency rule generators would be confounded by this situation, since they'd have no way of knowing the object file dependencies of each tool. (However, smart tools would probably generate correct dependency rules for the include files used by each source file.)

The main conclusion to be drawn from these two examples is that makefile dependency generators can handle include file dependencies that are expressed in the source code by #include statements. However, they can't figure out object file dependencies without additional help in the form of standard conventions, assumptions, or other explicit information.

The solutions in this book generate dependency rules for both the include files and object files that are used in the construction of software products. This is possible only because the code management conventions of this book require a separate product subtree for each software product. They disallow the production of multiple software products from one subtree (such as in the RCS 5.5 example above).

2. **How do you automatically generate complete makefiles?** Automatic makefile generation for different product types on different platforms is not a simple task. There are many requirements that must be satisfied in order to produce a workable system.

   The three key issues in this area are the three conventions that define the structure, the content, and the operating environment of the makefiles. These assumptions make it possible to define and construct the tools and procedures for automatically generating makefiles. Since defining such conventions is a complex task (a large part of this book is already devoted to describing just one possible set of such conventions), sets of alternative conventions won't be described here.

   The solutions in this book isolate platform, product, and environment dependent information into separate files. Standard default processes are specified for constructing, exporting, and cleaning up after standard software products. Product subtree conventions restrict both the number and the form of products that can appear in a subtree.

   I emphasize that it's the entire set of these conventions, and not just a few important ones in particular, that makes it possible to write tools that automatically generate entire makefiles.

3. **How do you preserve special targets when regenerating makefiles?** If a user has entered custom targets and commands in the appropriate place(s) in your standard makefile structure, how are those commands preserved when the makefiles are regenerated? (It's common to regenerate makefiles to pick up new targets, changes, or defaults made to the clonable templates. That way, the whole product tree picks up the new changes.)

   There are two main approaches. The first is to make the generation tools smart enough to parse all the makefiles that the user might have changed, and to copy custom commands into the newly generated makefiles. But this is difficult to do, because of the internal complexity of both makefiles and the user's custom targets and commands. Rigorous conventions would probably be required to simplify the internal structure and content of the makefiles for the benefit of the tools.

   A second, much simpler approach is to define a convention that requires all custom user commands to be located in a special include file. Then the custom targets and commands that are placed in such special makefiles can be the responsibility of the user. In this book, the special include file is called *imports.imp*.

Source Code Issues

This section considers source code content and format issues that affect the design and operation of code management systems.

Should you disallow platform-dependent `#ifdefs`? The `#ifdef` approach has many disadvantages that have been mentioned already.

One problem that hasn't been mentioned before is that the `#ifdef` approach doesn't distinguish between pi and pd source files. Thus developers who are porting code are forced to search all source files every time they want to review all pd `#ifdef` statements, instead of examining only the pd source files in pd source directories.

Another problem is that the use of pd `#ifdefs` usually forces developers to modify existing source files to add support for new platforms that require `#ifdef`'d code. In comparison, the approach used in this book normally allows developers to add support for new platforms without modifying any existing code. This strictly reduces the opportunity of introducing new defects into existing code, while adding support for new platforms.

Note that some of these disadvantages are directly caused by the use of pd `#ifdef` statements, whereas others are caused by having only one set of source files (in one directory) for multiple platforms.

How to Compare Code Management Systems

This section provides you with a list of questions that can help you evaluate the features of various code management approaches. You may want to use this list to compare your system with the system described in this book.

Each question below is accompanied by an answer that's based on the solutions described by this book.

1. **How complex is the proposed code management system?** I can still remember when I first encountered some of the ideas that are now being explained in this book. As I learned about them, I felt that the system being presented to me was very complex compared to what I had experienced before.

   I said so to one of the most experienced people on the development team. His response was, "Sure it's complex, especially compared to having one makefile and all the source code files in one directory. But it's less complex than other systems that do similar things." I thought this statement over for a while, and found myself agreeing with him.

   I admit that I didn't take his word for it. Instead I sat down and enumerated all the code management things that a simple system could do, and then compared them with an enumeration of all the things the more complex system could do. There was a huge difference in functionality. And after only one day of using the complex system, I also found out that the system wasn't so complex, either.

If you're like me, and you really want to understand the difference between two code management systems for yourself, you should probably try an approach like the one I used. That is, enumerate the relevant code management issues, and then compare the system features that resolve the issues. You might want to use the summary checklists at the end of this chapter as a starting point.

2. **How do you identify platform-dependent code and files?** This is a big issue in multi-platform code management systems—maybe even the biggest issue of all. So when you're comparing systems, be sure to take the time to fully understand the system's treatment of platform-dependent code and files. It's a very crucial issue.

   The solutions in this book store pd code in separate pd files, in separate directories, in each product subtree. Therefore pd code and pd files are easily identified by their physical location—any file that's stored below a platform directory contains pd code, and is a pd file.

3. **How do you minimize porting costs?** This is another big issue, and is one that can be affected by many of the little policies in a code management system.

   The solutions in this book help to reduce costs by making it easier to identify, clone, modify, and integrate code for supporting new platforms. This is because platform-dependent code is stored in separate pd files, in separate pd directories.

   In addition, the automatic makefile generation tools and the code management system directory structures reduce the costs of generating new makefiles that will compile and export newly ported software products.

4. **How do you minimize the cost of determining who owns a file?** In this book, the term "owner" refers to the product for which the file was originally created. It doesn't refer to the file system owner who can set file system permissions.

   The solutions in this book minimize the cost of identifying the "product owner" of a file because the owner can be determined by the physical location of the file. And for shared files that have been exported out of their owning product tree into the *$CMHTREE/share* directory, owners can easily be identified by using the *cmlsr* tool to inspect the export log files.

5. **How do you minimize the cost of determining who uses a file?** The question of "who uses this file" is the reverse side of the question "who owns this file." On large projects, the question is meaningful because changing a frequently used file can affect (and perhaps break) many other products.

   The *cmlsr* tool significantly reduces the cost of identifying products that share a file (by inspecting the import log files).

6. **How do you minimize the cost of directory and file reorganizations?** The solutions in this book minimize the cost of reorganizations in two significant ways.

First, they only place a few restrictions on the structure of product subtrees. One restriction is that there must be a source directory either beside or underneath each platform directory. The source directory must be beside the platform directory for pi products, or must be immediately underneath the platform directory for pd products. And the other restriction is that platform directories and source directories must have standard names that are known to the code management system. The structure of all other directories is arbitrary.

And second, reorganizations are supported by automated tools that can create or regenerate product subtrees, platform directories, makefiles, and tree walker scripts.

7. **How convenient is the system? What tools does it provide?** Many automated tools are provided for use with the code management system in this book. See Appendix A, *Code Management Software Tools* for a complete list.

Summary of Issues

The section summarizes the issues discussed in this chapter. They are for your convenience—use them as a checklist when you are designing your own code management environment.

Platform Issues

> Multiple development platforms
> What are the limitations of each development platform?
> Symbolic links versus file copy operations
> Newsgroups versus flat files for log messages

Corporate Issues

> Maintenance by replacement or maintenance by repair?
> Multiple developers
> File sharing support
> File releasing support
> Support for testing

Basic Directory Structure

> Is there a place in the directory structure designated for each of the following?

>> Source files for each product
>> Include files for each product
>> Version control files for each product
>> Makefiles for each product
>> Compilations for each product
>> Object files for each product

Alpha test product files
Officially released product files
Current baseline product files
Current baseline source files
Old released product and source files

Multiple Developers

How do you isolate and stabilize developer trees?
How do you control conflicting source modifications?
How do you log and communicate changes among developers?
How do you support multiple developers with tools?

Multiple Platforms

How do you represent platform-dependent code?
How do you isolate platform-dependent source files?
How do you isolate platform-dependent binary files?
How do you isolate platform-dependent scripts and makefiles?
How do you share platform-dependent files?
How do you share normal files with platform-dependent files?
How do you support porting source code to multiple platforms?
How do you support multi-platform development with tools?

Include Files

How do you store include files?
What forms of **#include** references should be allowed?

Documentation Files

How do you store documentation files?

Test Program Files

How do you store test program files?
Should test programs be treated as individual software products?
Who should maintain test program files?

Software Products with Special Needs

How will you store products that have special needs?
What are acceptable costs for converting programs?

Sharing and Releasing

How do you support sharing?
How do you support releasing?

Makefiles

What standard makefile targets should be used?
How do you support different types of products (exe, lib, script)?
How do you support multiple platforms?
How do you support special targets for individual products?
How do you support default sharing and releasing operations?
How do you support automated traversals of product trees?

Minimizing Sensitivity to Change

How do you minimize sensitivity to filename changes?
How do you accomodate different commands for different platforms?
How do you minimize sensitivity to directory reorganizations?

Automatic Generation of Makefiles

How do you automatically generate makefile dependency rules?
How do you automatically generate complete makefiles?
How do you preserve special targets when regenerating makefiles?

Source Code

Should you disallow platform-dependent `#ifdef` statements?

Evaluation Issues

How complex is the code management system?
How do you identify platform-dependent files?
How do you minimize porting costs?
How do you minimize the cost of determining who owns a file?
How do you minimize the cost of determining who uses a file?
How do you minimize the cost of directory and file reorganizations?
How convenient is the system? What tools does it provide?

In This Chapter:
• The CMTREE
• The CMHTREE
• Source Trees
• RCS Directories
• Evaluation

5

Directory Structures

This chapter describes a directory structure that effectively organizes files in multi-person, multi-platform environments. Three major tree structures comprise the system. Their relationships appear in Figure 5-1.

- The CMTREE (code management tree) holds platform-dependent makefile templates that are used by the makefile generation tools.

- Source trees hold files that are used to produce software products. These trees provide storage for many types of files including source files, include files, object files, executable files, script files, and makefiles. They also provide storage for other files associated with the software product. Source trees hold the main "inputs" to the code management system.

- The CMHTREE (code management holding tree) is a holding area for shared, alpha test, and released files. This tree holds the "outputs" of the code management system—finished products.

The main advantage of these particular tree structures is that they've been designed for use with the other makefile, sharing, and procedural solutions described in this book. Together, these solutions form a competent, integrated code management system that satisfies the requirements listed in the previous chapter.

In particular, the directory structures make it easier to develop tools that automate many common software development and maintenance tasks. The structures also make it easier for humans to identify and locate files within any one of the three trees.

The following sections discuss directory structure policies, directory contents, and important issues associated with directory structures. The chapter concludes with a short evaluation of the solutions presented.

The CMTREE

The CMTREE is a relatively small tree structure that contains the *makefile.tre* include file and the makefile templates for different platforms. The file *makefile.tre* is included by all makefiles in the code management system and contains macros that define the directories and filenames that are used by all makefiles. The makefile templates are

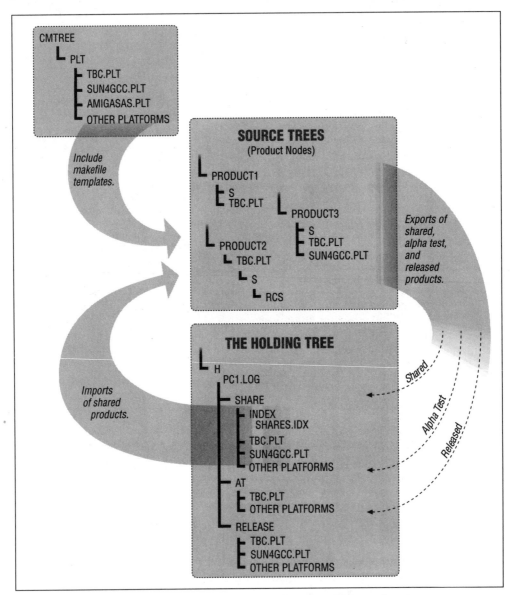

Figure 5-1. Macro information flow among the CMTREE, CMHTREE, and source trees

used by the makefile generation tools to generate complete makefiles for different kinds of software products.

Directory Structure

Figure 5-2 shows the structure of the CMTREE on my personal computer. The filenames in only one platform directory are shown, but all platform directories contain similar files.

The tree contains an extra *misc* directory, which has nothing to do with the CMTREE policies in this book. I've included the *misc* directory because it demonstrates that you can add arbitrary directories to the CMTREE without harm. In the directory, I keep a documentation file having to do with naming conventions in the CMTREE (*misc/names.txt*). This file helps me remember which files I have to change if I want to change the names or locations of various components of the code management system. You'll want to browse this file too if you're contemplating name changes to the code management system.

The only required directory in the CMTREE is the *plt* directory, which must contain some number of appropriate subdirectories and corresponding makefile template files.

The names of the subdirectories are important—you get to define them, but they must be consistently used throughout the code management system. Later, I will list some recommended policies for platform names.

Note that there's an RCS subdirectory below each platform directory in Figure 5-2. The tools in this book assume the presence of an RCS subdirectory directly underneath the files that are being protected.

The tools also assume that the RCS filenames are identical to the filenames of the protected files. The two-character RCS suffix (*,v*) that was traditionally used to identify RCS files on UNIX can't be used on other operating systems such as DOS. (Newer versions of RCS allow a choice—you don't have to use *,v.*)

The tools always use (lowercase) *rcs* for the RCS subdirectory names. Lowercase names are easier for them to work with than mixed-case pathnames that may or may not contain uppercase RCS directory names.

Directory Contents

Each platform directory contains makefile templates that are used by the makefile generation tools to create makefiles for the typical kinds of software products found on that platform. Not all kinds of software products are found on each platform. For example, makefiles for generating a binary library file on the *sun4gcc.plt* platform aren't appropriate for the *sun4sh.plt* platform, since one platform compiles with a C compiler and the other platform interprets with an interpreter (*/bin/sh*). So each platform directory contains only the makefile templates that are appropriate for that platform.

The seven template files that are commonly found in the CMTREE platform directories are listed in Figure 5-2. However, since they aren't related to directories, they aren't

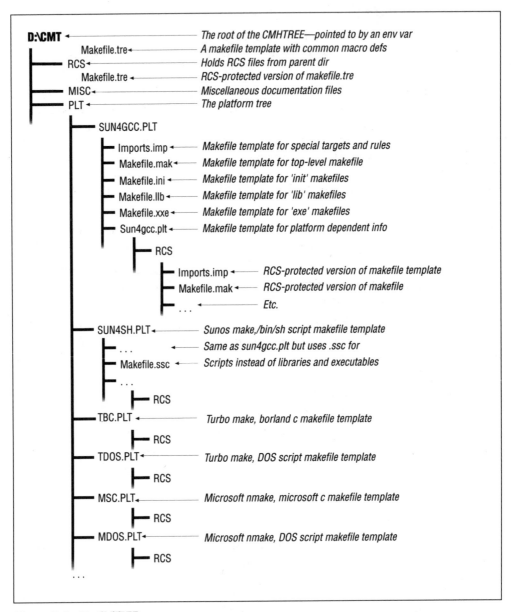

The following describes the structure shown in the figure:

D:\CMT ← The root of the CMHTREE—pointed to by an env var
    Makefile.tre ← A makefile template with common macro defs
    RCS ← Holds RCS files from parent dir
    Makefile.tre ← RCS-protected version of makefile.tre
    MISC ← Miscellaneous documentation files
    PLT ← The platform tree

      SUN4GCC.PLT
        Imports.imp ← Makefile template for special targets and rules
        Makefile.mak ← Makefile template for top-level makefile
        Makefile.ini ← Makefile template for 'init' makefiles
        Makefile.llb ← Makefile template for 'lib' makefiles
        Makefile.xxe ← Makefile template for 'exe' makefiles
        Sun4gcc.plt ← Makefile template for platform dependent info
          RCS
            Imports.imp ← RCS-protected version of makefile template
            Makefile.mak ← RCS-protected version of makefile
            ... ← Etc.

      SUN4SH.PLT ← Sunos make,/bin/sh script makefile template
        ... ← Same as sun4gcc.plt but uses .ssc for
        Makefile.ssc ← Scripts instead of libraries and executables
        ...
        RCS

      TBC.PLT ← Turbo make, borland c makefile template
        RCS

      TDOS.PLT ← Turbo make, DOS script makefile template
        RCS

      MSC.PLT ← Microsoft nmake, microsoft c makefile template
        RCS

      MDOS.PLT ← Microsoft nmake, DOS script makefile template
        RCS
   ...

Figure 5–2. My CMTREE

explained in this chapter. They are explained in detail in Chapter 6, *Makefile Architectures.*

Recommended Policies

This is a list of recommended policies for the CMTREE:

1. The environment variable CMTREE must point at the root of the CMTREE so the makefiles and tools can find the tree and the files that it contains. In Figure 5-2, the root of the tree is *d:\cmt.*

2. The CMTREE must contain a child directory called *plt.* This name is hardcoded in the file *makefile.tre* in the CMTREE. It's also hardcoded in at least one software tool (*getmakes*).

3. The *plt* directory must contain a subdirectory for each platform supported by the code management system. (The platform directories should also contain RCS subdirectories so that the makefile templates can be protected under RCS.)

4. Platform directory names should have two components. The first component name should be named after the *make* tool and the compiler used on the platform (e.g., *sun4gcc*) because the *make* tool and the compiler are the two things that change most often between platforms. The first component of the platform name should be less than or equal to eight characters in length so that it can be used on DOS systems.

5. The second component of the platform name must be *.plt.* The tools use this suffix to distinguish platform directories from other directories. This restriction also means that the tools will be confused if you happen to let any other "non-code management" directories in your filesystem end in *.plt.*

The CMHTREE

The CMHTREE holds products and shared files that have been exported from source trees. Conceptually, the CMHTREE holds the main "outputs" of the code management system, just as the source trees contain the main "inputs." (The makefile templates in the CMTREE can also be viewed as "inputs" to the code management system.)

Directory Structure

Figure 5-3 shows the structure of the CMHTREE on my small network of computers. The tree has three main subtrees: one for shared files (*share*), one for alpha test files (*ai*), and one for released files (*release*). Each of three main subtrees is further divided into platform-dependent subdirectories.

An environment variable named **CMHTREE** must point to the root of the CMHTREE so that the tools can find the tree.

The names of most directories in the CMHTREE are arbitrary, except for the platform directories, which must agree with the platform names used in the CMTREE. The

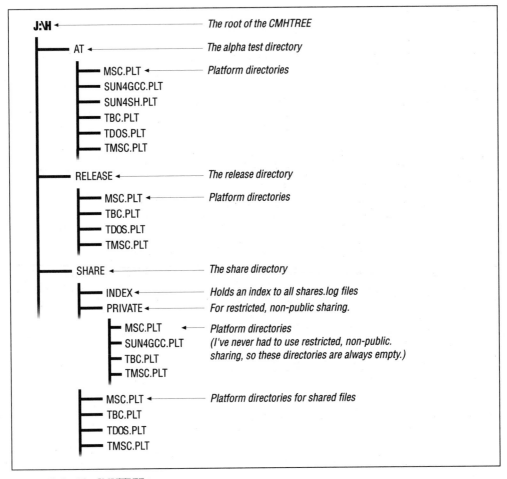

Figure 5-3. My CMHTREE

names of all other CMHTREE directories are defined in makefile macros in *makefile.tre* (stored in the CMTREE).

The CMHTREE can contain any other directories that you want to add, so long as the names of your directories don't confuse the tools. The tools use only the directories that are shown in Figure 5-3.

Directory Contents

Files are generally stored in two types of places in the CMHTREE, depending on whether the file is platform dependent or platform independent.

Platform-dependent (pd) files are exported *into* a platform directory (e.g., *share/sun4gcc.plt*), whereas platform-independent files are exported into a directory *above* a platform directory (e.g., *share*).

The *share* subtree holds software products that are used in the construction of other products.

The *at* (alpha test) directory and the *release* directory are structured identically, but the products exported into each directory could be different, of course. For example, the alpha test product might be compiled with debugging code included, whereas the release version might be compiled with compiler optimizing turned on.

I've found that I can save time and effort by placing the alpha test directories in my **PATH** environment variable so that I can run my alpha test programs right out of the alpha test directories. This approach can also work for teams of developers. They can add either the alpha test or the release directories (or both) to their **PATH**, depending on which versions of the products they want to use first.

One approach that might work well for your environment is to add both sets of directories to the **PATH** variable, with the alpha test directories being first. That way, friendly developers can use the experimental versions of products as long as they're stored in the alpha test directory. Then, if the alpha test versions are deleted when the products are officially released, everyone will automatically begin to use the officially released versions from the *release* directories (because the release directory is in the **PATH** variable after the alpha test directory).

The *share/index* directory contains an index file that lists the locations of all *shares.log* files in the code management system. (Recall that the *shares.log* files record import and export operations.) This index file is used by the file sharing tools (*cmi, cmx,* and *cmlsr*) to log and inspect file sharing relationships.

Files in the *share* and *share/platform.plt* directories are available for unrestricted sharing. No one has to ask anyone else for permission to share files that are stored in the *share* directory. The exporters of files into the *share* directory have already assumed that anyone can use the files.

In contrast, the *share/private* directory holds files that are available for restricted, non-public sharing. Files in this subtree should not be used without first obtaining permission from the human owner of the file. The *share/private* directory was created to share private files among closely related products.

For example, suppose you had an include file that defined common internal data structures used in several related software products. As a consequence of this, you'd want to share the file between these products, but you wouldn't want everyone to have access to the format of your internal data structures. So you'd share your files by exporting them to the *share/private* directory, where the other related products could access them. People who imported your files from this subtree without your permission (as the file's human owner) would be breaking the conventions of the code management system.

Recommended Policies

This is a list of recommended policies for the CMHTREE:

1. The environment variable **CMHTREE** must point at the root of the CMHTREE. In Figure 5-3, the root of the tree is *j:/h* ("h" stands for holding tree).

   I keep the names of the directories as short as feasible because DOS has limited space in its **PATH** variable. (Recall that I like to put the two DOS alpha test platform directories (*tdos.plt* and *tbc.plt*) in my **PATH** variable.) If I let the alpha test directory names get too long, they take up too much space in my **PATH** variable.

2. The CMHTREE must contain a child directory called *index*. This name is hardcoded into the file sharing tools. This directory contains a file called *shares.idx*, which contains a list of the pathnames (one per line) of all known *shares.log* files in the code management system.

3. The CMHTREE must contain a subdirectory called *share* and should contain subdirectories called *at* and *release*. These three directories hold shared, alpha test, and releasable files. The names of these directories are defined in the *makefile.tre* file in the root directory of the CMTREE.

4. The *share*, *at*, and *release* directories must contain subdirectories for each platform supported by the code management system. Platform directory names must agree with the platform names used in the CMTREE. No RCS subdirectories are required under the platform directories in the CMHTREE, since the CMHTREE holds finished products.

Source Trees

Source trees hold all the files that are used in the construction of software products. There can be an arbitrary number of source trees. This section explains the conventions for constructing and using source trees.

Directory Structures

To help with the following discussion, here are three sample tree structures for you to look at. A simple multi-platform product tree is shown in Figure 5-4. A more complex multi-product, multi-platform source tree is shown in Figure 5-5. For a large source tree containing many software products, look back at Figure 1-6.

Simple product trees

Consider the simple source tree shown in Figure 5-4. The root of the tree represents the product—in this case, a product named *ci* (the RCS checkin command). The source tree is also called a *product node*.

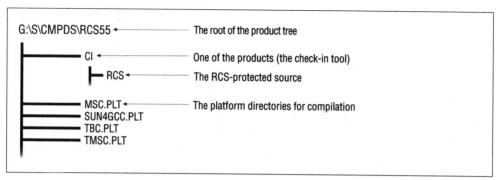

Figure 5–4. A simple multi-platform, pi source tree

There are three important things to notice about this simple source tree. First, there's only one *sibling* source directory, located beside—not underneath—the platform directories. This is important because it identifies the product as a platform-independent product.

Second, the platform directories are immediate children of the product node. The software tools define the product node to be the parent of the platform directories. They first find a platform directory by its *.plt* suffix, and then go up one directory to look at the name of the product node. If platform directories are more than one level under a product node, then the *twalker* tool won't use the proper product node name (which may include a *.ini*, *.lib*, or *.scr* suffix) for determining relative build order among products.

And third, the name of the product node doesn't end in *.ini*, *pd.lib*, *pid.lib*, or *.lib*. This is important because the tree walker tools are programmed to visit product nodes in sequential order, according to the names of the suffixes on the product node directories. The tools visit product nodes in a particular order to ensure that up-to-date files are exported by nodes early in the visiting sequence. The up-to-date files are then available for reuse in products that occur later in the visiting sequence.

Pi, pd, and pid nodes

Recall that pi, pd, and pid nodes were first introduced in Chapter 2, *A Hands-on Tour: Part 1*. Pi nodes contain only platform-independent files, pd nodes contain only platform-dependent files, and pid nodes can contain both types of files.

The simple source tree shown in Figure 5-4 is a pi tree because it contains only platform-independent source code. Since the same code can be used by all the platforms in the tree, only one source directory is required to hold the code. It follows that the best location for the source directory is beside the platform directories as a sibling directory.

However, the situation for pd and pid nodes is considerably different. Since at least some of the source code for these products is platform dependent, the source code for each different platform should be stored within that platform's subtree. As a consequence, many source directories are required, one below each platform directory.

See the *rcs_pi.lib* and *rcs_pd.lib* subtrees in Figure 5-6 for a clear picture of the structural differences between pi and pd product trees.

Complex product trees

Figure 5-5 shows an example of a more complex source tree—the RCS tools tree provided with this book. This source tree contains multiple software products, shared pi and pid libraries, and a few extra miscellaneous directories. The expanded structure of two of the product directories is shown in Figure 5-6.

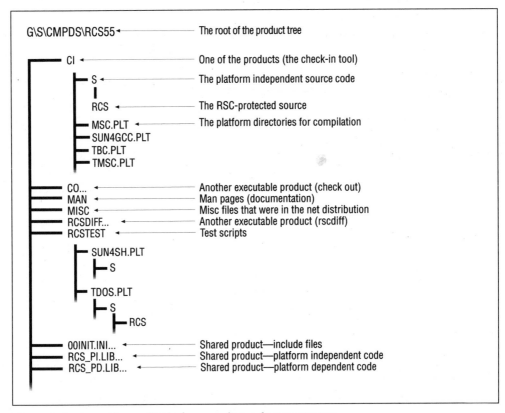

```
G\S\CMPDS\RCS55 ◄──────────────── The root of the product tree

        CI ◄──────────────────── One of the products (the check-in tool)

            S ◄──────────────── The platform independent source code

            RCS ◄────────────── The RSC-protected source
            MSC.PLT ◄────────── The platform directories for compilation
            SUN4GCC.PLT
            TBC.PLT
            TMSC.PLT

        CO... ◄────────────────── Another executable product (check out)
        MAN ◄─────────────────── Man pages (documentation)
        MISC ◄────────────────── Misc files that were in the net distribution
        RCSDIFF... ◄──────────── Another executable product (rscdiff)
        RCSTEST ◄─────────────── Test scripts
            SUN4SH.PLT
                S

            TDOS.PLT
                S
                    RCS

        OOINIT.INI... ◄────────── Shared product—include files
        RCS_PI.LIB... ◄────────── Shared product—platform independent code
        RCS_PD.LIB... ◄────────── Shared product—platform dependent code
```

Figure 5–5. A complex multi-platform, multi-product source tree

The RCS tools tree has several important features. First, note that all product directories are children of the main *rcs55* directory. Thus, according to the rules for recognizing product nodes that were explained earlier, the *rcs55* directory is NOT a product directory. That's because it isn't the parent of a platform directory. Instead, only the parent directories of platform directories are recognized as legitimate product directories. The structural conventions of this code management system allow many related products to be collected together under a single user-named directory.

A second interesting feature of the tree is that it contains two directories (*man* and *misc*) that are unrelated to the code management system. I created these two directories to move non-code files out of the main product directory. The *man* directory contains documentation (manual pages) for the RCS tools, and the *misc* directory contains miscellaneous old makefiles, copyright notices, and other such files that belong to the original RCS network distribution. The point here is that you can create your own directories within a product node if you want to. The code management system doesn't limit you to creating only source and platform directories.

A third interesting feature of the tree is that it contains a product subtree whose name contains the special *.ini* suffix: *00init.ini* (see Figure 5-6). Such directories are called *initialization directories*. Their purpose is to export shared files (usually include files) *before* the files are referenced by other products for compilation purposes.

One of the main problems solved by initialization directories is the ownership of shared files. Posed as questions, the problems are:

- Which product should own include files that are shared among several products?

- Where should the include files be stored?

- When automated tree walking tools are used to walk a product group subtree, how can they ensure that the shared include files are exported to the sharing directory before compilation begins?

Initialization (*.ini*) directories were designed to solve these problems. There are two main aspects of the solution.

First, the initialization product directory owns any include files that are commonly shared by members of the product group. (When a product node owns a file, both the file and its corresponding RCS file are stored within the product node.)

And second, the tree walker tools visit all initialization directories in a group before visiting any other product nodes in the group. This ensures that the shared include files will be exported to the *share* directory *before* compilations begin in other product directories.

Compilations are disallowed in initialization directories, because their purpose is to initialize (or set up) the product tree by exporting crucial include files.

Build order dependencies

Another interesting aspect of the tree in Figure 5-6 is that it contains two library directories whose names end in the suffix *.lib*. These directories, like the *.ini* directories, receive special treatment from the tree walker tools.

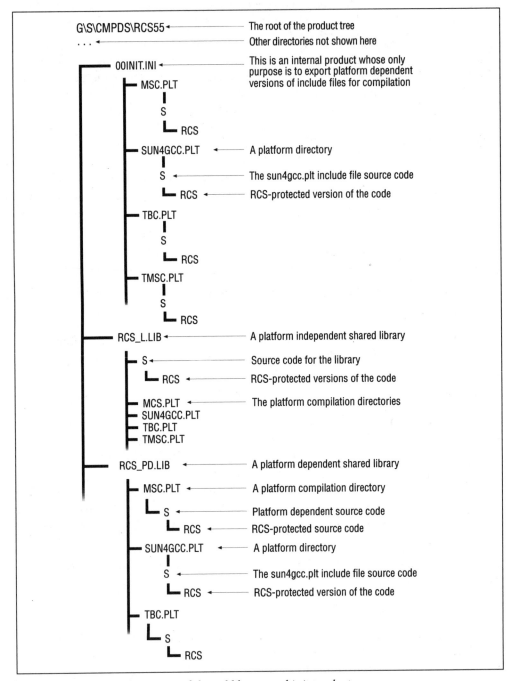

Figure 5–6. Expanded structure of shared library and init products

Specifically, the tree walker tools always visit *.ini* directories first, *pd.lib* and *pid.lib* directories second, *.lib* directories third, and other products last.

This ranking strategy implements the normal build-order sequence for software products: include files required for compilation are exported first, libraries required for linking are constructed next, and the products themselves are constructed last.

Figure 1-6 shows the top-level structure of one of the main source trees provided with this book. As you can see, the tree is comprised of several products that follow these structural conventions.

Directory Contents

The file contents of most of the directories that we've discussed have already been shown earlier in this book (in the tour chapters). I'll briefly restate the rules to make this discussion complete.

Top-level product directories never contain any files that are of interest to the code management system (although they may contain files that are of interest to human users).

Source directories contain source code files, and usually also contain an RCS subdirectory that contains RCS-protected versions of the source files.

Platform directories normally contain makefiles, object files, and completed binary files. Platform directories in pd and pid nodes may also contain source and RCS subdirectories.

Recommended Policies

This is a list of recommended policies for source trees:

1. Source trees are composed of four types of distinguished directories: product directories, platform directories, source directories, and RCS directories. All other types of directories are ignored by the code management system.

2. Product directories are defined as being the immediate parents of platform directories. The tools locate product directories by looking one level above platform directories.

3. Product directories may have special suffixes in their names. Special suffixes include *.ini* for initialization directories, and *pd.lib, pi.lib,* or *.lib* for library directories. Product node names that end in *pd.lib* or *pid.lib* are considered to be special types of library directories. (Recall that the suffixes are used by the tree walker tools to determine traversal order.)

4. Product nodes that contain pd source files are either pd or pid nodes. Pd and pid nodes must have one child source directory beneath each platform directory.

5. Product nodes that contain only pi source files are pi nodes. Pi nodes can only contain one source directory, and it must be a *sibling* of all platform directories.

6. Platform directories must follow the standard platform directory naming conventions. They must end with the suffix *.plt*.

7. Source directories must be named *s*.

RCS Directories

This section describes conventions for using the modified version of Tichy's Revision Control System that is provided by—and used by—this book. (The comments below also apply to the MKS RCS product, since that product has also been modified for use on DOS systems.)

Other source code control systems such as SCCS can be used if policies and tools are adjusted accordingly. This book, however, assumes that RCS is used.

Location and Structure

RCS subdirectories are optional, but if they exist they must be named *rcs* because the lowercase name is hardcoded into the tools. Mixed case pathnames are more difficult to work with in the tools than are purely lowercase pathnames.

Naming Conventions

In this code management system, RCS filenames have the same filenames as the original (RCS-protected) working files. Some operating systems such as DOS can't support the standard UNIX RCS file-naming convention of appending *,v* to the name of the original working file. Also, the new POSIX standard discourages commas in filenames, because it doesn't guarantee that such filenames will be portable.

It follows that the RCS files must be stored in a different directory than the original working files. This code management system specifies that RCS files should be stored in an RCS subdirectory named *rcs*, directly underneath the directory that holds the original working files. The RCS tools provided with this book have been modified to follow this convention.

Evaluation

This section informally evaluates the directory structure with respect to its intended goals. First, a short history of the directory structure is given, and then some possible objections are discussed.

Discussion

The most significant idea in the directory structure is using platform directories to separate platform-dependent files of all kinds. This physical separation of files naturally leads to the ideas of pi, pd, and pid product nodes, and to the placement of source directories within those nodes. As far as I know, the ideas of platform directories and distinct pi and pd nodes is almost two decades old. It may even be older.

The second most significant idea in the directory structure is using RCS files and RCS subdirectories (below all source directories) to track the evolution of all source code files. This idea leads naturally to the technique of cloning main source trees to make private developer trees in multi-person environments, and to the technique of checking modified source code files back into the main source tree. These ideas are also probably at least a decade old.

In addition to the ideas mentioned above, there are several other minor ideas worthy of mention. These are the presence of a standard holding tree (CMHTREE) for shared, alpha test, and released files; the presence of a standard tree (CMTREE) for holding standard makefile templates; the technique of generating tree walking scripts based on recognizable platform directory names; and the presence of the well defined policies and software tools that support the directory structure. Probably most of these ideas aren't totally new as individual ideas, but the integrated collection of these ideas seems relatively new.

Possible Objections

This section considers possible objections to the directory structures presented above.

- **The code management system is too complex.** One possible objection to the directory structure is that it's too complex when compared to traditional directory organizations such as those found in freeware program distributions.

  One might argue that many of those freeware programs have also been developed in multi-person, multi-platform environments, so those programs—and thus their directory structure techniques—can legitimately be called valid and useful. But their directory structures are much simpler than the ones shown here. They have no CMTREE, no CMHTREE, and no sprawling source trees with multiple levels of platform directories, source directories, and RCS subdirectories.

  However, a closer examination of the two approaches shows that the two techniques are not even close to having equivalent functionality. Both techniques can be used to store multi-platform code well enough, but the similarity ends there.

  For example, the traditional approach doesn't provide for the *simultaneous* existence or compilation of multiple platforms. It doesn't provide a standard mechanism for sharing files among either people or products. It doesn't support the automated generation of makefiles on multiple platforms. It doesn't support the logging or inspection of sharing relationships. It doesn't support the automated generation of tree walker scripts that can execute arbitrary commands in a set of selected directories. And so on. The two approaches are very different in their capabilities.

Instead, it's more reasonable to evaluate the complexity of the directory structures above in the context of the improved functionality that they offer. From that point of view, they don't seem to be unnecessarily complex at all, because it's difficult to imagine a *less* complex system that would provide equivalent functionality.

- **The code management system is too slow and requires extra work.** I can meet this objection by pointing out that the code management system is heavily automated (see the examples in the hands-on tour). As a consequence, common tasks can be performed both quickly and easily.

  As a case in point, the system described here is very much easier and faster than traditional techniques when bulk tree operations are considered. The tools (combined with the directory structure conventions) make it possible to generate and execute tree walker scripts for hundreds of products, all at computer speeds. For example, I once updated the makefile templates and completely regenerated 187 makefiles (for some 60 or 70 products) in 15 minutes on my old 386-16MHz personal computer.

  However, there is one noticeable little bit of extra work—typing pathnames requires more effort than in traditional situations. This code management system tends to have more directories and subdirectories than traditional directory structures do. But this is a very small inconvenience in comparison to the overall benefits of the entire system.

- **It's hard to port existing programs into the code management system.** This claim could be true for some programs in some situations. For example, it could take a lot of work to untangle programs that have a large number of nested `#ifdef` statements. It might also take a significant amount of work to duplicate the function of complex makefiles using the simple makefile templates and tools provided with this system.

  The claim certainly isn't true for most programs that have only a few `#ifdefs`, or are platform independent (because they have no `#ifdefs` at all), or have normal makefile requirements. So the claim only applies to a restricted set of programs.

  To be picky, the main point of the objection above is *not* that the code management disallows platform-dependent `#ifdefs`. Instead, the objection is concerned with the amount of work it takes to undo or port tangled `#ifdefs` statements.

  It has always required a lot of work to port programs that contain a lot of nested `#ifdefs`, no matter what code management system is used. The particular claim being discussed here isn't just aimed at the particular code management system in this book. It's aimed at all code management systems, everywhere.

6

Makefile Architectures

This chapter describes a six-part makefile architecture that effectively supports the automatic generation of makefiles. This is an important achievement because it significantly reduces the cost of generating and maintaining makefiles. It also helps to make the treatment of products more uniform within the development environment by virtue of more uniform makefile targets and command sequences.

The main idea behind the six-part makefile architecture is to separate and encapsulate different kinds of makefile knowledge into separate template files. Then custom makefiles for different needs can easily be assembled by including the appropriate templates into a top-level makefile.

The following sections describe the six makefile templates, a set of recommended makefile targets, and some important makefile policies. A special discussion on tree walking techniques is also included. Finally, the chapter concludes with an informal evaluation of the makefile system.

A Six-part Makefile Architecture

Table 6-1 summarizes the names and information content of the six different templates.

Table 6–1: The Six Makefile Templates and their Contents

Makefile Name	Type of knowledge	Description
makefile	Default Targets	The top-level makefile
makefile.tre	Environment	CMHTREE structure and filename macros
makefile.plt	Platform	Platform-dependent compile/link commands
makefile.xxe/lib/ssc	Product type	Commands for building exes, libs, etc.
makefile.pi/pd/pid	Program	Automatically generated dependency rules
imports.imp	Program	Import commands, special targets, custom commands

makefile—The Top-level Makefile

The top-level makefile is named *makefile*. Its main purpose is to include the other makefile templates. It also contains a few default makefile targets such as the default **build** target, the default **exports** target, and the default **release** target. It doesn't contain any program, platform, or product-dependent information.

Normally, there is only one top-level *makefile* in each platform directory. Since it contains no program-dependent information, it can be automatically generated (or regenerated) by the *getmakes* tool at any time.

Example 6-1 shows the top-level makefile for the *cmi* tool under the *sun4gcc.plt* platform.

Example 6–1: The cmi Tool's Makefile File

```
# $Id: makefile.mak 1.7 1993/01/25 19:54:37 jameson Exp $

# the makefile platform name, and the export platform name
MP=sun4gcc.plt
EP=sun4gcc.plt

# where to get the source tree definitions for this whole makefile system
TREE_DEFS=$(CMTREE)/makefile.tre

# the default thing to do when you just type 'make'
default: build

include $(TREE_DEFS)          # always need this
include $(MDIR)/$(MP)/$(MP)   # always need this
include $(IMPORTS_IMP)        # program unique defs
include $(MAKEFILE_PI)        # use for building pi products
include $(MAKEFILE_XXE)       # use for building executables

full: imports build
```

Example 6–1: The cmi Tool's Makefile File (continued)

```
all: imports build exports

exports: exports.spe
        $(CMX) -nl $(PROG)$(X) -dd $(ALPHA_DIR)/$(EP)

release: release.spe
        $(CMX) -nl $(PROG)$(X) -dd $(RELEASE_DIR)/$(EP)
```

makefile.tre—The Tree-specific Makefile

makefile.tre is the first included makefile. It contains makefile macros that define the internal structures of the CMTREE and the CMHTREE. As a consequence, makefile commands in the standard templates can include, import, and export files to and from the proper places in the CMTREE and the CMHTREE.

Only one copy of the *makefile.tre* file is required per code management system, because the same copy of *makefile.tre* is included by all makefiles. The file is stored in the root directory of the CMTREE. Example 6-2 shows the *makefile.tre* for the *cmi* tool under the *sun4gcc.plt* platform.

Example 6–2: The cmi Tool's makefile.tre File

```
# $Id: makefile.tre 1.9 1993/04/15 16:12:17 jameson Exp $

# This makefile defines the structure of the holding tree and the
# names of common filenames.
 ... (lines deleted to save space)

# this misc dir holds platform makefiles, etc
MDIR=$(CMTREE)/plt
MDIR_B=$(CMTREE_B)\plt

# the place to put all software for release
RELEASE_DIR=$(CMHTREE)/release
RELEASE_DIR_B=$(CMHTREE_B)\release

# the place to put all software for alpha testing (inhouse testing)
ALPHA_DIR=$(CMHTREE)/at
ALPHA_DIR_B=$(CMHTREE_B)\at

# the share directory holds shared files
SDIR=$(CMHTREE)/share
SDIR_B=$(CMHTREE_B)\share

# the index directory holds share logs index
IDXDIR=$(SDIR)/index

# don't share things from this dir without permission from the owner
PVTSDIR=$(SDIR)/private
```

Example 6-2: The cmi Tool's makefile.tre File (continued)

```
# Object and filename macros
ALL_OBJS=
OBJ_PI=
OBJ_PD=
 . . .
# standard names of platform independent and dependent makefiles
IMPORTS_IMP=imports.imp
 . . .
MAKEFILE_LLB=makefile.llb          # makefile for building libraries
 . . .
```

makefile.plt—The Platform-dependent Makefile

The *platform.plt* file (e.g., *tbc.plt, sun4gcc.plt*) is usually the second file included by the top-level makefile. It defines platform-dependent information such as the names of platform-dependent software tools, file suffixes, default compiler options, and implicit makefile rules.

The filename is always identical to the platform directory name that it represents. So the name of this file is *sun4gcc.plt* for the *sun4gcc.plt* platform, *tbc.plt* for the Borland C *tbc.plt* platform, and so on.

There's only one copy of the *platform.plt* file per code management system, since it is included by all makefiles for that particular platform. Example 6-3 shows the platform-dependent makefile for the *cmi* tool under the *sun4gcc.plt* platform.

Example 6-3: The cmi Tool's sun4gcc.plt File

```
# $Id: sun4gcc.plt 1.5 1993/04/15 16:21:58 jameson Exp $

# FILE SUFFIX NAMES
#
# suffixes for this environment; object,executable,library,archive,shell,etc
O=.o
X=
L=.a
A=
S=.sh
AWKS=.awk
SEDS=.sed

# TOOL NAMES
# Define the location of tools that should be used for makes.
# Okay to use hardcoded locations to avoid personal search path effects.
# The undefined log arg macro is for forcing logging on the command
# line. Type 'make -Dlog=-f' to force share log updates.

CMI=cmi $(log)
GENDEP=gendep
SED=sed
```

Example 6-3: The cmi Tool's sun4gcc.plt File (continued)

```
  . . .

# Override these flags in the imports.imp file. If you do, watch for
# incorrect macro expansion effects in your make tool.
CCFLAGS = -ansi -I. -I- -c

# can use different flags for lex and yacc if you like
CCLEXFLAGS  = $(CFLAGS)
CCYACCFLAGS = $(CFLAGS)

# Linker command (LD), flags, and libraries (LL).
# Include any initialization and library files required by the linker.
lb=
LDFLAGS =
LD=${CC} -o $(PROG) -L$(ALPHA_DIR)/$(EP) $(ALL_OBJS) $(lb3) $(lb)
  . . .
```

imports.imp—The Program-dependent Makefile

The *imports.imp* file is the third file included by the top-level makefile. It contains custom, program-dependent information for the software product being constructed. For example, it contains the names of both the product and the link libraries that are required to build the product. The file also contains any special importing, exporting, and release instructions.

There are many *import.imp* files in the code management system—one for each of the platform directories in each of the product subtrees. This is because the *imports.imp* file might contain unique custom instructions for each different product on each different platform.

The *imports.imp* file is never automatically regenerated because it contains custom, manually generated, program-dependent information. The regeneration tools will always ignore it, even though they'll replace the other makefile templates in the directory. Example 6-4 shows the *imports.imp* makefile for the *cmi* tool under the *sun4gcc.plt* platform.

Example 6-4: The cmi Tool's imports.imp File

```
# $Id: imports.imp 1.8 1993/04/16 19:41:32 jameson Exp $

# This file defines unique information for the program.
# The other makefiles can be automatically generated around it.

# The name of the thing being built on this platform (omit suffixes)
# eg. cmx cm_pd
PROG=cmi

# special libraries to include (full paths if they aren't in std places)
lb3=-lcm_pi -lcm_ro -lcm_pd
```

Example 6–4: The cmi Tool's imports.imp File (continued)

```
imports:
        $(CMI) -nl s_const.h
        $(CMI) -nl ../s/version.h
          . . .

imports.rev:
        $(RM) s_const.h
        $(RM) version.h
          . . .

# non-standard exporting instructions go here
exports.spe:

# special non-standard release instructions go here
release.spe:

# commands to update compilation dependencies go here
depends:
        $(GENDEP) pi

# special build instructions go here
build.spe:

# special clean instructions go here
clean.spe:
  . . .
```

makefile.pi/pd/pid—The Dependency Rules Makefile

The files *makefile.pi*, *makefile.pd*, and *makefile.pid* contain makefile dependency rules
for the software product being constructed. Normally, only one of the files is ever used
at any one time.

At least one of these files is required for each software product. Complex products
with subdivided source directories may have several of these files. They would normally be named *makefile.s1*, *makefile.s2*, etc. Later in this chapter, I explain how to
create multiple dependency files from subdivided source directories.

Example 6-5 shows the *makefile.pi* file for the *cmi* tool under the *sun4gcc.plt* platform.
Example 6-6 shows the *makefile.pd* file for the *cm_pd.lib* library under the *sun4gcc.plt*
platform.

Example 6–5: The cmi Tool's makefile.pi File

```
# this makefile is automatically generated.

# the relative path from compilation dir to source dir
PI=../s/
```

Example 6-5: The cmi Tool's makefile.pi File (continued)

```
cmi$(O): $(PI)ami.c s_const.h s_types.h s_macros.h s_sysdep.h \
        s_debug.h cecmdenv.h version.h
    $(CC) $(CCFLAGS) $(PI)cmi.c

ceinit$(O): $(PI)ceinit.c s_const.h s_types.h s_macros.h s_errno.h \
        cecmdenv.h
    $(CC) $(CCFLAGS) $(PI)ceinit.c

ceparse$(O): $(PI)ceparse.c s_const.h s_types.h s_macros.h s_debug.h \
        cecmdenv.h
    $(CC) $(CCFLAGS) $(PI)ceparse.c

    . . .

# a list of all files processed in this invocation
OBJ_PI= cmi$(O) ceinit$(O) ceparse$(O) ceusage$(O) cevalid$(O) \
        ceworker$(O)
```

Example 6-6: The cm_pd.lib Library's makefile.pd File

```
# this makefile is automatically generated.

# the relative path from compilation dir to source dir
PD=s/

copyfile$(O): $(PD)copyfile.c s_const.h s_types.h s_macros.h
    $(CC) $(CCFLAGS) $(PD)copyfile.c

getcwd$(O): $(PD)getcwd.c
    $(CC) $(CCFLAGS) $(PD)getcwd.c

getdrive$(O): $(PD)getdrive.c
    $(CC) $(CCFLAGS) $(PD)getdrive.c

    . . .

# a list of all files processed in this invocation
OBJ_PD= copyfile$(O) getcwd$(O) getdrive$(O) setdrive$(O) spltpath$(O)
```

makefile.llb/xxe/ssc—The Product Type Makefile

The three files *makefile.llb, makefile.xxe,* and *makefile.ssc* contain makefile instructions for building three types of products: binary executables, libraries, and scripts.

Only one of these files is ever included into the top-level makefile for any one product, because only one type of product can be produced by any one product node.

Producing only one product per product node is good policy because it greatly simplifies the tasks to be performed by the makefile generation tools. Automatically generating a makefile to produce a single product of a particular type is much easier than generating a makefile that can produce several products of different types.

All three of these makefile templates are platform dependent. As a consequence, one of them is required for every platform directory in every product node (the same as for top-level makefiles).

Example 6-7, Example 6-8, and Example 6-9 show examples of these three template files for the *sun4gcc.plt* platform.

Example 6-7: The cmi Tool's makefile.xxe File

```
# $Id: makefile.xxe 1.3 1993/01/15 23:09:25 jameson Exp $


###############################################################
# Standard Targets
###############################################################

clean: clean.spe imports.rev
        $(RM) *$(O)

empty: empty.spe clean
        $(RM) $(PROG)$(X) $(SHARESLOG)


###############################################################
# Standard Build Targets
###############################################################

# If these names are insufficient, add your own names too
ALL_OBJS=$(OBJ_PI) $(OBJ_PD) $(OBJ_YAC) $(OBJ_LEX) \
        $(OBJ_S1) $(OBJ_S2) $(OBJ_S3) $(OBJ_S4) $(OBJ_S5) \
          $(OBJ_S6) $(OBJ_S7) $(OBJ_S8) $(OBJ_S9) $(OBJ_S10)

build: build.spe $(PROG)$(X)

$(PROG)$(X): $(ALL_OBJS)
        $(LD)
```

Example 6-8: The CM_L.LIB Library's makefile.llb File

```
# $Id: makefile.lib 1.4 1993/01/15 23:09:27 jameson Exp $


###############################################################
#  Standard Targets
###############################################################

clean: clean.spe imports.rev
        $(RM) *$(O) $(LIBLIST)

empty: empty.spe clean
        $(RM) $(PROG)$(L) $(SHARESLOG)
```

Example 6-8: The CM_L.LIB Library's makefile.llb File (continued)

```
###################################################################
#  Library Building Rules
###################################################################

# If these names are insufficient, add your own names too
ALL_OBJS=$(OBJ_PI) $(OBJ_PD) $(OBJ_YAC) $(OBJ_LEX) \
        $(OBJ_S1) $(OBJ_S2) $(OBJ_S3) $(OBJ_S4) $(OBJ_S5) \
          $(OBJ_S6) $(OBJ_S7) $(OBJ_S8) $(OBJ_S9) $(OBJ_S10)

build: build.spe $(PROG)$(L)

$(PROG)$(L): $(ALL_OBJS)
        @echo Building $(PROG)$(L) ...
        @$(RM) $(PROG)$(L)
        @$(LIB) rcv $(PROG)$(L) $(ALL_OBJS)
        @$(RANLIB) $(PROG)$(L)
        @echo Done building $(PROG)$(L).
```

Example 6-9: The gendep Tool's makefile.ssc File

```
# $Id: makefile.ssc 1.1 1993/01/15 23:12:04 jameson Exp $

###################################################################
# Standard Targets
###################################################################

clean: clean.spe imports.rev

empty: empty.spe clean
       $(RM) $(PROG)$(S) $(SHARESLOG)

###################################################################
#  Building Targets
###################################################################

build: build.spe $(PROG)$(S)

$(PROG)$(S): $(ALL_OBJS)
```

Naming Conventions

The names of the makefile templates have been chosen to avoid wildcard matching problems when files are being deleted in the platform directories. The unusual names allow you to easily select the most commonly referenced groups of files in the directory. Table 6-2 lists some common wildcard expressions, the files that they delete, and the purposes of the deletions.

Table 6–2: Deleting Makefiles and Products with Starname Expresssions

Wildcard Expression	Files Deleted
*rm makefile**	Deletes auto-generated makefiles; saves *imports.imp*.
*rm makefile.**	Deletes *makefile.pi/pd/pid*. Use to rebuild dependency rules.
*rm *.imp*	Deletes *imports.imp* file. Use to create a new *imports.imp*.
*rm *.lib*	Deletes final products. Use when rebuilding final products.
*rm *.exe*	Deletes final products. Use when rebuilding final products.
*rm *.bat*	Deletes final products. Use when rebuilding final products.

Several platform-dependent makefile macros have been defined in the makefile templates to hold the most common filename extensions for different platforms. Some common suffixes for DOS include *.obj*, *.exe*, *.sed*, *.awk*, and *.bat*. In addition, the *imports.imp* file defines a makefile macro named **PROG** to hold the name of the current product.

Using platform-dependent suffix macros such as these makes it possible for the makefile templates to symbolically reference filenames without regard for platform-dependent filename conventions.

For example, the expression **$(PROG)$(X)** refers to an executable filename on all platforms, where **PROG** is the root name of the executable file, and **X** is the extension name of the executable file (if one is required).

Table 6-3 shows a sample list of macros that are defined in the *platform.plt* template file for each platform. The list of support suffixes can be modified simply by changing the appropriate *platform.plt* makefile template. Empty values indicate that the suffix isn't used on that platform.

Table 6–3: Filename Suffixes by Platform

Platform	S	O	X	L	AWKS	SEDS	LEXS	YACS
tbc.plt	.bat	.obj	.exe	.lib	.awk	.sed	.l	.y
tdos.plt	.bat	.obj	.exe	.lib	.awk	.sed	.l	.y
msc.plt	.bat	.obj	.exe	.lib	.awk	.sed	.l	.y
mdos.plt	.bat	.obj	.exe	.lib	.awk	.sed	.l	.y
sun4gcc.plt		.o		.a	.awk	.sed	.l	.y
sun4sh.plt		.o		.a	.awk	.sed	.l	.y

Standard Makefile Targets

The makefile templates contain three types of standard targets: normal targets, shadow targets, and reversing targets. Table 6-4 lists the standard targets used by the makefiles in this code management system.

Table 6–4: Standard Targets in Makefile Templates

Target Name	Template	Description
Normal Targets		
imports	*imports.imp*	Imports files required for a build
depends	*imports.imp*	Recreates dependency rules (mf.pi/pd)
lint	*imports.imp*	Runs source files through lint
protos	*imports.imp*	Generates a file of prototypes from source files
build	*mf.xxe/llb/ssc*	Builds the product (e.g., compiles)
exports	*makefile*	Exports products to CMHTREE alpha test dir
release	*makefile*	Exports products to CMHTREE release dir
full	*makefile*	Calls imports and build
all	*makefile*	Calls imports, build, and exports
clean	*mf.xxe/llb/ssc*	Remove object files/imports; saves products
empty	*mf.xxe/llb/ssc*	Calls **clean**, then removes products, too
Shadow Targets		
build.spe	*imports.imp*	Executes special build commands
exports.spe	*imports.imp*	Executes special exporting commands
release.spe	*imports.imp*	Executes special releasing commands
clean.spe	*imports.imp*	Executes special cleanup commands
empty.spe	*imports.imp*	Executes special empty commands
Reversing Targets		
imports.rev	*imports.imp*	Deletes all imported files

Normal targets represent the default common tasks in software development environments. These include importing files, building products, exporting or releasing products, deleting intermediate object files, and deleting the final product files after exporting.

Shadow targets are a place to record the special command sequences that are sometimes needed to carry out custom processing requirements. Shadow targets are always placed in the dependency lists of the normal targets so that invoking the normal targets will automatically invoke the shadow targets. For example, the shadow target **exports.spe** is always placed in the dependency list of the normal target **exports** (see Example 6-1).

This approach allows developers to perform common tasks with a very standard makefile interface (the normal targets), even though there might be special processing tasks taking place behind the scenes (the shadow targets). Shadow targets are named after the normal targets, except that the shadow targets have a **.spe** suffix.

Reversing targets undo the work done by normal targets. For example, the **imports.rev** target reverses the work done by the **imports** target. It deletes all files that were imported by the **imports** target. Actually, **import.rev** is the only reversing target in the templates. I've never found a need for any other reversing targets. (Although I suppose you could argue that the **clean** and **empty** targets are reversing targets for **build**.)

In this book, the names of normal targets are limited to one component of eight characters or less, because of restrictions imposed by Microsoft *nmake* under MS-DOS. First, *nmake* disallows target names with three components (e.g., **x.y.z**), as well as names that don't fit within the MS-DOS filename length limits (8+3). Second, shadow target names are formed by adding a special **.spe** suffix to the name of the corresponding normal target. This implies that normal targets can't have suffixes, because if they did, shadow target names would have three components, which is not allowed.

Target Placement in Makefile Templates

As shown in Table 6-4, the three types of normal, shadow, and reversing targets are spread throughout the six makefile templates.

The **exports**, **release**, **full**, and **all** targets appear in the top-level makefile because they're the same for all products. They're the same because they represent very stable default actions that can normally be applied to all software products. (Special processing needs for these normal targets are carried out by the corresponding shadow targets in the *imports.imp* file.)

Placing these targets in the top-level makefile also makes it easier to update them automatically with the makefile generation tools. You just have to edit the top-level template and then regenerate all the makefiles in the system. (In contrast, it's usually far more difficult to update all the *imports.imp* files in the system. You can't just replace all the *imports.imp* files with updated templates. Instead, you have to *edit* each existing *imports.imp* file, either manually or with *sed* scripts. This can be tricky or unfeasible if the editing changes are significant.)

The **imports** and **depends** targets and all the shadow and reversing targets are placed in the *imports.imp* file. This file is intended to contain all the product-dependent makefile information for any particular product. All other templates are automatically generated and rarely have to be changed once they've been created.

The **build**, **clean**, and **empty** targets are placed in the *makefile.xxe/llb/ssc* files. These particular targets tell how to build—and how to clean up after—the different product types (executables, libraries, scripts). These targets also call corresponding shadow targets in the *imports.imp* file to carry out any special processing requirements.

Special Targets and Special Processing Needs

As described above, the most desirable way of carrying out special processing needs is to use the targets in the *import.imp* file. Both normal and shadow targets can be placed into *imports.imp*.

If the special targets or actions in the *imports.imp* file are common enough in your work environment, perhaps you should relocate them as normal targets in the appropriate makefile templates. However, before doing that you should ensure that your new targets offer identical (or very similar) services on all platforms. Otherwise the uniformity of the multi-platform code management system described here will be destroyed, and you'll end up with nothing more than a collection of distinctly different single-platform code management systems.

If you want to make permanent custom changes to the command-line options or to the command sequences within a product's makefile, then place the changes in *imports.imp*. That way, your custom changes won't be overwritten the next time you regenerate all the makefiles in the system.

If you want to make temporary custom changes to the command-line options or to the command sequences within a product's makefile, then place the changes in the *makefile* if possible. That way, you can easily get rid of the temporary changes by regenerating the makefile. (Otherwise, you'd have to manually edit the *imports.imp* file to back out your changes and restore default behavior.)

Creating Makefile Templates for New Platforms

The process of creating new makefile templates for new platforms was described in the section called "Creating a New Platform".

Here's an overview of how to create templates for a new platform:

1. In the *CMTREE/plt* directory, make a new platform directory to hold the templates for the new platform. The directory name should be representative of the platform, and should end in *.plt*. (Platform naming conventions are discussed in the section called "Recommended Policies" in **UNKNOWN XREF**.)

2. Generate a new set of makefile templates by cloning the templates from an existing platform directory.

3. Edit the templates one by one to suit the characteristics of the new platform. You may have to change filename suffix macros, compiler and linker options, and the algorithms for constructing particular product types.

4. Verify that the templates work properly by constructing and exporting an existing software product. (You can use *makeplt* to make a new platform directory in the existing product node.)

5. Create a short message file describing the new platform and check the new templates into RCS with a command such as *rcsdo ci_u_initial msg -log default.*

Creating new templates should be a very simple and straightforward process, since most *make* tools use approximately the same syntax. As a result, the clone-and-modify approach is usually very effective.

Perhaps you'll have to invent new targets and special command sequences to suit the needs of your situation. If that's the case, you're on your own. You might be able to get some ideas by scanning through existing templates.

If the *make* tool on the new platform requires a different syntax for the dependency rules, you'll have to modify the *gendep* tool to generate the syntax that you need.

Special Compilation Options

Sometimes you might want to pass special compilation options to *make*. For example, you might want to turn on special debugging **#ifdefs** or use special compilation options.

The following paragraphs discuss several techniques for passing special arguments to *make*. They are arranged in order of least permanent to most permanent.

The easiest and least permanent way of passing options is to pass them on the *twalker* or *make* command line. For example, you could use a command such as *make "-Ddebug -DLEVEL=4" all* to enable your debugging code and define the C preprocessor symbol LEVEL to have a value of 4.

A slightly more permanent way is to override the compiler option defaults that are set in the makefile templates. You can do this by redefining or adding statements to the top-level *makefile* in your compilation directory. For example, you could add the statement *CCFLAGS= -Ddebug -DLEVEL=4 . . .* to turn on debugging, as in the previous point.

If you redefine compiler options in the top-level *makefile* in your compilation directory, the options will be lost if the makefiles are ever regenerated because the whole file is replaced.

If you'd rather keep the options around for a longer time, then you can place the redefinition statment in the *imports.imp* file, which is never replaced. Then you can enable or disable different sets of options as you please, simply by editing the *imports.imp* file.

Of course, you have to put the redefinitions in the proper place in the makefile so that they override the default values. This can be a problem sometimes because some *make* tools perform macro expansion at definition time, rather than at runtime. In that case, your overridden definitions won't have the desired effect.

For example, suppose your platform makefile template file (*myplat.plt*) has the following two lines in it:

```
CCFLAGS=-c
CC=cc $(CCFLAGS) -c ...other arguments...
```

Suppose also that you later redefine **CCFLAGS** in the top level makefile as shown below, in the hopes that your definition of **CCFLAGS** will override the original definition before any files are compiled.

```
# the default thing to do when you just type 'make'
include $(TREE_DEFS)                    # always need this
include $(MDIR)/$(MP)/$(MP)             # always need this
include $(IMPORTS_IMP)                  # program unique defs
include $(MAKEFILE_PI)                  # use for pi files
include $(MDIR)/$(MP)/$(MAKEFILE_XXE)   # use for building executables

# override CCFLAGS options that were set in the platform template file
CCFLAGS=-c -Ddebug
```

Suppose your make tool performs macro expansion "incorrectly" at definition time. Then the value of **CC** in the example above would always contain the the value of **CCFLAGS** that existed at the time **CC** was defined ("-c"). This type of behavior might be called something like "static expansion" or "definition-time expansion".

On the other hand, suppose your make tool performs macro expansion just before it issues the expanded commands to the operating system. Then the value of **CC** would contain the value of **CCFLAGS** that existed when the **CC** command was passed to the operating system (**-c -Ddebug**). This type of macro expansion behavior might be called "dynamic expansion" or "runtime expansion."

If you use the same sets of options over and over again on multiple products, then put the alternative statements in the *imports.imp* makefile template in the CMTREE. That way, whenever you generate the first set of makefiles for a new product, the alternative option statements will be available for enabling when you need them.

If none of these solutions is appropriate, then you can make up your own CMTREE to hold your own custom makefile templates (and options) within it. To use your private CMTREE, reset your **CMTREE** environment variable to point to it.

You may encounter problems when you try to pass combinations of arguments that contain whitespace between them to the *twalker* tool. For example, I had trouble passing the string *-Dlog=-f -nocopy* from the *twalker* command line to *make* on UNIX. (The string is useful for regenerating *shares.log* entries, as described in Chapter 7, *File Sharing*.)

I had to modify the *mwalker* tool to generate the appropriate */bin/sh* magic to get the quoting to work. You may have to do the same, if you port the tools to other platforms.

Generating Makefiles from Subdivided Source Directories

Sometimes large software products contain so much source code that it makes sense to subdivide the files into smaller groups located in subdirectories of the original source directory.

Subdivisions can be a convenience to developers because they separate large collections of possibly unrelated source files into smaller groups of more closely related files. For example, in some situations it may make sense to place the user-interface code, the database-interaction code, and the input/output code into separate subdirectories.

Because the structure of subdivided source directories can be arbitrary, the makefile generation tools in this book cannot completely generate a full set of makefiles by themselves. Some manual intervention is required. The following example shows you how to manually generate dependency rules for source files in subdivided source directories.

We'll use the *gendep* tool to generate a file of makefile dependency rules (*makefile.pi/pd/pid*) from the source files that it reads. *gendep* usually looks in the *../s* directory (the pi source directory, as referenced from the compilation directory) and in the *s/* directory (the pd source directory, as referenced from the compilation directory).

The following example shows how to get the *gendep* tool to look in arbitrary directories.

Suppose you had a subdivided source directory for a library of subroutines that looked like this:

```
G:S
+---DIR          library functions to do with directories
+---FILE         library functions to do with files
+---LIST         library functions to do with lists
+---STRING       library functions to do with strings
```

Change to a platform directory within the same product node as the subdivided source directories. Then manually provide the name of the subdirectory containing the source code to the *gendep* tool, as shown below. Invoke the *gendep* tool once for each subdirectory to be processed.

```
gendep s1 ../s/dir/ *.c        creates dependency rules in makefile.s1
gendep s2 ../s/file/ *.c       creates dependency rules in makefile.s2
gendep s3 ../s/list/ *.c       etc.
gendep s4 ../s/string/ *.c
```

The pathname for each subdivided source directory should be a relative pathname from the current platform directory. Use *s1* for the first subdirectory, *s2* for the second subdirectory, and so on. (These names are predefined in the *makefile.tre* template file.)

For each invocation of *gendep*, a new file (*makefile.s1, makefile.s2, ...*) will be created in the platform directory. Each file contains the makefile dependency rules for one of the subdivided source directories.

Then manually include the generated makefiles in the *imports.imp* file—not in the top-level *makefile*. This is important, because any custom include statements in the top-level makefile would be lost whenever the makefiles were next regenerated.

```
include $(MAKEFILE_S1)          these lines go in imports.imp!
include $(MAKEFILE_S2)
include $(MAKEFILE_S3)
include $(MAKEFILE_S4)
```

If you want to automate the dependency generation process in the future, put the *gendep* commands under the **depends** target in the *imports.imp* file. Then you can regenerate the dependencies by typing *make depends*. (Notice that I've used a macro to invoke the *gendep* tool. This is important on MS-DOS systems because the macro contains some special command-line arguments.)

```
# automate the generation of dependency rules from subdivided directories:
depends:
    $(GENDEP) s1 ../s/dir/ *.c          creates dependency rules in makefile.s1
    $(GENDEP) s2 ../s/file/ *.c         creates dependency rules in makefile.s2
    $(GENDEP) s3 ../s/list/ *.c         etc.
    $(GENDEP) s4 ../s/string/ *.c
```

Evaluation

This section informally evaluates the makefile architecture and tools that were presented in this chapter. First, a short history of the makefile architecture is given, and then some possible objections are discussed.

Discussion

The most significant idea in the makefile architecture presented in this chapter is the separation of different kinds of makefile knowledge into separate files. The separation is also a key factor in making it possible to create automated tools to support common makefile operations.

As far as I know, the idea of separating different kinds of makefile knowledge is almost two decades old—roughly the same age as the idea of platform directories. I say this because I learned about both of these ideas from someone who's been using them for 15 years or more. However, the idea of separating makefile knowledge into the six specific parts shown here is probably new with this book (unless someone else unknown to me has already done it this way).

The second most significant idea associated with the makefile architecture is the use of automated tools to perform common makefile maintenance operations. Of course, the idea of generating individual makefiles isn't new, nor is the idea of automatically generating dependencies. Freeware tools for performing both of these tasks have been available for many years on the net. But the overall capabilities of the freeware tools are substantially below the capabilities of the toolset provided with this book.

Advantages

The main advantage of the makefile architecture shown here is that it reduces project maintenance costs by isolating different kinds of makefile information into separate files. This permits developers to use efficient automated tools to generate and maintain makefiles in a multi-platform environment. Here is a list of several other advantages:

- Uniformity. The makefile architecture is more convenient for developers because makefiles are the same everywhere in the project, across both products and platforms.

- Convenience. The makefile architecture is a convenience to developers because many common development tasks are heavily supported with automated tools.

- Structural flexibility. The architecture has a flexible structure because it continues to work even after large-scale directory reorganizations (tree walker scripts can be easily regenerated as needs require).

- Procedural flexibility. The procedures in the architecture are flexible because it provides two places for adding custom makefile targets: in the default makefile templates, or in the *imports.imp* file. In addition, the tree walker scripts can execute arbitrary commands in selected directories in a subtree.

- Multi-platform support. The architecture (and the tools) help to reduce the cost of creating and maintaining makefiles for different platforms.

- Ease of understanding. The six-part architecture in this book isolates and separates different kinds of makefile knowledge into separate makefile template files. This makes it easier for developers to understand the detailed operation of whole sets of similar makefiles that must achieve the same computational goals, but on different platforms.

Efficiency and convenience issues

The makefile system described here is efficient because it reduces the cost of generating and maintaining makefiles. Also, it's convenient because most of the work is done by automated tools with simple user interfaces. The overall convenience of the system is also enhanced by the standard form of the makefiles, even across different platforms and product types.

The main cost associated with the makefile system is setting up the initial default templates for your work environment. After that, the only significant ongoing cost is that of modifying *imports.imp* files to satisfy the special processing needs of particular products. (Developers have to do that anyway, no matter what makefile system is used.)

Possible Objections

The initial feeling of most people is that the makefile system described here is overly complex compared to other makefile systems that they've used. This is primarily because of the educational costs that are required of them when they first start using the system. For example, they're required to learn about the six-part makefile architecture, about the interactions between templates, and about the tools that generate the final makefiles.

But it's also interesting to consider what you *don't* have to learn when using this system. For example, you don't have to learn a different makefile architecture for every platform—the one shown here is nearly identical across all platforms. You don't have to learn a separate set of tools for every platform—the tools shown here will work on almost any platform. And you don't have to learn a separate set of makefile syntaxes for each platform—this system isolates you from most of the peculiarities of the syntaxes on all platforms.

So in the end, it's very possible that you might have to learn *less* by using this single system on all platforms than by using any other combination of multiple makefile systems that are only available on some platforms.

Anyway, it's reasonable to expect more complexity in a system with more functionality, isn't it? So the real question should be, "Is the observed increase in complexity an unreasonable cost to pay for the associated benefits of increased functionality?"

7

File Sharing

This chapter describes a simple solution for common file sharing problems. The solution is to keep track of which products use which files, so you can see how changes to a file will ripple throughout your whole code management system.

The hub of the solution is a central directory, the CMHTREE holding tree, where the most up-to-date versions of all shared files are stored. Developers work on their own products and copy (export) the latest versions into the central *share* directory when the products are ready for sharing. Then other people who want to use the shared files can copy (import) them from the central *share* directory. Because the copying operations are implemented by special tools, it's easy to record all exporting and importing operations in a file. That makes it easy to find out which products are using shared files.

Three tools are central to this solution. *cmx* records a log entry as it exports (copies) a file from one location to another. *cmi* records a log entry as it imports (copies) a file from one location to another. *cmlsr* allows people to list the sharing relationships that are recorded in the *share.log* files. The tools answer questions such as "Which product exports file X for sharing?" and "Which products import file X for sharing?"

The product that exports a file is the owner of the file. This means that the file is stored in (and exported from) that product's subtree.

Common Sharing Situations

This section describes some common file sharing problems that can be treated by the solutions in this book. Three sharing situations are discussed:

- Sharing include files among multiple products. The tour examples showed how to manage shared pi and pd data files by exporting them from *.ini* nodes. A more detailed discussion is given in this chapter.

- Sharing source or object files among products. The tour examples show how to manage shared pi and pd files by exporting them into the *share* subtree. A discussion of other possible options will be given here.

- Sharing source subsystems among releasable products and non-releasable, private developer tools. This last situation arises when developers want to reuse some of the source code contained in releasable software products.

Sharing Include Files Among Products

There are several ways to share a single copy of an include file between multiple programs and libraries. Probably the worst way is to hardcode the absolute (or relative) pathname of the include file into all the source files that use the include file. This is bad because it couples the location of the source file to the location of the include file. If absolute pathnames are used, what happens if you have to relocate the include file? And if relative pathnames are used, what happens if you have to relocate *either* file?

Another way of sharing, much preferred, is to tell the compiler (through its **-Idirectory** command-line argument) where to look for the include files. The include files can either be placed in a special directory for holding such files, or they can stay in the source directory of the product that owns the file.

However, neither of these two directory methods is ideal. If you put the file in a special include directory, it can become difficult to maintain ownership relationships—years later, you may wonder which product originally owned the file. And if you leave include files in their original source directories, future directory reorganizations will invalidate the absolute pathnames in the **-Idirectory** arguments of the affected makefiles. The **-Idirectory** technique is also less than ideal because it doesn't automatically force recompilations of products if include files are changed.

The only way to trigger an automatic recompilation of the products in these cases is to put the full pathname of the include file in the appropriate makefile dependency rules. But this usually doesn't happen for include files that are stored in remote directories, for several reasons. For example, the "makedepend" tool may not be capable of working with remote include directories. Or the developers may not want to manually name dozens of include files for each object file built in the makefile (which can often be the case if the source file includes many include files from window system libraries). Nested include files also defeat automatic recompilation mechanisms, because the timestamp of the top-level nested include file rarely changes. Instead, it's the files included by the top-level include file that change.

The sharing solution offered by this book doesn't have any of these problems. Instead, it recommends that you leave the shared file in the source directory of the owning product, and then export the file (logging the operation) into the *share* subtree. Then any product that wants to share the file can import it (logging the operation) to the directories where it's going to be reused. All operations are under the control of makefiles. That way, whenever the original include file is updated, the export and import tools will ensure that a new copy of the changed file is propagated to all the directories where the file is being shared. This will trigger recompilations where they're appropriate.

Sharing Source Files Among Programs and Libraries

Sharing include files is easier than sharing source files because you can usually tell a compiler (with its **-Idirectory** command-line argument) where to look for include files without introducing too much sensitivity to directory reorganizations. In addition, most programmers find it easy to accept the idea of using a special *include* directory to hold any include files that are used by many products.

But consider the equivalent idea of using a special **-Idirectory** source directory to hold all the source code files used by multiple products. That's another matter entirely, isn't it? Most programmers would feel very uncomfortable about losing the ownership relationships between products and their shared source files.

Acceptable solutions for sharing source files are few in number. You could maintain multiple copies of the source code, but most programmers would rightly reject the idea. Or you could modify the makefiles for all the sharing products to contain absolute (or relative) pathname references to the location of the shared source files in their original product node. But this would introduce unwanted sensitivities to directory reorganizations.

This book suggests the following solution. Shared source files should be stored in the source directories of their original, or owning products. Then, for sharing, they can be exported (logging the operation) to the *share* directory for public sharing, or to the *share/private* directory for restricted sharing. And to complete the process, users of shared files can import the files (logging the operation) to the directories where the files are to be reused.

This solution solves the ownership problem—you always know which product owns a file. It also solves the file updating problem, because the importing and exporting tools will re-import or re-export shared files whenever the timestamp on the original file changes. This solution also makes it easy to list the sharing relationships of shared files (with the *cmlsr* "list sharing relationships" tool).

Sharing Source Subsystems Within the Company

A third—and common—sharing situation occurs when developers within a company would like to reuse some of the source code from a releasable software product. For example, developers often want to reuse common data structures such as linked-list packages in their own personal software tools. Ideally, the developers would like to reuse the latest version of the code automatically.

The main difficulty with this situation is that the shared files must be shared *outside* of the set of releasable software products. For most code management systems, this can be difficult, because the private developer's tools aren't part of the code-managed software.

The quick and dirty solution to this problem is to copy the files of interest directly out of the code management system into a location where the developers can easily get to them. The normal consequence of this solution is that each of the developers makes a copy of the files in his or her own source tree. (Recall the story in the introduction about the six expert C++ developers who each had their own copy of the same linked-list package.)

The main point here is that unless a formal mechanism is provided for reuse of such code, multiple copies of shared files will proliferate as reuse is implemented in non-efficient ways. For example, none of the C++ developers was able to automatically pick up changes in the releasable product's version of the linked-list package. And the reverse was also true—improvements made to a developer's copy rarely made it back into the releasable version.

For these reasons, it's important to provide a formal, workable method for reusing releasable code in private developers' tools. For example, you could export reusable code into a standard public *share* directory using the standard exporting techniques described in this book. Then developers could efficiently reuse the code in their own personal tools. To go even further, you could define a special subdirectory in the *share* subtree for this particular purpose, as well as a corresponding macro in the *makefile.tre* file. Then you could create separate directories for groups of related files (such as linked-list packages). Regardless of the techniques used, supporting this kind of reuse is a good idea because it saves resources, and promotes consistency.

It's worth saying that you'll have to face personal ownership issues if you start sharing linked-list packages among commercial products and personal developer tools. Developers won't want to base their personal software tools on reusable corporate linked-list packages if they can't take a copy of the linked-list package with them when they go somewhere else. This type of problem will totally kill reuse within the company.

My personal opinion is that the managers in corporations should adopt a more cooperative attitude than I've seen in the past. Most of the managers that I've known have a knee-jerk response to this type of thing—NO! But none of them have been able to explain why it's bad for the company, either.

I recommend that when reuse occurs, both parties should agree that both parties can have a complete copy of the reused code. That way, corporations can gain a wealth of reusable code and tools from programmers at no charge, and programmers can reuse bits of code from the corporation's products at no charge. (You might even consider making the reusable software into freeware, by posting it to the net with an appropriate copyright notice.) Trade secret algorithms and source files are excepted from this recommendation, of course.

Requirements

This section summarizes several desirable characteristics of file sharing mechanisms.

- The sharing mechanism should promote reliable code reuse. This means that files shouldn't get lost, product-ownership relationships are preserved, and shared files are updated whenever the original file is changed.

- The sharing mechanism should record sharing (coupling) relationships between products that share files. The form of the recorded representation doesn't matter, so long as it's useful and convenient. For example, it can take the form of a copy statement in a script, an import (*cmi*) or export (*cmx*) statement in a makefile, or an entry in an ASCII logfile. It should list the names of the participating products and the files being shared.

  Explicit representations of sharing relationships are important because they help both people and software tools to efficiently recognize and carry out the sharing relationship. Explicit sharing relationships help to reduce the number of hidden surprises that may cause problems after directory reorganizations or file modifications.

- File sharing operations should be undoable and redoable to support convenient code and directory reorganizations. This is a practical requirement that I discovered only through experience. Theory alone didn't predict it (sigh).

  For example, let's say that you want to re-import all the imported files in a compilation directory. And, to make it really bad, let's say you have many imported and non-imported files to deal with. The problem is that you have to delete the imported files without destroying the non-imported files (because you don't want to have to recompile the many object files that *don't* depend on the imported files).

  To make this task easier, I've added a default makefile target called **imports.rev** to the *imports.imp* file. I use it as follows. For every file that I import under the **imports** target, I also put a deletion command under the **imports.rev** target. Then when I want to undo my imports, I can just type *make imports.rev*. This an excerpt from one of my makefiles, which illustrates the symmetry in the importing and exporting commands.

```
imports:
        $(CMI) -nl s_const.h        the -nl means no logging
        $(CMI) -nl s_types.h
        . . .

imports.rev:
        $(RM) s_const.h
        $(RM) s_types.h
        . . .
```

Implementation

This section describes the implementation of the sharing mechanism advocated by this book. The implementation consists of three tools (*cmi, cmx,* and *cmlsr*) and their associated logfiles, a logfile index file, and some default makefile targets.

Logging Share Operations

The importing (*cmi*) and exporting (*cmx*) tools implement sharing by copying a file from a source location (usually a source tree) to a destination location (usually *CMHTREE/share*).

For export operations, the default source directory is the current directory, and the default destination directory is the *CMHTREE/share* directory. For import operations, the reverse is true. The default source directory is the *CMHTREE/share* directory, and the default destination directory is the current directory. All defaults can be overridden with command-line arguments.

Both types of operations are logged by recording the source and destination pathnames into a *shares.log* file in the current platform directory. The absolute pathname of the *shares.log* file itself is also recorded, but in the *shares.idx* index file in the *CMHTREE/share/index* directory.

The logs can be inspected with the *cmlsr* (list sharing relationships) tool by giving it search criteria in the form of command-line arguments. It will then apply the search criteria to each *shares.log* file named in the index file.

The *cmlsr* tool ignores any invalid pathnames in the index file. (Invalid pathnames can occur when you delete or move the *shares.log* files.) Furthermore, the *cmlsr* tool will remove the invalid pathnames from the index file if the –u (update) control argument is given.

Examples of file sharing operations

The following examples show some typical file sharing operations. Samples are shown for both interactive command-line operations and operations driven by makefiles. The only difference is that the makefile examples use default macros to specify the default tool names, platform names, and directory names in the code management system.

First, here are some simple exporting commands that illustrate some of the options and defaults of the *cmx* tool.

```
cmx foo.bar                          copies foo.bar to the default share dir
cmx -nl foo.bar                      specify no logging
cmx foo.bar -for my own comment      -for records the comment in the log entry
```

The following command shows how to export a file from a remote directory to the share directory:

> **cmx /remote/foo.bar**   *export from a remote dir to the share dir*

You can use this technique to export an include file right out of a source directory (such as *../s* or */s*) without first importing the file into the current platform directory. I sometimes use this approach to export include files directly out of the source directories in initialialization nodes, since there's no point in importing them into the platform directory first. (No compilations occur in initialization nodes.)

This next example shows how to export a file into an arbitrary remote directory instead of into the default *share* directory. I frequently use this technique to copy batch files, *sed* scripts, and *awk* scripts between "identical" platforms (within the same product node) that only differ in their *make* tools. That way, I have to maintain only one copy of the original file that I'm exporting around inside the product node.

For example, I'll use these commands to export a batch file for the *tdos.plt* platform (Borland *make*, DOS batch files) into the source directory for the *mdos.plt* platform (Microsoft *make*, DOS batch files):

> **cmx foo.bar –dd /my/dir**   *specify a non-default target directory*
> **cmx s/foo.bat –dd ../mdos.plt/s**   *copy identical file from tdos.plt to mdos.plt*

Now, I'll show you what the typical export command looks like in a makefile. The main difference is that the tool names, the filenames, and the directories are all referenced by makefile macros. The use of makefile macros makes it easier to maintain the makefile templates, because one change made to the macro will affect all the makefiles that include the template.

> $(CMX) –nl $(PROG)$(X) –dd $(ALPHA_DIR)/$(EP)   *a typical makefile entry*

CMX defines the name of the export tool. (Once upon a time it was named "export," and not *cmx*, but that name conflicted with the export commands in UNIX shells, so I changed it to *cmx*.) **PROG** contains the name of the current product (which is also the last parameter given to the *getmakes* command). **X** contains the suffix for an executable file on the current platform (**X** is ".exe" on DOS, and null on UNIX). **ALPHA_DIR** contains the pathname of the *CMHTREE/at* directory. And **EP** contains the platform name of the current export platform.

To import a file, the command syntax is the same. Only the tool name changes.

> **cmi foo.bar**   *copies foo.bar from default share dir*
> **cmi foo.bar –for see you later**   *-for records the comment in the log entry*
> **cmi –nl foo.bar**   *specify no logging*
> **cmi –nl foo.bar –dd /my/dir**   *copy from share to a non-default target directory*
> **cmi /remote/foo.bar**   *import from a remote dir to current dir*
> $(CMI) –nl s_sysdep.h   *typical makefile cmd for a shared include file*
> $(CMI) –nl ../s/version.h   *typical makefile cmd for a local include file*

There's one other trick that you can sometimes use if you dislike the idea of creating pd source directories just to hold a single include file that has the same name for all platforms. In this situation, you'd put the include files for all platforms in the pi source directory. Each include file would be named after its associated platform—*sun4gcc.h* for the *sun4gcc.plt* platform, and so on. Then you'd simply rename the include file as you imported it into the platform directory, using a command like this:

```
cmi sun4gcc.h -df flip.h          specify a new destination file name
```

I used this technique in the makefiles for the *cmpds/flip* tool included with this book. (But I don't use this technique any more because it's very non-standard. It means that you can't remove support for a platform just by deleting all the appropriate platform directories. Some of the pd source will still be in a pi source directory!)

Both tools are described in detail in the appendices.

Angle-bracket Include Files

The sharing solutions in this book usually ignore include files referenced with angle brackets in the code (e.g., `#include <stdio.h>`). This is because include files referenced with angle-brackets are usually very stable, owned by the compilation system, are available on every platform, and are used by almost every program.

For all of these reasons, it usually makes little sense to put such files in makefile dependency rules, to import the files from the compiler installation directories, or to record the files (if they were ever imported) in the sharing logs. (But the code management system can do all of those things if the need arises.)

ASCII Logfiles

The import and export tools work with two ASCII log files. The first file is the *shares.log* file, whose format is shown in the example below. Each line in the file represents one sharing operation. Each line has five parts: the operation type (import or export), the source pathname, the direction indicator, the destination pathname, and the comment field.

For example, here's how you could find out which products are sharing files. You'd list the relevant sharing relationships with the *cmlsr* tool.

```
K:\> cmlsr foo.bar
export g:/s/amtools/foo.bar -> j:/h/share/foo.bar (my own purpose)
import j:/h/share/foo.bar -> g:/s/amtools/foo.bar (see you later)
```

The second log file is the *shares.idx* index file that's stored in the *share/index* directory of the CMHTREE. Each line in this file is an absolute pathname of a once-valid *shares.log* file. Hopefully, some of the pathnames are still valid. Pathnames that point to non-existent files are ignored by the *cmlsr* tool.

Here's an example from the *shares.idx* file on my personal computer:

```
g:/s/cm/cmtools/cm_pd.lib/sun4gcc.plt/shares.log
g:/s/cm/cmtools/cm_pd.lib/msc.plt/shares.log
g:/s/cm/cm_pds/ed/edmain/tbc.plt/shares.log
g:/s/cm/cm_pds/rcs55/rcs_pi.lib/msc.plt/shares.log
. . .
```

Globally Regenerating Log Files

This section explains how to globally regenerate share log files without triggering recompilations. This discussion may be useful to you if you reorganize your source trees or change the location of the CMHTREE, since both these actions will invalidate entries in the index *shares.log* files.

The ability to regenerate share log files depends heavily on the design of the control arguments for the *cmi* and *cmx* commands. The control arguments are the same for both commands and are briefly explained in Appendix A, *Code Management Software Tools*.

Let's consider an example and see how the control arguments support the efficient regeneration of the share log files (and index).

Suppose that you're working on a very large project where it takes a full 24-hour day (or more) to walk the product trees and recompile all the products. That is something you want to avoid. Furthermore, suppose that you've just reorganized the source trees on the project, thus invalidating all pathnames in the share logs and the index file (*share/index/shares.idx*). But you've left all the object files alone and haven't changed any of the timestamps on any files, so there should be no need for new importing, exporting, or recompilation operations.

How do you update the sharing logs and the *shares.idx* file in an optimal and accurate way, without consuming any more time than is necessary?

First, to remove all the invalid *shares.log* files in the source trees, you could use a tree walker script to walk all platform directories with the command *rm shares.log*. (You could use the *find* command such as *find . -name shares.log -print -exec rm {} \;*, if you preferred.)

To clean up the index file you could type *cmlsr -u*, which would delete all invalid pathnames from the index file. This would leave you with an empty index file, since we've assumed that you relocated all source trees during the reorganization.

Now let's consider the more difficult problem of how to regenerate new *share.log* files without triggering recompilations. This is where the control arguments help.

It's easy to see that the only feasible way to rebuild the share logs is to use the make-files to execute the *cmi* and *cmx* commands for each software product. That way, the tools will regenerate the share log entries. There's just no other efficient alternative.

It's also our goal to update the share logs without triggering any unwanted recompilations or file copying actions (imports or exports). Avoiding file copying operations is important, because copying operations can sometimes change timestamps that will in turn trigger recompilations.

Let's consider some obvious solutions and their associated problems.

One very inefficient way to regenerate the share logs would be to run *make empty all* on all the product trees. This would delete all imported files and rebuild the *shares.log* files as part of the complete rebuild. But then you'd have to wait for the recompilations to complete before you could use the share log files, so we'll reject this solution.

A second way would be to just run *make all* over the whole set of trees. As the *cmi* and *cmx* tools were executed, they could update the missing logs. The problem is that they don't do this by default, or they'd end up rewriting all the log entries every time you ran *make* during development, even if no importing or exporting actions were necessary. That would be very inefficient, so the default behavior of the tools is to update the log entries only when a physical copy operation (import or export) is performed. So we must reject this solution too. (But it was close.)

We could use the **-f** argument to force both copying operations and logging operations to take place. (This is what the **-f** argument does—it forces both actions, which are independent actions within the code.) We'd regenerate the logs, but we'd also trigger recompilations by copying files.

The solution is to use both the **-f** and the **-nocopy** arguments. This forces logging to occur, but disables file copying operations. The **-nocopy** overrides the **-f** argument, which overrides the default behavior.

To enable this drastic action (rebuilding all the share logs), you must either redefine or override the default (null) value of the "log" makefile macro used in the definitions of the **CMI** and **CMX** makefile macros. The new value of the log macro should be **"-f -nocopy"** instead of the null string.

To edit the macro definitions, edit the appropriate *CMTREE/plt/platform.plt* files. To temporarily override the default value, redefine the log macro on the command line. The command *make log="-f -nocopy" all* works for me on the *sun4gcc.plt* platform, and the command *make -Dlog="-f -nocopy" all* works for me on the *tbc.plt* platform.

Recommended Policies

Here's a list of recommended policies for file sharing operations.

- Use the **-Idirectory** argument to the compiler to search standard include directories (such as */usr/include/X11* on UNIX systems) for standard include files. You don't want to import large numbers of standard include files (such as from the X11 include directory) into your compilation directories. (Besides, even if you did import them while logging the operation, the resulting logs would get cluttered with hundreds or thousands of log records. That would slow the tools down, but you could still use the tools to pick out exactly the log entries that you were interested in.)

- Use import (*cmi*) commands in makefiles to import application-dependent include files that are required for compilation. Don't log imports from local source directories to local platform directories because they're so numerous and intuitive. Do log imports that occur between platforms or product nodes because they're few in number, often unintuitive, and therefore unexpected.

  An alternate solution that you may want to adopt is to put **-I../s** and **-I./s** directives in the compilation command line defined in the *platform.plt* makefile template in the CMTREE. This would tell the compiler to look in the pi and pd source directories in a product node for all include files, saving you the trouble of importing local include files from those source directories. This approach harms nothing and reduces the number of import statements required in the *imports.imp* file.

  However, my preference is not to use this shortcut, for several reasons. First, I like to have a list of *all* the import dependencies listed in the *imports.imp* file, rather than just a list of imports from outside the product node. Second, I sometimes like to modify include files in the compilation directory during debugging without having to mess up the checked-out copy in the source directory. Third, if I have to export include files into the CMHTREE for sharing, I like to export them from the current directory, not directly from their source directories. That way I can change the permissions on the files if I like, after importing but before exporting.

- Add a deletion command under the **imports.rev** target in *imports.imp* for every import command that you add under the **imports** target in the *imports.imp* file. This is required if all imported files are to be deleted when the **clean** or **empty** targets are called.

- Platform-independent products should be exported for sharing into either the main *share* directory or the *share/private* directory. (See the shortcut described below.)

- Platform-dependent products should be exported for sharing to a *share/platform.plt* directory or into a *share/private/platform.plt* directory. (See the short cut below.)

- **Shortcut:** Export link library products to the alpha test platform directories, and then use the alpha test platform directories in the default linker search rules in the *makefile.xxe* file. This shortcut means that you'll be able to use the same copy of the library for both sharing (linking) and for alpha testing.

  If you don't use this shortcut, you'll have to put a second copy of each library into the appropriate *share/platform.plt* directory if you want to share the library with any other products. That's because all products should properly use the *share* directories for *all* sharing operations, period. But as you can see, this approach requires you to have two copies of every releasable library, one in the *share* directory for sharing, and one in the alpha test directory for alpha testing.

The non-shortcut approach also means that the link command in your *makefile.xxe* template would have to search the *share* directory instead of the alpha test directory. Since all this duplication seems pointless to me, I just do all my library sharing out of the alpha test directory. That way I avoid the inefficiencies of having two copies of the libraries around.

- Enable logging for sharing operations that cross product-node boundaries. These types of sharing operations are worth tracing to help you when products are reorganized. It's the "long distance" sharing operations that are hard to anticipate, and the shares that occur between remote parts of the filesystem will be the ones that cause you trouble, not the local shares within a product node. Sharing operations that take place within a product node just aren't that interesting or troublesome.

- Disable logging in the following cases, because it's of such little value:

  - Disable export logging when exporting products to the alpha test or release directories. It's reasonable to assume that all products will eventually end up in these two directories.

  - Disable import logging when importing from the local source directories. Shares inside of a product node are usually uninteresting because they're so easy to spot by looking in the *imports.imp* file.

  - Disable import logging when importing heavily shared files from the share directories. These are uninteresting because almost everyone uses them. For example, I've disabled import logging for all the *s_const.h* files in the makefiles in the software that accompanies this book because I can't see the point of logging it. It's easy to see that if I ever used *cmlsr* to list the programs that used the *s_const.h* file, I'd probably get a complete list of all platform directories for all tools in the source tree. Almost every program uses the file, and that's why recording the share operations doesn't seem to be useful—I already know that every program uses the file.

Evaluation

This section informally evaluates the sharing mechanisms that were described above. First a short history of the sharing strategy is given, and then possible objections are discussed.

Discussion

The most important idea in the sharing mechanism described above is the use of an explicit represention (log entries) of sharing relationships. This idea naturally leads to software tools that can create and inspect a database of sharing relationships.

The second key idea in the sharing mechanism described above is the use of default *share* and *share/platform.plt* directories to hold shared files. Default directories like these significantly simplify both the policies and the tools that are required for managing the file sharing mechanism.

As far as I know, the idea of explicitly representing sharing relationships in this way is a novel idea because I invented it specifically for this book. Perhaps other people have also independently invented similar mechanisms.

Advantages

The sharing mechanism described in this book offers several benefits:

- It is very simple. It uses standard makefiles to explicitly represent sharing relationships in the form of import and export commands. The associated software tools are also simple; they copy product files and update ASCII log files. This simplicity is an advantage because it means that the tools can be used in non-standard situations where more complex tools would fail.

- It's general. It can be used for any kind of computer file at all—source files, include files, binary files, text files, and so on. As a consequence, the sharing tools can probably be used in situations that weren't considered in the original design of the system.

- It's efficient. Since the tools don't copy files with identical timestamps, unnecessary copying operations are avoided.

- It's insensitive to directory reorganizations. It doesn't break when files and directories are renamed or reorganized. Instead, pathnames to non-existent *shares.log* files are ignored and can easily—and automatically—be removed from the index file.

- It saves time. It does this by helping developers to identify coupling relationships between software products. For example, the mechanism can quickly answer the common software question "Which products use this file?"

- It promotes reliable code reuse. It can export any number of related files (such as a linked-list package) to any set of destination directories and record all such exports. It can also continue to update the remote files as a normal part of the software maintenance process.

- The sharing mechanism uses an ASCII "database" file that can be read by tools on multiple platforms. This isn't always true for binary database files, because not all filesystems use the same byte ordering when they store binary files.

The sharing mechanism helps to promote project stability and product reliability by making all shared-file dependency relationships explicit and obvious. Developers can thus work in an information-rich environment that gives them access to information about sharing relationships that affect the products they're working on. As a consequence of this information, developers are less likely to make changes that inadvertently affect other software products.

Possible Objections

This subsection considers possible objections to the sharing mechanism presented above.

- **The sharing mechanism requires too much work.** This is a possible objection because the mechanism requires developers to explicitly encode interesting sharing relationships in product makefiles.

  However, it's reasonable to expect that a sharing mechanism with more functionality would require more work. That's because if you want to be able to create, maintain, and query a database of sharing relationships using software tools, then it's very reasonable to request that developers enumerate those relationships in a file somewhere.

  Therefore, the small extra effort required to enter importing commands into makefiles—once—seems to be a reasonable cost for the benefits gained. The default exporting commands are already in the makefile templates.

- **The sharing mechanism is too complex.** This is a possible objection because the sharing mechanism involves several *share* directories, several tools, and many log files.

  Again, one must compare the additional costs against the additional benefits. It's true that the sharing approach here is more complex than traditional sharing techniques such as absolute pathname references and search rule specifications to *make* tools, compilers, and linkers. But the approach described here also offers many more benefits.

  It makes coupling relationships explicit. It allows you to easily identify all the users of a shared file. And it takes nothing away from the traditional techniques. (You can still use absolute pathnames or search rule specifications to tools, compilers, and linkers for situations that you feel are appropriate for such techniques.)

8

A Hands-on Tour:
Part 3

This is the last chapter in the hands-on tour. It contains three examples:

- Example 5 shows you how to build batch file products (instead of compilable libraries and programs).

- Example 6 shows you how to perform bulk RCS operations on entire trees of source files.

- Example 7 shows you how to support multiple developers with one central source tree. (This example assumes that you're working on a UNIX system.)

Example 5: Managing Batch File Products

In this simple example, I'll show you how to build and export shell scripts under the code management system.

The main difference between compilable code products and shell script (or batch file) products is that shell scripts require no compilation. This means that the corresponding makefiles for shell scripts are a bit less complex and that a different platform is required for shell scripts than for compilable programs, because the makefiles are different. In the example, I'll be using the *tdos.plt* platform. On UNIX, the corresponding platform that I'd use would be the *sun4sh.plt* platform.

The second most common difference I've found is that shell scripts are often accompanied by auxiliary files such as *awk* and *sed* scripts. This means that a few extra import and export statements must be added to the *imports.imp* file.

Other than these two differences, working with shell scripts is the same as working with compilable programs and libraries.

In this example, we'll build and export a script that prints "hello world."

First, we'll generate a pd node to hold the script. Scripts always require pd nodes because they are interpreted languages and are usually very different on different platforms. (For example, the DOS batch file language is very different from the UNIX shell script language.) Notice also that I name the subtree *myhello.scr*—the "scr" suffix helps the *newmakes* tool determine the type of product being produced by the node.

```
K:\MAIN> makenode myhello.scr pd tdos.plt
```

We've seen the structure of several pd nodes already, and this one's no different. Here's what it looks like:

```
K:\MAIN> tree /a myhello.scr
K:\MAIN\MYHELLO.SCR
\---TDOS.PLT              a place for makefiles, imports, etc.
    \---S                a place for pd source files
        \---RCS          a place for the corresponding RCS files
```

Now create the batch file.

```
K:\MAIN> cd myhello.scr\tdos.plt\s
K:\MAIN\HELLO.SCR\TDOS.PLT\S> emacs myhello.bat     create the batch script
K:\MAIN\HELLO.SCR\TDOS.PLT\S> type myhello.bat      show its contents
@echo off
echo Hello from myhello.bat.
```

Check in the source file once you've created it.

```
K:\MAIN\HELLO.SCR\TDOS.PLT\S> echo This is a sample script.> msg
K:\MAIN\HELLO.SCR\TDOS.PLT\S> rcsdo ci_u_initial msg -log default
K:\MAIN\HELLO.SCR\TDOS.PLT\S> del msg
```

Now generate some makefiles, and build, export, and test the product. You don't have to customize the *imports.imp* this time because no imports are required.

```
K:\MAIN\HELLO.SCR\TDOS.PLT\S> cd ..
K:\MAIN\HELLO.SCR\TDOS.PLT> getmakes tdos.plt pd scr myhello

K:\MAIN\HELLO.SCR\TDOS.PLT> make all
K:\MAIN\HELLO.SCR\TDOS.PLT> cd ..          leave the current working dir so we can
K:\MAIN\HELLO.SCR> myhello                 invoke the alpha dir copy of myhello
Hello from myhello.bat.
```

This script didn't use any auxiliary files (such as *sed* or *awk* scripts), so we didn't have to add any extra import or export statements. But if the batch file did use auxiliary files (like *rcsdo* does, for example), here's what the import statements might look like. The following lines are taken from the *rcsdo.scr\tdos.plt\imports.imp* file. They show how to properly import and export auxiliary *rcsdo.awk* files:

```
PROG=rcsdo                              this defines the product name
imports:
    $(CMI) -nl s/$(PROG)$(S)            S='.bat' under DOS, S='null' under UNIX
    $(CMI) -nl s/$(PROG)$(AWKS)         AWKS='.awk' under both DOS and UNIX
```

```
imports.rev:
    $(RM) $(PROG)$(S)
    $(RM) $(PROG)$(AWKS)

exports.spe:
    $(CMX) -nl $(PROG)$(AWKS) -dd $(ALPHA_DIR)/$(EP)    EP=tdos.plt, the export platform
```

You can see by examining the makefile templates that they define macros, such as **S** and **AWKS**, for the suffixes of platform-dependent filenames. Common suffixes for MS-DOS include *.obj*, *.exe*, *.sed*, *.awk*, and *.bat*. A summary of filename suffix macros is shown in Table 6-3 in Chapter 6, *Makefile Architectures*.

Batch file products must use absolute pathnames to reference any auxiliary *sed* or *awk* scripts because the *sed* and *awk* tools can't use the PATH variable to locate their interpreted script files.

For more examples of how I use and maintain absolute pathnames in scripts, examine the source code for the *mvawkdir* script, and for any of the other scripts that are named inside of the *mvawkdir* source code. You'll see that I reference all auxiliary files from the alpha test directory with a pathname like this:

```
sed -f \%cmhtree_b%\at\tdos.plt\myfile.sed
```

(Recall that **CMHTREE_B** is an environment variable that you had to define in order to use the code management tools.) This way, all the absolute pathnames in the scripts actually point into the CMHTREE, wherever it happens to be. In addition, this method also causes the tools to use the most recently exported copy of the auxiliary *sed* and *awk* files.

The Final Source Trees

Here's a complete picture of our final source trees now that we've completed all of the tour examples that will modify the overall tree structure. I've included filenames in the tree listing, so that you can see where the various files are stored. I've also shown the CMHTREE structure, so that you can even see where the shared files are stored.

The duplicate copies of include files in the platform directories are imported copies of the original source files. Some of these duplicate copies come from the local source directory, and some of them come from the *CMHTREE\share* directories.

I've divided the tree structure printout into sections, since it's a big tree structure.

Tree Structures Only (No Files)

At this point in the tour, the overall tree structure should look like the two pictures shown in this section. I've removed the empty *rcs* directories below the platform directories, since we never used them. (They are created by *makenode* and *makeplt* so that you can check your *imports.imp* files into RCS, if you so desire.)

This is the structure of the original *tool1* tree. Recall that it contained all eight types of information in one file, in one directory.

```
C:MAIN
+---TOOL1              the original "how not to" structure
|   +---S              lines 0-8 of the program are stored here
|   |   \---RCS
|   \---TBC.PLT
```

We cloned the original *tool1* program into two other programs, *tool2* and *tool3*, so that we could demonstrate the concepts of sharing.

```
+---TOOL2              a clone of tool1, but much improved
|   +---S              lines 5 (pi local code), 6 (pi local data)
|   |   \---RCS
|   +---TBC.PLT        imported lines 3,4,7,8 (pi/pd shared code/data)
|   |   \---S          lines 0, 1 (pd local code), 2 (pd local data)
|   |       \---RCS
|   \---TB2.PLT
|       \---S
|           \---RCS
```

```
+---TOOL3              a clone of tool2, to demonstrate sharing
|   +---S              pi source code locally shared by tbc.plt, tb2.plt
|   |   \---RCS
|   +---TBC.PLT
|   |   \---S          pd source code for platform tbc.plt
|   |       \---RCS
|   \---TB2.PLT
|       \---S          pd source code for platform tb2.plt
|           \---RCS
```

Here are the tree structures of the shared products.

```
+---TOOL_PI.INI       pi include file (line 8)
|   +---S             tool_pi.h for all tools, all platforms
|   |   \---RCS
|   +---TBC.PLT
|   \---TB2.PLT
```

```
+---TOOL_PI.LIB       pi subroutine (line 7)
|   +---S             pi_sub.c, pi_sub.h for all tools, all platforms
|   |   \---RCS
|   +---TBC.PLT
|   \---TB2.PLT
```

```
+---TOOL_PD.LIB       pd subroutine (line 3)
|   +---TBC.PLT
|   |   \---S         pd_sub.c, pd_sub.h for tbc.plt
|   |       \---RCS
|   \---TB2.PLT
|       \---S         pd_sub.c, pd_sub.h for tb2.plt
|           \---RCS
```

```
+---TOOL_PD.INI          pd include file (line 4)
|    +---TBC.PLT
|    |    \---S          tool_pd.h for tbc.plt
|    |         \---RCS
|    \---TB2.PLT
|         \---S          tool_pd.h for tb2.plt
|              \---RCS
```

We also just created a simple batch file.

```
|
\---MYHELLO.SCR          a pd batch file
     \---TDOS.PLT
          \---S          pd myhello.bat for tdos.plt
               \---RCS
```

Tree Structures (with Files)

The original tool1 tree

This next listing shows the files as well as the directories.

```
K:> tree /a/f main          the command used to print this tree

K:MAIN
|    WALKSRC.BAT            walks source directories
|
+---TOOL1                   the first pi product node that we
|    +---S                  built—note that the source directory
|    |    | . TOOL1.C       is a sibling of the platform directory
|    |    |   TOOL1.H       working copies of source files
|    |    |   TOOLS.H
|    |    |
|    |    \---RCS
|    |         TOOL1.C      rcs copies of the source files
|    |         TOOL1.H
|    |         TOOLS.H
|    |
|    \---TBC.PLT
|         MAKEFILE          this file includes other makefiles
|         IMPORTS.IMP       such as this one containing custom targets
|         MAKEFILE.PI       and this one containing dependency rules
|         TOOL1.H           imported from ../s
|         TOOLS.H           imported from ../s
|         TOOL1.OBJ         a tbc.plt object file
|         TOOL1.EXE         a tbc.plt executable file
|
```

The tool2 product tree

The tree structures for *tool2* and *tool3* are clones of each other. We did this because we only wanted to use *tool3* to show how to share files between *tool2* and *tool3*.

Among all the changes we made to change *tool1* to *tool2*, we can pick out a few major differences:

- *tool2* is a pid node because it holds both pi and pd source files.

- It has two platform directories because we ported it to a second platform.

- It contains source files in the platform directories that have been imported from the *CMHTREE\share* directories.

The *k:\main\tool2* tree structure is a pid node since it has source directories that are both siblings (pi) and children (pd) of the platform directories.

The following diagram shows the pi source directory in the *main\tool2* subtree.

```
|                              continued from K:MAIN
|
+---TOOL2                       a pid node, since platform dirs have both
|   +---S                       sibling and child source directories
|   |   |   T2_SUB.C
|   |   |   TOOL2_PI.H           working copies of the pi source files
|   |   |
|   |   \---RCS
|   |           T2_SUB.C         rcs versions of the pi source files
|   |           TOOL2_PI.H
|   |
```

The following diagram shows the contents of the first platform directory *main\tool2\tbc.plt*. Notice that the pd source files for the *tbc.plt* platform for the *tool2* program are stored *below* the platform directory.

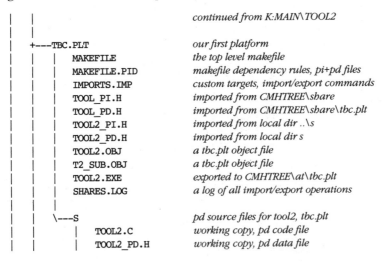

```
|   |                          continued from K:MAIN\TOOL2
|   |
|   +---TBC.PLT                 our first platform
|   |   |   MAKEFILE            the top level makefile
|   |   |   MAKEFILE.PID        makefile dependency rules, pi+pd files
|   |   |   IMPORTS.IMP         custom targets, import/export commands
|   |   |   TOOL_PI.H           imported from CMHTREE\share
|   |   |   TOOL_PD.H           imported from CMHTREE\share\tbc.plt
|   |   |   TOOL2_PI.H          imported from local dir ..\s
|   |   |   TOOL2_PD.H          imported from local dir s
|   |   |   TOOL2.OBJ           a tbc.plt object file
|   |   |   T2_SUB.OBJ          a tbc.plt object file
|   |   |   TOOL2.EXE           exported to CMHTREE\at\tbc.plt
|   |   |   SHARES.LOG          a log of all import/export operations
|   |   |
|   |   \---S                   pd source files for tool2, tbc.plt
|   |       |   TOOL2.C         working copy, pd code file
|   |       |   TOOL2_PD.H      working copy, pd data file
```

```
  |   |       |
  |   |       \---RCS                    rcs versions of working files
  |   |             TOOL2.C
  |   |             TOOL2_PD.H
  |   |
```

The next diagram shows the contents of the second platform directory *main\tool2\tb2.plt*. This second platform directory is a clone of the *tbc.plt* platform directory. The main difference is that the contents of the *tb2.plt* pd source files are slightly different from the corresponding pd source files for the *tbc.plt* platform. (The *tb2.plt* pd source files print out "tb2.plt" instead of "tbc.plt.")

```
  |   |                                  continued from K:MAIN\TOOL2
  |   |
  |   \---TB2.PLT                         our second platform
  |       |   MAKEFILE
  |       |   MAKEFILE.PID
  |       |   IMPORTS.IMP                 these files are the same as for
  |       |   TOOL2_PD.H                  the tbc.plt platform, except that
  |       |   TOOL2_PI.H                  (1) the pd source code is different
  |       |   TOOL_PI.H                   (2) the compiled products could be
  |       |   TOOL_PD.H                       different (if the compiler options
  |       |   TOOL2.OBJ                       for tb2.plt were different from
  |       |   T2_SUB.OBJ                       those used for tbc.plt.
  |       |   TOOL2.EXE                   exported to CMHTREE\at\tb2.plt
  |       |   SHARES.LOG
  |       |
  |       \---S                           pd source files for tool2, tb2.plt
  |           |   TOOL2.C
  |           |   TOOL2_PD.H
  |           |
  |           \---RCS
  |                   TOOL2.C
  |                   TOOL2_PD.H
  |
```

The tool3 product tree

The *k:\main\tool3* tree structure is a pid node since it has source directories that are both siblings (pi) and children (pd) of the platform directories.

The *tool3* tree structures and files are clones of the corresponding *tool2* tree structures and files. The main difference, as usual, is that the contents of some of the source files are slightly different. For example, files for *tool3* contain names that end in 3 (for *tool3*) rather than names that end in 2 (for *tool2*). But in all other respects, you'll find that the *tool3* and *tool2* subtrees are identical.

```
|                                            continued from K:MAIN
|
|
+---TOOL3
|   +---S                                    pi source files for tool3, all platforms
|   |   |   T3_SUB.C
|   |   |   TOOL3_PI.H
|   |   |
|   |   \---RCS
|   |           T3_SUB.C
|   |           TOOL3_PI.H
|   |
|   +---TBC.PLT                              tool3 for tbc.plt is compiled here
|   |   |   MAKEFILE
|   |   |   IMPORTS.IMP
|   |   |   MAKEFILE.PID
|   |   |   TOOL_PI.H                         imported from CMHTREE\share
|   |   |   TOOL3_PI.H                        imported from local ..\s
|   |   |   TOOL_PD.H                         imported from CMHTREE\share\tbc.plt
|   |   |   TOOL3_PD.H                        imported from local s
|   |   |   TOOL3.OBJ
|   |   |   T3_SUB.OBJ
|   |   |   TOOL3.EXE                         exported to CMHTREE\at\tbc.plt
|   |   |   SHARES.LOG                        records all logged share operations
|   |   |
|   |   \---S                                pd source files for tool3, tbc.plt
|   |       |   TOOL3.C
|   |       |   TOOL3_PD.H
|   |       |
|   |       \---RCS
|   |               TOOL3.C
|   |               TOOL3_PD.H
|   |
|   \---TB2.PLT                              tool3 for tb2.plt is compiled here
|       |   MAKEFILE
|       |   MAKEFILE.PID
|       |   IMPORTS.IMP
|       |   TOOL_PI.H                         imported from CMHTREE\share
|       |   TOOL3_PI.H                        imported from local ..\s
|       |   TOOL_PD.H                         imported from CMHTREE\share\tbc.plt
|       |   TOOL3_PD.H                        imported from local s
|       |   TOOL3.OBJ
|       |   T3_SUB.OBJ
|       |   TOOL3.EXE                         exported to CMHTREE\at\tb2.plt
|       |   SHARES.LOG
|       |
|       \---S                                pd source files for tool3, tb2.plt
|           |   TOOL3.C
|           |   TOOL3_PD.H
|           |
|           \---RCS
|                   TOOL3.C
|                   TOOL3_PD.H
|
```

The tool_pi.ini product tree

The *k:\main\tool_pi.ini* tree structure is a pi node since its single source directory is the sibling of the platform directories.

This tree just exports pi data files—no compilations take place here.

```
|                                      continued from K:MAIN
|
+---TOOL_PI.INI                        a pi node
|   +---S                              pi source files for *.plt, to export
|   |   |   TOOL_PI.H                  exported to CMHTREE\share
|   |   |
|   |   \---RCS
|   |           TOOL_PI.H
|   |
|   +---TBC.PLT                        simple makefiles to export the .h file from tbc.plt
|   |       MAKEFILE
|   |       IMPORTS.IMP
|   |       TOOL_PI.H
|   |       SHARES.LOG
|   |
|   \---TB2.PLT                        simple makefiles to export the .h file from tb2.plt
|           MAKEFILE
|           IMPORTS.IMP
|           TOOL_PI.H
|           SHARES.LOG
```

The tool_pd.ini product tree

The *k:\main\tool_pd.ini* tree structure is a pd node since its source directories are children of the platform directories.

The main thing to look for in this tree is that it only exports pd data files—no compilations take place here.

```
|                                      continued from K:MAIN
|
+---TOOL_PD.INI                        pd source files for global sharing
|   +---TBC.PLT                        the first platform
|   |   |   MAKEFILE                   this simple makefile only exports files
|   |   |   IMPORTS.IMP
|   |   |
|   |   \---S                          pd source files for tbc.plt, to export
|   |       |   TOOL_PD.H              exported to CMHTREE\share\tbc.plt
|   |       |
|   |       \---RCS
|   |               TOOL_PD.H
|   |
|   \---TB2.PLT                        our second platform directory
|           MAKEFILE                   simple makefiles to export the .h file from tb2.plt
|           IMPORTS.IMP
|   |
```

```
|          \---S                    pd source files for tb2.plt, to export
|              |   TOOL_PD.H        exported to CMHTREE\share\tb2.plt
|              |
|              \---RCS
|                      TOOL_PD.H
|
```

The tool_pi.lib product tree

The *k:\main\tool_pi.lib* tree structure is a pi node since its single source directory is the sibling of the platform directories.

Compilations do take place in this node. This node exports a single pi binary library file to the *CMHTREE\at* directory.

```
|                                  continued from K:MAIN
|
+---TOOL_PI.LIB                    pi code for global sharing
|    +---S
|    |   |   PI_SUB.C              pi source files
|    |   |   PI_SUB.H
|    |   |
|    |   \---RCS
|    |           PI_SUB.C
|    |           PI_SUB.H
|    |
|    +---TBC.PLT                   the first platform, and compilation dir
|    |       IMPORTS.IMP
|    |       MAKEFILE
|    |       PI_SUB.H              imported locally from ..\s\pi_sub.h
|    |       PI_SUB.OBJ
|    |       MAKEFILE.PI
|    |       TOOL_PI.LIB
|    |
|    \---TB2.PLT                   the second platform
|            IMPORTS.IMP
|            MAKEFILE
|            PI_SUB.H              imported locally from ..\s\pi_sub.h
|            PI_SUB.OBJ
|            MAKEFILE.PI
|            TOOL_PI.LIB
|
```

The tool_pd.lib product tree

The *k:\main\tool_pd.lib* tree structure is a pd node since it contains source directories that are children of the platform directories.

Compilations do take place in this node. This node exports a single pd binary library file to the *CMHTREE\at* directory.

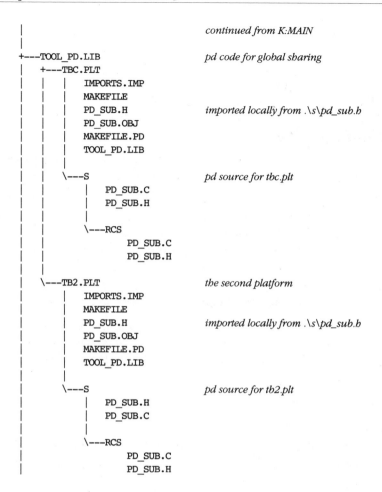

```
|                                       continued from K:MAIN
|
+---TOOL_PD.LIB                         pd code for global sharing
|   +---TBC.PLT
|   |   |   IMPORTS.IMP
|   |   |   MAKEFILE
|   |   |   PD_SUB.H                    imported locally from .\s\pd_sub.h
|   |   |   PD_SUB.OBJ
|   |   |   MAKEFILE.PD
|   |   |   TOOL_PD.LIB
|   |   |
|   |   \---S                          pd source for tbc.plt
|   |       |   PD_SUB.C
|   |       |   PD_SUB.H
|   |       |
|   |       \---RCS
|   |               PD_SUB.C
|   |               PD_SUB.H
|   |
|   \---TB2.PLT                         the second platform
|       |   IMPORTS.IMP
|       |   MAKEFILE
|       |   PD_SUB.H                    imported locally from .\s\pd_sub.h
|       |   PD_SUB.OBJ
|       |   MAKEFILE.PD
|       |   TOOL_PD.LIB
|       |
|       \---S                          pd source for tb2.plt
|           |   PD_SUB.H
|           |   PD_SUB.C
|           |
|           \---RCS
|                   PD_SUB.C
|                   PD_SUB.H
|
```

The myhello.scr product tree

Last, here's a picture of the *k:\main\myhello.scr* tree structure. This tree is a pd node since it contains a source directory underneath a platform directory. No compilation takes place in the platform directory because a script file is being exported.

```
\---MYHELLO.SCR                        pd batch file
    \---TDOS.PLT                       the pd tdos.plt platform directory
        |   IMPORTS.IMP
        |   MAKEFILE
        |   MYHELLO.BAT                imported locally from .\s\myhello.bat
        |
        \---S                          pd source code
            |   MYHELLO.BAT
            |
            \---RCS
                    MYHELLO.BAT
```

Example 6: Bulk Operations

This example shows you how to perform various bulk operations on entire source trees. Specifically, it will show you how to regenerate makefiles and modify *imports.imp* files—in bulk—throughout the entire source tree.

Bulk Regeneration of Makefiles

To regenerate all the makefiles in a source tree, go to the top of the subtree of interest, generate a batch file with the *newmakes* tool, and then run the generated batch file. Figure 8-1 shows what *newmakes* does.

The following commands show how to regenerate the makefiles for all the software products in our example source tree. I've included several platform names on the command line, because I want the script to visit all the platform directories in our entire source tree.

```
K:\MAIN\HELLO.SCR> cd \main                                   go to the tree top
K:\MAIN> newmakes doit.bat tbc.plt tb2.plt tdos.plt           generate a walker script
```

The *newmakes* tool generates a tree walking script that automatically executes a pre-calculated *getmakes* command in each visited directory. The *newmakes* tool calculates the *getmakes* command for each visited directory to generate the proper kind of makefiles for that node's product.

Now let's run the generated script to regenerate all the makefiles in our source tree.

```
K:\MAIN> doit
```

To test the new makefiles, we'll generate a normal tree walker script to visit all the platform directories in the tree. Then we'll use it to rebuild all of the products in our source tree.

I've used several different *make* commands below to demonstrate some of the common experiences that I've had with this technique.

```
K:\MAIN> twalker walkplts.bat tbc.plt tb2.plt tdos.plt
K:\MAIN> walkplts make all                 many recompilations due to rcs checkins.
K:\MAIN> walkplts make all                 should be no recompilations this time.
K:\MAIN> walkplts make empty               delete everything
K:\MAIN> walkplts make all                 rebuild everything from scratch.
K:\MAIN> del doit.bat                       clean up
```

Bulk Modifications to imports.imp Files

I've found that in rare circumstances I want to upgrade or modify all the *imports.imp* files in my source trees. Usually, this is because I want to change the name of a makefile macro in all makefiles and templates, or because I want to add a new target to all of the *imports.imp* files in my source trees.

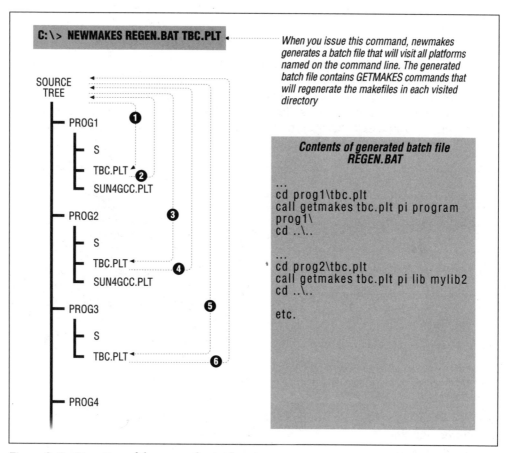

Figure 8–1. Operation of the newmakes tool

The main problem with this is that the makefile generation tools can't regenerate an *imports.imp* file. Instead, they leave the existing *imports.imp* files alone because the files usually contain custom, manually-entered import and export information that the tools can't regenerate.

The solution that I usually use is to walk the platform directories with a tree walker script. The tree walker script then invokes a second script—a "worker" script—that performs the necessary editing operations on exactly one *imports.imp* file. The worker script usually edits the *imports.imp* file by invoking an auxiliary *sed* or *awk* script.

Remember to use absolute pathnames in the worker script and on the tree walker script command line. This is necessary because the worker script is invoked in many different directories throughout the source tree—a situation which prevents the use of relative pathnames.

In the following example, I'll demonstrate bulk modifications of *imports.imp* files by making a harmless text string change in each of the *imports.imp* file in our example source trees.

First, let's create and test the worker script. I'll just use the one that I've used many times before, because I know that it works. It's called *edit1imp*. I'll show the interesting part of the *edit1imp* code below to help you understand what's going on, but you don't have to type it in. *edit1imp* is already available as one of the software tools that accompanies this book. It modifies the *imports.imp* file and saves a backup copy of the file in *imports.old*.

```
This is part of the edit1imp tool that's provided with the book. Don't type it in.
...
if exist imports.old attrib -r imports.old          make file writeable
if exist imports.old del imports.old                and then delete it
if exist imports.imp attrib -r imports.imp          make file writeable
if exist imports.imp ren imports.imp imports.old    save the old file
if exist imports.old sed -f
```

The parameter in the last line of *edit1imp* specifies the absolute pathname of the *sed* script that should be used for the editing. The use of a parameter in *edit1imp* is a good idea because it allows us to reuse the same worker script time after time. Then we only have to change the *sed* script for each new editing situation.

This is the *sed* script that will make the harmless text string change.

```
K:\MAIN> emacs change1.sed
# this sed script changes the string "automatic" to "AUTOMAGIC-SED"
s/automatic/AUTOMAGIC-SED/
```

All that's left to do is to generate the walker script and then turn it loose on the entire source tree. But that takes guts, doesn't it, without having first tested the worker script? So instead, let's test the worker script on a dummy file *before* we let it run rampant through our costly, hand-modified *imports.imp* files.

First, we'll test the *sed* script by itself, manually, and then we'll test the worker script. Only after that will we use the tree walker.

Using a bottom-up testing strategy is a smart thing to do here, because it's risky to modify every *imports.imp* file in the source tree with an automated, untested *sed* script. That's why we're going to test ours first, before sending it out to chew up files in our source trees at computer speeds.

(This reminds me of a cartoon—a bunch of big business executives are at a computer show, looking in awe at the console of the latest, huge, impressive computer. The sign on the console says, "This computer can make 931,456,732 mistakes in 0.0001 seconds.")

Be sure before you turn your tree walkers loose on a source tree. If you've armed them with defective *sed* scripts, it could take you a long time to clean up the mess.

So let's perform the first bottom-up manual test of our *sed* script.

```
K:\MAIN> copy tool2\tbc.plt\imports.imp         get a file to sacrifice
K:\MAIN> sed -f change1.sed imports.imp >junk   manually invoke the sed script
K:\MAIN> diff imports.imp junk                  see if it worked
K:\MAIN> del junk                               get rid of the file
```

Now, try step 2 of the bottom-up testing strategy.

```
K:\MAIN> edit1imp change1.sed                   now the automated way
K:\MAIN> diff imports.old imports.imp           show the changes
K:\MAIN> del imports.old
K:\MAIN> del imports.imp
```

Now, turn the tested *sed* script loose on the source tree under the guidance of a tree walker script. I always generate a completely new tree walker script whenever I'm globally editing files because I don't want to risk using an old—and possibly edited or obsolete—tree walker script on such an important task.

```
K:\MAIN> twalker editimps.bat tbc.plt tb2.plt tdos.plt   create a new tree walker script
K:\MAIN> editimps call edit1imp k:\main\change1.sed      use absolute path
K:\MAIN> editimps grep AUTOMAGIC-SED imports.imp         check results
K:\MAIN> editimps make all                               does make still work?
```

If you prefer to keep your *imports.imp* files under RCS control, you'll have to use a tree walker script to check them all out of RCS before you can edit them with *edit1imp*. Then you can use the same tree walker to perform the edit operation, to check the modified files back in, and to delete the old *imports.old* files.

Here's an example of a *sed* script that you can use to add a new makefile target to an *imports.imp* file. (This is the same script that I once used to upgrade the hundreds of *imports.imp* files on my PC.)

```
# sed script to append two new targets to the end of the imports.imp file.
# All newlines except the last one should be escaped with a backslash.
#
# The 'nothing' command is required for a make tool that I use—it
# does nothing (it's an empty shell script), but it stops the make tool
# from protesting about empty targets. If your make tool doesn't need
# it, then you can leave it out.
#
$a\
\
# special instructions for installation go here\
install:\
    @nothing\
\
# special instructions for linting the source files go here\
lint:\
    @nothing
```

This particular *sed* script appends all text following the *sed* append command ("a" in the script) to the end of the *imports.imp* file. The only tricky thing to watch for in the script is that all newlines in the text to be appended must be escaped with a back-slash. The *sed* program stops appending when it sees the first non-escaped newline character.

One final tip on changing *imports.imp* files. In very rare cases, I've had to manually edit all the *imports.imp* files in my system because the required changes were too awkward to make with an automated script. I recommend that you use the *find* tool to generate a list of all the files to be modified, and then figure out some way of using that list to save you keystrokes.

I do this by working from the top of the source tree and reading the list of pathnames into my editor. Whenever I'm ready to read in another file, I cut and paste the path-name of the next file into the editor's file-read prompt buffer. That way I don't have to type long pathnames.

I also try to create an editor macro to perform the main editing changes to save more keystrokes. Then all I have to do is cut and paste a filename and invoke an editor macro. This approach can save you a great deal of time if you have to manually mod-ify all the *imports.imp* files on your system.

Example 7: Multiple Developers

This example, which requires a UNIX system to execute, shows you how multiple developers can clone trees and share RCS files.

Specifically, this example shows you how to clone a source tree, how to check out the entire set of the latest (or a particular) version of the source files into the cloned tree, how to regenerate makefiles in all directories of the cloned tree, and how to rebuild and export all of the software products produced by the source tree.

Most of the examples use tree walker scripts to apply commands to all the appropriate directories within the source tree.

Moving the Example Source Trees to UNIX

Before I can show you the techniques for multiple developers, we'll have to move our current source trees to a UNIX system that supports symbolic links. (The UNIX system must also have the code management tools installed, of course.)

We'll move the tree of examples by packing it up into an archive file, copying the file to a UNIX machine, and unpacking the archive file in the new environment.

But first, let's clean up the example source trees by deleting all the compiled object and executable files in the various platform directories. We'll also delete all of the batch files that we've created in the top-level *main* directory. That way we'll have fewer files to transfer to the UNIX system. (If you're working in a networked DOS-UNIX environment, you may want to take the DOS executables along too, so that you can have both types of executables in your tree at the end of the tour.)

```
K:\MAIN> twalker cleanup.bat tbc.plt tb2.plt tdos.plt
K:\MAIN> cleanup ls -l imports.*          check for imports.old files
K:\MAIN> cleanup del imports.old          edit1imp created these
K:\MAIN> cleanup make empty
```

If you want to save your DOS tree walker scripts for later use on a DOS-UNIX network with a shared filesystem, then skip this next step. But I'll delete mine, since tree walker scripts are easy to regenerate.

```
K:\MAIN> del *.bat
K:\MAIN> del *.sed                        delete the old sed script too
K:\MAIN> ls
 myhello.scr  tool2       tool_pd.ini  tool_pi.ini
 tool1        tool3       tool_pd.lib  tool_pi.lib
```

Next, pack up the example tree using the *tar* program that's provided on the disk.

```
K:\MAIN> tar cvf extree.tar *.*
```

Once you've transferred the archived file to a UNIX system, create a directory named *main* to match the DOS directory name that we've been using so far. Then go into that temporary directory and unpack the source trees.

```
/home/kj/> cd main
/home/kj/main> tar xvf extree.tar
/home/kj/main> rm extree.tar         do this only if it unpacked properly
```

Next, set up your **CMTREE**, **CMHTREE**, and **CMPCILOG** environment variables on the UNIX system. The easiest way to get this right is to follow the instructions printed out by the *cmrules* tool, which is an online help program. The commands shown below accomplish the same thing. I'm showing the commands as if I typed them on my UNIX command line, but of course I'd normally put them into my shell initialization file.

```
CMTREE=/local/cmtree              point to your cmtree, wherever it is
export CMTREE
CMHTREE=/local/cmhtree            point to your cmhtree, wherever it is
export CMHTREE
CMPCILOG=/local/cmhtree/pci.log   point to your log file
export CMPCILOG
PATH=$PATH:.                      add . to your PATH
```

That's all that's required for moving the example source trees to the UNIX system.

Porting to the sun4gcc.plt Platform

Before we can recompile the programs in the old source tree on the new system, we have to port the pd source code in all product nodes to the *sun4gcc.plt* platform. This will take some work. However, since there are many powerful and interesting commands and techniques to learn along the way, the process of porting won't be boring.

Our immediate purpose is to add *sun4gcc.plt* platforms to all the source trees, in the appropriate places, of course. Then we'll have to port the code, regenerate the makefiles, and rebuild the example programs under the new platform. After that's all done, we can move on to multiple-developer techniques.

So first, go to the directory above the example source trees:

```
/home/kj> cd main
/home/kj/main> ls
myhello.scr/ tool2/      tool_pd.ini/   tool_pi.ini/
tool1/       tool3/      tool_pd.lib/   tool_pi.lib/
```

Next, generate a tree walker script to walk the *tbc.plt* platform directories.

```
/home/kj/main> twalker walktbc.sh tbc.plt
```

We'll use the tree walker script to invoke the *addaplat* tool, which will create a new *sun4gcc.plt* platform directory beside each *tbc.plt* platform directory in the source tree.

The purpose of the *addaplat* tool is to reduce the cost of adding new platforms to entire source trees. It automates the process of creating new platform directories and cloning *imports.imp* files, and thereby saves typing. It's behavior is shown in Figure 8-2.

Specifically, whenever *addaplat* is invoked from within an existing platform directory, it calls *makeplt* to create a new sibling platform directory (whose name is provided by the user). Then *addaplat* copies the *imports.imp* file from the current platform directory into the newly created sibling platform directory. This usually saves you from having to retype the import statements that are contained in the original *imports.imp* file.

So by using a tree walker script to invoke the *addaplat* tool, you can add new platform directories to entire source trees with very little effort. It's the fastest way that I can think of to add new platform directories to a source tree.

```
/home/kj/main> walktbc.sh addaplat sun4gcc.plt          invoke the addaplat tool
walktbc.sh addaplat sun4gcc.plt
*********************
/netshare/home/kj/main/tool_pi.ini/tbc.plt
addaplat sun4gcc.plt
*********************
/netshare/home/kj/main/tool_pd.ini/tbc.plt
addaplat sun4gcc.plt
  . . .
7 directories visited.
```

The main thing that you have to watch for when using *addaplat* to generate UNIX platforms (such as *sun4gcc.plt*) from DOS platforms (such as *tbc.plt*) is that different *make* tools may be involved. In other words, the syntax of the two *imports.imp* files may be different.

The two most common problems that I've encountered concern tabs and carriage returns. My DOS *make* tool isn't fussy about either problem, whereas the SunOS 4.1.3 *make* tool is fussy about both. The Sun *make* tool requires a tab before every

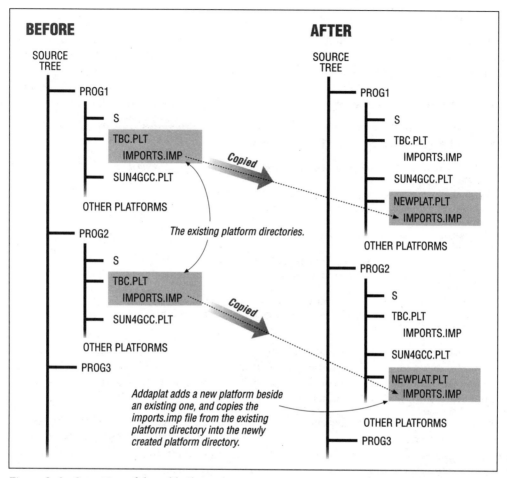

Figure 8–2. Operation of the addaplat tool

command that's below a target in the makefile, and it doesn't like carriage returns after tabs on blank lines below targets. (It happily accepts newlines after tabs on empty command lines.) So we're going to fix those two problems right now.

The carriage return problem can be solved by invoking the *flip* tool from a tree walker script. The *flip* tool is provided with the book. It either adds carriage return characters to the ends of lines (*-m*, for "MS-DOS"), or removes them (*-u*, for "UNIX").

We'll use the *-u* argument to remove the carriage returns from the ends of all the lines in all of the *imports.imp* files that we copied from *tbc.plt* platform directories into *sun4gcc.plt* platform directories.

```
/home/kj/main> twalker walksun.sh sun4gcc.plt        visit new sun4gcc.plt platform dirs
/home/kj/main> walksun.sh flip -u imports.imp        and remove CRs from import.imp files
```

The tab problem, unfortunately, can only be solved by manually editing the copied *imports.imp* files. And we don't know which files, if any, need editing to fix their tabbing problems. (If you inserted only tabs when you were editing files during all the previous tour examples, there should be no tab problems.) So we'll have to wait until we get error messages from *make* before we know which files need editing.

Let's continue on. To create new makefiles, use the *newmakes* tool to create a script that invokes *getmakes* in each visited directory.

```
/home/kj/main> newmakes doomakes.sh sun4gcc.plt        create the script
/home/kj/main> doomakes.sh                             run it to generate makefiles
getmakes sun4gcc.plt pi prog tool1 ./tool1/sun4gcc.plt
getmakes sun4gcc.plt pid prog tool2 ./tool2/sun4gcc.plt
s/*.c not found
getmakes sun4gcc.plt pid prog tool3 ./tool3/sun4gcc.plt
s/*.c not found
getmakes sun4gcc.plt pd ini tool_pd.ini ./tool_pd.ini/sun4gcc.plt
getmakes sun4gcc.plt pd lib tool_pd ./tool_pd.lib/sun4gcc.plt
s/*.c not found
getmakes sun4gcc.plt pi ini tool_pi.ini ./tool_pi.ini/sun4gcc.plt
getmakes sun4gcc.plt pi lib tool_pi ./tool_pi.lib/sun4gcc.plt
7 platforms processed.
```

The error messages that were printed out are from *gendep*, which was called by *getmakes* to generate makefile dependency rules for *tool2*, *tool3*, and *tool_pd.lib*. The errors were printed out because *gendep* couldn't find any C files to generate dependency rules from in those product nodes.

There aren't any platform-dependent C source files in the pd source directories of these product nodes yet. This is because we haven't yet cloned and modified some existing pd source code files to use as a starting point in the newly created pd *sun4gcc.plt/s* source directories.

Normally, I would have copied over all the pd source files *before* running the *newmakes* script. (But if I'd done that, you wouldn't have had the chance to see what the error message looked like.)

Let's fix the error message problem by cloning the appropriate *tbc.plt* pd source files for use in the *sun4gcc.plt/s* pd source directories. We'll port the cloned files in the next step.

```
/home/kj/main> cp tool_pd.ini/tbc.plt/s/*.* tool_pd.ini/sun4gcc.plt/s
/home/kj/main> cp tool_pd.lib/tbc.plt/s/*.* tool_pd.lib/sun4gcc.plt/s
/home/kj/main> cp tool2/tbc.plt/s/*.* tool2/sun4gcc.plt/s
/home/kj/main> cp tool3/tbc.plt/s/*.* tool3/sun4gcc.plt/s
```

Now, port the cloned pd source files to the new platform by changing the platform names from *tbc.plt* to *sun4gcc.plt* in all of the copied pd source files. No other source code changes are required.

You might have to make the following files writable if they were marked read-only during the transfer.

```
/home/kj/main> emacs tool_pd.ini/sun4gcc.plt/s/tool_pd.h      change tbc.plt to sun4gcc.plt
/home/kj/main> emacs tool_pd.lib/sun4gcc.plt/s/pd_sub.h
/home/kj/main> emacs tool_pd.lib/sun4gcc.plt/s/pd_sub.c
/home/kj/main> emacs tool2/sun4gcc.plt/s/tool2.c
/home/kj/main> emacs tool2/sun4gcc.plt/s/tool2_pd.h
/home/kj/main> emacs tool3/sun4gcc.plt/s/tool3.c
/home/kj/main> emacs tool3/sun4gcc.plt/s/tool3_pd.h
```

Notice that we didn't edit any files in the *tool1* tree. That's because all the files in the *tool1/s* directory are supposed to be platform independent.

When to use tree walkers and sed scripts

Note that I've used a manual editing approach here, instead of using a tree walker script with a *sed* script. After all, the editing change was trivial ("s/tbc.plt/sun4gcc.plt/", in *sed* terminology), and we have the *twalker* and *edit1imp* programs to help us with the details. Not all bulk editing situations are suitable for treatment by tree walking *sed* solutions, however.

The determining reason for avoiding the *sed* technique in this case is that the *edit1imp* script was designed specifically for use on *imports.imp* files. So it's not useful for editing a series of source files that each have a different name, which is the situation we face here.

Another reason for avoiding the tree walking technique is the small number of files. You can usually edit a small number of files in less time than it would take you to create a tree walker script and a *sed* script, test the *sed* script, test the *sed* script using the *edit1imp*, and then run the entire combination of the tree walker, the *edit1imp* program, and the *sed* script over a source tree.

A third reason for avoiding the tree walker technique here is that it's a bit awkward to generate a tree walker script to visit only the *sun4gcc.plt* source directories. You could create the script in two ways. One way is to create a script that visits all source directories, and then edit the script to remove all visits to non-*sun4gcc.plt* directories. This would take a fair amount of editing in our case, however, because there are 18 source directories in our little tree.

A second way would be to use *find*, *fgrep*, and *sed* to create a list of *sun4gcc.plt* directories, and then use the *mwalker* ("make a tree walker") tool to generate the final script. (The *mwalker* tool is actually called by *twalker* to generate a tree walker script from a list of directories created by *twalker*. The *mwalker* tool is also discussed at length later on in this example.)

This second technique is educational and interesting, so let's take a minute to try it out. We'll use *find* to generate a list of all directories in the source tree. Then we'll pipe that list to *grep*, which will in turn select and print all the *sun4gcc.plt/s* source

directories. Last, we'll redirect the output of *grep* into a file, and then use *mwalker* to
generate a tree walker script from the list of directories contained in the file.

```
/home/kj/main> find . -type d -print | grep sun4gcc.plt\/s$ > mydirs
/home/kj/main> cat mydirs
./tool2/sun4gcc.plt/s
./tool3/sun4gcc.plt/s
./tool_pd.ini/sun4gcc.plt/s
./tool_pd.lib/sun4gcc.plt/s

/home/kj/main> mwalker mydirs > visit4.sh
/home/kj/main> more visit4.sh                    have a look at what's inside
```

Now we can revisit the determining reason for why the tree walker technique isn't
useful in this case. How do we write a new *edit1imp* script to edit a series of files
when we don't know the names of the files? I couldn't think of a good solution fast
enough, so I just manually edited the files.

The main implication of this experience is that tree walkers and *sed* scripts work best
on trees of files where the files all have the same name. This makes it easy to clone
and modify the *edit1imp* script to use the required filename instead of *imports.imp*.

Finishing the port to the sun4gcc.plt platform

Now back to the task at hand—finishing the port of our programs to the *sun4gcc.plt*
platform. We've just finished porting the *sun4gcc.plt/s* pd source files (by manually
editing) to the *sun4gcc.plt* platform.

We can rerun the *doomakes.sh* script to generate makefiles again. This time *gendep*
shouldn't generate any error messages when it tries to generate makefile dependency
rules from missing source files.

```
/home/kj/main> doomakes.sh
```

We're ready to compile the software now, because the source files and makefiles are
ready to go.

We can expect at least two kinds of errors because we've copied DOS *imports.imp*
files. The first error was described above: tabs may be required before commands
under makefile targets in UNIX makefiles. The solution is to manually replace leading
spaces with a single tab.

The second kind of error occurs because of differences between the linker command-
line syntaxes on the *tbc.plt* (DOS) and *sun4gcc.plt* (UNIX) platforms. The problem has
to do with the library naming conventions on the two different platforms.

On DOS, the standard library naming syntax is *filename.lib*, where filename uniquely
identifies the library. On UNIX, library names are automatically prefixed with "lib" to
give names like *libfilename.a*. The tools handle this convention by adding the prefix
automatically. Thus, the *sun4gcc.plt* makefiles in our *tool_pi.lib* node will automatically
build a library named *libtool_pi.a*.

Now we can talk about the real problem. On DOS, to get the linker to search libraries, you put the library names on the linker command line, after an appropriate control argument. (For example, *tlink /L ... mylib1 mylib2.*) But on UNIX, you have to prefix each library name with a *-l* control argument (meaning that we need to put *-ltool_pi* on the UNIX linker command line).

However, since we copied the UNIX *imports.imp* files from a DOS platform, the library names listed in the **lb3** macro of the copied *imports.imp* files won't have the necessary *-l* prefix. As a result, the *sun4gcc.plt* linker won't be able to find the libraries when it tries to link *tool2* and *tool3*.

The solution is to prepend a **-l** to the library names listed in the **lb3** macro of all of the copied *imports.imp* files.

Let's continue now by using a tree walker script to rebuild all the tools on the new *sun4gcc.plt* platform. We'll run *make*, and it will tell us where the errors are. If you encounter any tab errors, fix them. I won't show any of them in the text here. (The error messages for tabs usually say "Missing separator" on my workstation.) I'll show the corrections for the linking errors below.

```
/home/kj/main> walksun.sh make all          build all tools on sun4gcc.plt
```

Now fix up the two library name problems. They arise because the UNIX linker requires the *-l* argument to be prepended to all library names on the command line. So we have to prepend a *-l* to the front of the library names listed in the **lb3** macros of the *imports.imp* files for *tool2* and *tool3*. Specifically, change the library references in the referencing *imports.imp* files to be **-ltool_pi** and **-ltool_pd**.

```
/home/kj/main> emacs tool2/sun4gcc.plt/imports.imp
lb3= -ltool_pi -ltool_pd
/home/kj/main> emacs tool3/sun4gcc.plt/imports.imp
lb3= -ltool_pi -ltool_pd
```

The linker should now be able to find the two libraries (*libtool_pi.a* and *libtool_pd.a*). The makefile templates will automatically generate the proper library name with the "lib" prefix.

Walk the tree and rebuild once again under the *sun4gcc.plt* platform.

```
/home/kj/main> walksun.sh make empty all
```

Let's test the compiled products to make sure that we've ported the tools correctly to the *sun4gcc.plt* platform.

```
/home/kj/main> tool1
0  This is tool1 compiled on platform (tbc.plt).
1  (tbc.plt) This is pd local  code from tool1/s/tool1.c.
2  (tbc.plt) This is pd local  data from tool1/s/tool1.h.
3  (tbc.plt) This is pd shared code from tool1/s/tool1.c.
4  (tbc.plt) This is pd shared data from tool1/s/tools.h.
5  (pi)      This is pi local  code from tool1/s/tool1.c.
6  (pi)      This is pi local  data from tool1/s/tool1.h.
```

```
7 (pi)     This is pi shared code from tool1/s/tool1.c.
8 (pi)     This is pi shared data from tool1/s/tools.h.
```

The *tool1* program still prints out the original bad output, which is the correct thing to do because we never intended to port *tool1*. Recall that the main purpose of *tool1* is to provide contrast with the *tool2* and *tool3* programs.

Let's check out *tool2* for *sun4gcc.plt*. This time, the output should contain *sun4gcc.plt* platform names.

```
/home/kj/main> tool2
0 This is tool2 compiled on platform (sun4gcc.plt).
1 (sun4gcc.plt) This is pd local  code from tool2/sun4gcc.plt/s/tool2.c.
2 (sun4gcc.plt) This is pd local  data from tool2/sun4gcc.plt/s/tool2_pd.h.
3 (sun4gcc.plt) This is pd shared code from tool_pd.lib/sun4gcc.plt/s/pd_sub.c.
4 (sun4gcc.plt) This is pd shared data from tool_pd.ini/sun4gcc.plt/s/tool_pd.h
5 (pi)     This is pi local  code from tool2/s/t2_sub.c.
6 (pi)     This is pi local  data from tool2/s/tool2_pi.h.
7 (pi)     This is pi shared code from tool_pi.lib/s/pi_sub.c.
8 (pi)     This is pi shared data from tool_pi.ini/s/tool_pi.h.
```

The *tool2* program output is correct. Now test *tool3*.

```
/home/kj/main> tool3
0 This is tool3 compiled on platform (sun4gcc.plt).
1 (sun4gcc.plt) This is pd local  code from tool3/sun4gcc.plt/s/tool3.c.
2 (sun4gcc.plt) This is pd local  data from tool3/sun4gcc.plt/s/tool3_pd.h.
3 (sun4gcc.plt) This is pd shared code from tool_pd.lib/sun4gcc.plt/s/pd_sub.c.
4 (sun4gcc.plt) This is pd shared data from tool_pd.ini/sun4gcc.plt/s/tool_pd.h
5 (pi)     This is pi local  code from tool3/s/t3_sub.c.
6 (pi)     This is pi local  data from tool3/s/tool3_pi.h.
7 (pi)     This is pi shared code from tool_pi.lib/s/pi_sub.c.
8 (pi)     This is pi shared data from tool_pi.ini/s/tool_pi.h.
```

The output from the *tool3* program is also correct. This means that we've successfully ported our example software programs to a third new platform (*sun4gcc.plt*) under a completely different operating system.

The final step in the port is to check in the ported files under RCS. Notice that the same message file is used for all check-in operations in the sequence below. That's why the absolute pathname is used.

(The "->" signs below are placeholders that represent the rest of the (long!) current directory name that would normally appear in the prompts. The pathnames were too long to fit on the page in one line. In each case, the missing piece of the pathname appears in the *cd* command on the previous line.)

```
/home/kj/main> echo This is part of the sun4gcc.plt port.>msg
/home/kj/main> cd tool_pd.ini/sun4gcc.plt/s
/home/kj/main/-> rcsdo ci_u_initial /home/kj/main/msg -log default

/home/kj/main/-> cd ../../../tool_pd.lib/sun4gcc.plt/s
/home/kj/main/-> rcsdo ci_u_initial /home/kj/main/msg -log default
```

```
/home/kj/main/-> cd ../../../tool2/sun4gcc.plt/s
/home/kj/main/-> rcsdo ci_u_initial /home/kj/main/msg -log default

/home/kj/main/-> cd ../../../tool3/sun4gcc.plt/s
/home/kj/main/-> rcsdo ci_u_initial /home/kj/main/msg -log default

/home/kj/main/-> cd ../../..
/home/kj/main> walksun.sh make empty
/home/kj/main> walksun.sh make all
/home/kj/main> walksun.sh make empty
```

This completes the initial setup of the source tree in the UNIX environment. Now I can show you how to clone source trees and perform RCS check-ins in a true multi-developer environment.

An Overview of Multi-person Environments

In a multi-developer environment, working with private (cloned) source trees is exactly the same as working with the main source trees that we've been working with so far. The same commands are used in the same ways.

There a couple of differences between the cloned trees and the main source trees themselves. One difference is that the private, cloned trees don't really have RCS subdirectories. Instead, the RCS "subdirectories" are symbolic links that point back to the real RCS directories in the main source tree.

A second difference is that in multi-developer environments, *imports.imp* files must also be stored under RCS. The *imports.imp* file contains custom, manually generated information that can't be reconstructed by automated tools. As a consequence, developers must be able to check out an official copy of the *imports.imp* file at the same time they check out official copies of the source files.

As it happens, these two differences don't affect the operation of the code management tools in any way.

Bulk Manual Check-ins of the imports.imp Files

In preparation for demonstrating some multiple-developer techniques, let's check in all the *imports.imp* files in our example source trees.

I'm not going to use *rcsdo* for this task, for two reasons. First, you already know how to use *rcsdo*. You wouldn't be learning anything new if I used *rcsdo ci_u_initial* to check in all the *imports.imp* in all the *sun4gcc.plt* platform directories.

The second and major reason is that logging all the *imports.imp* file check-in operations would be a tedious task because *rcsdo ci_u_initial* will try to check in all files in the platform directories and not just the *imports.imp* files. (You may want to visit each directory and try to check in only the *imports.imp* file with *rcsdo* to fully appreciate how awkward the task is.) So instead of using *rcsdo*, I'm going to walk the platform directories and "manually" check in the files. It'll be a lot cleaner and a lot faster.

Here's a tip to keep in mind when you're performing bulk check-ins manually (that is, by using a tree walker script and the raw RCS checkin (*ci*) command). The tree walker script will walk the source directories, and the RCS *ci* command will expect to find an RCS directory beneath each visited source directory.

A problem might occur if the raw RCS *ci* command can't find an RCS subdirectory below the currently visited source directory. Specifically, the *ci* program might try to create an RCS file in the source directory. (This would cause a name conflict between the working file and the RCS file on DOS.) The main problem with this kind of situation is that it's tedious to correct (as are all bulk mistakes made by bad tree walkers).

To avoid such events, I always manually create *rcs* subdirectories under each platform directory just before I perform bulk manual check-ins. That way, I know for sure that RCS subdirectories exist. (If you can guarantee that you'll always use the *makenode* and *makeplt* tools to create platform directories, you'll never have to perform the manual check that we're performing here. They will create the *rcs* directories for you.)

The *walksun.sh* script (which we created at the beginning of our UNIX porting effort) visits all the *sun4gcc.plt* platform directories in the source tree.

```
/home/kj/main> walksun.sh mkdir rcs   create RCS subdirs everywhere
```

Now that we know for sure that RCS subdirectories exist everywhere, we can perform the bulk manual check-in of all *imports.imp* files. The *-u* argument tells *ci* to unlock (make read-only) the working file after performing the check-in. The *-t* argument defines the pathname of a text file that contains the RCS file description message (not the log message). (If it bothers you that the same original check-in message will be given to all files, remember that we're checking in the same file (*imports.imp*) everywhere—so having the same message isn't a big problem.)

```
/home/kj/main> echo Support multiple developers by checking in this file.>msg
/home/kj/main> walksun.sh ci -u -t/home/kj/main/msg imports.imp   check in all imports.imps
/home/kj/main> rm msg
```

Notice that these manual RCS operations weren't recorded in the global RCS check-in log file named by the **CMPCILOG** environment variable. It doesn't really matter though, since we're just checking in a bunch of *imports.imp* files. All future changes to the *imports.imp* files will be recorded in the normal way.

Now the *imports.imp* files are checked in, and can be checked out by developers into newly cloned trees.

Cloning Private Developer Trees

The next command sequence shows you how to create a private developer's source tree by cloning the main source tree (our main tree is called *main*).

```
/home/kj/main> mkdir ../clone1
/home/kj/main> cptrio /home/kj/main /home/kj/clone1
```

At this point, we have an empty, cloned tree that's named *clone1*. Pretend that the cloned tree is your private source tree, and that the original tree (*main*) is the main source tree. We'll check out the source files and *imports.imp* files from the main tree into our private tree, and then rebuild all the software products from within the cloned tree.

To check out the source files into the cloned tree, we could use a tree walker script to walk all the appropriate source directories in the cloned tree. We're faced with a small problem though, since we only want to check out files in the pi directories and *sun4gcc.plt* pd source directories. That is, we don't want to visit the *tbc.plt*, *tb2.plt*, and *tdos.plt* source directories, but the *twalker* tool isn't smart enough to let us visit only this particular set of directories.

We have two alternatives, just as we did a little earlier on in this chapter, when we faced the same problem.

The first alternative is to create a tree walker script in the normal way, and then edit the resulting script to remove all references to the unwanted directories (*tbc.plt*, *tb2.plt*, and *tdos.plt*). This is how we should do it if we only had a few directories to delete from a tree walker script, because manual editing can be quick and efficient. But when we're faced with manually removing tens of directories—as in this example—the manual editing technique can be tedious.

Instead, I'll show you a second method that's much better for these kinds of situations. It'll also allow me to show you how to use the *mwalker* tool.

Creating Custom Tree Walker Scripts

To create a custom tree walker script, we'll generate a list of directories to visit and then manually generate a tree walker script from the list by using the *mwalker* (make a tree walker) tool. (This is exactly how *twalker* creates scripts too—it creates a list of directories to visit, and then calls *mwalker* to create the final script.)

Let's use *find* to create a full list of source directories, and then use *sed* to delete the directories that we don't want to visit.

```
/home/kj/main> cd ../clone1
/home/kj/clone1> find . -type d -name s -print >  foo
/home/kj/clone1> sed -e "/tbc.plt/d" -e "/tb2.plt/d" -e "/tdos.plt/d" foo > mydirs
```

Here's the list of directories that we want to visit.

```
/home/kj/clone1> cat mydirs

./tool1/s
./tool2/s
./tool2/sun4gcc.plt/s
./tool3/s
./tool3/sun4gcc.plt/s
./tool_pd.ini/sun4gcc.plt/s
./tool_pd.lib/sun4gcc.plt/s
./tool_pi.ini/s
./tool_pi.lib/s
```

Use *mwalker* to create a tree walker script from the list of directories. Note that we have to manually set the execute file-permission bits on the generated tree walker script because *mwalker* doesn't know the name of the generated script file. (The *twalker* tool also has to set the execute bits on the script that's produced by *mwalker*.)

```
/home/kj/clone1> mwalker mydirs > walksrc.sh        create the script
/home/kj/clone1> chmod 755 walksrc.sh               set execute permission
/home/kj/clone1> rm foo mydirs                      discard old working files
/home/kj/clone1> ls
./              rcs@            tool3/          tool_pi.ini/
../             tool1/          tool_pd.ini/    tool_pi.lib/
myhello.scr/    tool2/          tool_pd.lib/    walksrc.sh*
```

Now we're ready to check out both the source files and *imports.imp* files from the symbolically linked RCS directories.

```
/home/kj/clone1> walksrc.sh rcsdo co_u_f        check out source files
/home/kj/clone1> twalker walksun.sh sun4gcc.plt for walking sun4gcc.plt dirs
/home/kj/clone1> walksun.sh rcsdo co_u_f         check out imports.imp files
```

Next, generate new *sun4gcc.plt* makefiles for all of the checked-out source files by using the *newmakes* tool. (Recall that the *newmakes* tool will generate a tree walker script that automatically calls *getmakes* to generate the proper kind of makefiles for each product node visited by the tree walker script.)

```
/home/kj/clone1> newmakes walkmake.sh sun4gcc.plt   generate makefile maker script
/home/kj/clone1> walkmake.sh                        generate new makefiles
```

Now we can rebuild the example software programs in the cloned tree.

```
/home/kj/clone1> walksun.sh make all                rebuild everything
```

This ends the preparation of the cloned source tree. We now have *two* complete source trees (*main* and *clone1*) that share a common set of RCS files. The common RCS files are stored in the original *main* tree.

Sharing Code Changes with Other Developers

In this section I'll show you that code changes checked in from the cloned tree will show up as changes in the RCS files of the main tree.

To show this, we'll make a code change in the cloned tree, check it into RCS from the cloned tree, and then check the changed file out from within the *main* source tree.

(In practice, however, we wouldn't want to check out files directly into the main source tree in a multi-person development environment. Normally, you're not supposed to let anyone work directly within the main source tree—some files might get damaged or might get confused with the latest official versions in the RCS files.)

Let's change the *clone1/tool2/sun4gcc.plt/s/tool2.c* file in the cloned tree and observe the change in the main tree.

To make the change very visible, let's put exclamation marks after several words in line 0 of the *tool2.c* file.

```
/home/kj/clone1> cd tool2/sun4gcc.plt/s          go into the cloned tree
clone1/tool2/sun4gcc.plt/s> co -l -f tool2.c      check out a file
clone1/tool2/sun4gcc.plt/s> emacs tool2.c         change line 0 to 'compiled! on! cloned!'
```

Now update the RCS files. This action will affect the RCS files that are in the main source tree even though we're working within the cloned tree.

```
clone1/tool2/sun4gcc.plt/s> echo Changed tool2.c in the cloned tree.> msg
clone1/tool2/sun4gcc.plt/s> rcsdo ci_u_locked msg -log default
clone1/tool2/sun4gcc.plt/s> rm msg
```

We'll rebuild the *tool2* program *in the cloned tree* to convince ourselves that the change is visible in the output of the modified *tool2* program.

```
clone1/tool2/sun4gcc.plt/s> cd ..
clone1/tool2/sun4gcc.plt> make all                 rebuild the modified program
clone1/tool2/sun4gcc.plt> tool2
0 This is tool2 compiled! on! cloned! platform (sun4gcc.plt).
. . .
```

Yes, the change is visible. This verifies that the change has been checked in and tested from within the cloned tree. Now let's go back to the main tree to see if the change is available there too.

I'll show that the change is *not* in the current copy of the *tool2.c* program. I'll do this by showing that a search for the word "cloned" in the working file fails, the RCS version number of the current *tool2.c* program is different from the latest checked-in version, and that differences exist between the working file and the latest checked-in version.

First, show that a search for the word "cloned" in the working file fails (no lines are matched).

```
clone1/tool2/sun4gcc.plt> cd /home/kj/main
/home/kj/main> cd tool2/sun4gcc.plt/s
/home/kj/main/tool2/sun4gcc.plt/s> grep cloned tool2.c     the cloned word is missing
```

Now use *rcsdo* to check for locked and changed files.

```
/home/kj/main/tool2/sun4gcc.plt/s> rcsdo ls_locked       and the file isn't locked
/home/kj/main/tool2/sun4gcc.plt/s> rcsdo ls_changed      but we can detect changes
tool2.c has changed.
/home/kj/main/tool2/sun4gcc.plt/s> rcsdiff tool2.c       this shows the code changes
9c9
<     printf("0  This is tool2 compiled! on! cloned! (sun4gcc.plt).\n");
---
>     printf("0  This is tool2 compiled on platform (sun4gcc.plt).\n");
```

The results from *rcsdo* mean that the working file hasn't changed—instead, the RCS file has changed!

Now let's show that there's a difference in RCS version numbers between the working file and the latest checked-in version of the RCS file. The version number of the working file will be *lower than* (that is, behind) the version number of the latest version in the RCS file.

The following comands are RCS commands. The *ident* tool prints out the RCS version number of the named file. (The version number is usually stored in the RCS version string—the keyword **Id** surrounded by dollar signs—that we put at the head of the file.) The *rlog* tool prints out the modification history that's stored in the RCS file.

```
/home/kj/main/tool2/sun4gcc.plt/s> ident tool2.c         show the version of our file
/home/kj/main/tool2/sun4gcc.plt/s> ident rcs/tool2.c     show the version of the RCS file
/home/kj/main/tool2/sun4gcc.plt/s> rlog tool2.c          this shows the RCS log entries
```

Let's check out the latest version of the file, now that we've inspected the changes in several different ways.

```
/home/kj/main/tool2/sun4gcc.plt/s> co -u -f tool2.c      check out the new modifications
/home/kj/main/tool2/sun4gcc.plt/s> grep cloned tool2.c   see? the cloned word is here
```

Now let's rebuild the *tool2* program in the platform directory of the main tree to verify that we've been able to access the changed file from within the main tree.

```
/home/kj/main/tool2/sun4gcc.plt/s> cd ..
/home/kj/main/tool2/sun4gcc.plt> make all                rebuild the tool2 program.
/home/kj/main/tool2/sun4gcc.plt> ./tool2
This is tool2 compiled! on! cloned! platform (sun4gcc.plt).
 . . .
```

The key to sharing—the structural solution, you might say—is to have a central tree for source control files and separate development directories for each programmer. But a procedural solution is also required. You need a way to direct each programmer's check-ins and check-outs to the central tree. The system used in this book does this through a feature offered on all modern UNIX systems, symbolic links.

Summary

The examples in this chapter showed you how to use the *addaplat* tool to add new platforms to an entire source tree. (The *rmaplat* tool removes platforms using a similar technique.)

The example also showed you how to clone a source tree, how to use the *mwalker* tool to generate custom tree walker scripts from an arbitrary list of directories, and how to check out the latest source code files into a cloned tree. It also showed you how to generate new makefiles for new platform directories throughout the entire cloned tree.

Finally, the example showed you how to generate, how to inspect (*ident, rlog, rcsdiff*), and how to share code changes among multiple source trees.

This concludes the tour.

9

Code Management Environments for DOS and UNIX

This chapter contains two simple case studies based on the requirements and issues that were described earlier in Chapter 4, *Designing a Code Management System*. They quickly summarize the decisions that made it possible to create the code management system included with this book. Once you understand the decisions that are described in this chapter, you'll be able to apply the same principles to your own working environment.

An Environment for DOS

The environment described here is definitely not the only one that can be used on DOS systems, but I know that it's a practical one. I've used it for two years to manage the code for over 100 multi-platform programs, libraries, and scripts on my personal computer network.

The following sections discuss the issues, the policies, the procedures, and some special cases of the DOS code management environment.

Environment Overview

This section enumerates and explains the issues that helped to create this environment for DOS. The issues themselves are listed in Chapter 4.

The environment described here is a single-person, multi-platform environment for DOS computers. And because it doesn't assume the presence of symbolic links or newsgroups, it should also be a good model for single-person, multi-platform development environments on other machines (including UNIX and mainframes).

It's also a maintenance-by-replacement environment. This means that the descriptions below don't talk about how to store and modify old releases of the software.

I chose this particular single-person, multi-platform, maintenance-by-replacement environment as the first model for this book, because it's a simple, practical, and very common development environment. That is, it represents the typical kind of development environments that many people use. And it doesn't require special hardware or operating-system features, either—it can be implemented on any computer that's at least as smart as DOS. (Which isn't a lot to ask!)

The following subsections enumerate and explain the many issues that define this environment for DOS computers. Each point below addresses one of the issues listed in Chapter 4.

Platform issues

1. **Multiple platforms will be used.** This is because many people want their software products to run on multiple platforms (for various reasons).

2. **There are DOS platform limitations.** The main limitation that concerns us here is that *make* tools don't handle recursion well under DOS. This is because the standard DOS computer has only 640K bytes of memory available for both the *make* tool and the tools that it calls (such as compilers and linkers). This means that DOS has a limited ability to support programs that invoke other programs, for the same reason. (EMS (expanded/extended) memory swapping techniques can mitigate this problem to some extent, if they're actually used by the calling programs.)

3. **No symbolic links.** DOS doesn't support symbolic links. As a consequence, all sharing operations must be carried out by physically copying files, instead of by linking to them.

   The techniques in this book call for the use of links only in multi-developer UNIX environments. There, symbolic links are used to link the RCS directories in private developer trees back to the RCS directories in the main source tree. (Since there's only one developer and one source tree in a single-person DOS environment, symbolic links aren't required.)

4. **No newsgroups to distribute change log messages.** On networked DOS systems, the consequence of this limitation is that RCS log entries must be put into an ASCII log file instead of a newsgroup. However, if you have some kind of a newsgroup facility on your DOS computer, you can modify the *pci* (post check-in information) tool to use your newsgroup facility. The only difference between using a file and using a newsgroup is that the newsgroup facility may make it more convenient to view new log entries. On single-user, non-networked DOS systems, of course, a log file works just fine.

Corporate issues

1. **Maintenance by replacement.** This policy makes things easier because only one copy of the source tree—the main source tree—has to be managed in the development environment. As a consequence, the problems of working with multiple versions of old software releases can be avoided. Besides, it's rare for DOS products to be released under a maintenance-by-repair policy. Instead, most DOS products are shrink-wrapped products, produced in maintenance-by-replacement environments.

2. **No multiple developers.** The environment described here is a single person environment, such as a developer might have on a PC at home. This decision precludes the multi-person problems of creating and maintaining private developer source trees, locking source code files, constructing official baseline versions of the products each week, and so on. All those problems are discussed in the UNIX part of this chapter.

3. **File sharing is supported.** This environment supports file sharing for the standard reasons that were mentioned earlier. These include the need to share common source and include files, the desire to reuse source code and binary files, and the need to export files for alpha testing and for release.

4. **File releasing is supported.** You can assume that released software products are different in some way from alpha test products. For example, they may have been compiled with different options, or may contain a different set of software features. Or they may have been put through a different software process that involved much more quality assurance testing than do alpha test products. Because they were derived through a different construction process, released files must be stored in a different place from alpha test files.

5. **Tested code is separate from untested code.** This means that only tested code should be checked into the RCS files, implying that a working, tested version of the product can always be extracted from the RCS files. To accomodate this policy, you should always make sure that your source files work properly on all platforms before checking them into the RCS system.

   The main goal of this policy decision is to ensure that the baseline version of the software product will always work properly. (The baseline version of the product is always built from the latest checked-in versions of product files.)

   The consequences of checking untested (and possibly defective) code into the RCS files is that the baseline might fail during testing. On small projects, this might cause a night of testing time to be wasted. And on large systems, several days of quality assurance tests might be lost.

Tree structures

1. **Source files are stored in the source directories of product nodes.** If the source files are stored in either the pi *s* directory or the pd *platform.plt/s* directories, the makefile generator tools can automatically generate dependency rules. But if the source is stored in subdivided source directories such as *s/part1*, *s/part2*, etc., you'll have to construct the appropriate *gendep* commands to generate dependency rules yourself. (Generating dependency rules from source files in subdivided source directories was explained in Chapter 6, *Makefile Architectures*.)

2. **Include files are stored in the product owner's source directory.** This decision works well with most include files. However, a special difficulty can arise where one include file is used by all products in a product group. Then it's hard to

choose a single "owner" of the file, because it's shared. Moreover, the file must be made available for sharing before any of the products—including the owning product—can be compiled.

To get around these kinds of problems, I usually create a pseudo-product called *product.ini* to act as owner for the files. That way, the tree walker scripts ensure that the include files owned by *product.ini* are exported for sharing before any of the other products are compiled. (See Chapter 5, *Directory Structures*, for more information on build-order dependencies.)

3. **Version control files are stored in RCS subdirectories.** By default, the *makenode* tool creates an RCS subdirectory below any directory that contains files requiring version control.

4. **Makefiles are stored in platform directories.** This approach has the advantage of storing all of a product's platform-dependent makefiles within the product subtree. This makes it easier to reorganize directories, because makefiles are physically stored within the product trees that use them. It also makes it easier for developers to change makefile compilation options, since the makefiles are stored in the same directory where compilations, debugging, and tests take place. Last, storing makefiles in platform directories also makes it easier for the makefile generator tools to find the information that they need to generate makefiles and dependency rule files.

    The alternative to this, storing makefiles for all products in one directory, would preclude all these advantages.

5. **Compilations are performed in the platform directories.** The use of a separate platform directory for each platform allows you to simultaneously store files for multiple platforms.

6. **Object files are stored in the platform directories.** The advantage of storing all platform specific makefiles, object files, and finished products in the same platform directory is that all platform specific files are contained in one subtree. This makes it easier to add, remove, and support multiple platforms.

7. **Alpha test files are stored in the alpha test directory.** By default, all makefiles export finished products to the platform-specific alpha test directories. This means that if you add the alpha test directories to your **PATH** variable, you can use the latest alpha test copy of all products in your daily work. This is a particularly convenient technique for managing the (usually very many) non-releasable, in-house software tools that are found in most typical software development environments.

8. **Released files are stored in the release directory.** The main difference between released files and alpha test files is that the released files may have been passed through a release procedure. Such procedures vary widely among environments, but they typically involve a bit more testing and perhaps the removal of some conditionally compiled debugging code.

9. **The alpha test version of the product is defined to be the latest baseline version of the product.** This means that no special procedures are required to generate an alpha test version of the software. Instead, new alpha test versions can be generated simply by checking out, compiling, and exporting the latest versions of the source files from the RCS system.

10. **The alpha test source is the baseline source.** Since the alpha test products are defined to be the baseline products, the source used to build the alpha test products is, by definition, the baseline source code. And we already have a place to store that.

11. **Old releases are not stored.** This is because the DOS environment described here has adopted a maintenance-by-replacement policy.

Multiple developers

The DOS environment described here is intended to be a single-person environment, so it can be used as an example of a very simple code management system. For this reason, the multiple-developer issues discussed in Chapter 4 are not relevant to this discussion.

Multiple platforms

1. **#ifdefs are not allowed for platform specific code.** The main benefit of this decision is that it forces developers to remove platform-dependent code from platform-independent source files. This enhances the readability of source files, and makes it easier for the makefile tools to generate dependency rules.

2. **Platform-dependent source files are stored in *platform.plt/s* directories.** This decision follows the conventions described earlier.

3. **Platform-dependent binary files are stored in platform directories.** This decision follows the conventions described earlier.

4. **Makefiles and test scripts are stored in platform directories.** Simple test scripts (which are actually *scripts* instead of programs) can be stored in the platform directory, with their RCS files in an RCS subdirectory below the platform directory. But if the scripts are complex, or if they're actually compiled programs, it's probably better to store them in their own standard product nodes.

5. **Platform-dependent files are shared via the *share/platform.plt* directories.** This decision follows the conventions described earlier.

6. **Normal files are shared via the *share* directory.** This decision follows the conventions described earlier.

7. **Code is ported to new platforms by cloning and modifying existing platform-dependent files.** This decision follows the conventions described earlier.

8. **Multi-platform development is supported with the tools in this book.** This issue isn't a very big one if you decide to use the tools and procedures that I've described in this book. But it *is* a big issue if you decide not to use the techniques described in the book.

   In that case, you should explain how you intend to support multi-platform development with your own techniques. You may want to review Chapter 4 to help you to define requirements for your site.

Include files

1. **Include files are stored with the product owner's source files.** The product owner of an include file is the product tree that stores (and possibly exports) the file.

2. **Absolute and relative pathnames are not allowed in include statements.** It's a bad practice because it makes the code more sensitive to directory reorganzations.

Documentation files

1. **Storage is provided for technical and user documentation.** Test program documentation can be stored with other technical documentation.

2. **User documentation is stored in a separate directory.** This is because user documentation files are often stored in a special word processor file format. For this reason, it's easiest to keep them in a separate directory that is only used for word processing.

   The user documentation directory can be a peer of the platform directories (perhaps named *udoc*), or it can be stored in some remote location, as you see fit.

3. **Technical documentation is stored in the product node.** Technical maintenance and programming documentation can be kept near the source code by placing it in a documentation subdirectory in the product node. I usually name the documentation directory in a product node *doc.*

Test program files

1. **Simple test scripts are stored in the platform directories.** This decision is consistent with the presentation of this simple, single-person DOS environment. But it may be the case that this decision doesn't meet your needs. If that's so, you should review the test program issues discussed in Chapter 4 and make a decision to suit your needs.

2. **Larger test programs are treated as separate products.** If a test program has to be compiled, I don't put it in or below the platform directories. Instead, I make the test program a peer of the software products that it tests. Sometimes I end up creating a new parent directory to hold both the test programs and the tested products.

3. **The single developer maintains the test programs.** This decision is simple in single person environments—one person has to do everything.

Non-standard software products

The decisions associated with handling non-standard software products are discussed later, in the section on special cases. The main thing for you to decide is when, why, and how much you should convert non-standard software products into the standard forms supported by your code management environment.

This book argues that you should *not* spend a lot of time converting non-standard software unless there's a good reason for it.

Sharing and releasing

The DOS environment uses the mechanisms described in Chapter 7, *File Sharing*, to implement sharing and releasing.

Makefile issues

1. **A set of standard makefile targets is used.** The targets that I use are listed in Table 6-4. However, you might want to use a different set of standard targets for your environment. If so, just change the makefile templates in the CMTREE.

2. **Different product types are supported with different makefile templates.** Sample templates for executables, libraries, and scripts are explained in this book.

3. **Different platforms are supported with different makefile templates.** Sample templates for common (DOS and UNIX) compilers and *make* tools are provided with this book.

4. **Special targets are supported in the *imports.imp* file.** The *imports.imp* file is the appropriate place to put special makefile targets for a particular product. This is because *imports.imp* files are never modified by the makefile generation tools.

5. **Default operations are supported with standard makefile targets.** The makefiles in this book support many common build activities.

6. **Automated product tree traversals are supported with tree walker scripts.** The tree walker tools were described in the tour chapters and are explained in detail in Appendix A, *Code Management Software Tools*.

Minimizing sensitivity to change

1. **Makefile macros are used for common filenames and tool names.** The platform-dependent macros are defined in *makefile.plt*, and platform-insensitive filename macros are defined in *makefile.tre*.

2. **Platform-dependent makefile templates are used to build products.** Specifically, the contents of the *makefile.llb*, *makefile.xxe*, and *makefile.ssc* can be different for different platforms. This approach minimizes the sensitivity of standard makefiles to platform changes by encapsulating platform-dependent knowledge in separate files.

3. **Automated tools are used to regenerate tree walker files after reorganizations.** The recommended approach is to use the *newmakes, getmakes*, and tree walker tools to regenerate makefiles and rebuild products after directory and filename reorganizations.

As you already know, makefiles in this environment are commonly generated with makefile generation tools.

Source code issues

Disallow platform-dependent #ifdefs in source files. The issue was also discussed above, under multiple platform issues.

Policies

Here's a list of recommended policies for the DOS single-person environment:

- **The baseline product must always work for all platforms.** The baseline version of the product is created from the latest checked-in versions in the RCS files. The idea behind this policy is that once you get a working version of the product, you should never allow it to stop working. Instead, continued development should proceed unidirectionally forward, and should always enhance the operation of the product, rather than destroy it.

  This policy also means that you should test your modifications thoroughly before checking them into the RCS files. (Assuming that you *have* a test suite, of course.)

- **If you modify one file in a pd node, modify the corresponding files for all platforms.** This simple rule helps to ensure that developers don't just modify the code for one platform. (Modifying code for one platform can happen quite easily if individual developers use different platforms as their daily working machines. For example, if a developer works on a Sun4 workstation, it's likely that the Sun4 platform will be the first one modified, the first one tested, and so on. This is because it's usually more convenient (faster) for developers to work on their personal workstations than it is for them to work across a network, on a foreign machine that has an unfamiliar and different behavior.)

- **Test modifications on all platforms before doing any check-ins.** This will help to ensure identical product behavior on all platforms. If this policy isn't followed—especially in a multi-person environment—then the product's behavior can become platform dependent.

  This approach also makes it easy for you to stop and discard your partially completed modifications should you encounter huge difficulties on one particular platform. That is, since your modifications for previously modified platforms haven't yet been checked in, they don't have to be backed out while you figure out how to fix the code for the current (troublesome) platform. And by modifying all platforms before checking in *any* of the modified files, you'll protect the baseline from developing platform-dependent behavior.

- **The normal state of all source files is checked-in and read-only.** This is a good practice because it makes it easier for you to identify source files that have been modified (but not checked in). This practice also helps you to ensure that all modifications have been checked in before doing a product release.

  (Recall that during the tour chapter, we used a tree walker script to list the file access modes on all files in the source directories. Any writable source files were suspect, because they might have contained modifications that hadn't been checked in.)

- **Try to make small, incremental changes to products instead of big ones.** This technique was described earlier in the section called "Checking in RCS Files as You Go" in Chapter 3, *A Hands-on Tour: Part 2*. It helps you keep the baseline working by allowing you to make a steady series of small, working improvements in the code. It's a much less risky approach than checking out files for days, and then checking in huge chunks of new code.

- **Log all check-ins with the *rcsdo* tool.** This policy encourages me to make up more detailed log message files for each modification, thus improving my work records. It also helps me to keep a record of all the software modifications that I do, anywhere on my system. Then when I'm trying to evaluate my progress or the source code changes that have occurred over some period of time, I can easily find the answer in a few ASCII log files. (I also use this same approach to manage the ASCII text files that form this book.)

Procedures

This section describes a few particular procedures that work well with the MS-DOS environment described in this chapter.

Working with RCS branches. Many people use RCS branches to support either old releases (maintenance by repair) or platform-dependent versions of the software. But since the maintenance-by-replacement environment described here uses a different technique for platform-dependent code, adding branch support to *rcsdo* seemed unnecessary to me at the time that I wrote the tool.

However, the *rcsdo* source code has been provided with this book, so you can add such support if you so desire.

Release procedures

Since the individual steps in most release procedures vary enormously among development environments, this book makes no attempt to describe and justify a detailed release procedure. Instead, it only offers some general guidelines. The details of creating a good release procedure for your own environment are best defined by you, since you're the person that knows the most about the specific requirements of your environment.

Here's a list of some steps that you might want to include in your release procedures:

1. **Decide what to include in the release.** In this step you should identify the new features and the bug fixes that will be fixed in the next release. It's best if you can use some kind of a formal change control system for this step, because such systems can help you to manage the many possible changes that could be made.

   Change control systems are frequently called bug tracking systems, but I think that's too narrow a term for their role. Systems that I have used not only kept track of bugs, but they also kept track of possible new features and improvements too. In fact, the systems that I've had experience with tended to collect all sorts of "non-bug" information about current products, future products, bugs, new features, questions and answers, and so on.

   Maybe it would be best to call these systems *change management* systems, because they help to manage many different kinds of *requests for change*.

2. **Install the selected changes into the software.** This step consists of normal development and maintenance activities. The logs created by the *rcsdo* tool are a useful by-product of this step.

3. **Completely rebuild the release software.** Most people that I know like to completely rebuild all products from the baseline source files for each new release. This is because they're afraid that their baseline source code won't build correctly functioning products. So they like to prove to themselves that what they *think* are the latest source files will actually produce what they want to release. And a second reason for rebuilding is that they want to find out about any construction problems *before* the new release goes out the door. For these reasons, I've included this step in the guidelines for release procedures.

4. **Verify that the intended changes have been made.** Now that the release has been constructed, you should verify that the intended changes actually made it into the final software. There are two ways to check this: by examining the *rcsdo* logs, and by testing the software. Neither one of these two ways is perfect, but if you use both of them you should be able to convince yourself that the changes have been made.

   The *rcsdo* check-in logs are useful because not all changes produce testable differences. For example, cosmetic code cleanups (such as reformatting the source code) should definitely not produce testable differences in product behavior.

5. **Check that the main source tree is in a consistent state.** I do this by using a tree walker script to list the file permissions of all the source files in the product tree. The permissions should all be read-only, since all source files should have been checked in for the release. So any source files that aren't read-only are suspect, because they might contain changes that haven't yet been checked into the RCS files.

6. **Generate the release directly from the RCS files.** If you're really paranoid about release procedures (which is the smart way to be if you want to avoid handing out those free product upgrades), always generate the final releasable products directly from the RCS files. Don't just generate the products from the source files that happen to be in the main source tree, because they might be the wrong ones, for reasons that no one on your team will ever be able to explain :-).

   Instead, check out the latest versions of all source files from the RCS files, and then generate and test the release from those source files.

   This approach ensures that whatever is in the release is also in the RCS files, and that you'll always be able to recreate the exact products that you sent out to customers. And no customer will get a "special development product" that was inadvertently left around by a developer.

7. **Test and label the source files for the new release.** Once you're convinced that the newly generated products work properly, assign an appropriate symbolic name to all RCS files in the new release.

Special Cases

A few special situations are worthy of discussion here. These include working with subdivided source directories and freeware products obtained from the net.

Subdivided source directories

The first special case occurs when there are too many source files in the single source directory of a product. In such cases, most people subdivide the source directory into several subdirectories and regroup the files in the new subdirectories.

I recommend that you avoid this practice unless it is absolutely necessary, because the makefile tools in this book don't completely support subdivided source directories.

But if you have to do it, the example in Chapter 6 shows how to generate dependency rules for subdivided source directories.

Managing freeware products

A special case arises when you get a freeware product from the net. Should you install it in a product node in your code management system, or leave the original distribution alone?

Several factors affect the answer—many of the same factors that were relevant to the question of whether to put test programs under the code management system. (Test programs were discussed in Chapter 4.) Here are a few reasons to think about:

1. If you're going to seriously enhance or rewrite the product, or port it to other platforms, then install it in the code management system. You'll probably recover your installation work several times over.

2. If installation requires a trivial amount of effort, install it under the code management system. Installation is a small price to pay for the convenience of being able to maintain the product using standard policies and tools.

Summary

The single-person, multi-platform, maintenance-by-replacement MS-DOS environment described here is modeled after the working environment on my personal computer.

I've used the described environment for more than a year, to maintain over 100 software products of different kinds (pi and pd libraries, C programs, scripts, documentation files), in two different environments (UNIX and MS-DOS), and on several different compilation platforms. (Recall that a platform is a combination of a *make* tool and a compiler or interpreter.)

This experience has convinced me that the environment described here is significantly better than traditional MS-DOS development environments.

An Environment for UNIX

This section describes one possible code management environment for UNIX systems. It's a superset of the DOS environment described in the previous section, and provides for multiple platforms and multiple developers. It's been used for over five years to manage about 100,000 lines of executable code under a maintenance-by-replacement policy, on three different computing platforms, with good results.

In particular, the environment did a good job of managing two very different types of platforms. One of the platforms was a 64-processor Transputer machine, which meant that it was very specialized. You didn't run compilers on that machine—you ran only finished programs on it. So we used cross compilers to generate binaries for it, and then downloaded the binaries to it from a Sun workstation.

The first section gives an overview of the UNIX code management environment, and discusses the differences between the UNIX and DOS environments. The second section contains a list of recommended policies. A third section outlines several important multi-person, multi-platform procedures for the UNIX environment. Last, this chapter closes with a brief summary.

Environment Overview

The UNIX environment is very similar to the DOS environment described earlier. As a consequence, only the differences between it and the DOS environment will be described here.

Summary of differences: DOS/SPMP versus UNIX/MPMP

The UNIX environment described here is a multi-person, multi-platform, maintenance-by-replacement environment that's suitable for UNIX computers.

The main conceptual difference between the UNIX and the DOS environments is that UNIX environments can typically support multiple developers, whereas DOS environments usually support only one developer.

The main technical difference is that the UNIX environment uses symbolic links. It uses them to connect the RCS directories in private developer source trees to the corresponding RCS directories in the main source tree. This makes it possible for developers to perform RCS operations on the main source tree simply by applying the desired RCS operations directly to their own private trees. The symbolic links propagate the operations to the RCS files in the main source tree.

A second, less important technical difference is that the UNIX environment uses newsgroups to record the RCS check-in messages provided by *rcsdo*. (Recall that the DOS version of *rcsdo* puts RCS check-in messages in an ASCII log file.)

A third (and optional) technical difference is that recursive makefile techniques can be easily used on UNIX systems. However, I don't recommend this option, because linear tree walking scripts work on more platforms, and offer more operational flexibility. Note that even though recursive makefile techniques aren't recommended by this book, they *are* compatible with the tools and methods of the book. So if you want to use recursive techniques, just modify the makefile templates accordingly.

Summary of issues

- **Platform issues.** These issues are completely different from the DOS environment. The UNIX platform provides both links and newsgroups, and has no significant limitations.

- **Corporate issues.** These issues are the same in the DOS environment, except that the UNIX environment supports multiple developers.

- **Directory issues.** These issues are the same as in the DOS environment, with the exception of multiple developer issues. Multiple developer issues are discussed separately in the following section.

- **Makefile issues.** These issues are the same as in the DOS environment, with the exception of recursive makefiles. Recursive makefile techniques aren't discussed by this book.

- **Source code issues.** These issues are the same as in the DOS environment.

Multiple developer issues

UNIX systems are often multi-person environments, so they typically require different policies from DOS environments.

1. **Private trees are created by cloning the main tree.** Private developer trees are created by copying the main source tree to a private area, and then by linking the RCS directories of the new tree back to the RCS directories of the main source tree.

    This approach lets developers stabilize their working environments by controlling the movement of updated files from the main tree into their trees. If they want to pick up new changes from the main source tree, they can check out the latest copies of the relevant files. Otherwise, their working environments will be unaffected by new checkins in the main source tree.

2. **Check-in conflicts are controlled with tools and procedures.** In a multi-person environment, it's possible for multiple developers to simultaneously modify the same source code file. This is awkward because checking in one person's modifications may overwrite another person's changes.

    The most common technique for avoiding this is for each developer to lock the file while they're performing their modifications. This approach imposes a serial order on the changes by allowing only one developer at a time to work on the file.

    However, it's often the case (for business, personal, or other non-technical reasons) that multiple developers do work on the same code at the same time. In such cases, two cases arise: either the developers change the same part of the source file, or they change different parts of the source file.

    If the developers change different parts of the source file, then their changes don't conflict with each other. Then it's possible to automatically merge the non-conflicting changes with a tool such as *rcsmerge*.

    But if the developers change the same part of the file, then their changes conflict. As a consequence, the conflicting code changes can't be merged automatically, and must be reconciled by a developer.

3. **A newsgroup is used to communicate source code changes to developers.** It's important to keep everyone on the development team aware of the changes that are being made to software products. The tools provided with this book support this goal by collecting all RCS check-in log messages into a central location (either a file or a newsgroup).

4. **Multiple developers are supported with the tools described in this book.** For efficiency, convenience, and uniformity reasons, multiple developers should probably be supported with automated tools. This book lists several.

Policies

The policies for the UNIX environment are the same as those for DOS.

1. The baseline product must always work for all platforms.

2. If you modify one file in a pd node, modify the corresponding files for all platforms.

3. Test modifications on all platforms before doing any checkins.

4. The normal state of all source files is checked-in, and read-only.

5. Try to make small, incremental changes to products instead of big ones.

6. Log all checkins with the *rcsdo* tool.

Converting to a Multi-person UNIX Environment

Two things are required to convert source files from a DOS single-person, multi-platform environment to a UNIX multi-person, multi-platform environment. First, the standard DOS line-termination characters (CR+LF) must be converted to the standard UNIX line-termination character (LF only). And second, new platform directories must be added to all product trees to support the UNIX platform.

The RCS tools provided with this book behave differently when compiled under DOS and UNIX. Specifically, the DOS versions expect each line in the RCS files to end in the standard, two-character DOS line termination sequence: carriage return plus newline. In contrast, the UNIX versions of the tools expect the standard UNIX line-termination sequence: a single newline character.

This doesn't cause a problem in DOS-only systems or in UNIX-only systems because then the tools and the line-termination sequences in the files are consistent with each other. But if editors and tools from both platforms are used on the same source code files, problems can occur because the platform-dependent tools and line-termination sequences may disagree with each other.

For example, suppose version 1 of a file is checked in under UNIX. Then the file will have no carriage returns at the end of its lines. Now suppose that the file is checked out under DOS, trivially modified on one line, and checked back in, still under DOS.

This sequence should cause RCS to detect a difference in just the one line that was modified. (You can see this for yourself using *rcsdiff*.) But in practice, RCS will think that the whole file has been modified, because the second (DOS-modified) version will have carriage returns at the end of all lines. This is because most DOS editors will add carriage returns as they write out modified files. (So in fact, RCS is right—every line in the file is different.)

It also follows that all development tools on each platform will follow the platform-dependent carriage return convention. And that's a problem when you're sharing files between platforms, because the tools for one platform may not work with the carriage return convention of another platform. Let's consider two possible solutions:

1. Consider the solution of modifying the RCS tools in this book so that they follow a uniform carriage return convention (whichever one pleases you) on all platforms. That way, all the RCS files would have the same carriage return convention, regardless of which platform-dependent tools were used to check them in. But that isn't a solution that I can use, because the tools in this book are intended to work with third party RCS tools (such as the MKS RCS tools for UNIX and DOS).

2. Suppose now that the RCS *ci* and *co* tools (for all platforms) were wrapped in a script, so that the files were always converted to a uniform carriage return convention before the files were checked in, or after they were checked-out. Then the RCS tools wouldn't have to be modified. This solution would also allow people to edit the files on any platform with their favorite editor, without having to worry about carriage return conventions.

    But unfortunately, this still doesn't solve the problem, because the RCS tools themselves may add or remove carriage returns to the incoming or outgoing files. (This is what happens under DOS, for example.) So to solve the problem, you'd have to modify the RCS *ci*, *co*, and *rcsdiff* tools for at least one of the platforms to follow your chosen carriage return convention. But we can't do that either. That's the same problem that we disallowed above—modifying the RCS tools!

So as you can see, I don't have a good solution to this problem that I can use in this book. (The only apparent solution is to arrange your work habits so that you consistently modify your source files from platforms that use the same carriage return conventions.) But I can certainly tell you how to solve the problem using non-standard techniques, if you're willing to accept them.

If you really want to solve the problem, first modify all the RCS tools (on all platforms) in your environment to follow the same carriage return convention. Then create wrapper scripts for all the RCS tools (including *rcsdiff*) to convert all checked out files to agree with the traditional carriage return conventions for each platform in the environment. That way, checked out files will look normal to the editors used in each environment, and when the files are checked in again, the RCS tools will convert them back to your chosen carriage return convention. That should solve the problem.

Summary

This section described a code management environment suitable for UNIX systems. The environment described for UNIX was almost identical to the DOS environment, with the exceptions that the UNIX environment used newsgroups and symbolic links.

This similarity in structure and form between the two environments makes it easier for developers to move between development platforms in heterogeneous DOS/UNIX work environments.

In This Chapter:
- *Summary of Key Ideas*
- *Conclusions*
- *Future Directions*

10

Conclusion

This chapter summarizes the key ideas of the book and interprets their overall significance. It also identifies the problems that were successfully addressed by this work, as well as the problems that still remain. The chapter concludes with a brief discussion of possible future directions in code management systems.

Summary of Key Ideas

The four major ideas of this book were about directory structures, makefile structures, file sharing mechanisms, and automated tool support for the previous three ideas. Each idea is discussed separately in the sections below.

Directory Structures

Chapter 5, *Directory Structures*, described a set of directory structure conventions for effectively organizing computer files in MPMP (multi-person, multi-platform) development environments. The structure has been used to manage about 100,000 lines of executable code on three platforms in an MPMP UNIX environment, and about 100 smaller software tools on two platforms in a single-person, multi-platform DOS environment.

The advantages of the directory structure conventions are numerous. Specifically, the directory structures isolate specific kinds of files for both practical and conceptual convenience. They promote the use of automated tools by imposing a regular, uniform structure on the entire source tree. They work well on different platforms. They reduce the project's sensitivity to directory reorganizations by using standard directory names for product nodes. And the directory structures are flexible enough to support simple, individual software products, as well as groups of complex, related products.

The main disadvantage of the conventions is that they impose (minor) naming restrictions on product directories and on some of the associated subdirectories. But these minor restrictions are easy costs to bear, given the advantages that can be gained.

The operational costs of using the directory structure conventions are minimized by the directory construction and traversal tools that are provided with this book.

The philosophical value of the directory structure conventions may be that they represent a near-optimum way of separating and managing the different kinds of information in a code management environment. That's because the directory structures seem capable of storing most, if not all, software products of different kinds. (The structures are capable of storing all the products that I've ever seen.)

In my opinion, the main value of the directory structures is that they impose enough uniformity on the development environment to promote the development of useful automated tools. This is a very significant advantage because it opens the door to possibly huge improvements in efficiency as tools become increasingly more powerful.

Makefile Architectures

Chapter 6, *Makefile Architectures*, described a set of makefile conventions for effectively isolating different kinds of makefile knowledge in separate template makefiles. This encapsulation imposed enough uniformity on the makefile architecture to allow the development of useful automated makefile generation tools. The makefile architecture (or earlier versions of it) has been used by a variety of developers to support hundreds of software products of different kinds on different platforms for many years.

Several conceptual and economic advantages are provided by the makefile architecture. It encapsulates standard types of makefile knowledge, and so promotes uniformity, reuse of makefile templates, and reduced maintenance costs. It decreases the costs of upgrading makefiles. It can easily be extended to support new kinds of software products and different kinds of makefile knowledge. It's operationally efficient because it's supported by tools.

Also, since the makefile architecture provides an arbitrary amount of room for custom makefile targets and commands, it doesn't restrict the use of traditional makefile techniques. The makefile architecture has no significant disadvantages that I'm aware of.

It seems to me that the philosophical meaning of the makefile architecture is that it helps to separate general procedural knowledge from specific product knowledge. By this, I mean that the makefile architecture physically and conceptually separates the knowledge of compiling, linking, library building, exporting, and so on, from any knowledge about the specific software product itself.

For example, all the knowledge (instructions) required for building software products is stored in standard makefile templates in the CMTREE. In contrast, all the knowledge about which files make up a specific product is stored within the product node.

File Sharing Mechanisms

Chapter 7, *File Sharing*, described a set of conventions and tools for sharing files among software products. The tools implemented file sharing by physically copying files and by optionally logging the copy operation.

The sharing technique has been used to support file sharing among about 100 small programs, on multiple platforms, for about one year.

The main advantages of this approach are that it's simple, flexible, general, efficient, and practical. Furthermore, it provides a means of explicitly representing and inspecting file sharing relationships among software products in the code management system described here. And importantly, it doesn't restrict the use of traditional file sharing techniques. Instead, it can co-exist peacefully with them.

The main disadvantage of the approach is that it's more complex than other file sharing methods. However, this is reasonable because the file sharing approach described here offers many advantages that other methods do not. (The approach also creates multiple copies of every shared file. But this isn't so bad, since programmers are likely to create multiple copies of shared files anyway. At least in this method you know where the shared copies are and can keep them up to date automatically.)

To me, the philosophical value of the file sharing approach is that it acts as a general conceptual glue for joining together separately maintained subproducts. This is important because it means that large software products and systems can be more easily constructed out of smaller, shareable, and reusable subproducts.

Automated Tool Support

The fourth major idea in this book was to provide automated tool support for the directory, makefile, and file sharing conventions discussed above.

The main advantages of the tools are their simplicity, convenience, and efficiency, as shown by the examples presented in earlier chapters. Furthermore, since source code has been provided, it's possible to extend the tools to fit the particular needs of special development environments.

The main functional disadvantage with the tools is that they're still relatively new, and therefore immature. Like any software producer, I have had to budget my time and leave out some features that I knew would be useful to some users.

The main shortcoming in the implementation of the tools is that many of them are shell scripts that use *sed* and *awk* scripts. (One can easily imagine that compiled C programs could be made both more efficient and more intelligent.) But converting these scripts to C programs and testing them would require far more time and effort than I have at present.

The philosophical meaning of the tools, in my opinion, is that they demonstrate by example that it's possible to define and construct a standard code management environment for multiple platforms. It seems obvious to me that future code management environments will exceed both the convenience and the capabilities of the code management conventions and tools that I've described here.

Conclusions

The main conclusion of this book is that the directory structure, makefile, and file sharing conventions are all worthwhile. They reduce the cost of organizing and maintaining files in multi-platform software development environments.

A second conclusion, prompted by the presence of the tools, is that it's possible to provide a significant amount of automated support to a well-defined code management environment based on uniform directory and makefile structures.

Problems Successfully Addressed

The methods described in this book successfully address or solve the following problems:

- **Separating and isolating platform specific code from platform-independent code.** This was addressed by the directory structure conventions and `#ifdef` restrictions.

- **Generating and maintaining makefiles.** This was addressed by the makefile generation tools. In particular, the platform specific `#ifdef` restrictions and directory structure conventions made it easier to automatically generate makefile dependency rules.

- **Sharing and reusing files.** This was addressed by the file sharing conventions and tools.

- **Representing and implementing build order dependencies.** This was addressed by the *twalker* tool and its built-in conventions for visiting nodes in the order *ini, pd.lib, pi.lib*, and so on.

- **Reorganizing directories and product trees.** This was primarily addressed by the file sharing conventions (which reduced the need for absolute or relative pathnames in makefiles). It was also addressed by tools (such as *twalker, getmakes,* and *gendep*) that could help to regenerate files that were sensitive to file and directory reorganizations.

Problems Still Remaining

There are two significant code management problems that haven't been addressed by this book. The first is maintenance-by-repair environments, which was discussed in Chapter 4, and the second is distributed code management environments.

Distributed code management systems support developers that don't use a centrally shared filesystem. Instead, the developers work on their own machines and store code on their local filesystems. For example, these local filesystems might be local disks on a personal computer that is part of a network. That way, developers don't have to compile their code "across the network," a situation where the compiler runs on the local machine, but reads and writes files to remote filesystems across the network—which can be very slow on busy networks.

As another example, the distributed filesystems might be disks on machines that are located in different cities. The main point is that in a distributed code management system, not all developers use the same files on the same filesystem.

A third, less important problem is the need for a better way of treating build order dependencies. While the *twalker* tool does a reasonable job for most situations, it's incapable of handling arbitrary build order depdendencies.

For example, the current *twalker* tool can't handle situations that involve linking a series of dynamically linked libraries with each other (a necessity in some IBM environments). This is because the product node naming conventions (and as a consequence, the *twalker* tool) are inadequate for the job.

To solve this problem, a more competent *twalker* tool could be written. That way, users could specify a particular build order in an ASCII file, and give it to the new twalker tool as one of its inputs. The tool would produce an output script that followed the specific build order described in the ASCII input file.

Future Directions

This book has separated various kinds of code management knowledge into explicitly defined forms. This has been done by defining conventions for directory structures, makefile architectures, and file sharing mechanisms. Furthermore, the book has provided the source code for an initial set of code management tools that support the conventions.

The main consequence of this separation of code management ideas into explicit forms, in my view, is that these "code management subproducts" are now easily accessible for reuse. In other words, even though this book explains one possible way of combining the subproducts into a useful, integrated code management environment, there may also be other, better ways that could—and should—be investigated.

In particular, it may be possible to combine and share these code management ideas with other, more complex ideas that haven't been described here. For example, could configuration management systems be improved even further if they could assume the presence of the standard directory structures, makefile architectures, and file sharing models that were presented here?

This is a particularly interesting question because the solution of common configuration management problems seems like the next logical step toward improving code management environments. But that's the subject of another book, and of another (long!) publishing schedule.

Code Management Software Tools

This appendix describes the software tools that accompany this book.

The first section gives an overview of the software on the disks. It describes the contents, organization, and history of the tools on the disks.

The second section describes the code management tools that were discussed in the text of the book. It lists all the command-line options for each tool and gives simple examples of their use.

The third section describes the freeware tools that accompany the book. In particular, this section describes the RCS (Revison Control System) tools that are used.

The last section describes the DOS executables on the disks. DOS executables are provided as a convenience to DOS users, since not all DOS system users will have the necessary compilers to create executables. (In contrast, it's likely that UNIX system users will have—or can get—the necessary ANSI C compilers to compile the code. For example, the FSF (Free Software Foundation) provides freeware C compilers.)

Software on the Disks

I've provided source code for the code management tools that I wrote for this book and for the freeware RCS tools.

Overview

The software on the disks is organized into four groups. Each of the four groups is stored in a separate directory tree on the disks. The four trees are:

- The *cmtree*, which contains makefile templates.

- The *cmtools* tree, which contains the code management tools such as *getmakes* and *rcsdo*.

- The *cmpds* tree, which contains freeware tools with source code, such as the RCS tools, *flip*, and *ed*.

- The *cmdosexe* tree, which contains DOS executables for all of the tools. There are three subtrees in the *cmdosexe* tree. The *dos_exe1* subtree contains DOS executables for the code management tools, the *dos_exe2* subtree contains executables for the RCS tools, and the *dos_exe3* subtree contains executables for several freeware tools (such as *gawk, sed, find*, and others).

The Ported RCS Software

I ported the standard UUNET distribution of RCS version 5.5 to DOS for the purposes of this book. Then I ported the non-standard, DOS-ported software back to UNIX so that the same non-standard version of the software would run on both platforms.

I did it this way for several reasons. First, I wanted to use the RCS software for multi-platform support for the tools described in this book.

Second, I thought that porting the RCS source code using the ideas of this book would be a validation of those ideas.

Third, managing the RCS code would also help to test the code management tools. Managing the RCS tools involves pi and pd code and data, local and global files, file sharing, multiple platforms, and so on.

And fourth, the ported RCS source code would be a good example of the techniques described in the book. Readers could use the ported RCS tools as a realistic, working example of a standard product tree.

Porting Notes

The behavior of the RCS tools that accompany this book is different from the behavior of the original UUNET version in several ways because the UUNET version of RCS was never designed to run on DOS.

All platform-dependent changes are contained within the *rcs_pd.lib* product tree. Other changes, because they're platform independent, can be found in the pi source directories of other nodes.

Here's a list of some of the changes I made during the port to DOS:

- **Filenames**. File naming conventions in the RCS tools were changed because standard RCS filenames (such as *myfile.xyz,v*) are not allowed under DOS. The RCS tools can't add the traditional RCS *,v* suffix to DOS filenames that already have three characters in their filename extension. (RCS versions 5.6 and later can create filenames without the *,v* suffix, for POSIX compliance. POSIX discourages commas in filenames because it doesn't guarantee the portability of the resulting filenames.)

As a consequence, the RCS tools were modified to use the same filename for both the original filename and the RCS filename. Furthermore, the RCS tools always assume that RCS files will be in an *rcs* subdirectory immediately below the directory containing the original working file. This is true for both UNIX and DOS systems.

Note the use of lowercase letters in the *rcs* subdirectory name. This made it easier to write some of the code management tools (particularly batch scripts) that had to work with pathnames containing the "rcs" character string. For example, batch-file string comparisions between "RCS" and "rcs" were a headache.

- **File locations**. The RCS tools (as well as the code management tools) create their temporary files in the current working directory since not all DOS systems have */tmp* directories.

- **File operations**. Several file manipulation operations were changed because they assumed the presence of a UNIX system. For example, the common UNIX technique of opening a temporary file and then immediately unlinking it fails miserably under DOS. UNIX won't delete the temporary file until the program closes the file, but DOS will delete the file right away. If this occurs, and if the DOS program writes to the deleted file, the program trashes the file allocation table on the DOS hard disk.

- **File mode bits**. The semantics and procedures of changing file mode bits and deleting files were modified to work properly under both operating systems.

- **rcsmerge**. The original *rcsmerge* tool was modified to use *diff, diff3*, and *ed* to implement the merging function, on both DOS and UNIX. (The original UNIX version of *rcsmerge* called the UNIX *merge* tool.)

Since I ported RCS 5.5 a year or two ago, a new version of RCS has become available on the net (RCS 5.6). This version has been ported to several different operating systems, including MS-DOS.

Tools in the CMTOOLS Tree

This reference section describes the code management tools in detail. The purpose, function, and possible options of each tool are described. Freeware tools are described in the next section.

addaplat—Add a platform to an existing node

The purpose of the *addaplat* tool is to add new platform directories to entire trees of product nodes.

To add a new platform directory to all product nodes within a particular subtree, generate a tree walker script to walk one of the existing platform directories in the subtree. Try to walk a platform directory whose *imports.imp* files will work with the new platform's *make* tool, since *addaplat* will copy the *imports.imp* file from the existing platform directory into the new platform directory that it creates. This saves you some editing. Then invoke the tree walker script with a command line that calls *addaplat*.

This is the online help from the *addaplat* tool. (You can get online help for all the tools by invoking the tool with no arguments.)

```
K:\W\WRITE\CM> addaplat
Usage:  addaplat platform
        addaplat newplat.plt

        Invoke this program from a twalker script to create a peer
        platform from an existing platform. For example:

            twalker walkp1.bat platfrml.plt
            walkp1 call addaplat platfrm2.plt
```

The *addaplat* tool will create a new platform directory (?troff \^>*platfrm2.plt* in the online help shown above) beside the existing platform directory (?troff \^>*platfrm1.plt*), and then copy the *imports.imp* file from the existing directory into the new directory.

At that point—assuming that no platform-dependent files were involved—you could run the *newmakes* tool to generate new makefiles in all the new platform directories within the tree. Last, you could generate a tree walker script to walk the new platform directories and use it to invoke *make all* to build the products for the new platform.

cmi—Import a file

The purpose of the *cmi* tool is to import shared files from the *share* directories to the current working directory (usually a platform directory). Imports are carried out by physically copying the imported file. Import operations can be logged. For efficiency, identical timestamps on both the source and destination file will normally block the physical file copy operation. However, this behavior can be overridden with the appropriate command-line arguments.

The *cmi* tool assumes that the default source directory is *CMHTREE/share* and that the default destination directory is the current directory.

(The *cmx* tool assumes the reverse—that the default source directory is the current directory, and the default destination directory is *CMHTREE/share*.)

This is the online help information for the *cmi* tool:

```
K:\W\WRITE\CM> cmi
Usage:  cmi [ctl_args] srcpath [dest_spec] [idx_spec] [comment]

Where ctl_args are:
  -v            prints program version
  -db level     enables debug messages at levels 1,2,4,8, . . .
  -nl,-nolog    discourages logging to the share log file
```

```
    -f              encourages physical import, forces logging
    -nc,-nocopy     blocks physical import, overrides -f
    -p platform     name of platform subdirectory below share dir

Where dest_spec and idx_spec are:
    -dd path        the destination directory
    -df path        the destination filename
    -id path        the index share directory
    -if path        the index share filename

Where comment is:
    -c   words      words describing the reason for the share
    -for words      words describing the reason for the share

Default file locations are obtained from the CMHTREE environment variable.
Example:  set CMHTREE=/root/of/holding/tree/
          import myfile.h -for program 2
```

Here are some examples of how to use the tool. More examples of how to use the *cmi* tool are given in Chapter 7, *File Sharing*.

cmi mypifile.h	*import from default share dir in CMHTREE*
cmi -p tbc.plt mypdfile.h	*import from share/tbc.plt dir in CMHTREE*
cmi -nl myfile.h	*don't log it*
cmi -nl -f myfile.h -for some reason	*add a log comment*

Now let's have a closer look at some of the command-line options.

-db level

This option is a convenience for debugging. Several different types of debugging messages are printed, with each type being controlled by one bit in the "level" number. Using a level of 1 will turn on messages about the command-line arguments; 2 will turn on messages about filenames and directories; 4 will turn on messages about internal data processing steps; 8 will turn on general informational messages.

Because each bit in the level number is independent of other bits, the bits can be combined to turn on messages about more than one type of message. For example, 15 (binary 1111) will turn all four types of messages.

-p platform

This option can be used to import files from one of the platform directories below the default *share* directory in the CMHTREE. Conceptually speaking, this control argument implements "default" (CMTREE) platform-dependent sharing operations.

-dd, -df, -id, -if

These arguments are all provided just in case you don't want to use the default directories and filenames that are programmed into the source code of the tools. These four arguments let you move files to and from arbitrary places in the filesystem and log the operations in an arbitrary index file. They're the same for both the *cmi* and *cmx* tools, so I'll use export examples in the discussion below. (That way I won't have to repeat myself in the descriptions for the *cmx* tool.)

The *-dd path* argument is used to copy a file to a non-standard directory, while keeping the original filename. For example, I use this argument to duplicate DOS batch files in multiple platform directories (e.g., *tdos.plt* and *mdos.plt*). Since the imported and exported batch files are identical for both platforms, I only want to maintain one copy.

The *-df path* argument is used to copy a file to a non-standard directory while changing the original filename. There are two situations in which you can use this.

First, you may have a collection of files with different names (such as a collection of pd include files within one directory) from which you must choose one file that must end up with a particular name. This is the technique that I used to import the *flip.h* file for the freeware *flip* tool on the disks. The final include file must have the name *flip.h* (because that's what *flip.c* expects), but I store the pd versions of this include file as *msc.h*, *tbc.plt*, and *sun4gcc.h*. (Recall that I've mentioned this case earlier and identified it as a non-standard practice that I now avoid. I've left it in the book to show you how to do it anyway. It might not bother you as much as it bothers me.)

Second, you may have one file that must be used in multiple places with different filenames. I use this technique to reuse the *cmpwd* program that accompanies this book. The product is named *cmpwd* instead of *pwd* because it has a different behavior than the standard UNIX *pwd* tool. The scripts provided with this book can therefore call the correct *cmpwd* tool for their needs. But I'd also like to have a *pwd* command on my own computer, so I use the *-df path* argument to export the *cmpwd* program and rename it to *pwd* during the export. That way I don't have to change my old UNIX habit of typing *pwd* to see the current directory even though I'm using a program with a different name. This is an example of how developers can reuse releaseable product code within their own development environments.

The defaults for both the *cmi* and *cmx* tools are to use the *CMHTREE/share* directory, to copy the named file if the timestamps on the source and destination files are out of date, and to log the relationship only if a file copy operation occured.

cmlsr—List sharing relationships

The *cmlsr* tool lists sharing relationships that have been recorded in the sharing logs. This can help developers identify products that share files.

The *cmlsr* tool lists sharing relationships by searching the share logs for entries that contain the match string given on the command line. Lines in the logs that contain the match string are printed to the display screen.

This is the online help information for the *cmlsr* tool:

```
K:\W\WRITE\CM> cmlsr
Usage:  cmlsr [ctl_args] match_string

        -v              prints program version information
        -db level       enables debug messages at level 1,2,4,8
        -id path        the directory containing the index file
        -if path        the full pathname of the index file
        -f path         the specific filename to match
        match_string    the specific log entry string to match
        -u              removes non-existent files from index file
```

Here are some examples of how to use the tool.

cmlsr myfile.h	*use default index and logs*
cmlsr -u	*update index, rm non-existent share log pathnames*
cmlsr foo	*match foo as a directory or a filename*
cmlsr -f foo	*match foo only as a filename*

Since the command-line arguments for this tool are modelled after those used in the *cmi* tool, see the *cmi* description for more information on how these arguments work.

cmpwd—Print current working directory

The *cmpwd* tool is a simple tool that prints the working directory in either UNIX or DOS styles. The *cmpwd* tool is used by the *twalker* tool to generate tree traversal scripts.

Here are some examples of its use:

```
K:\W\WRITE\CM> cmpwd                    no args, so give default style for the platform
k:\w\write\cm
```

```
K:\W\WRITE\CM> cmpwd dos                force DOS backslash style
k:\w\write\cm
```

```
K:\W\WRITE\CM> cmpwd unix               force UNIX forward slash style
k:/w/write/cm
```

cmx—Export a file

The *cmx* tool is identical to the *cmi* tool, except that the *cmx* tool exports files instead of importing them. Specifically, the major difference between the tools is in their assumptions about the default source and destination directories for imported and exported files.

The *cmx* tool assumes the default source directory is the current directory, and the default destination directory is *CMHTREE/share*. (The *cmi* tool assumes the reverse—the default source directory is *CMHTREE/share*, and the default destination directory is the current directory.)

This is the online help for the cmx tool:

```
K:\W\WRITE\CM> cmx
Usage:  cmx [ctl_args] srcpath [dest_spec] [idx_spec] [comment]

Where ctl_args are:
   -v             prints program version
   -db level      enables debug messages at levels 1,2,4,8, . . .
   -nl,-nolog     discourages logging to the share log file
   -f             encourages physical export, forces logging
   -nc,-nocopy    blocks physical export, overrides -f
   -p platform    name of platform subdirectory below share dir

Where dest_spec and idx_spec are:
   -dd path       the destination share directory
   -df path       the destination share filename
   -id path       the index share directory
   -if path       the index share filename

Where comment is:
   -c    words    words describing the reason for the share
   -for words     words describing the reason for the share

Default file locations are obtained through the CMHTREE environment
variable.
Example:  set CMHTREE=/root/of/holding/tree/
          export myfile.h -c for program 2
```

For more information on the command-line arguments for the cmx tool, see the description of the *cmi* tool.

cptrio—Copy a source tree

The *cptrio* tool clones a source tree by creating a new tree that contains the same directory structure as the original tree. No files are copied.

Cloning trees on DOS systems is a useless activity because you don't really need them in a single-person development environment. The single developer can reliably work in the main source tree without ill effects. Also, working with cloned trees in development environments that don't support symbolic links requires a different set of code management tools.

On UNIX platforms, *cptrio* creates RCS directories in the new tree as symbolic links that point back to the RCS directories in the main tree.

This is the online help information for the *cptrio* tool:

```
jameson[unix]: cptrio
Usage:  cptrio abs_path_src_path absolute_dest_path
        cptrio /s/main/tree /s/myspace/mytree

        The destination directory must already exist.
```

This is an example of how to use the tool on UNIX:

```
cd /myspace
mkdir newtree
cptrio /oldtree/products /myspace/newtree
```

edit1imp—Automatically edit one imports.imp file

The purpose of the *edit1imp* tool is to help developers modify all the *imports.imp* files within a source tree. It does this by applying a *sed* script to the *imports.imp* in the current directory. A backup copy of the original *imports.imp* file is made in the current directory before the editing changes are applied. The name of the backup copy is *imports.old*.

To modify all the *imports.imp* files in a source tree, first create a *sed* script to perform the necessary editing changes. Test the *sed* script manually to ensure that it works. Then test the *sed* script again, but this time pass the name of the script as an argument to the *edit1imp* tool. Again verify that the editing changes are correct.

Last, generate a tree walker script to walk all platform directories of interest. Use the tree walker script to invoke the *edit1imp* tool from every directory visited by the script (with the name of your *sed* script as an argument, of course). Be sure to use an absolute pathname for the *sed* script. This is required because the *sed* script will be invoked from many different directories in the source tree.

You can delete all the backup *imports.old* files by passing an appropriate deletion command (such as *rm imports.old*) to the tree walker script.

This is the on-line help information from the *edit1imp* tool.

```
K:\W\WRITE\CM> edit1imp
Usage:  edit1imp sed_scriptname
        edit1imp k:\temp\change1.sed
        edit1imp change1.sed

Use an absolute pathname when calling this program from
within a tree walker script. For example:

        twalker walkdirs.bat tdos.plt mdos.plt
        walkdirs call edit1imp k:\temp\change1.sed
```

This command is used in the sixth tour example in Chapter 8, *A Hands-on Tour: Part 3*.

existdir—Test if a directory exists

The *existdir* tool is used in batch files to test for the existence of specific directories. For example, it's used by the following tools: *addaplat*, *gendep*, *nodetype*, and *rmaplat*.

This is the online help for the *existdir* tool.

```
K:\W\WRITE\CM> existdir
Usage:   existdir pathname
         existdir g:\s\amtools
         existdir /s/amtools

         Returns 1 if the directory exists.
         Returns 0 if the directory does not exist.
```

gendep—Generate makefile dependency rules

The purpose of the *gendep* tool is to automatically generate makefile dependency rules for the source files stored in the standard source directories of the product node. It does this by individually reading all source files in the named (or default) source directory.

Since *gendep* can't recognize #ifdefs, it always generates dependency rules that list *all* of the include files included by the original source file. This means that it will produce incorrect results from files that contain #include statements bounded by #ifdefs of any kind.

By default, the *gendep* tool is automatically invoked by the *getmakes* tool when *getmakes* is creating a complete set of makefiles. However, *gendep* must be invoked manually to create dependency rules from source files stored in subdivided source directories. *getmakes* doesn't understand subdivided source directories.

This is the online help information for the *gendep* tool. Note that the last few command-line arguments are optional.

```
K:\W\WRITE\CM> gendep
Usage:      gendep id [source_directory] [names] [makefile_dep_name]

Example:    gendep pi
            gendep pd
            gendep pid
            gendep lex
            gendep yac
            gendep pi ../s/ *.c
            gendep pi ../s/ *.c makefile.pi
            gendep pd    s/ *.c makefile.pd
            gendep s1 ../s/subdir1/ *.c makefile.s1
            gendep sN ../s/subdir1/ *.c makefile.sN

The trailing forward slash on the source directory is required.
Defaults: directory = ../s/, names = *.c, *.l, or *.y.
```

There are four possible arguments to the *gendep* command. The last three arguments are optional under particular circumstances.

The first argument, *id*, is a short identifier that's used by *gendep* in several places. First, it's used inside the generated makefiles as a makefile macro name to hold a list of the names of all files for which dependency rules are generated. Look inside the makefiles to see how the name is used. Second, the identifier is used in the filename of the generated list of dependency rules. Recall that dependency rules are normally stored in makefiles named *makefile.pi, makefile.pd,* and *makefile.pid.* And third, the identifier is used to control default actions inside the *gendep* tool. This is why the last three arguments are optional, as long as a known identifier such as pi, pd, pid, lex, or yac is used.

The second argument (e.g., *../s*) is a directory pathname. The *gendep* tool should generate dependency rules for all source files in this directory. The directory pathname must be a relative pathname from the current platform directory.

The third argument is a wildcard expression that tells *gendep* which files to consider in the selected directory. For example, this expression is different for C files (**.c*), *lex* files (**.l*troff \^>), and *yacc* files (**.y*).

The fourth argument is the filename of the generated makefile template that contains the generated dependency rules.

See the discussion in Chapter 6, *Makefile Architectures,* on generating dependency rules from files in subdivided source directories for more information on how to use the *gendep* tool.

getmakes—Generate complete makefiles

The *getmakes* tool generates complete makefiles in the platform directories of standard product nodes. It does this by copying and then modifying several standard makefile templates from the CMTREE. *getmakes* then calls the *gendep* tool to generate makefile dependency rules from the source files in the source directory of the product node.

The *getmakes* tool should always be run from within a platform directory.

Makefiles can be generated for pi (platform independent), pd (platform dependent), and pid (both platform independent and dependent) nodes.

Makefiles can also be generated for several different types of products: compilable programs, compilable libraries, batch scripts, or initialization products.

This is the online help information for the *getmakes* tool:

```
K:\W\WRITE\CM> getmakes
Usage:  getmakes  platform  node   product name
        getmakes  tbc.plt   pi     program  my_c_program_name
        getmakes  tdos.plt  pd     script   my_batch_file_name
        getmakes  msc.plt   pid    library  my_c_library_name
        getmakes  tbc.plt   pid    ini      my_init_name
```

Many examples of how to use the *getmakes* tool are provided in the tour examples.

hasslash—Determine if a pathname contains a slash

The *hasslash* tool is used internally by the *rcsdo* tool to test for the existence of a slash (forward or backward) in the pathname of the RCS log message file. The processing of the argument depends on the presence of a slash.

This is the online help for *hasslash*:

```
K:\W\WRITE\CM> hasslash
Usage:  hasslash pathname
        hasslash /tmp/msg
        hasslash \temp\msg
        hasslash msg


        Returns 1 if the pathname contains a slash.
        Returns 0 if the pathname does not contain a slash.
```

longdate—Print out a date string

The *longdate* tool is a simple utility program that prints out a date-time string that looks like this: **1993–05–10__15:13:47**. This tool is used by other tools (such as *pci*) to generate a timestamp in a known format.

This is an example of how to use *longdate*.

```
K:\W\WRITE\CM> longdate
1993-09-19__12:06:27
```

makenode—Make a product node

The *makenode* tool creates standard pi, pd, and pid nodes for holding product files. The directory structures of the three types of nodes are shown at the beginning of the first tour example in Chapter 2, *A Hands-on Tour: Part 1.*

This is the online help information for the *makenode* tool. An arbitrary number of platforms can be placed on the command line, limited only by the length of the longest command line accepted by the command-line interpreter (e.g., 128 characters on MS-DOS).

```
K:\W\WRITE\CM> makenode
Usage:  makenode name       style  platform1  plt2 ... pltN
        makenode hello      pi     tbc.plt    msc.plt
        makenode myscript   pd     tdos.plt   mdos.plt
        makenode myprog     pid    tdos.plt   mdos.plt
```

makeplt—Make a platform node

The *makeplt* tool is almost identical to the *makenode* tool, except that *makeplt* creates only the platform subtree part of a product node. As a consequence, the *makeplt* tool should be used only to add new platform subtrees to existing product nodes. Like *makenode*, the *makeplt* tool can create platform subtrees for pi, pd, or pid products.

You should be in the root directory of the product node when you issue this command, since it creates the platform subtrees as children of the current directory. An arbitrary number of platforms can be placed on the command line, limited only by the length of the longest command line accepted by the command-line interpreter (e.g., 128 characters on MS-DOS).

This is the online help information for the *makeplt* tool:

```
K:\W\WRITE\CM> makeplt
Usage:  makeplt  style  plat_1    plat_2  ...  plat_n
        makeplt  pi     tbc.plt   sun4gcc.plt
        makeplt  pd     tdos.plt  sh.plt
        makeplt  pid    tdos.plt  sh.plt
```

Examples of how to use the *makeplt* tool are provided in Chapter 3, *A Hands-on Tour: Part 2*.

mvawkdir—Reset hardcoded awk pathnames

The *mvawkdir* tool is provided as a convenience to readers who want to move their code management tool executables out of the CMHTREE into some other directory.

Relocating the scripts out of the CMHTREE can be awkward because some of the scripts contain hardcoded pathnames that reference the location of various *sed* and *awk* scripts. By default, the scripts contain references to platform directories in the CMHTREE, which is where both the batch scripts and the *sed* and *awk* scripts are stored after a normal installation.

The *mvawkdir* tool mitigates the awkwardness of relocating the scripts by automatically changing the hardcoded pathnames in all of the appropriate script files. To use the tool, move all the batch, *sed*, and *awk* scripts to the new location. Then invoke *mvawkdir* as shown below.

There are two things that you'll have to watch for. First, on DOS systems, be sure to use two backslashes for each one that you want in the final pathname (e.g., *g:\\my\\new\\dir*). You need to escape backslashes in *sed* to make them show up as literal characters. On UNIX systems, no special actions are required. You can type in a pathname such as */local/bin* without modification.

Second, watch out for file permissions. If you're moving the scripts on a UNIX system, you might need superuser permissions in order to edit the files. Also, in a networked environment, you might require other permissions.

This is the online help information for the DOS *mvawkdir* tool:

```
K:\W\WRITE\CM> mvawkdir
Usage:  mvawkdir new_directory
        mvawkdir c:\\my\\batch\\dir
```

This file should be run when you move the executable script files to a new directory. It modifies the installed versions of the programs, *not* the original versions in the source tree. The *new_directory* argument must be at least two characters long and must *not* end in a trailing slash.

This program should be executed in the new executable directory that contains all the files that have been moved there.

Double backslashes are required for DOS, e.g., *mvawkdir d:\\rc\\e.* No backslashes are required for UNIX, e.g., *mvawkdir /local/bin.*

This is an example of how to use the tool on DOS:

```
cd CMHTREE\at\tdos.plt        go to where batch executables are
mv *.* my\new\exe\dir         move everything to a new directory
cd my\new\exe\dir             go there
mvawkdir my\\new\\exe\\dir    update all hardcoded pathnames
```

This is an example of how to use the tool on UNIX:

```
chdir CMHTREE/at/tdos.plt     go to where batch executables are
mv *.* my/new/exe/dir         move everything to a new directory
chdir my/new/exe/dir          go there
mvawkdir my/new/exe/dir       update all hardcoded pathnames
```

mwalker—Help twalker

The *mwalker* tool is a helper tool that's used by the *twalker* tool to generate tree traversal scripts. Its precise function is to generate a traversal script from a file that contains a list of the directories that should be traversed. (*twalker* just generates a list of directories to be modified and then calls *mwalker.*)

The main situation in which *mwalker* can be used to advantage by itself is when your product trees contain build-order dependencies that are beyond the ranking capabilities of *twalker.* In such cases, you may be able to generate a relatively permanent file that contains a list of product directories to visit in proper build order. Then *mwalker* can be used to automatically generate a tree traversal script from that file.

This is the online help information for the *mwalker* tool:

```
K:\W\WRITE\CM> mwalker
Usage:  mwalker filename
        mwalker mydirs
```

Here is an example of how to use the tool:

```
K:\W\WRITE\CM> echo /my/good/directory/one > junk
K:\W\WRITE\CM> echo /my/good/directory/two >> junk
K:\W\WRITE\CM> mwalker junk > walktwo.bat
K:\W\WRITE\CM> walktwo.bat ls
```

newmakes—Generate a script for generating new makefiles

The purpose of the *newmakes* tool is to upgrade all the makefiles in a subtree. It does this by generating a batch script (which calls *getmakes*) to regenerate all the makefiles within a particular subtree.

When the output batch script is invoked with no arguments, it generates new makefiles by changing to successive platform directories and invoking *getmakes* with appropriate command-line arguments.

This is the online help information for the *newmakes* tool:

```
K:\W\WRITE\CM> newmakes
Usage:  newmakes outfilename  platform_1 plat_2 ... plat_8
        newmakes programs.bat tbc.plt tmsc.plt sun4gcc.plt
        newmakes scripts.bat  tdos.plt sun4sh.plt
```

Here's an example of how to use the tool:

```
K:\W\WRITE\CM> cd /top/of/my/source/tree
K:\W\WRITE\CM> newmakes doit.bat tbc.plt msc.plt sun4sh.plt
K:\W\WRITE\CM> doit.bat
K:\W\WRITE\CM> twalker rebuild.bat tbc.plt
K:\W\WRITE\CM> rebuild.bat make all
```

nodetype—Return the node type of a node (pi, pd, or pid)

The purpose of the *nodetype* tool is to help the *newmakes* tool determine what kind of makefiles it should regenerate for a product node. The *newmakes* tool parses the answer provided by the *nodetype* tool and puts the appropriate pi, pd, or pid argument into the *getmakes* command line.

This is the online help for the *nodetype* tool.

```
K:\W\WRITE\CM> nodetype
Usage:  nodetype pathname     platform [resultfile]
        nodetype ./mydir      tbc.plt
        nodetype k:\temp      tbc.plt
        nodetype k:/temp/foo  tbc.plt  output.tmp
```

Note that the type of a node can be different for different platforms within the node. Different platforms within the same product node may or may not have platform-dependent source directories. However, the nodetype of a product node is *usually* identical for all platforms within that node.

nothing—Do nothing

This software tool is an empty batch file that does nothing. I use it as a placeholder command for unused default targets in makefiles. Some *make* programs (such as Borland's *make*) generate error messages for targets that have no commands under them.

nullfile—Indicate if named file is null

The *nullfile* tool is used in batch scripts to test whether files have a byte count (file length) of zero. In particular, the tool is used to check the lengths of files that may or may not contain output from various kinds of searches performed by batch files.

For example, consider the *gendep* tool for generating makefile dependency rules. It generates a list of source files to process by redirecting the output of the *ls* command into a file. Then it uses *nullfile* to verify that the output file contains at least one filename. If *nullfile* reports that the file has a non-zero length, *gendep* continues. If *nullfile* reports a zero-length file, *gendep* prints an error message and halts.

The *nullfile* tool has an optional command-line argument that reverses the two possible status codes that *nullfile* can return. For example, *nullfile* usually returns a value of 1 if the file has a zero length, and 0 if the file has a non-zero length. But if the *-r* option is given, *nullfile* returns 0 for zero-length, and 1 for non-zero length. The capability to reverse the return codes makes it more convenient to test for both zero-length and non-zero-length files in batch files.

This is the online help information for the *nullfile* tool:

```
K:\W\WRITE\CM> nullfile
Usage: nullfile [-r] filename

Exit value is:
     0 if the file size is 0 bytes,
     1 if the file size is greater than 0 bytes, and
     2 if the file doesn't exist (or invocation error).

     -r reverses the 0 and 1 error codes.
```

Here are some examples of how to use the tool:

```
K:\W\WRITE\CM>echo hi > foo          create a file with something in it
K:\W\WRITE\CM>nullfile foo
K:\W\WRITE\CM>errlevel
Error level is 1.

K:\W\WRITE\CM>touch iamempty         touch creates a zero-length file
K:\W\WRITE\CM>nullfile iamempty
K:\W\WRITE\CM>errlevel
Error level is 0.
```

```
K:\W\WRITE\CM>nullfile -r iamempty        use -r for errlevel=1 on 0-length files
K:\W\WRITE\CM>errlevel
Error level is 1.
```

pci—Post check-in information

The *pci* tool posts bulk *rcsdo* check-in information to either an ASCII file (on DOS systems) or to a newsgroup (on UNIX systems).

Under DOS, *pci* adds a timestamp to the current log message and appends it to the end of the existing log file. (If a log file doesn't exist, *pci* will create one). Under UNIX, *pci* adds a timestamp and posts the resulting current log message file to a named (or default) newsgroup.

This is the online help information for the *pci* tool:

```
K:\W\WRITE\CM> pci
Usage:  pci filelist msgfile logfile_name
        pci myfiles  msg     my_history_log
        pci myfiles  msg     project_news_group
```

rcsdo—Do bulk RCS operations

The *rcsdo* tool is an important tool because it's the main code management interface to the RCS revision control system. Many useful bulk operations are provided by *rcsdo*.

This is the online help information for the *rcsdo* tool:

```
K:\W\WRITE\CM> rcsdo
Usage: rcsdo options

rcsdo  ls_changed                list files different from rcs version
rcsdo  ls_locked                 list files locked under rcs
rcsdo  ls_names                  list all labels in all files
rcsdo  ls_name label             list files bound to this label

rcsdo  ci_u_initial [msgf -log fn] check in (w/unlock) all files in dir
rcsdo  ci_d_locked  [msgf -log fn] check in (w/delete) locked files
rcsdo  ci_l_locked  [msgf -log fn] check in (w/relock) locked files
rcsdo  ci_u_locked  [msgf -log fn] check in (w/unlock) locked files

rcsdo  co_l   [label]            check out (locked)        all files
rcsdo  co_l_f [label]            check out (locked,force)  all files
rcsdo  co_u   [label]            check out (unlocked)      all files
rcsdo  co_u_f [label]            check out (unlocked,force) all files

rcsdo  dl_unchanged              delete unchanged files (override locks)
rcsdo  add_name label            add a symbolic name to all files
```

Many examples of how to use the *rcsdo* tool are provided in the tour.

rmaplat—Remove a platform directory

The purpose of the *rmaplat* tool is to remove platform directories from entire trees of product nodes. It performs the opposite function of the *addaplat* tool.

To remove an existing platform directory, platform A, from all product nodes within a particular subtree, S, follow these steps. First, generate a tree walker script that will visit a platform directory, platform B, in each product node that contains the platform A, which you want to remove.

Use the tree walker script to visit each platform B in the subtree S and pass the following command to the tree walker script: *call rmaplat A* (where A is the name of the platform that you want to delete).

This is the online help for the *rmaplat* tool:

```
K:\W\WRITE\CM> rmaplat
Usage:  rmaplat platform
        rmaplat oldplat.plt

Invoke this program from a twalker script to remove a peer
platform from an existing platform. For example:

        twalker walkpl.bat platfrml.plt
        walkpl call rmaplat platfrm2.plt
```

In the above example, *platfrm2.plt* is the platform being deleted.

twalker—Generate a tree traversal script

The purpose of the *twalker* tool is to generate a batch script that will traverse a tree and execute an arbitrary command in each directory visited by the script.

Directories are selected for traversal by naming them as command-line arguments. Typically the names are platform directory names.

Directories that are selected for traversal are ranked in an order that attempts to satisfy common build-order dependencies among products. In other words, the batch file created by the *twalker* tool will visit product nodes in the order required to get everything built properly.

The output script ranks directories to visit according to the name of the product directory. Products whose names in *ini* are visited first, followed by products whose names end in *pd.lib*, *pid.lib*, and *lib*, followed by all other products (in no particular order).

This is the online help information for the *twalker* tool. An arbitrary number of platforms that can be placed on the command line, limited only by the operating system (128 characters on DOS).

```
K:\W\WRITE\CM> twalker
Usage:  twalker outfile platform_1 plat_2 ... plat_n
        twalker wbc.bat tbc.plt tdos.plt msc.plt mdos.plt

        Directories ending in    '.ini' appear first in the output file.
        Directories ending in 'pd.lib' appear  next in the output file.
        Directories ending in 'pid.lib' appear  next in the output file.
        Directories ending in    '.lib' appear  next in the output file.
        Directories ending in anything else are last in the output file.
```

The *twalker* tool recognizes the directories to be traversed by performing simple string comparisons between command-line arguments and absolute directory pathnames. In particular, *twalker* only looks at the last component of an absolute directory pathname. As a consequence of this strategy, *twalker* files can be generated for directories other than platform directories. For example, I commonly generate *twalker* scripts for walking source directories.

Many examples of how to use the *twalker* tool are provided in the tour.

Here are two suggestions that might help you to manage your *twalker* scripts:

The first is that you leave your tree walker scripts in the same directory in which you created them. This is the most convenient place to store them because you have to be in that same directory again in order to use them. In addition, it saves you the trouble of moving them to a directory on your **PATH** after you've generated them. Leaving them in the same directory also makes it easier to replace old scripts with newly generated versions.

The second suggestion is about choosing names for your *twalker* scripts. I usually name all mine so that the name always begins with a "w" and ends with a platform name (or some reference to platform names). That way, when I list the files in the directory, I can easily spot the *twalker* scripts. The leading "w" in the filename usually makes all the *twalker* scripts show up (in one convenient place) at the end of the listing. The embedded platform names make it easy for me to recognize which scripts traverse which platform directories.

This is a list of some common *twalker* names that I use. I've given the entire *twalker* commands too, by way of example.

```
twalker wtbc.bat tbc.plt                    walk tbc.plt only
twalker wmsc.bat msc.plt                     walk msc.plt only
twalker wdos.bat tbc.plt tdos.plt msc.plt    walk all dos platforms
twalker wsun.sh sun4gcc.plt sun4sh.plt       walk all sun4 platforms
```

Tools in the CMPDS Tree

The CMPDS tree on the disks contains RCS manual pages and other freeware tools.

RCS Tools

The disks contain the original RCS manual pages. They're stored in the *cmpds/rcs55/man* directory. For this reason, they won't be reproduced here. Instead, you can read them online or print them off on hardcopy paper.

Here's just one tip, in case you don't want to read the RCS manual pages. Don't forget to set your **USER** environment variable to the login name that you want the RCS tools to use when locking files. For example, I have the following line in my *autoexec.bat* file:

```
set user=jameson
```

If you do that, then you'll probably be able to get away with just following the examples that I've given in the tour. You might not ever have to read the RCS manual pages.

Other Freeware Tools

A variety of other freeware tools have also been provided with the software on the disks. They're used behind the scenes by some of the code management tool batch scripts.

Documentation for these tools isn't provided here because it's beyond the scope of this book. If you want to find out more about these freeware tools, look for some good introductory books on the UNIX operating system. In particular, the two most complex tools are described in the O'Reilly & Associates book *sed & awk* by Dale Dougherty.

This is a short list of where I use the freeware tools in this book. Most of the tools are already available on UNIX, so if you're running a UNIX system, you probably won't need to acquire any of them.

- *chmod* is used in the tour examples.
- *cmp* is used by *rcsdo*.
- *diff3* is used by *rcsdiff*.
- *diff* is used by *rcsdiff*, and in some of the tour examples.
- *fgrep* is used by *gendep* and *newmakes*.
- *find* is used by at least *cptrio*, *getmakes*, *newmakes*, *rcsdo*, and *twalker*. It's also used in the tour examples.

- *gawk* is used by at least *cptrio, getmakes, newmakes,* and *rcsdo* on DOS. UNIX versions of the tools use *awk*.

- *ls_tk* is used by *gendep* and *rcsdo* on DOS.

- *ls* is *ls_tk.com* by another name.

- *rm* is used during installation, by the tour examples, and by the *rmaplat* and *rcsdo* tools.

- *sed* is used by *cptrio, edit1imp, getmakes, mvawkdir, newmakes, rcsdo,* and *twalker.*

- *sort* is used by *cptrio, newmakes,* and *rcsdo.*

- *tar* is used during installation and in the tour examples.

B

Other Useful Tools

This appendix describes the tools that I use in my working environment in the hopes that my experiences can help other people save time, effort, and money in selecting tools for their environments.

I currently work on a small network consisting of two PCs and a Sun4 Sparc IPC workstation. One PC is a Compaq LTE 386/20 laptop computer (with a docking station), and the other is an old IBM 386/16 Model 80, recently upgraded to a 486/32 with a Cyrix 386-to-486 clock doubler chip (which was inexpensive, and which works very well).

UNIX Tools

On my UNIX machine, I use the entire set of GNU tools published by the Free Software Foundation. I was able to install hundreds of megabytes of GNU code on my Sun thanks to the X11/GNU CD-ROM that I purchased from Walnut Creek CDROM. I was especially lucky, since they provide precompiled binaries for the operating system that I'm running (Sun OS 4.1.3). It was a painless installation. You can contact them at:

Walnut Creek CDROM
1547 Palos Verdes Mall
Suite 260
Walnut Creek, CA 94596
Phone: 800-786-9907
Fax: 510-674-0821
orders@cdrom.com

The combination of the native Sun OS tools and the X11/GNU tools is more than enough for my work. The only extra software that I added was *Tex* and *Latex*, so I could do some text formatting in a familiar language.

DOS Tools

This section describes the tools that I use on my DOS computers for both software development and documentation. Many of the tools are freeware and are available for UNIX as well. Being able to use the same tools on both DOS and UNIX machines is important to me because I can use the same work habits on any machine on the network.

Since my personal computer is over seven years old, it's somewhat underpowered by today's standards. The lack of power hasn't bothered me much, though, I only miss having more power when I do long compilations.

I vouch that the tools described below have provided me with a very responsive development environment for many years. I have usually been the limiting factor, not the machine or software.

Operating System Tools

I use Desqview-386 2.4/QEMM 6.02 and MS-DOS 5.0 because together they provide a very responsive, pre-emptive, multitasking work environment. I highly recommend Desqview-386.

It also provides more conventional DOS memory to my programs than I would have thought possible. For example, Desqview/QEMM gives me almost 630K of free memory at the DOS prompt, 588K free in the first Desqview DOS window, and 567K in each Desqview DOS window after the first. (Memory values are sensitive to the machine configuration, so they may be different on your machine.)

I have 10 megabytes of RAM installed, so I can easily have many DOS work sessions open and running simultaneously. In practice, I always have at least two windows open (one for editing, one for compiling), and often a third for miscellaneous tasks. I often put file transfers, database, and spreadsheet applications in separate (background) windows as well. Even on my old 386, I can edit with ease while running a background file transfer at 19.2K bits per second (actually, my Kermit measurements tell me I only get 17.6K bits per second throughput.)

I've also started to try Desqview/X, which is a multi-tasking X Windows environment for PCs. Desqview/X is slow on my machine, but my machine just doesn't have the horsepower to paint graphics screens. When I'm in a DOS window the speed is quite acceptable. (Desqview-386 in text mode is much faster, of course.)

I'm confident that the slowness is a limitation of my machine, and not of the DVX implementation. When I use DVX to dial into my Sun workstation at the office over a 14.4K PPP (point to point protocol) link being driven at 38.4K by my PC, the screen display is only slightly slower than the transmission rate. I'm confident that the feel of Desqview/X on a more powerful 486 machine that had a faster video system would be much snappier.

Desqview-386 and Desqview/X are available from:

> Quarterdeck Office Systems
> 150 Pico Boulevard
> Santa Monica, CA 90405
> *info@qdeck.com*

I also use an inexpensive shareware product called Tame 2.61 that drastically increases the multitasking performance of my old machine under Desqview. Tame works by minimizing the CPU cycles consumed by inactive applications in background windows. This frees up the cycles for use by the foreground window and active background windows.

Some applications consume large numbers of CPU cycles—even when they're inactive—by polling the mouse or the keyboard buffer. These polling actions put a surprising amount of load on a computer and very obviously slow down the performance of active foreground applications.

Tame improves performance by minimizing the useless polling load that's placed on the computer by inactive programs. It does this by telling the multitasker (such as Desqview) to move on to the next task whenever an application does too many polls within its multitasking time slice. Once this happens a few times, Tame becomes less patient and tells Desqview to move on after only a few polls. This action frees up the rest of the time slice for other, more productive tasks.

Tame is available from:

> David Thomas
> PowerSoft Inc.
> P.O. Box 956338
> Duluth, GA 30136

You can also get it from various net archive sites such as *msdos/desqview/tame261.zip*.

Together, Desqview and Tame provide an excellent DOS multitasking work environment, and if they ever do get in the way for applications that require more conventional memory, it's very easy to leave Desqview just long enough to run the big application. I highly recommend both of these programs, as well as the technical support service that I've received from both vendors over the several years that I've used these products.

Software Development Tools

Developers use their software development tools so frequently that they usually become an ingrained part of a person's work habits. Thus most developers tend to have strong opinions about tools that they've tried.

Accordingly—since I doubt that I'm any different in this regard—the paragraphs below contain a list of the tools that I use and my reasons for using them.

Compilers and Linkers

I used the Borland C++ 2.0 and Microsoft C 6.0 compilers to compile the software tools for this book.

The Borland compiler is much faster than the Microsoft compiler, but the Microsoft compiler seems to produce more error messages. I've also had problems with the Microsoft compiler running out of memory under Desqview and crashing my machine.

I use the Microsoft Quick Help tool for looking up standard C library functions because it's so fast. It's also a standalone program, which means that it's faster to pop it up in a Desqview window than it is to load the entire Borland C environment in another window. But if I'm doing a lot of lookups while working with the Borland compiler, I'll take the time to load up the Borland environment and use the help tool in there. I almost always use the Borland compiler for the initial development work on any software that I write, because I can't stand the editor in Borland 2.0.

Lint

For checking out my C code, and especially for finding portability problems in code that I've obtained from the net, I use a product called PC Lint from Gimpel software. If you're like I was, you'll find it truly amazing to see how many problems *lint* can help you find and fix in a piece of C code. In particular, I find *lint* very useful for the following two tasks. The first task is finding data type inconsistencies in freeware code. A lot of freeware code was written using the forgiving compilers on UNIX systems. My experience has been that almost all non-ANSI-compliant UNIX C compilers will "do the right thing" with almost any kind of C statement construct that's in the right ballpark.

The bad news is that these constructs usually fail to work when I try to port them from UNIX to DOS. *lint* has helped me many times in the past to find obscure data conversion errors in grotty C code.

The second task is generating C function prototypes. The presence of C prototypes in C programs helps compilers to perform correct data type conversions. This is generally a good thing to do because it helps avoid unexpected data conversions that may cause programs to fail on new platforms. Furthermore, if the prototypes are placed in a separate include file that's included by all the source files in a software product, incompatible definitions and uses of C functions are much less likely to occur.

I recommend PC Lint because it has saved me many hours of time in debugging code, in porting code, and in developing extracting prototypes from existing code. PC Lint is available from Gimpel Software, 3207 Hogarth Lane, Collegeville, PA 19426. They now have a new version out for C++.

Code Management Tools

I use the code management tools described in this book almost every day for managing both software files and documentation files. I haven't had to write a makefile for almost two years.

Editors

Since people usually have very strong personal preferences for their favorite text editors, I won't make the mistake of trying to justify my choices of editors. Instead, I'll simply identify the editors that are present in my environment. I use the Mutt Editor V2.4 (by Craig Durland) on both DOS and UNIX, and GNU Emacs (by Richard Stallman) on UNIX.

The Mutt Editor is small, powerful, free, starts up quickly, and has fast response times on both DOS and UNIX. In contrast, the GNU Emacs editor is extremely enormous, extremely powerful, starts up extremely slowly, and only has an acceptable response time on personal computers and on small UNIX systems.

Both the Mutt and GNU Emacs editors are freeware, both have an Emacs interface, and both are very extensible with Lisp or Lisp-like extension languages. Both are available—with source code—from the net.

File Compression Programs

It is common practice these days to compress files to save disk space, both on personal computers and on UNIX workstations. I've found that the *zip* family of programs work on all the machines I use and will properly unpack files across the network in DOS-UNIX environments.

Documentation Tools

I use Latex and Emtex 3.0 (by Eberhard Mattes) for documentation work on DOS. Emtex is an implementation of Donald Knuth's TeX program. Latex is a documentation preparation system (a macro package) that was written by Leslie Lamport. All three are freeware. Commercial user guides for TeX and Latex are available.

The main advantages of using Latex are that it's free, it runs on both UNIX and DOS systems (as well as others), and it uses ASCII source files. These advantages mean that it's easy to share documents among different systems and that you get to use your favorite editor to prepare documents. In addition, the underlying TeX implementation produces a device-independent output file. This means that document files compiled on one machine can be printed or displayed on many different printers and display screens.

This book was originally written in Latex.

One of the main shortcomings of working with Latex on DOS is the difficulty of including pictures in the body of the text. TeX and Latex aren't particularly convenient for typesetting pictures.

This isn't a problem on UNIX however, because the freeware *xfig* tool is convenient both for drawing pictures and for automatically generating a file of TeX commands that can be included by the main Latex document.

MKS Tools for DOS

I also use several tools from Mortice Kern Systems (MKS). They produce several excellent products that provide the convenience of popular UNIX tools in a DOS environment. I have three of their products: the MKS Toolkit, MKS RCS, and MKS Lex and Yacc.

The MKS Toolkit contains implementations of over 150 UNIX tools such as *cp, rm, find, sed, awk, which, tar, sort, compress, grep, egrep, fgrep, spell, look, touch,* and many more. In particular, the toolkit contains a complete implementation of the Korn shell interpreter that's compatible with the Bourne Shell.

The MKS RCS product contains MKS *make* and about 30 other tools (including the standard RCS tools). In contrast to the RCS tools provided with this book, the MKS RCS tools are of commercial quality. As a consequence, they have features that go well beyond the freeware RCS tools that are provided here. For example, many of the MKS RCS tools can accept a list of filenames (contained in a *filelist* file) for checking in, checking out, etc. Many of the tools can also access options that have been set in a configuration file.

The MKS Lex and Yacc product contains about 20 tools that are useful for parser construction, including *lex* and *yacc,* of course. As with the RCS tools, MKS Lex and Yacc are high-quality commercial products. They come with a 450 page manual that includes tutorials on constructing parsers, performing error handling, and debugging parsers.

I wish that I'd known about these two MKS tools before I spent so much time trying to port GNU *bison* to DOS, and to modify the skeleton parsers for *bison* and *flex* for compilation under ANSI C, Microsoft C, and Borland C. I'm sure that if I had a dollar for every hour that I've spent trying to get freeware *lex* and *yacc* tools to work on DOS, I could have paid for the MKS commercial DOS versions of the tools at least once. I think the MKS *lex* and *yacc* tools are excellent investments that will pay for themselves in a very short time if you plan to do any reasonable amount of parsing work.

MKS RCS Compatibility with My CM Tools

The MKS RCS tools for DOS are compatible with the *rcsdo* tool provided with this book. I know this because I specially modified the *rcsdo* tool to work with the MKS RCS tools.

(I had to turn on the **strictlocking** option in the MKS configuration file and set the two-character year option. MKS allows you to select four-character year values (1994) or two-character year values (94) in the options list. In contrast, the RCS 5.5 tools in this book use two-character year values—which means they will break in six years.)

This compatibility is an important advantage because it gives you the opportunity to use high quality, commercially supported RCS tools underneath the code management tools provided with this book. For example, some people may not want to trust their source code to the modified, non-standard, freeware RCS programs that I've provided here. The ongoing costs of maintaining these modified RCS programs may also be a deterrent to some people.

The MKS RCS tools are available for several operating systems (UNIX, DOS, Windows NT, and OS/2), and share the same internal (RCS 5.4) format for RCS storage files. In my opinion, this makes the MKS tools a very good choice if you want to use commercially supported RCS tools in a multi-platform work environment. The decision is up to you because I've made sure that *rcsdo* will work with both my modified RCS toolset and with the commercially supported MKS RCS toolset.

The MKS DOS Lex and Yacc tools are also compatible with the makefile templates that are included with this book. In fact, the the MKS *lex* and *yacc* tools were used to test both the implicit rules in the makefile templates and the explicit rules generated by *gendep*. (Both the implicit and explicit rules should work with UNIX and POSIX *lex* and *yacc* tools as well.)

Useful Tool Capabilities

This section briefly describes some useful capabilities in tools that are commercially available.

Compilers

Most compilers accept a command-line argument (such as **-Idirectory**) that tells them where to look for include files. This is a useful feature if you have a large number of include files that are referenced by a large number of software products.

For example, you might not want to import large numbers of include files to the platform compilation directory. The tradeoff is that if you don't import the files, then you can't log the sharing relationships either.

This usually isn't a problem however, since large groups of include files are usually associated with products—such as window systems—that are heavily used by almost all programs. In that case, logging so many sharing relationships is of doubtful value.

Make Tools

Some *make* tools allow you to tell them where to search for source files by specifying a list of directories in a **VPATH** macro. This macro is similar to the **PATH** environment variable. That is, anytime *make* looks for a source file, it looks in the current directory first, and then searches all the directories specified in **VPATH**.

The main advantage of using a **VPATH** macro in a multi-person environment is that it may allow developers to use sparse private source trees instead of fully populated private source trees. (A sparse source tree is one that only contains files that you've checked out for modification.) Developers can use sparse private trees—and thus save disk space—if there's a baseline version of all source files maintained in a public directory somewhere.

For example, if baseline copies of the source files are available, developers only have to copy over (or check out) the files that they want to modify when they clone the main source tree. They don't have to check out all the rest of the product files because *make* can find those source files by using the **VPATH** macro.

A second useful feature that is sometimes provided with some *make* tools is the ability to automatically calculate dependency rules. This is a useful feature because it saves developers time and reduces the frequency of errors in human-generated makefile dependency rules.

Advanced dependency rule generators are more capable than the *gendep* tool because *gendep* doesn't understand nested include files or include file statements surrounded by **#ifdefs** (of any kind).

A third useful feature in some *make* tools is the ability to perform efficient internal recursions. This means that they don't call the operating system to recursively invoke themselves with a new set of command-line options. Instead, they just push their current internal data set on a stack, load the new set of makefile data into the current internal data space, and restart their internal processing from the beginning. Then when the recursive invocation ends, they load the previous set of internal data back into the internal data space and continue from where they left off.

The difference between these two approaches to recursion is significant on platforms that have limited memory space (such as DOS). This is because compiling a program from a recursive invocation of *make* can be impossible if the two copies of *make* (and the two copies of its internal data) don't leave enough free memory for the compiler and its required data space.

Index

Bibliography

Babich, Wayne. *Software Configuration Management.* Addison Wesley, Menlo Park, CA. 1986.

Berliner, Brian. "CVS II: Parallelizing Software Development." Published in the Proceedings of the USENIX conference, Washington, D.C., Winter 1990.

DuBois, Paul. *Software Portability with Imake.* O'Reilly & Associates, Sebastopol, CA. 1993.

Harbison, Samuel P. and Steele, Guy L. Jr. *C: A Reference Manual, 3rd Ed.* Prentice Hall, Inglewood Cliffs, NJ. 1991.

MacKenzie, David, et. al. *Autoconf.* Free Software Foundation, 1992.

> Autoconf is a tool for producing shell scripts that automatically configure software source code trees for compilation on many different Unix platforms. In practice, Autoconf creates a configuration script from a template file that lists the operating system features that the configured application wants to use. Then, when the configuration script is run, it configures the source tree for compilation on a specific platform.

MKS. *MKS Lex and Yacc.* Mortice Kern Systems, Ontario, Canada. 1992.

MKS. *MKS RCS: Revision Control System Tools.* Mortice Kern Systems, Ontario, Canada. 1991.

MKS. *MKS Toolkit.* Mortice Kern Systems, Ontario, Canada. 1991.

Oram, Andy, and Talbot, Steve. *Managing Projects with Make.* O'Reilly & Associates, Sebastopol, CA. 1991.

Tichy, W. *RCS: A Revision Control System.* Department of Computer Sciences, Purdue University, Indiana. 1985.

About the Author

Kevin Jameson is a software engineer whose main focus since 1982 has been to improve the quality and productivity of the software development process. His approach to the problem is very pragmatic: keep trying out new productivity ideas until you find some that work.

He has two main current projects. The first is to improve, extend, and commercialize the software tools that accompany this book, *Multi-Platform Code Management*. The second is to write a modeling tool that can understand and usefully manipulate domain knowledge objects, so people can reuse ideas and knowledge interactively to improve their productivity.

At various times in his several careers, Kevin has studied electronics (diploma in industrial electronic technology, Southern Alberta Institute of Technology), chemical physics (B.S., general studies, University of Calgary), and computer science (M.S., University of Calgary).

Kevin currently splits his time between consulting, research, and learning how to play the violin, and as often as possible, he tries to write more code for his small network of Suns and PCs. Then, he waits with anticipation for the morning productivity and quality report of the nightly coding style and metrics daemon.

Colophon

Our look is the result of reader comments, our own experimentation, and feedback from distribution channels.

Distinctive covers complement our distinctive approach to technical topics, breathing personality and life into potentially dry subjects.

Trapeze artists are featured on the cover of *Multi-Platform Code Management*. Acrobats appeared in art as early as 2500 B.C., when several were depicted in a painting on the wall of a tomb in the Nile Valley. The art of tightrope walking is thought to have originated in China, and Marco Polo described fantastic acrobatics displays, including "rope dancing," that he witnessed in the court of Kublai Khan. The Roman emperor Carinus is credited as being the first to sponsor a formal performance by acrobats, in the third century.

The trapeze entered the modern age in 1859, thanks to two French trapeze artists. On June 30, 1859, Emile Gravelet, who called himself Blondin, crossed Niagara Falls on a tightrope for the first time. He repeated this feat numerous times throughout the summer of 1859, drawing huge crowds each time. News of these crossings created such a sensation that high-wire acts came into great demand throughout the world.

That same year another young Frenchman named Jules Leotard, assisted by his father, developed a routine in which he "flew" from one device to another. He is believed to be the first flying trapeze artist. He not only created a sensation that would forever become a staple of circus acts, he also gave his name to the costume acrobats and dancers continue to wear to this day.

Danger has always been an integral part of the appeal of the trapeze, with sometimes tragic results. Some of the most legendary trapeze artists to die while performing their art are Lillian Leitzel, in 1931, and several members of the Flying Wallenda family, including Willy Wallenda in 1933 and Karl Wallenda in 1978.

Edie Freedman designed this cover using a nineteenth-century engraving from the Dover Pictorial Archive. The cover layout was produced with QuarkXPress 3.3 using the ITC Garamond font. Edie also designed the interior layout.

Text was prepared in SGML (Standard Generalized Markup Language) using the DocBook 2.1 DTD. The print version of this book was created by translating the SGML source into a set of gtroff macros using a filter developed in-house by Norman Walsh. Steve Talbott designed and wrote the underlying macro set on the basis of the GNU gtroff -gs macros; Lenny Muellner adapted them to SGML and implemented the book design. The GNU groff text formatter version 1.08 was used to generate PostScript output.

The figures were created in Aldus Freehand 4.0 by Chris Reilley and Karla Tolbert. The colophon was written by Clairemarie Fisher O'Leary with help from Michael Kalantarian.

Programming

UNIX, C and DCE

Books from O'Reilly & Associates, Inc.

Summer 1994

High Performance Computing

By Kevin Dowd
1st Edition June 1993
398 pages, ISBN 1-56592-032-5

High Performance Computing makes sense of the newest generation of workstations for application programmers and purchasing managers. It covers everything, from the basics of modern workstation architecture, to structuring benchmarks, to squeezing more performance out of critical applications. It also explains what a good compiler can do——and what you have to do yourself. The book closes with a look at the high-performance future: parallel computers and the more garden-variety shared memory processors that are appearing on people's desktops.

ORACLE Performance Tuning

By Peter Corrigan & Mark Gurry
1st Edition September 1993
642 pages, ISBN 1-56592-048-1

The ORACLE relational database management system is the most popular database system in use today. This book shows you the many things you can do to increase the performance of your existing ORACLE system, whether you are running RDBMS Version 6 or 7. You may find that this book can save you the cost of a new machine; at the very least, it will save you a lot of headaches.

Understanding Japanese Information Processing

By Ken Lunde
1st Edition September 1993
470 pages, ISBN 1-56592-043-0

There are many complex issues surrounding the use of the Japanese language in computing. Unlike English, which has 26 letters in a single alphabet, Japanese has thousands of characters in three scripts. The issues around handling such an unwieldy collection of data are formidable and complex. Up to now, researching and understanding the relevant issues has been a difficult, if not unattainable task, especially to a person who doesn't read or speak Japanese. *Understanding Japanese Information Processing* is a book that provides detailed information on all aspects of handling Japanese text on computer systems. It brings all of the relevant information together in a single book. It covers everything from the origins of modern-day Japanese to the latest information on specific emerging computer encoding standards. There are fifteen appendices which provide additional reference material, such as a code conversion table, character set tables, mapping tables, an extensive list of software sources, a glossary, and more.

"Understanding Japanese Information Processing is a Rosetta Stone for those concerned about how Japanese is handled on computer systems. It removes the mystique and creates understanding."
—Dr. Jun Murai, Keio University, WIDE Project

Guide to Writing DCE Applications

By John Shirley, Wei Hu & David Magid
2nd Edition May 1994
462 pages, ISBN 1-56592-045-7

A hands-on programming guide to OSF's Distributed Computing Environment (DCE) for first-time DCE application programmers. This book is designed to help new DCE users make the transition from conventional, nondistributed applications programming to distributed DCE programming. In addition to basic RPC (remote procedure calls), this edition covers object UUIDs and basic security (authentication and authorization). Also includes practical programming examples.

"This book will be useful as a ready reference by the side of the novice DCE programmer."
—*;login*, March/April 1993

Distributing Applications Across DCE and Windows NT

By Ward Rosenberry & Jim Teague
1st Edition November 1993
302 pages , ISBN 1-56592-047-3

This book links together two exciting technologies in distributed computing by showing how to develop an application that simultaneously runs on DCE and Microsoft systems through remote procedure calls (RPC). Covers the writing of portable applications and the complete differences between RPC support in the two environments.

Understanding DCE

By Ward Rosenberry, David Kenney & Gerry Fisher
1st Edition October 1992
266 pages, ISBN 1-56592-005-8

A technical and conceptual overview of OSF's Distributed Computing Environment (DCE) for programmers and technical managers, marketing and sales people. Unlike many O'Reilly & Associates books, *Understanding DCE* has no hands-on programming elements. Instead, the book focuses on how DCE can be used to accomplish typical programming tasks and provides explanations to help the reader understand all the parts of DCE.

Migrating to Fortran 90

By James F. Kerrigan
1st Edition November 1993
389 pages, ISBN 1-56592-049-X

Many Fortran programmers do not know where to start with Fortran 90. What is new about the language? How can it help them? How does a programmer with old habits learn new strategies? This book is a complete overview of the new features that Fortran 90 has brought to the Fortran standard, with examples and suggestions for use. It discusses older ways of solving problems, and contrasts them with the new ways provided by Fortran 90. Topics include array sections, modules, file handling, allocatable arrays and pointers, and numeric precision. Two dozen examples of full programs are interspersed within the text, which includes over 4,000 lines of working code.

"This is a book that all Fortran programmers eager to take advantage of the excellent feature of Fortran 90 will want to have on their desk."
—*FORTRAN Journal*

UNIX for FORTRAN Programmers

By Mike Loukides
1st Edition August 1990
264 pages, ISBN 0-937175-51-X

This book provides the serious scientific programmer with an introduction to the UNIX operating system and its tools. The intent of the book is to minimize the UNIX entry barrier and to familiarize readers with the most important tools so they can be productive as quickly as possible. *UNIX for FORTRAN Programmers* shows readers how to do things they're interested in: not just how to use a tool such as *make* or *rcs*, but how to use it in program development and how it fits into the toolset as a whole.

"An excellent book describing the features of the UNIX FORTRAN compiler f77 and related software. This book is extremely well written."
— *American Mathematical Monthly*, February 1991

Using C on the UNIX System

By Dave Curry
1st Edition January 1989
250 pages, ISBN 0-937175-23-4

Using C on the UNIX System provides a thorough introduction to the UNIX system call libraries. It is aimed at programmers who already know C but who want to take full advantage of the UNIX programming environment. If you want to learn how to work with the operating system and to write programs that can interact with directories, terminals, and networks at the lowest level you will find this book essential. It is impossible to write UNIX utilities of any sophistication without understanding the material in this book.

"A gem of a book. The author's aim is to provide a guide to system programming, and he succeeds admirably. His balance is steady between System V and BSD-based systems, so readers come away knowing both."
—*SUN Expert*, November 1989

Practical C Programming

By Steve Oualline
2nd Edition January 1993
396 pages, ISBN 1-56592-035-X

C programming is more than just getting the syntax right. Style and debugging also play a tremendous part in creating programs that run well. *Practical C Programming* teaches you not only the mechanics of programming, but also how to create programs that are easy to read, maintain, and debug. There are lots of introductory C books, but this is the Nutshell Handbook®! In the second edition, programs now conform to ANSI C.

Understanding and Using COFF

By Gintaras R. Gircys
1st Edition November 1988
196 pages, ISBN 0-937175-31-5

COFF—Common Object File Format—is the formal definition for the structure of machine code files in the UNIX System V environment. All machine-code files are COFF files. This handbook explains COFF data structure and its manipulation.

Checking C Programs with lint

By Ian F. Darwin
1st Edition October 1988
84 pages, ISBN 0-937175-30-7

The *lint* program checker has proven itself time and again to be one of the best tools for finding portability problems and certain types of coding errors in C programs. *lint* verifies a program or program segments against standard libraries, checks the code for common portability errors, and tests the programming against some tried and true guidelines. *Linting* your code is a necessary (though not sufficient) step in writing clean, portable, effective programs. This book introduces you to *lint*, guides you through running it on your programs, and helps you interpret *lint's* output.

"The book is short, useful, and to the point. I recommend it for self-study to all involved with C in a UNIX environment, as it certainly goes beyond the standard documentation on *lint* and makes this important tool much more accessible."
—*Computing Reviews*, August 1989

lex & yacc

By John Levine, Tony Mason & Doug Brown
2nd Edition October 1992
366 pages, ISBN 1-56592-000-7

Shows programmers how to use two UNIX utilities, lex and yacc, in program development. The second edition contains completely revised tutorial sections for novice users and reference sections for advanced users. This edition is twice the size of the first, has an expanded index, and now covers Bison and Flex.

"The book is...well-written and thorough. I had the pleasant surprise numerous times of reading some passage, thinking to myself, 'Oh, they've missed this perhaps subtle point, make a note,' and then the next sentence or paragraph would cover exactly that point... I'm glad I'll finally have a good book to recommend to folks."
—Vern Paxson, Developer of Flex

Software Portability with imake

By Paul DuBois
1st Edition July 1993
390 pages, 1-56592-055-4

imake is a utility that works with *make* to enable code to be complied and installed on different UNIX machines. This Nutshell Handbook®—the only book available on *imake*—is ideal for X and UNIX programmers who want their software to be portable. The book covers a general explanation of *imake*, how to write and debug an *Imakefile*, and how to write configuration files. Several sample sets of configuration files are described and are available free over the Net.

Managing Projects with make

By Andrew Oram & Steve Talbott
2nd Edition October 1991
152 pages, ISBN 0-937175-90-0

make is one of UNIX's greatest contributions to software development, and this book is the clearest description of *make* ever written. It describes all the basic features of *make* and provides guidelines on meeting the needs of large, modern projects. Also contains a description of free products that contain major enhancements to *make*.

Power Programming with RPC

By John Bloomer
1st Edition February 1992
522 pages, ISBN 0-937175-77-3

RPC, or remote procedure calling, is the ability to distribute the execution of functions on remote computers. Written from a programmer's perspective, this book shows what you can do with RPC's, like Sun RPC, the de facto standard on UNIX systems. It covers related programming topics for Sun and other UNIX systems and teaches through examples.

POSIX Programmer's Guide

By Donald Lewine
1st Edition April 1991
640 pages, ISBN 0-937175-73-0

Most UNIX systems today are POSIX-compliant because the Federal government requires it for its purchases. Given the manufacturer's documentation, however, it can be difficult to distinguish system-specific features from those features defined by POSIX. The *POSIX Programmer's Guide*, intended as an explanation of the POSIX standard and as a reference for the POSIX.1 programming library, helps you write more portable programs.

Programming with curses

By John Strang
1st Edition 1986
76 pages, ISBN 0-937175-02-1

Curses is a UNIX library of functions for controlling a terminal's display screen from a C program. It can be used to provide a screen driver for a program (such as a visual editor) or to improve a program's user interface. This handbook will help you make use of the curses library in your C programs. We have presented ample material on curses and its implementation in UNIX so that you understand the whole as well as its parts.

Building a Successful Software Business

By Dave Radin
1st Edition April 1994
394 pages, ISBN 1-56592-064-3

This handbook is for the new software entrepreneur and the old hand alike. If you're thinking of starting a company around a program you've written—and there's no better time than the present—this book will guide you toward success. If you're an old hand in the software industry, it will help you to sharpen your skills, or provide a refresher course. It covers the basics of product planning, marketing, customer support, finance, and basic operations.

"A marvelous guide . .the Swiss Army Knife of high-tech marketing."
—Jerry Keane, Universal Analytics Inc.

GLOBAL NETWORK NAVIGATOR

The Global Network Navigator™ (GNN) is a unique kind of information service that makes the Internet easy and enjoyable to use. We organize access to the vast information resources of the Internet so that you can find what you want. We also help you understand the Internet and the many ways you can explore it.

Charting the Internet, the Ultimate Online Service

In GNN you'll find:

- *The Online Whole Internet Catalog*, an interactive card catalog for Internet resources that expands on the catalog in Ed Krol's bestselling book, *The Whole Internet User's Guide & Catalog*.

- *Newsnet*, a news service that keeps you up to date on what's happening on the Net.

- *The Netheads Department*, which features profiles of interesting people on the Internet and commentary by Internet experts.

- *GNN Metacenters*, special-interest online magazines aimed at serving the needs of particular audiences. GNN Metacenters not only gather the best Internet resources together in one convenient place, they also introduce new material from a variety of sources. Each Metacenter contains new feature articles, as well as columns, subject-oriented reference guides for using the Internet, and topic-oriented discussion groups. Travel, music, education, and computers are some of the areas that we cover.

All in all, GNN helps you get more value for the time you spend on the Internet.

Subscribe Today

GNN is available over the Internet as a subscription service. To get complete information about subscribing to GNN, send email to **info@gnn.com**. If you have access to a World Wide Web browser such as Mosaic or Lynx, you can use the following URL to register online: `http://gnn.com/`

 ## The Best of the Web

The *O'Reilly Resource Center* was voted "**Best Commercial Site**" by users participating in "Best of the Web' 94."

GNN received "Honorable Mention" for "**Best Overall Site**," "**Best Entertainment Service**," and "**Most Important Service Concept**."

The *GNN NetNews* received "Honorable Mention" for "**Best Document Design**."

If you use a browser that does not support online forms, you can retrieve an email version of the registration form automatically by sending email to **form@gnn.com**. Fill this form out and send it back to us by email, and we will confirm your registration.

FOR INFORMATION: **800-998-9938**, 707-829-0515; **NUTS@ORA.COM**

BOOK INFORMATION
AT YOUR FINGERTIPS

O'Reilly & Associates offers extensive online information through a Gopher server (*gopher.ora.com*). Here you can find detailed information on our entire catalog of books, tapes, and much more.

The O'Reilly Online Catalog

Gopher is basically a hierarchy of menus and files that can easily lead you to a wealth of information. Gopher is also easy to navigate; helpful instructions appear at the bottom of each screen (notice the three prompts in the sample screen below). Another nice feature is that Gopher files can be downloaded, saved, or printed out for future reference. You can also search Gopher files and even email them.

To give you an idea of our Gopher, here's a look at the top, or root, menu:

```
O'Reilly & Associates (The public Gopher server)

    1.  News Flash! -- New Products and Projects/

    2.  Feature Articles/

    3.  Product Descriptions/

    4.  Ordering Information/

    5.  Complete Listing of Titles

    6.  Errata for "Learning Perl"

    7.  FTP Archive and Email Information/

    8.  Bibliographies/


    Press ? for Help, q to Quit, u to go up a menu
```

The heart of the O'Reilly Gopher service is the extensive information provided on all ORA products in menu item three, "Product Descriptions." For most books this usually includes title information, a long description, a short author bio, the table of contents, quotes and reviews, a gif image of the book's cover, and even some interesting information about the animal featured on the cover. (One of the benefits of a Gopher database is the ability to pack a lot of information in an organized, easy-to-find place.)

How to Order

Another important listing is "Ordering Information," where we supply information to those interested in buying our books. Here, you'll find instructions and an application for ordering O'Reilly products online, a listing of distributors (local and international), a listing of bookstores that carry our titles, and much more.

The item that follows, "Complete Listing of Titles," is helpful when it's time to order. This single file, with short one-line listings of all ORA products, quickly provides the essentials for easy ordering: title, ISBN, and price.

And More

One of the most widely read areas of the O'Reilly Gopher is "News Flash!," which focuses on important new products and projects of ORA. Here, you'll find entries on newly published books and audiotapes; announcements of exciting new projects and product lines from ORA; upcoming tradeshows, conferences, and exhibitions of interest; author appearances; contest winners; job openings; and anything else that's timely and topical.

"Feature Articles" contains just that—many of the articles and interviews found here are excerpted from the O'Reilly magazine/catalog *ora.com*.

The "Bibliographies" entries are also very popular with readers, providing critical, objective reviews on the important literature in the field.

"FTP Archive and Email Information" contains helpful ORA email addresses, information about our "ora-news" listproc server, and detailed instructions on how to download ORA book examples via FTP.

Other menu listings are often available. "Errata for 'Learning Perl,'" for example, apprised readers of errata found in the first edition of our book, and responses to this file greatly aided our campaign to ferret out errors and typos for the upcoming corrected edition (a nice example of the mutual benefits of online interactivity).

Come and Explore

Our Gopher is vibrant and constantly in flux. By the time you actually log onto this Gopher, the root menu may well have changed. The goal is to always improve, and to that end we welcome your input (email: **gopher@ora.com**). We invite you to come and explore.

Here are four basic ways to call up our Gopher online.

1) If you have a local Gopher client, type:
   `gopher gopher.ora.com`

2) For Xgopher:
   `xgopher -xrm "xgopher.root\`
   `Server: gopher.ora.com"`

3) To use telnet (for those without a Gopher client):
   `telnet gopher.ora.com`
   login: **gopher** (no password)

4) For a World Wide Web browser, use this URL:
   `http://gopher.ora.com:70/`

LISTING OF TITLES

from O'Reilly & Associates, Inc.

INTERNET
The Whole Internet User's Guide & Catalog
Connecting to the Internet: An O'Reilly Buyer's Guide
!%@:: A Directory of Electronic Mail Addressing & Networks
Smileys

USING UNIX AND X
UNIX Power Tools (with CD-ROM)
UNIX in a Nutshell: System V Edition
UNIX in a Nutshell: Berkeley Edition
SCO UNIX in a Nutshell
Learning the UNIX Operating System
Learning the vi Editor
Learning GNU Emacs
Learning the Korn Shell
Making TeX Work
sed & awk
MH & xmh: E-mail for Users & Programmers
Using UUCP and Usenet
X Window System User's Guide: Volume 3
X Window System User's Guide, Motif Edition: Volume 3M

SYSTEM ADMINISTRATION
Essential System Administration
sendmail
Computer Security Basics
Practical UNIX Security
System Performance Tuning
TCP/IP Network Administration
Learning Perl
Programming perl
Managing NFS and NIS
Managing UUCP and Usenet
DNS and BIND
termcap & terminfo
X Window System Administrator's Guide: Volume 8
    (available with or without CD-ROM)

UNIX AND C PROGRAMMING
ORACLE Performance Tuning
High Performance Computing
lex & yacc
POSIX Programmer's Guide
Power Programming with RPC
Programming with curses
Managing Projects with make
Software Portability with imake
Understanding and Using COFF
Migrating to Fortran 90
UNIX for FORTRAN Programmers
Using C on the UNIX System
Checking C Programs with lint
Practical C Programming
Understanding Japanese Information Processing

DCE (DISTRIBUTED COMPUTING ENVIRONMENT)
Distributing Applications Across DCE and Windows NT
Guide to Writing DCE Applications
Understanding DCE

BERKELEY 4.4 SOFTWARE DISTRIBUTION
4.4BSD System Manager's Manual
4.4BSD User's Reference Manual
4.4BSD User's Supplementary Documents
4.4BSD Programmer's Reference Manual
4.4BSD Programmer's Supplementary Documents
4.4BSD-Lite CD Companion

X PROGRAMMING
The X Window System in a Nutshell
X Protocol Reference Manual: Volume 0
Xlib Programming Manual: Volume 1
Xlib Reference Manual: Volume 2
X Toolkit Intrinsics Programming Manual: Volume 4
X Toolkit Intrinsics Programming Manual, Motif Edition: Volume 4M
X Toolkit Intrinsics Reference Manual: Volume 5
Motif Programming Manual: Volume 6A
Motif Reference Manual: Volume 6B
XView Programming Manual: Volume 7A
XView Reference Manual: Volume 7B
PEXlib Programming Manual
PEXlib Reference Manual
PHIGS Programming Manual (softcover or hardcover)
PHIGS Reference Manual
Programmer's Supplement for R5 of the X Window System

THE X RESOURCE
A quarterly working journal for X programmers
The X Resource: Issues 0 through 11

OTHER
Building a Successful Software Business
Love Your Job!

TRAVEL
Travelers' Tales Thailand

AUDIOTAPES
Internet Talk Radio's "Geek of the Week" Interviews
The Future of the Internet Protocol, 4 hours
Global Network Operations, 2 hours
Mobile IP Networking, 1 hour
Networked Information and Online Libraries, 1 hour
Security and Networks, 1 hour
European Networking, 1 hour

Notable Speeches of the Information Age
John Perry Barlow, 1.5 hours

INTERNATIONAL DISTRIBUTORS

Customers outside North America can now order O'Reilly & Associates' books through the following distributors. They offer our international customers faster order processing, more bookstores, increased representation at tradeshows worldwide, and the high quality, responsive service our customers have come to expect.

EUROPE, MIDDLE EAST, and AFRICA
except Germany, Switzerland, and Austria

—INQUIRIES—

International Thomson Publishing Europe
Berkshire House
168-173 High Holborn
London WC1V 7AA
United Kingdom
Telephone: 44-71-497-1422
Fax: 44-71-497-1426
E-mail: danni.dolbear@itpuk.co.uk

—ORDERS—

International Thomson Publishing Services, Ltd.
Cheriton House, North Way
Andover, Hampshire SP10 5BE
United Kingdom
Telephone: 44-264-342-832 (UK orders)
Telephone: 44-264-342-806 (outside UK)
Fax: 44-264-364418 (UK orders)
Fax: 44-264-342761 (outside UK)

GERMANY, SWITZERLAND, and AUSTRIA

International Thomson Publishing GmbH
O'Reilly-International Thomson Verlag
Königswinterer Strasse 418
53227 Bonn
Germany
Telephone: 49-228-445171
Fax: 49-228-441342
E-mail (CompuServe): 100272,2422
E-mail (Internet): 100272.2422@compuserve.com

ASIA except Japan

—INQUIRIES—

International Thomson Publishing Asia
221 Henderson Road
#05 10 Henderson Building
Singapore 0315
Telephone: 65-272-6496
Fax: 65-272-6498

—ORDERS—

Telephone: 65-268-7867
Fax: 65-268-6727

AUSTRALIA

WoodsLane Pty. Ltd.
Unit 8, 101 Darley Street (P.O. Box 935)
Mona Vale NSW 2103
Australia
Telephone: 61-2-9795944
Fax: 61-2-9973348
E-mail: woods@tmx.mhs.oz.au

NEW ZEALAND

WoodsLane New Zealand Ltd.
7 Purnell Street (P.O. Box 575)
Wanganui, New Zealand
Telephone: 64-6-3476543
Fax: 64-6-3454840
E-mail: woods@tmx.mhs.oz.au

THE AMERICAS, JAPAN, and OCEANIA

O'Reilly & Associates, Inc.
103A Morris Street
Sebastopol, CA 95472 U.S.A.
Telephone: 707-829-0515
Telephone: 800-998-9938 (U.S. & Canada)
Fax: 707-829-0104
E-mail: order@ora.com

How to Order by E-mail

E-mail ordering promises to be quick and easy. Because we don't want you sending credit card information over a non-secure network, we ask that you set up an account with us before ordering by e-mail.

To find out more about setting up an e-mail account, you can either call us at (800) 998-9938 or select `Ordering Information` from the Gopher root menu.

O'Reilly & Associates Inc.
103A Morris Street, Sebastopol, CA 95472

(800) 998-9938 • (707) 829-0515 • FAX (707) 829-0104 • order@ora.com

How to get information about O'Reilly books online

• If you have a local gopher client, then you can launch gopher and connect to our server:
`gopher gopher.ora.com`

• If you want to use the Xgopher client, then enter:
`xgopher -xrm "xgopher.rootServer: gopher.ora.com"`

• If you want to use telnet, then enter:
`telnet gopher.ora.com` login: `gopher`   [no password]

• If you use a World Wide Web browser, you can access the gopher server by typing the following http address:
`gopher://gopher.ora.com`

WE'D LIKE TO HEAR FROM YOU

O'Reilly & Associates Inc.

(800) 998-9938 • (707) 829-0515 • FAX (707) 829-0104 • order@ora.com

How to order books by e-mail:

1. Address your e-mail to: order@ora.com
2. Include in your message:
   - The title of each book you want to order
     (*an ISBN number is helpful but not necessary*)
   - The quantity of each book
   - Your account number and name
   - Anything special you'd like us to know about your order

_____

O'Reilly Online Account Number

Use our online catalog to find out more about our books (see reverse).

BUSINESS REPLY MAIL
FIRST CLASS MAIL   PERMIT NO. 80   SEBASTOPOL, CA

Postage will be paid by addressee

O'Reilly & Associates, Inc.
103A Morris Street
Sebastopol, CA 95472-9902